MW00715888

EDITORS: Karen Davis, Michael Kuta
STATISTICIANS/RESEARCH: Greg Innis, Morris Moorawnick
ADVERTISING SALES: John Pettit, Bill Ley, Jeff Ajluni, Mike Mazurek,
                   Dan Frank, Scott Miller, Andy Loughnane
PRODUCTION: North American Graphics, Inc.
PRINTER: Scott Publishing
INSIDE PHOTOS: Mark Hicks

For a free demonstration of the clarity
of Ameritech's new ClearPath Cellular, have
someone read this ad into your ear.

CLEARPATH™
SO CLEAR, IT'S LIKE YOU'RE THERE

DETROIT RED WINGS, INC.

Joe Louis Arena — 600 Civic Center Drive — Detroit, MI 48226
Phone: (313) 396-7544   P.R. FAX: (313) 567-0296

Owner .... Mike Ilitch
Owner/Secretary-Treasurer .... Marian Ilitch
Vice-Presidents .... Atanas Ilitch, Christopher Ilitch
Senior Vice-President .... Jim Devellano
General Manager .... Ken Holland
Assistant General Manager .... Don Waddell
Head Coach .... Scotty Bowman
Associate Coaches .... Barry Smith, Dave Lewis
Goaltending Consultant .... Jim Bedard
NHL Scout .... Dan Belisle
Director of Player Development/AHL Scout .... Jim Nill
Pro Scout/Minor League Player Development .... Mark Howe
Eastern Scout .... Joe McDonnell
Western Scout .... Bruce Haralson
Eastern, USA, High School and College Scout .... Mark Leach
Director of European Scouting .... Hakan Andersson
Czech and Slovak Republic Scout .... Vladimir Havluj
Russian Scout .... Ruslan Shabanov
Scouts .... Paul Crowley, Marty Stein
Executive Assistant .... Nancy Beard
Administrative Assistant .... Kristin Armstrong
Director of Finance .... Paul MacDonald
Accounting Assistant .... Cathy Witzke
Marketing Director .... Ted Speers
Marketing .... Kevin Vaughn, Lori Shiels
Public Relations .... Karen Davis, Michael Kuta
Joe Louis Arena General Manager/V.P. of Operations .... John Pettit
General Sales Manager .... Bill Ley
Manager, Arena Signage, Print & Promotions .... Jeffrey Ajluni
Manager, Media and Interactive Sales .... Michael Mazurek
Account Executives .... Dan Frank, Scott Miller
Advertising Sales Coordinator .... Andy Loughnane
Broadcasting Coordinator .... Jason O'Connell
Box Office Manager .... Bob Kerlin
Season Ticket Sales Manager .... Brad Ebben
Season Ticket Coordinator .... Chuck Smith
Hockey Group Sales Coordinator .... Mary Greener
Athletic Therapist .... John Wharton
Equipment Manager .... Paul Boyer
Assistant Equipment Manager .... Tim Abbott
Team Physicians .... John Finley, D.O.; David Collon, M.D.
Team Dentist .... C.J. Regula, D.M.D.

Team Transportation:
  Chief Pilot – Aviation Manager .... Dennis Gease
  Senior Captain .... Rob Mintari
  Chief Maintenance .... George Zuchelkowski
  Flight Attendants .... Michelle Wojcik, Kelly Haass
  Pilots .... Jeff Hanes, Pat White
  Flight Engineer/Mechanic .... Greg Vineyard
  Flight Operations Assistant/Office Manager .... Amy Schmaltz
Team Founded 1926
Home Ice .... Joe Louis Arena
Seating Capacity 19,983
Press Box/Radio-TV booths .... Jefferson Avenue side of arena, top of seats
Media Lounge .... First-floor hallway near Red Wings' dressing room, Atwater Street side of arena
Rink Dimensions .... 200 feet by 85 feet; S.A.R. Plastic above boards
Uniforms .... Home: Base color white, trimmed in red
                                              Road: Base color red, trimmed in white
Radio flagship station .... WJR-AM (760)
TV stations .... WKBD (Channel 50); Fox Sports Detroit (cable)
Radio announcers .... Ken Kal, Paul Woods
TV announcer .... Mickey Redmond

3

SCORE
TWICE

With
Pizza! Pizza!®

Little Caesars®

MIKE ILITCH
Owner

MARIAN ILITCH
Owner/Secretary-Treasurer

...BE GLAD YOU'RE JUST WATCHING

YOUR RED WINGS.
FOX ATTITUDE.™
CHECK LOCAL CABLE TV LISTINGS.

www.foxsports.com

ATANAS ILITCH
Vice-President

CHRISTOPHER ILITCH
Vice-President

UNSCREW A
FIRE
BREW

Red Wings senior vice-president Jim Devellano can be credited with carefully building Detroit's 1997 Stanley Cup championship team through 15 years of successful draft selections and savvy trade and free agent acquisitions. Entering his 16th season with the Red Wings, Devellano has been a driving force behind Detroit's steady rise from one of the NHL's weakest teams into the powerful club that has reached the Stanley Cup finals two of the last three years, culminating with last season's championship, giving Devellano his fourth Stanley Cup ring (three with the New York Islanders, one with Detroit).

Devellano was the first individual hired by owners Mike and Marian Ilitch after purchasing the Red Wings in June of 1982. He was the team's general manager for eight seasons before ascending to his current position of senior vice-president July 13, 1990. An excellent judge of talent throughout his 31 years in the NHL, Devellano believes that building a solid foundation begins with a capable scouting staff and strong Entry Draft selections. An impressive fourteen players on last season's club were drafted under the Devellano regime.

Jim Devellano was one of the first NHL general managers to assemble a strong European scouting staff back in 1984 which has produced high caliber players such as Sergei Fedorov, Slava Kozlov and Vladimir Konstantinov. From Sweden came a strong defenseman in Nicklas Lidstrom and promising young players such as Tomas Holmstrom and Anders Eriksson.

Through the course of Devellano's tenure with the Red Wings, Detroit has participated in five conference finals ('87, '88, '95, '96, '97) and two Stanley Cup Finals ('95, '97), collected two Presidents' Trophies ('95, '96), three regular season Western Conference championships ('94, '95, '96) and six division championships ('88, '89, '92, '94, '95, '96). In addition, the Red Wings American League farm team has won three Calder Cup Championships ('86, '89, '92) as the AHL's playoff champions.

Devellano's lengthy tenure as head of hockey operations for the Red Wings is second only to the 35 years served by the late Jack Adams, the legendary G.M. credited with building the Red Wing dynasty of the 1950's. In addition to his duties as senior vice-president, Jim serves as the team's alternate on the NHL's Board of Governors. Currently there are three NHL general managers who have succeeded under Devellano's tutelage — Detroit's new general manager Ken Holland, Neil Smith of the New York Rangers and Darcy Reiger in Buffalo.

Devellano, 54, did not play professional hockey but rose through the ranks in various capacities in his native Toronto. Joining current Red Wings coach Scotty Bowman, he became a scout with the St. Louis Blues in 1967 when the NHL expanded from six to 12 teams. The Blues reached the Stanley Cup final in each of their first three seasons. Also, it was Devellano who strongly recommended the hiring of Scotty Bowman to Mike Ilitch that led to Bowman's hiring with the Wings.

Joining the New York Islanders as a scout when that club was founded in 1972, Devellano's scouting skills helped to build a team that won four consecutive Stanley Cup titles (1980-83). In 79-80, he became G.M. of the Islanders' Indianapolis (CHL) farm club and was named Minor League Executive of the Year by The Hockey News in his first year. He returned to New York in '81 as the Islanders' assistant general manager.

Entering his 14th year with the Detroit Red Wings, Ken Holland begins his tenure as the club's general manager after serving as assistant general manager for the previous three seasons. Holland was elevated to his present position July 18, 1997.

In his new and expanded role, he oversees all aspects of hockey operations including all matters relating to player personnel, development, contract negotiations and player movements. Because of his expanded duties, Holland will now take a less prominent role at the NHL Entry Draft, after being the main point person for the past seven years. In that capacity, he was instrumental in selecting some of Detroit's best young talent, including Vyacheslav Kozlov, Darren McCarty, Chris Osgood and Martin Lapointe, along with several other top prospects.

Holland, 42, has deftly handled several different front-office duties for the club over the past 13 years. At the conclusion of his playing days as a goaltender spending most of his pro career at the American Hockey League level, Holland began his off-ice career in '85 as a western Canada scout followed by five years as amateur scouting director before promotions leading to his current position as general manager.

A native of Vernon, BC, Holland played in the junior ranks for Medicine Hat (WHL) in 74-75. He was Toronto's 13th pick (188th overall) in the '75 draft but never saw action with the Maple Leafs. Holland twice signed with NHL teams as a free agent — in '80 with Hartford and '83 with Detroit. He spent most of his pro career with AHL clubs in Binghamton and Springfield, along with Adirondack, but did appear in four NHL games, making his debut with Hartford in 80-81 and playing three contests for Detroit in 83-84.

Ken and wife Cindy have four children, Brad, Julie, Rachel and Greg, and reside in suburban Detroit.

The newest addition to Detroit's management team is assistant general manager Don Waddell. A native of Detroit, Waddell comes to the Red Wings from the Orlando Solar Bears of the International Hockey League where he served as general manager for the two-year old franchise. During the 1995-96 season, Waddell carefully crafted the expansion Solar Bears into a championship team, marking the first time in the IHL's 52-year history that an expansion club reached the Turner Cup Finals. Waddell's achievements were recognized as he was awarded the Andy Mulligan Trophy as the 1995-96 IHL Executive of the Year. It was the second time in four seasons that he received the award.

Orlando was not Waddell's first experience in beginning a successful expansion team. Prior to joining the Solar Bears on June 9, 1995, he was hired to build the IHL expansion San Diego Gulls in 1990. After their inaugural season, Waddell assumed the head coaching duties in addition to his front-office responsibilities and led the Gulls to their first playoff berth.

The next season, Waddell stepped aside as coach to concentrate on the G.M. duties and built a team which posted the then best regular season record in professional hockey as the Gulls went 62-12–8 in 1992-93, setting a victory mark which was matched by the Red Wings in the 1995-96 season.

Before his days in management, Don Waddell was drafted by the Los Angeles Kings in the 1978 Entry Draft. He earned a spot on the 1980 U.S. Olympic Team, but a broken leg kept him out of play. He played for three different IHL teams in the 1980s — Saginaw, Toledo and Flint. His best season came in 1981-82, when he earned the Governors' Trophy as the league's top defenseman.

Waddell and his wife, Cheryl, have one daughter, Chelsea.

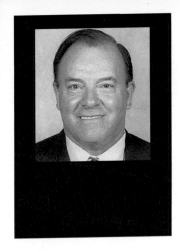

Last season, Scotty Bowman led the Detroit Red Wings to their eighth Stanley Cup championship in the franchise's 71 year history, ending the team's 42 year drought since the 1955 title. Individually, Bowman now has won eight Cups (seven as coach, one as director of player development) over the course of his 26 seasons as an NHL coach and becomes the first to win the Cup with three different teams. Entering his fifth season as Detroit's head coach, Scotty Bowman aims to match one of the few remaining NHL records he does not already own — the most Stanley Cup titles as coach (8), held by the legendary Toe Blake. Already a Hall of Famer and the winningest coach in National Hockey League past and present, Bowman met a seemingly unreachable milestone upon recording his 1000th regular-season victory Feb. 8, 1997 at Pittsburgh. Among his other remarkable achievements, Bowman is also the only coach in NHL history to guide a team to a 60-win season; achieving it twice ('77, '96).

In 1995-96, he led the Red Wings to their second consecutive Presidents' Trophy, posting a 62-13–7 mark for a franchise-best 131 points. Their 62 wins set an NHL record for wins in a season topping the 19-year old record of 60 set by Bowman's 1976-77 Montréal Canadiens. The four best victory and point totals in NHL history belong to Bowman coached teams (62 wins — 131 points by Detroit in 95-96, 60 wins — 132 points by Montréal in 76-77, 59 wins — 129 points by Montréal in 77-78, and 58 wins — 127 points by Montréal in 75-76). Also in the 95-96 campaign, Detroit captured it's third consecutive Central Division title and led the Western Conference in points.

On December 29, 1995 at Dallas he set a new NHL record for most games coached with 1607, surpassing Al Arbour. He is the only coach to register 1,000 victories overall in the regular season and playoffs combined. The total was 1191 entering this season — 1013-461–262 in 1736 regular-season games and 178-105 in 283 playoff contests. He reached the 900 mark in regular-season victories March 25, 1995 at Vancouver after posting his 1,000th overall triumph the season before on Feb. 2, 1994, at Tampa Bay. He has the best regular-season winning percentage (.659) of anyone who has coached at least 600 regular-season games.

Eleven times in 25 seasons, Bowman has been to the Cup final, second behind Dick Irvin (16). Scotty ranks first on the all-time playoff coaching ledger in victories, games, playoff series, and series won. He has coached in 55 series and won 39. Among those coaching a minimum of 65 postseason games, Bowman's .629 winning percentage is third after Glen Sather (.706) and Blake (.689). In the Stanley Cup finals, Bowman is third in victories with a 28-21 mark in 49 games, trailing Irvin and Blake (32 wins each), and Bowman is second in games in the finals after Irvin (77), yet surpassing Blake (48) last season.

Bowman, 63, became the 22nd head coach in Detroit history June 15, 1993, signing a two-year deal, and on June 24, 1994, he added the title of director of player personnel, a post which he held through the 1996-97 season. At the conclusion of the 1996-97 Cup-winning season, Bowman signed a two-year contract to return as head coach.

Before coming to Detroit, Bowman had coached Pittsburgh the previous two seasons, including a Cup title in 1992. Scotty had earned another Stanley Cup ring in 1991 when he was Pittsburgh's director of player development and recruitment. In 1991-92, Bowman took the reins as the Penguins' coach when the late Bob Johnson became ill. Scotty remained in the dual role through the 92-93 season.

When Detroit won the Central Division in 1995-96, it was Bowman's 13th division title. Seven times his teams have been first overall in the NHL, and one of his clubs tied for best record. Bowman's teams have amassed 100 or more points 12 times and missed the playoffs only twice.

Bowman broke into the NHL coaching ranks with the St. Louis Blues in the 1967-68 season, when the NHL expanded from six to 12 teams. The Blues advanced to the Cup final in each of their first three seasons and won two division titles.

Moving in 1971 to Montréal — where he earlier had worked and coached in the Canadiens' minor league system — Bowman achieved remarkable success. He won the Stanley Cup five times (1973 and '76 through '79) and rang up six division titles in eight seasons. In seven of his eight seasons in Montréal, the Canadiens notched more than 100 points and missed the mark once with 99. The 76-77 club holds the league record for fewest defeats (8) in a season of 70 or more games.

Bowman went to the Buffalo Sabres in 1979, where he was general manager and shared coaching duties until 1987. He won a division title in his first year behind the Buffalo bench in 79-80.

After leaving the Sabres, Bowman worked for CBC-TV's "Hockey Night in Canada" from 1987 until joining Pittsburgh's front office in June of '90.

Bowman is also a proven winner at the international level, coaching Team Canada to the 1976 Canada Cup title. He also guided Team Canada in the '81 Canada Cup and the NHL All-Stars in a three-game series against the Soviet Union in '79. Scotty was inducted into the Hockey Hall of Fame in 1991.

William Scott Bowman was born Sept. 18, 1933 in Montréal. He and wife Suella have five children, Alicia, David, Stanley, Bob and Nancy, and spend the off-season in suburban Buffalo.

NHL COACHING RECORD

Season	Team	Regular Season							Playoffs			
		GC	W	L	T	PTS	PCT	FIN	GC	W	L	PCT
1967-68	St. Louis	58	23	21	14	60	.517	3rd	+18	8	10	.444
1968-69	St. Louis	76	37	25	14	88	.579	1st	+12	8	4	.667
1969-70	St. Louis	76	37	27	12	86	.566	1st	+16	8	8	.500
1970-71	St. Louis	28	13	10	5	31	.554	2nd	6	2	4	.333
1971-72	Montréal	78	46	16	16	108	.692	3rd	6	2	4	.333
1972-73	Montréal	78	52	10	16	120	.769	#1st	*17	12	5	.706
1973-74	Montréal	78	45	24	9	99	.635	2nd	6	2	4	.333
1974-75	Montréal	80	47	14	19	113	.706	@1st	11	6	5	.545
1975-76	Montréal	80	58	11	11	127	.794	#1st	*13	12	1	.923
1976-77	Montréal	80	60	8	12	132	.825	#1st	*14	12	2	.857
1977-78	Montréal	80	59	10	11	129	.806	#1st	*15	12	3	.800
1978-79	Montréal	80	52	17	11	115	.719	1st	*16	12	4	.750
1979-80	Buffalo	80	47	17	16	110	.688	1st	14	9	5	.643
1981-82	Buffalo	35	18	10	7	43	.614	3rd	4	1	3	.250
1982-83	Buffalo	80	38	29	13	89	.556	3rd	10	6	4	.600
1983-84	Buffalo	80	48	25	7	103	.644	2nd	3	0	3	.000
1984-85	Buffalo	80	38	28	14	90	.563	3rd	5	2	3	.400
1985-86	Buffalo	37	18	18	1	37	.500	5th	–	–	–	–
1986-87	Buffalo	12	3	7	2	8	.333	5th	–	–	-	–
1991-92	Pittsburgh	80	39	32	9	87	.544	3rd	*21	16	5	.762
1992-93	Pittsburgh	84	56	21	7	119	.708	#1st	*12	7	5	.583
1993-94	DETROIT	84	46	30	8	100	.595	1st	7	3	4	.429
1995	DETROIT	48	33	11	4	70	.729	#1st	+18	12	6	.667
1995-96	DETROIT	82	62	13	7	131	.799	#1st	19	10	9	.526
1996-97	DETROIT	82	38	26	18	94	.573	5th	*20	16	4	.800
DETROIT TOTALS		**296**	**179**	**80**	**37**	**395**	**.667**		**64**	**41**	**23**	**.641**
NHL TOTALS		**1736**	**1013**	**461**	**262**	**2289**	**.659**		**283**	**178**	**105**	**.629**

*-Won Stanley Cup   +-Lost Stanley Cup final   #-First overall in NHL   @-Tied for first overall in NHL

Barry Smith's coaching career has included stops at the collegiate, international and National Hockey League levels, all of which combined have made him invaluable as the Red Wings associate coach for the past four years. His variety of experiences has enabled him to employ innovative ideas that have greatly improved an already successful Red Wing hockey team.

Smith was largely responsible for implementing the "left wing lock" defensive system he discovered while watching teams in Sweden. The entire team bought into the plan which stresses defensive play first, and the results were evident by Detroit's low goals-against average the last few seasons.

Smith, in his fifth season with Detroit, has found success at every level he has coached. In addition to last season's championship, he won two Stanley Cup rings as an assistant coach with the Pittsburgh Penguins and has won championships while coaching at collegiate and international levels. As a credit to his international reputation, he was selected to serve as assistant coach for Team Sweden in the inaugural World Cup of Hockey in the summer of '96. Later that season, Barry took a temporary leave from the Red Wings to assume the head coaching duties with Malmo of the Swedish Elite League, yet returned in time for Detroit's playoff run in the spring.

Smith, 46, came to Detroit July 28, 1993, after being an assistant at Pittsburgh for three seasons, first under the late Bob Johnson and then two years with Bowman while the Penguins won Stanley Cup titles in '91 and '92. Smith also spent three years as an assistant with the Buffalo Sabres.

Barry entered the coaching ranks in 1975 as head coach at Elmira (NY) College while earning a masters degree in education. His clubs won three Eastern Collegiate Athletic Conference titles and twice went to the NCAA Division III Finals.

Moving to Europe, Smith coached in Sweden from 1981-84 and Norway form 1984-86, serving as an assistant on the Norwegian club in the World Championships. He also scouted European prospects for the Sabres and in March of '86 he went to Buffalo as Bowman's assistant. Smith worked one year under Bowman and remained in Buffalo until 1989, when he journeyed to Italy for one season to coach the Alleghe club and the Italian National Team. He joined the Penguins in 1990-91 as Johnson's assistant, and also was an aide to Johnson on Team USA in the 1991 Canada Cup.

The Buffalo native received a degree in physical education in 1972 from Ithaca (NY) College where he starred in hockey and football. He was elected to the school's Hall of Fame in 1992.

Barry and wife Mary have a son, Ryan, and a daughter, Molly, and spend the off-season in suburban Buffalo.

Dave Lewis enters his tenth year as part of the Red Wings' coaching staff, having worked with three different head coaches beginning with Jacques Demers, followed by Bryan Murray and continuing with Scotty Bowman, he draws on his vast experiences while working to maintain Detroit's reputation as a solid defensive club. Lewis also relies on his 15 seasons as an NHL defenseman to help fine tune a defensive unit that has ranked among the top in the NHL over the last few seasons. His duties also include extensive video work used in pre-scouting opponents.

Lewis, 43, joined the coaching staff immediately after retiring as a player Nov. 6, 1987, amid his 15th NHL season. This is his eleventh year in the Detroit organization since signing as a free agent (no compensation) July 28, 1986. The 1996-97 Stanley Cup championship with Detroit was the first of his career.

A native of Kindersley, SK, Lewis played junior hockey for Saskatoon (WHL) and was the New York Islanders' second pick (33rd overall) in the 1973 Entry Draft (selected by Jim Devellano, the Islanders' chief scout at the time). Lewis jumped from the junior ranks to the NHL and never played in the minor leagues.

Dave's biggest milestone came when he played in his 1,000th regular-season game Apr. 1, 1987, against Philadelphia at Joe Louis Arena. In all, he played 1,008 regular-season games with the Islanders, Los Angeles, New Jersey and Detroit, recording 36 goals, 187 assists and 953 penalty minutes. He also appeared in 91 playoff games, with one goal, 20 assists and 143 penalty minutes.

Dave and wife Brenda live in suburban Detroit and have a son, Ryan, and daughter, Meagan.

Entering his 16th season with the Red Wings, and 12th as the club's top NHL Scout, Dan Belisle continues to provide valuable insight upon which the coaches and management rely when considering player personnel decisions. Belisle is called upon to provide key information used in making potential trade and free agent acquisitions or preparing for opponents.

Belisle, 60, joined the organization in 1982-83 as an assistant coach under Nick Polano. He remained as an assistant to Harry Neale and Brad Park, then assumed his present position in the summer of '86.

A successful minor-league coach, Belisle was appointed head coach of the Washington Capitals in 78-79, remaining there until early in the 79-80 season.

Dan returned to the minors in 80-81 as general manager/coach at Dallas (CHL), guiding that club to the regular-season title and winning the league's Coach of the Year award (one of four times he received such an honor in the minors).

Belisle made his pro coaching debut in 72-73 with Des Moines (IHL) and won the league title in his second season. He moved to Syracuse (NAHL) in 75-76, winning regular-season and playoff championships in his second year, then went to Philadelphia (AHL) in 77-78.

A native of South Porcupine, ON, Belisle spent most of his 15-year playing career as a right wing in the minors, although he played four games for the New York Rangers in the 60-61 season. He retired as a player in '71.

Dan and wife Carol reside in Sarasota, FL, and have three grown children, Debra, Dan Jr. and Dee.

Jim Nill is in his fourth season in the Red Wings' front office and third as director of player development/AHL scout. Following his playing days, Nill established a reputation as an outstanding scout with a sharp eye for talent which led him to his current position with the organization.

Nill oversees the development of all Detroit-owned players, with the exception of those at the team's Adirondack (AHL) farm club. He focuses on prospects in the junior leagues and Europe and also scouts the AHL for potential free agents and trades.

Nill, 38, joined the Red Wings' front office in the summer of 1994 after three seasons with the Ottawa Senators. Starting with Ottawa as an amateur scout, he was promoted to pro scout after only two years.

Jim was no stranger to Detroit when he moved into the executive level. He spent his final 2½ years as an NHL player with the Red Wings after being acquired from Winnipeg Jan. 10, 1988, for Mark Kumpel. Nill later went to Adirondack as a player/coach, retiring as a player after the 90-91 season. A right wing in nine NHL seasons, he recorded 58 goals, 87 assists and 854 PIM in 524 regular-season games.

The native of Hanna, AB, played for Medicine Hat (WHL) in the junior ranks, one year at the University of Calgary and was on the Canadian National and Olympic teams in 79-80. He was St. Louis' fourth pick (89th overall, fifth round) in the '78 Entry Draft and also played for Vancouver and Boston.

Jim and wife Bekki reside in Glens Falls, NY, with daughters Jenna and Kristin and son Trevor.

The tradition of Detroit Stanley Cup championships and the "Howe" name carries on as Mark Howe will have his name engraved on hockey's hallowed trophy as Detroit's pro scout. Although this is Mark's first Cup, his father Gordie's name appears on Detroit's previous four. Ironically, another Howe of no relation to Mark and Gordie, Syd Howe, was with the club for its first three championships meaning that Detroit has never won a Cup without a Howe.

Mark enters his sixth season with the organization, third in the front office. After ending his professional hockey career as an NHL defenseman on September 28, 1995, Howe joined the Red Wings front office as an assistant to the hockey department. In that capacity, he began scouting at the IHL and AHL level, however, his energies were primarily focused on preparing promising young defenseman for the NHL at Detroit's Adirondack (AHL) affiliate. He has worked with current Red Wing blueliners Jamie Pushor, Anders Eriksson and Aaron Ward. This year, Mark will continue to scout the IHL, but he will also add some NHL games to his schedule after being called on for some scouting reports on Detroit's playoff opponents last spring.

On July 8, 1992, Howe returned to his hometown of Detroit when he signed as a free agent (no compensation). He appeared in 122 regular-season games in three seasons for Detroit, collecting eight goals and 56 assists.

Playing first in the WHA and then the NHL, Howe is the second-highest-scoring defenseman in professional hockey after current Red Wing Paul Coffey with 1247 points — 742 in 929 NHL regular-season games on 197 goals and 545 assists after 505 points in the WHA (208-247–505).

Howe was a First Team NHL All-Star defenseman in '83, '86 and '87, when he also was runner-up for the Norris Trophy. In 85-86, he led the league with a plus-85 and followed with a plus-57 to pace all NHL defenseman in 86-87. He was selected for five NHL All-Star games ('81, '83, '85, '86 and '88).

Mark and wife Ginger reside in suburban Detroit with sons Travis and Nolan and daughter Azia.

SCOUTING STAFF

JOE McDONNELL
Eastern Scout

BRUCE HARALSON
Western Scout

MARK LEACH
Eastern USA, High School
and College Scout

HAKAN ANDERSSON
Director of
European Scouting

VLADIMIR HAVLUJ
Czech and Slovak
Republic Scout

PAUL CROWLEY
Scout

(not pictured)

RUSLAN SHABANOV
Russian Scout

MARTY STEIN
Scout

Entering his seventh full season as the Red Wings' athletic trainer, John Wharton has earned a reputation as one of the best in his field. His primary responsibility is to maintain the health and conditioning of Detroit's players. Wharton was hired in February of 1991 as strength and conditioning coordinator after five years in the Center for Athletic Medicine at Detroit's Henry Ford Hospital.

His latest endeavor is the opening of John Wharton's The Training Room, a dynamic fitness and sports medicine facility which will provide the public with a high caliber rehabilitation and fitness treatment usually only reserved for professional athletes. The Training Room will also serve as the official training center for the Wings. Expanding his reputation internationally, he received one of the greatest honors of his career in the summer of 1996 when asked to serve as head athletic trainer for Team Russia during the inaugural World Cup of Hockey tournament.

The Flint native has a bachelor of science degree in sports medicine from Central Michigan University and is a certified strength and conditioning specialist. He was hockey trainer at the '90 Goodwill Games and spent a season with the Detroit Lions. John and wife Jeanne reside in suburban Detroit with their son Luke and daughter Brookelyn.

Paul Boyer enters his fourth season as equipment manager, coming to Detroit after one season with the New Jersey Devils. A native of Sault Ste. Marie, ON, Paul earned a bachelor of science degree from nearby Lake Superior State University, then spent five years as the school's hockey trainer before heading for the NHL. Paul and his wife Helen reside in suburban Detroit.

Assistant equipment manager Tim Abbott is in his sixth season. The Mt. Clemens native attended L'Anse Creuse High School and Macomb Community College, then spent four years as assistant trainer for Adirondack. Tim, wife Kristen and son Tyler reside in suburban Detroit.

Lending a hand with the busy workload in the dressing room are assistants Wally Crossman and Mike Vella.

The Red Wings' medical staff is comprised of John Finley, D.O.; David Collon, M.D.; and C.J. Regula, D.M.D. Dr. Finley has a general practice in Southfield; Dr. Collon is director of orthopedic surgery at the Center for Athletic Medicine at Henry Ford Hospital and also serves the Tigers and Lions; Dr. Regula has a dental practice in Livonia.

JOHN WHARTON
Athletic Trainer

PAUL BOYER
Equipment Manager

TIM ABBOTT
Assistant Equipment Manager

WALLY CROSSMAN
Dressing Room Assistant

MIKE VELLA
Dressing Room Assistant

JOHN FINLEY, D.O.
Team Physician

DAVID COLLON, M.D.
Team Physician

C.J. REGULA, D.M.D.
Team Dentist

31 GOOD REASONS

WHY SO MANY PEOPLE IN METRO DETROIT

THINK FORD FIRST!

BLOOMFIELD HILLS
ALAN FORD
1845 South Telegraph
(248) 333-3000

CENTERLINE
BOB THIBODEAU
26333 Van Dyke
(810)755-2100

DEARBORN
FAIRLANE FORD SALES
14585 Michigan Avenue
(313) 846-5000

DEARBORN
VILLAGE FORD
23535 Michigan Avenue
(313) 565-3900

DETROIT
JORGENSEN FORD
8333 Michigan Avenue
(313) 584-2250

DETROIT
RIVERSIDE FORD SALES
1800 East Jefferson Avenue
(313) 567-0250

DETROIT
STARK HICKEY WEST
24760 West Seven Mile Road
(313) 538-6600

FARMINGTON HILLS
TOM HOLZER FORD
39300 West Ten Mile Road
(248) 474-1234

FERNDALE
ED SCHMID FORD
21600 Woodward Avenue
(248) 399-1000

FLAT ROCK
SUPERIOR FORD
22675 Gibralter Road
(734) 782-2400

LIVONIA
BILL BROWN FORD
32222 Plymouth Road
(734) 421-7000

MT. CLEMENS
MIKE DORIAN FORD
35900 Gratiot
(810) 792-4100

MT. CLEMENS
RUSS MILNE FORD
43870 Gratiot Avenue
(810) 293-7000

NORTHVILLE
MCDONALD FORD SALES
550 West Seven Mile Road
(248) 349-1400

OAK PARK
MEL FARR FORD
24750 Greenfield
(248) 967-3700

PLYMOUTH
BLACKWELL FORD
41001 Plymouth Road
(734) 453-1100

REDFORD
PAT MILLIKEN FORD
9600 Telegraph Road
(313) 255-3100

ROCHESTER
HUNTINGTON FORD
2890 South Rochester Road
(248) 852-0400

ROYAL OAK
ROYAL OAK FORD
27550 North Woodward Avenue
(248) 548-4100

SOUTHFIELD
AVIS FORD
29200 Telegraph Road
(248) 355-7500

SOUTHGATE
SOUTHGATE FORD
16501 Fort Street
(734) 282-3636

ST. CLAIR SHORES
ROY O'BRIEN
22201 Nine Mile Road
(810) 776-7600

STERLING HEIGHTS
JEROME-DUNCAN
Van Dyke at 17-1/2 Mile Road
(810) 268-7500

TAYLOR
RAY WHITFIELD FORD
10725 South Telegraph Road
(313) 291-0300

TROY
DEAN SELLERS FORD
2600 West Maple Road
(248) 643-7500

TROY
TROY FORD, INC.
777 John R
(248) 585-4000

WARREN
AL LONG FORD
13711 Eight Mile Road
(810)777-2700

WATERFORD
FLANNERY FORD, INC.
5900 Highland Road
(248) 356-1260

WAYNE
JACK DEMMER FORD
37300 Michigan Avenue
(313) 721-2600

WESTLAND
NORTH BROTHERS FORD
33300 Ford Road
(313) 421-1300

WOODHAVEN
GORNO FORD
22025 Allen Road
(734) 676-2200

Ford FORD

THINK FORD FIRST!

Metro Detroit Ford Dealers

CALL 1-800-NEW FORD FOR CURRENT OFFERS or, www.thinkfordfirst.com

Play-by-play announcer Ken Kal and analyst Paul Woods returning in their third season together behind the microphone on flagship station WJR-AM (760).

Before coming to the Red Wings, Kal, 39, had done radio play-by-play for University of Michigan hockey for 11 years on Ann Arbor AM stations — seven on WTKA after the first four on WAAM, during which time he also covered the Red Wings as a reporter. Born and raised in the city of Detroit, Kal graduated from Wayne State University in 1979 and immediately joined WAAM, doing sports and working as a disc jockey.

In addition to his on-air duties, Ken Kal is extremely active in the team's community relations efforts, often visiting schools or business groups. Kal is also a contributing writer to the team's official magazine, "Inside Hockeytown." Rounding out his administrative duties, one of Ken's newest assignments is to work with the broadcast department to expand the Red Wings radio network and maintain affiliate relations. Away from the office, he also earned most valuable player honors for his play in the Red Wings charity softball games.

Woods is returning for his 11th year as hockey broadcast analyst for WJR, a career which began shortly after the conclusion of his retirement from the NHL. The native of Hespeler, ON, was drafted by Montréal in '75 but never played for the Canadiens and was obtained by Detroit in the '77 waiver draft. His seven-year stint with the Red Wings began in 1977-78 and ended after the '83-'84 season. He had 72 goals and 124 assists in 501 regular-season NHL games.

Mickey Redmond enters his 12th year as color analyst on Red Wings television — UPN 50 (Channel 50) and the new Fox Sports Detroit. Redmond is a highly regarded analyst whose broadcast resume includes work on nationally televised games for the Fox Network, ESPN as well as CBC's Hockey Night in Canada. Mickey twice was a 50-goal scorer in five full seasons with Detroit after being acquired from Montréal with Guy Charron and Bill Collins for Frank Mahovlich in January of '71. He scored 52 goals and made the NHL's First All Star Team in '73, and netted 51 the next season to earn a Second-Team berth. He had 233 goals and 195 assists in 538 regular-season games in nine NHL seasons with Montréal and Detroit.

Toby Cunningham, winner of six local Emmy Awards and four Associated Press honors for production of Red Wings telecasts, is in his 18th season as executive producer for Channel 50 coverage.

Following is the team's radio network (some stations broadcast a limited number of games):

WMSB-AM, Alpena	WQSN/WKZO, Kalamazoo
WJR-AM, Detroit	WHCH-FM, Marquette
WCBY-AM, Cheboygan	WKBZ-AM, Muskegon
WCHT-AM, Escanaba	WNBY-AM, Newberry
WTRX-AM, Flint	WJML AM, Potocky
WMJZ-FM, Gaylord	WPHM-AM, Port Huron
WMFN-AM, Grand Rapids	WMAX-AM, Saginaw
WKHM-AM, Jackson	WSOO-AM, Sault Ste. Marie

KEN KAL

PAUL WOODS

MICKEY REDMOND

TOBY CUNNINGHAM

JOHN PETTIT
General Manager –
Joe Louis Arena/
V.P. of Operations
Joe Louis Arena

PAUL MacDONALD
Director of Finance

TED SPEERS
Marketing Director

BOB KERLIN
Box Office Manager

WILLIAM LEY
General Sales Manager

JEFFREY AJLUNI
Manager, Arena Signage,
Print & Promotions

MICHAEL MAZUREK
Manager, Media and
Interactive Sales

DAN FRANK
Senior Account Executive

SCOTT MILLER
Account Executive

ANDY LOUGHNANE
Advertising Sales
Coordinator

JASON O'CONNELL
Broadcast Coordinator

KEVIN VAUGHN
Marketing Coordinator

BRAD EBBEN
Season Ticket Manager

KAREN DAVIS
Public Relations
Coordinator

MICHAEL KUTA
Public Relations
Coordinator

LORI SHIELS
Marketing Assistant

NANCY BEARD
Executive Assistant

CATHY WITZKE
Accounting Assistant

KRISTIN ARMSTRONG
Administrative Assistant

GAME STAFF

P.A. Announcer . . . . Budd Lynch
Production Manager . . . . Beth Kangas
Event Producer . . . . Donna Westphal
Broadcast Engineer In Charge . . . . Sheldon Nueman
Video Coordinator . . . . Joe Ducharme
Team Photographer . . . . Mark Hicks
Game Staff Coordinator/Statistics & Research . . . . Grey Innis
Statistics & Research Assistant . . . . Morris Moorawnick
Game Staff Assistants . . . . Jerry Brown, Bucky Browning, Rich Clemente, Dennis Davidson, Marc DeRosiers,
Scott Glenn, Lowell Gumbert, Gary Hinds, Eric Hofner, Kurt Hofner, Lance Hofner,
Larry Kosiba, Gene Majtyka, Chip Molitor, Jim Omilian, Tom Shaw, Bill Waddell
Team Statistician . . . . Adam Mitchell
Media Lounge Receptionist . . . . Barbara Valade
Red Wings' Dressing Room Assistants . . . . Mike Vella, Wally Crossman
Visitors' Dressing Room Assistants . . . . Chad Youngblood, Henry Baker

NHL OFF-ICE OFFICIALS

Supervisor & Penalty Timekeeper . . . . Mike Hargraves
Official Scorer . . . . Bill Martin
Game Timekeeper . . . . Ron Idziak, Phil Blain
Goal Judges . . . . Jack MacRobert, Chuck Sneddon
Penalty Box Attendants . . . . Ken McFadden, Len Paquette
Real Time Scorers . . . . Ron Hayes, Steve Hosmer, Bob Dollas, Roy Finger,
Jerry Moran, Jerry McKelvey (*Alternate:* Mike Blair)
Video Goal Judges . . . . Matt Pavelich, Jerry Pateman
TV Commercial Coordinator . . . . John Vieceli

THE PLAYERS

BROWN Doug

BECAME RED WING: Obtained in NHL Waiver Draft January 18, 1995.

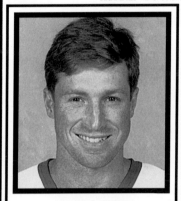

RIGHT WING

- 5-10 • 188 lbs.
- Shoots Right
- Born: New Haven, CT
  June 12, 1964
- Last Amateur Club:
  Boston College (HE)

Career vs. N.H.L.

Team	GP	G	A	PTS
Anaheim	12	2	4	6
Boston	22	8	8	16
Buffalo	18	6	7	13
Calgary	20	3	6	9
Chicago	29	2	4	6
Colorado	22	3	6	9
Dallas	29	2	7	9
Detroit	14	2	7	9
Edmonton	26	7	6	13
Florida	6	2	1	3
Hartford	25	16	5	21
Los Angeles	24	1	6	7
Montréal	19	0	3	3
New Jersey	5	0	0	0
NY Islanders	40	7	8	15
NY Rangers	39	11	14	25
Ottawa	8	0	3	3
Philadelphia	40	5	8	13
Phoenix	26	5	3	8
Pittsburgh	32	8	12	20
San Jose	15	4	5	9
St. Louis	27	7	4	11
Tampa Bay	6	1	5	6
Toronto	22	3	6	9
Vancouver	22	2	6	8
Washington	35	6	7	13

1996-97 SEASON — Scored two goals and posted two assists (one GWG) Nov. 4, 1996 vs. Hartford for first multiple-point effort of season which matched career-best performance (four assists) Dec. 11, 1993 at Tampa Bay while playing for Pittsburgh....Points in 10 of 49 regular-season contests....3-6–9 home, 3-1–4 road....1-1–2 on PPGs....0-1–1 on SHGs....0-1–1 on GWGs...Assisted on two game-winning goals in Conference Finals vs. Colorado....Scored three goals in three games in second round series vs. Anaheim....First Stanley Cup Championship.

CAREER — Collected an assist Jan. 20, 1995 vs. Chicago in Red Wings debut....First goal as Red Wing Jan. 30, 1995 at Edmonton....Most recent point streak: Feb 27-29, 1996 (1-2–3)....Never drafted, he signed with New Jersey as free agent in August of '86....NHL debut March 13, 1987 vs. NY Islanders....First point was assist Mar. 18, 1987 at Winnipeg....First full season in 87-88, named Devils' top rookie....First goal Oct. 9, 1987 vs. Pittsburgh....Played with Devils in '88 conference final, scoring first playoff OT goal....Led Devils' forwards with plus-18 in 90-91, third overall on team at plus-17 in 91-92....Scored penalty shot Nov. 23, 1991, at Philadelphia vs. Ken Wregget....Signed as free agent by Pittsburgh in Sept. of '93....Career highs in goals (18), assists (37), points (55) in lone season with Penguins (93-94), ranking third on club at plus-19....Team USA in '86, '89, '91 World Championships, '91 Canada Cup....Four seasons at Boston College, making Hockey East First All-Star Team in final two years (84-85, 85-86).

PERSONAL — Doug and his wife have two daughters and two sons....Spent off-season in New York....Enjoys golf, tennis....Brother Greg also played in NHL.

CAREER

Season	Team	League	Regular Season					Playoffs				
			GP	G	A	P	PM	GP	G	A	P	PM
1982-83	Boston College	ECAC	22	9	8	17	0	–	–	–	–	–
1983-84	Boston College	ECAC	38	11	10	21	6	–	–	–	–	–
1984-85a	Boston College	ECAC	45	37	31	68	10	–	–	–	–	–
1985-86a	Boston College	ECAC	38	16	40	56	16	–	–	–	–	–
1986-87b	New Jersey	NHL	4	0	1	1	0	–	–	–	–	–
	Maine	AHL	73	24	34	58	15	–	–	–	–	–
1987-88	New Jersey	NHL	70	14	11	25	20	19	5	1	6	6
	Utica	AHL	2	0	2	2	2	–	–	–	–	–
1988-89	New Jersey	NHL	63	15	10	25	15	–	–	–	–	–
	Utica	AHL	4	1	4	5	0	–	–	–	–	–
1989-90	New Jersey	NHL	69	14	20	34	16	6	0	1	1	2
1990-91	New Jersey	NHL	58	14	16	30	4	7	2	2	4	2
1991-92	New Jersey	NHL	71	11	17	28	27	–	–	–	–	–
1992-93	New Jersey	NHL	15	0	5	5	2	–	–	–	–	–
	Utica	AHL	25	11	17	28	8	–	–	–	–	–
1993-94c	Pittsburgh	NHL	77	18	37	55	18	6	0	0	0	2
1995d	DETROIT	NHL	45	9	12	21	16	18	4	8	12	2
1995-96	DETROIT	NHL	62	12	15	27	4	13	3	3	6	4
1996-97	DETROIT	NHL	49	6	7	13	8	14	3	3	6	2
DETROIT Totals			156	27	34	61	28	45	10	14	24	8
NHL Totals			583	113	151	264	130	83	17	18	35	20

a-Hockey East First All-Star Team.
b-Signed as free agent by New Jersey, August 6, 1986.
c-Signed as free agent by Pittsburgh, Sept. 28, 1993.
d-Acquired by DETROIT in Waiver Draft, January 18, 1995.

DANDENAULT Mathieu

BECAME RED WING: Second choice (49th overall) in 1994 Entry Draft.

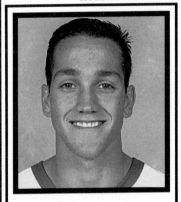

RIGHT WING/DEFENSE

- 6-1 • 200 lbs.
- Shoots Right
- Born: Sherbrooke, PQ
  February 3, 1976
- Last Amateur Club:
  Sherbrooke Fauçons (QMJHL)

Career vs. N.H.L.

Team	GP	G	A	PTS
Anaheim	4	0	0	0
Boston	3	1	0	1
Buffalo	3	1	0	1
Calgary	4	0	0	0
Chicago	6	0	1	1
Colorado	5	0	0	0
Dallas	7	1	2	3
Detroit	0	0	0	0
Edmonton	6	0	0	0
Florida	1	0	0	0
Hartford	2	0	0	0
Los Angeles	7	0	4	4
Montréal	4	3	1	4
New Jersey	3	0	0	0
NY Islanders	2	0	0	0
NY Rangers	2	0	0	0
Ottawa	4	1	1	2
Philadelphia	3	0	1	1
Phoenix	4	0	0	0
Pittsburgh	1	0	0	0
San Jose	4	0	1	1
St. Louis	4	0	0	0
Tampa Bay	3	0	0	0
Toronto	7	1	4	5
Vancouver	7	0	1	1
Washington	3	0	0	0

1996-97 SEASON — First goal of season Oct. 12 at Buffalo, first assist came Nov. 23 at Los Angeles...Had one two-game streak: Jan. 5-8 (0-2–2)....Had two two-point efforts on season....Was youngest player on team....0-4–4 home, 3-5–8 road....Assisted on one game-winning goal....First Stanley Cup Championship.

CAREER — NHL debut Oct. 8, 1995 at Edmonton...First NHL point was power play goal Nov. 2, 1995 at Boston....First NHL assist Nov. 14, 1995 at Los Angeles....First career two-goal outing Dec. 2, 1995 at Montréal....In 1994-95, led Sherbrooke (QMJHL) in goals, assists, points, was ninth in league scoring.

PERSONAL — Single....Spends off-season in hometown of Sherbrooke, PQ....Plays with the Red Wings' charity softball team in off-season.

CAREER

Season	Club	League	Regular Schedule					Playoffs				
			GP	G	A	P	PIM	GP	G	A	P	PIM
1993–94	Sherbrooke	QMJHL	67	17	36	53	67	12	4	10	14	12
1994–95	Sherbrooke	QMJHL	67	37	70	107	76	7	1	7	8	10
1995–96	DETROIT	NHL	34	5	7	12	6	–	–	–	–	–
1996-97	DETROIT	NHL	65	3	9	12	28	–	–	–	–	–
DETROIT and NHL Totals			**99**	**8**	**16**	**24**	**34**	–	–	–	–	–

Drafted by DETROIT in 1994 Entry Draft (2nd choice, 49th overall).

DRAPER Kris

BECAME RED WING: Obtained June 30, 1993, from Winnipeg for future considerations.

CENTER

- 5-11 • 190 lbs.
- Shoots Left
- Born: Toronto, ON
  May 24, 1971
- Last Amateur Club:
  Ottawa 67s (OHL)

Career vs. N.H.L.

Team	GP	G	A	PTS
Anaheim	9	0	1	1
Boston	2	0	0	0
Buffalo	3	1	0	1
Calgary	16	1	2	3
Chicago	17	4	4	8
Colorado	8	0	0	0
Dallas	15	1	2	3
Detroit	2	1	0	1
Edmonton	15	1	2	3
Florida	6	0	0	0
Hartford	4	1	0	1
Los Angeles	12	2	0	2
Montréal	5	2	1	3
New Jersey	5	0	0	0
NY Islanders	4	0	1	1
NY Rangers	4	1	0	1
Ottawa	4	0	3	3
Philadelphia	6	2	0	2
Phoenix	15	2	2	4
Pittsburgh	4	0	0	0
San Jose	12	2	2	4
St. Louis	13	1	2	3
Tampa Bay	3	0	1	1
Toronto	14	3	1	4
Vancouver	18	0	4	4
Washington	7	0	0	0

28

1996-97 SEASON – Registered career-best eight goals....1-2–3 at home...7-3–10 on road....1-2–2 on game-winning goals....Assisted on one shorthanded goal....Scored one power play goal....Scored two goals (one shorthanded) and collected game-winning assist in first round of playoffs vs. St. Louis....Posted a shorthanded assist in Stanley Cup Finals series vs. Philadelphia...First Stanley Cup Championship.

CAREER — April 7-14, 1996, posted career-high four-game streak (2-3–5) which included two game-winning assists....In '95 playoffs, dramatic GWG with 1:45 remaining in third period June 4 vs. Chicago gave Detroit 3-2 victory for 2-0 series lead en route to winning conference championship....Career bests in total points (7-9–16) in 1995-96....Scored goal in NHL debut Oct. 4, 1990, for Winnipeg vs. Toronto....First goal as Red Wing Feb. 12, 1994, at St. Louis....First NHL assist Jan. 27, 1993, at Chicago....Initially Winnipeg's fourth pick (62nd overall, third round) in '89 draft....Played two seasons for Canadian National Team.

PERSONAL — Single....Spends off-season in West Hill, ON....Enjoys golf and mountain biking....Plays for Red Wings charity softball team in summer.

CAREER

Season	Club	League	Regular Schedule					Playoffs				
			GP	G	A	P	PM	GP	G	A	P	PM
1988-89	Canadian	National	60	11	15	26	16	–	–	–	–	–
1989-90	Canadian	National	61	12	22	34	44	–	–	–	–	–
1990-91	Winnipeg	NHL	3	1	0	1	5	–	–	–	–	–
	Moncton	AHL	39	19	42	61	35	17	8	11	19	20
1991-92	Winnipeg	NHL	10	2	0	2	2	2	0	0	0	0
	Moncton	AHL	61	11	18	29	113	4	0	1	1	6
1992-93	Moncton	AHL	67	12	23	35	40	5	2	2	4	18
	Winnipeg	NHL	7	0	0	0	2	–	–	–	–	–
1993-94	Adirondack	AHL	46	20	23	43	49	–	–	–	–	–
	DETROIT	NHL	39	5	8	13	31	7	2	2	4	4
1995	DETROIT	NHL	36	2	6	8	22	18	4	1	5	12
1995-96	DETROIT	NHL	52	7	9	16	32	18	4	2	6	18
1996-97	DETROIT	NHL	76	8	5	13	73	20	2	4	6	12
DETROIT Totals			**203**	**22**	**28**	**50**	**158**	**63**	**12**	**9**	**21**	**46**
NHL Totals			**223**	**25**	**28**	**53**	**167**	**65**	**12**	**9**	**21**	**46**

Drafted by Winnipeg in 1989 NHL Entry Draft (4th choice, 62nd overall, 3rd round).
Traded to DETROIT from Winnipeg for future considerations, June 30, 1993.

1997-1998 DETROIT 44 RED WINGS

ERIKSSON Anders

BECAME RED WING: First choice (22nd overall, 1st round) in 1993 Entry Draft.

DEFENSE

- 6-3 • 218 lbs.
- Shoots Left
- Born: Bollnas, Sweden
  January 9, 1975
- Last Amateur Club:
  MoDo (Sweden)

Career vs. N.H.L.

Team	GP	G	A	PTS
Anaheim	0	0	0	0
Boston	1	0	0	0
Buffalo	1	0	0	0
Calgary	1	0	1	1
Chicago	2	0	0	0
Colorado	1	0	0	0
Dallas	5	0	0	0
Detroit	0	0	0	0
Edmonton	1	0	0	0
Florida	0	0	0	0
Hartford	1	0	1	1
Los Angeles	2	0	2	2
Montréal	2	0	0	0
New Jersey	1	0	0	0
NY Islanders	0	0	0	0
NY Rangers	0	0	0	0
Ottawa	1	0	0	0
Philadelphia	0	0	0	0
Phoenix	1	0	1	1
Pittsburgh	0	0	0	0
San Jose	0	0	0	0
St. Louis	2	0	0	0
Tampa Bay	0	0	0	0
Toronto	1	0	0	0
Vancouver	1	0	1	1
Washington	0	0	0	0

1996-97 SEASON — Finished with second best plus/minus (+10) on club with Adirondack (AHL)...Was third in scoring among Adirondack defensemen.

CAREER — NHL debut Apr. 14, 1996 at Dallas...Appeared in first NHL playoff contest May 23, 1996 at Colorado (Game 3 of Conference Finals)...In 1995-96, led Adirondack defensemen in points (6-36–42 in 75 games) and was sixth in overall team scoring...Earned silver medal in 1993 World Junior Championship and won 1992 European Championships with Swedish National Team....Voted Best Junior in Sweden in 1994....At age 15, won "Lill Strimmas" scholarship as top defenseman of the year.

PERSONAL — Single, resides in hometown of Bollnas, Sweden....Enjoys golf, fishing and paintball.

CAREER

Season	Club	League	Regular Schedule GP	G	A	P	PM	Playoffs GP	G	A	P	PM
1992-93	MoDo	Sweden	20	0	2	2	2	1	0	0	0	0
1993-94	MoDo	Sweden	38	2	8	10	42	–	–	–	–	–
1994-95	MoDo	Sweden	39	3	6	9	54	–	–	–	–	–
1995-96	Adirondack	AHL	75	6	36	42	64	3	–	–	–	–
	DETROIT	NHL	1	–	–	–	–	3	–	–	–	2
1996-97	Adirondack	AHL	44	3	25	28	36	4	0	1	1	4
	DETROIT	NHL	23	0	6	6	10	–	–	–	–	–
DETROIT and NHL Totals			**24**	**0**	**6**	**6**	**10**	**3**	**–**	**–**	**–**	**2**

Drafted by Detroit in 1993 NHL Entry Draft (1st choice, 22nd overall, 1st round).

1997-1998 DETROIT 91 RED WINGS

FEDOROV Sergei

BECAME RED WING: Fourth pick (74th overall) in 1989 Entry Draft.

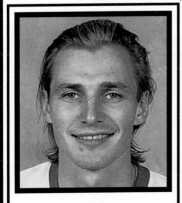

CENTER

- 6-1 • 200 lbs.
- Shoots Left
- Born: Pskov, Russia
  December 13, 1969
- Last Amateur Club:
  Central Red Army (USSR)

Career vs. N.H.L.

Team	GP	G	A	PTS
Anaheim	15	7	11	18
Boston	13	2	6	8
Buffalo	14	5	12	17
Calgary	24	13	15	28
Chicago	44	17	27	44
Colorado	17	5	11	16
Dallas	42	23	28	51
Detroit	0	0	0	0
Edmonton	23	8	15	23
Florida	6	3	1	4
Hartford	14	4	14	18
Los Angeles	25	14	15	29
Montréal	14	8	8	16
New Jersey	12	8	5	13
NY Islanders	14	8	12	20
NY Rangers	13	4	12	16
Ottawa	7	3	2	5
Philadelphia	12	7	12	19
Phoenix	30	14	27	41
Pittsburgh	14	11	9	20
San Jose	22	13	20	33
St. Louis	38	15	24	39
Tampa Bay	13	9	14	23
Toronto	43	18	29	47
Vancouver	23	13	15	28
Washington	14	10	6	16

1996-97 SEASON — Finished third in overall team scoring, second in goals and power play assists....Season-high six-game streak (8-5–13) Dec. 22-Jan. 5 included three consecutive multiple-point efforts....Recorded 14 goals in 15 games Dec. 1-Jan. 5....Scored a career-high five goals Dec. 26 vs. Washington (most goals by Red Wing in a single game since Syd Howe scored six goals Feb. 3, 1944 vs. NY Rangers) – outing marked Fedorov's third career hat trick....Had 16 multiple-point efforts (one five, one three, 14 twos)....Points in 43 of 74 games...."Plus" or "even" in 59 of 74 games....17-14–31 home, 13-19–32 road....9-5–14 on power play goals....4-2–6 on game winning goals....2-1–3 shorthanded goals....Led club in overall playoff points (8-12–20), assists and game winning goals (4)....First Stanley Cup Championship.

CAREER — In 1995-96, led club in points, goals, assists, tied for eighth in NHL scoring....Surpassed 100 point mark in 1993-94 and for 1995-96....Set club record for most game winning goals in a season (11) topping previous mark of ten set by Carson Cooper during the 1928-29 season....Finished second in NHL for game winning goals....Finished second in league and team in plus/minus (+49) behind teammate Vladimir Konstantinov....Career and season-best ten-game streak (6-10–16) Nov. 2-28, 1995, then matched ten-game stretch (5-8–13) Feb. 10-29, 1996....Recorded two five-point performances(Dec. 2, 1995 at Montréal and Mar. 19, 1996 vs. Toronto, which included two power play goals)....Scored or assisted on game winning goals eight times in span of 15 games (Jan. 6-Feb. 13, 1996)....Collected 500th career point with assist Mar. 8 1996 at Colorado....Tied for first on team in playoff scoring....Recorded points in 64 of 78 games....1995 NHL playoff leader in points and assists....Four goals Feb. 12, 1995 vs. Los Angeles (second career hat trick, first four-goal outing; first three in succession for "natural hat trick")....Top honors in 93-94: Hart Trophy as MVP (only European winner); Selke Trophy as best defensive forward; Lester B. Pearson Award as top performer in vote by Players' Association; First-Team All-Star; Player of Year by Hockey News, Sporting News, Hockey Digest....Second in NHL in scoring, third in goals, second at plus-48 in 93-94....Career highs that season in goals, assists, points, plus-minus, GWGs (10), equaled personal best in PPGs (13)....One of six Red Wings, second center, to notch 50-goal season; one of five, third center, to get 100 points....First NHL hat trick Mar. 1, 1994, vs. Calgary....NHL Co-Player of Month December, 1993, with Buffalo's Dominik Hasek....'92, '94, '96 All-Star games....Runner-up to Guy Carbonneau for 91-92 Selke Trophy despite more first-place votes (22-to-19) in total-points ballot....Second to Ed Belfour for 90-91 Calder Trophy....Four career regular season OT goals, one in playoffs....Tied club record for points in one period with 1-3–4 in second vs. Philadelphia Jan. 21, 1992....90-91 All-Rookie Team after pacing freshmen in goals, assists, points....PPG in NHL debut Oct. 4, 1990, at New Jersey....First two assists Oct. 10, 1990, vs. Calgary....Is seventh on Red Wings' all-time scoirng list....'91 Canada Cup....Played for Team Russia in 1996 World Cup of Hockey....Four years on Central Red Army team....Helped Soviet national team win gold medals in '89, '90 World Championships....Came to Detroit in July, 1990, after leaving Soviet team in Portland, OR (departed before Goodwill Games at Seattle).

PERSONAL — Single....Resides in suburban Detroit....Enjoys golf, boating, travel.

CAREER

			Regular Schedule					Playoffs				
Season	Club	League	GP	G	A	P	PM	GP	G	A	P	PM
1986-87	CSKA	Moscow	29	6	6	12	12	–	–	–	–	–
1987-88	CSKA	Moscow	48	7	9	16	20	–	–	–	–	–
1988-89	CSKA	Moscow	44	9	8	17	35	–	–	–	–	–
1989-90	CSKA	Moscow	48	19	10	29	10	–	–	–	–	–
1990-91a	DETROIT	NHL	77	31	48	79	66	7	1	5	6	4
1991-92	DETROIT	NHL	80	32	54	86	72	11	5	5	10	8
1992-93	DETROIT	NHL	73	34	53	87	72	7	3	6	9	23
1993-94bcde	DETROIT	NHL	82	56	64	120	34	7	1	7	8	6
1995	DETROIT	NHL	42	20	30	50	24	17	7	17	24	6
1995-96	DETROIT	NHL	78	39	68	107	48	19	2	18	20	10
1996-97	DETROIT	NHL	74	30	33	63	30	20	8	12	20	12
DETROIT and NHL Totals			**506**	**242**	**350**	**592**	**346**	**88**	**27**	**70**	**97**	**69**

a-NHL All-Star Rookie Team.
b-Won Hart Trophy.
c-Won Selke Trophy.
d-Won Lester B. Pearson Award.
e-NHL First All-Star Team.
Drafted by DETROIT in 1989 NHL Entry Draft (4th choice, 74th overall, 4th round).

FETISOV Viacheslav

BECAME RED WING: Obtained April 3, 1995, from New Jersey for third-round pick in 1995 Entry Draft.

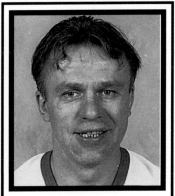

DEFENSE

- 6-1 • 215 lbs.
- Shoots Left
- Born: Moscow, Russia
  April 20, 1958
- Last Amateur Club:
  Central Red Army (USSR)

Career vs. N.H.L.

Team	GP	G	A	PTS
Anaheim	7	0	5	5
Boston	13	2	3	5
Buffalo	18	2	6	8
Calgary	13	0	5	5
Chicago	17	0	6	6
Colorado	17	2	9	11
Dallas	16	2	3	5
Detroit	11	0	5	5
Edmonton	16	0	3	3
Florida	5	0	1	1
Hartford	16	0	6	6
Los Angeles	15	1	3	4
Montréal	15	0	9	9
New Jersey	2	0	0	0
NY Islanders	28	0	9	9
NY Rangers	29	3	10	13
Ottawa	4	0	2	2
Philadelphia	32	2	9	11
Pittsburgh	34	3	12	15
St. Louis	17	5	13	18
San Jose	13	2	6	8
Tampa Bay	7	1	1	2
Toronto	16	1	6	7
Vancouver	15	0	4	4
Washington	30	1	8	9
Winnipeg	17	2	9	11

1996-97 SEASON — Posted season-high six-game streak (seven assists including two on power play) Mar. 1-15....Had consecutive two-assist performances Jan. 5-8....Recorded six multiple-point outings (1 three, 5 twos)....Scored two goals in as many games Oct. 17-19....Missed first five games of season following arthroscopic knee surgery in September....2-7-9 home, 3-15-18 road....Collected three power play assists, two on game winners...Finished fifth on club with plus-26....Special selection by the NHL Commissioner to play in 1997 All-Star Game in San Jose....In playoffs, collected four assists....First Stanley Cup Championship.

CAREER — In 1995-96, tied career-high 42 points for best NHL season since 1989-90 (first year in NHL)....Was seventh on team in assists....Career-best plus-37, third on club....Scored two goals (including game winner) and added two assists Mar. 31, 1996 vs. St. Louis for season-best four point effort and first two-goal outing of NHL career....Scored first shorthanded goal as Red Wing Mar. 22 vs. Colorado... In '95, set career-high six-game streak (2-8-10) Apr. 13-23....First goal as Red Wing with power play goal Apr. 16 at St. Louis....Became free agent after 94-95 season, sat out start in '95, but returned to New Jersey, signing as free agent with Detroit Feb. 23, getting assist that night vs. Boston...."Plus" player in all nine NHL seasons, with career-best plus-37 in 95-96....New Jersey's sixth choice (150th overall) in '83 draft, joined club in 89-90, when he had career highs in goals, assists, points....Assist in NHL debut Oct. 5, 1989, at Philadelphia....First goal Oct. 18, 1989, vs. Flyers....Longtime captain of Central Red Army team, which he joined in 74-75, and where he was teammate of Sergei Fedorov, Vladimir Konstantinov....Earned Soviet "Honored Masters of Sport" award, equivalent of Hockey Hall of Fame....Three times ('84, '86, '90) won Gold Stick Award as Europe's top player....Soviet Player of Year three times ('82, '86, '88)....Nine-time Soviet League All-Star....Pravda Trophy four times as league's top-scoring defenseman....Played in three Olympics (silver medal in '80, golds in '84, '88)....Performed in 11 World Championships...Played for Team Russia in inaugural World Cup of Hockey in 1996.

PERSONAL — Slava and his wife have one daughter....Spends off-season in West Orange, NJ....Organized the Stanley Cup's first visit to Russia including stops at the Central Red Army hockey school and a walk through Red Square.

CAREER

Season	Club	League	Regular Schedule GP	G	A	P	PM	Playoffs GP	G	A	P	PM
1974-75	CSKR	USSR	1	0	0	0	0	–	–	–	–	–
1976-77	CSKR	USSR	35	9	18	27	46	–	–	–	–	–
1978-79	CSKR	USSR	29	10	19	29	40	–	–	–	–	–
1979-80	CSKR	USSR	37	10	14	24	46	–	–	–	–	–
1980-81	CSKR	USSR	48	13	16	29	44	–	–	–	–	–
1981-82ac	CSKR	USSR	46	15	26	41	20	–	–	–	–	–
1982-83ad	CSKR	USSR	43	6	17	23	46	–	–	–	–	–
1983-84a	CSKR	USSR	44	19	30	49	38	–	–	–	–	–
1984-85a	CSKR	USSR	20	13	12	25	6	–	–	–	–	–
1985-86abc	CSKR	USSR	40	15	19	34	12	–	–	–	–	–
1986-87ab	CSKR	USSR	39	13	20	33	18	–	–	–	–	–
1987-88ab	CSKR	USSR	46	18	17	35	26	–	–	–	–	–
1988-89	CSKR	USSR	23	9	8	17	18	–	–	–	–	–
1989-90	New Jersey	NHL	72	8	34	42	52	6	0	2	2	10
1990-91	New Jersey	NHL	67	3	16	19	62	7	0	0	0	17
	Utica	AHL	1	1	1	1	0	–	–	–	–	–
1991-92	New Jersey	NHL	70	3	23	26	108	6	0	3	3	8
1992-93	New Jersey	NHL	76	4	23	27	158	5	0	2	2	4
1993-94	New Jersey	NHL	52	1	14	15	30	14	1	0	1	8
1995e	New Jersey	NHL	4	0	1	1	0	–	–	–	–	–
	DETROIT	NHL	18	3	12	15	2	18	0	8	8	14
1995-96	DETROIT	NHL	69	7	35	42	96	19	1	4	5	34
1996-97	DETROIT	NHL	64	5	23	28	76	20	0	4	4	42
DETROIT Totals			151	15	69	84	174	57	1	16	17	90
NHL Totals			488	34	180	214	584	95	2	23	25	137

a-Soviet National League All-Star Team (1979, 1980, 1982-88).
b-Leningradskaya–Pravda Trophy–Top Scoring Defenseman (1984, 1986-88).
c-Soviet Player of the Year (1982, 1986, 1988).
d-Drafted by New Jersey in 1983 Entry Draft (sixth choice, 150th overall).
e-Signed with New Jersey as a free agent, Feb. 23, 1995.
Traded to DETROIT from New Jersey April 3, 1995 for 3rd round pick in 1995 Entry Draft.

GILCHRIST Brent

BECAME RED WING: Signed as free agent (no compensation) July 8, 1997

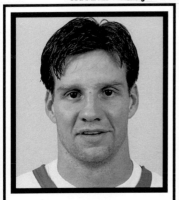

LEFT WING

- 5-11 • 180 lbs.
- Shoots Left
- Born: Moose Jaw, SK
  April 3, 1967
- Last Amateur Club:
  Spokane (WHL)

Career vs. N.H.L.

Team	GP	G	A	PTS
Anaheim	12	6	4	10
Boston	31	3	7	10
Buffalo	30	1	9	10
Calgary	28	6	8	14
Chicago	34	9	7	16
Colorado	32	6	5	11
Dallas	11	4	5	9
Detroit	31	7	6	13
Edmonton	20	7	7	14
Florida	6	1	4	5
Hartford	31	8	7	15
Los Angeles	28	6	5	11
Montréal	9	1	6	7
New Jersey	15	2	4	6
NY Islanders	15	7	1	8
NY Rangers	15	1	2	3
Ottawa	8	3	2	5
Philadelphia	40	2	5	7
Phoenix	30	6	8	14
Pittsburgh	19	2	2	4
San Jose	20	4	5	9
St. Louis	33	7	10	17
Tampa Bay	9	0	1	1
Toronto	26	5	4	9
Vancouver	32	7	7	14
Washington	13	1	7	8

1996-97 SEASON — Recorded ten goals, 20 assists with Dallas....Had seven multiple-point efforts (all twos)....Had one two-goal outing (Nov. 20 vs. Calgary)....Had two power play goals and two game winners....Collected two goals and two assists in six playoff contests.

CAREER — 1995-96: Recorded highest point total (42) since '91-92 season (50) and second highest of career....Was tied for third in goals and fourth in points with Stars....**1994-95:** Had two multi-goal games and tied for third in NHL in shorthanded tallies with 3....Missed 13 games (Feb. 28–Mar. 27) because of arthroscopic surgery to repair torn cartilage in his wrist....**1992-93:** Upon being acquired by Dallas, recorded two points in eight games with Stars before missing final 11 games of season after suffering separated shoulder Mar. 18 at Detroit....**1991-92:** Finished fifth in team scoring (50 points) with Montréal....Established single season highs in goals, assists, points, penalty minutes....Led Canadiens with +29....Had a career-high four assists vs. Vancouver Feb. 10 and then tallied first career NHL hat trick vs. Minnesota Feb. 17.... **Career transactions:** Originally Montréal's sixth choice, 79th overall, in 1985 Entry Draft....Acquired by Edmonton from Montréal Aug. 27, 1992 with Shayne Corson and Vladimir Vujtek for Vincent Damphousse and fourth round pick in 1993 Entry Draft.... Acquired by Dallas from Edmonton for Todd Elik on Mar. 5, 1993....Scored first NHL goal Nov. 11, 1988 at Vancouver....First NHL game: Oct. 29, 1988 vs. Pittsburgh....First NHL Point: Nov. 7, 1988 vs. St. Louis.

PERSONAL — Brent and his wife have two sons and spend off-season in western Canada....Hobbies include golf, tennis and water skiing.

CAREER

Season	Club	League	Regular Schedule					Playoffs				
			GP	G	A	P	PM	GP	G	A	P	PM
1983–84	Kelowna	WHL	69	16	11	27	16	–	–	–	–	–
1984–85	Kelowna	WHL	51	35	38	73	58	6	5	2	7	8
1985–86	Spokane	WHL	52	45	45	90	57	9	6	7	13	19
1986–87	Spokane	WHL	46	45	55	100	71	5	2	7	9	6
	Sherbrooke	AHL	–	–	–	–	–	10	2	7	9	2
1987–88	Sherbrooke	AHL	77	26	48	74	83	6	1	3	4	6
1988–89	MONTRÉAL	NHL	49	8	16	24	16	9	1	1	2	10
	Sherbrooke	AHL	7	6	5	11	7	–	–	–	–	–
1989–90	MONTRÉAL	NHL	57	9	15	24	28	8	2	0	2	2
1990–91	MONTRÉAL	NHL	51	6	9	15	10	13	5	3	8	6
1991–92	MONTRÉAL	NHL	79	23	27	50	57	11	2	4	6	6
1992–93	EDMONTON	NHL	60	10	10	20	47	–	–	–	–	–
	MINNESOTA	NHL	8	0	1	1	2	–	–	–	–	–
1993–94	DALLAS	NHL	76	17	14	31	31	9	3	1	4	2
1994–95	DALLAS	NHL	32	9	4	13	16	5	0	1	1	2
1995–96	DALLAS	NHL	77	20	22	42	36	–	–	–	–	–
1996–97	DALLAS	NHL	67	10	20	30	24	6	2	2	4	2
NHL Totals			**556**	**112**	**138**	**250**	**267**	**61**	**15**	**12**	**27**	**30**

HODSON Kevin

BECAME RED WING: Signed as free agent (no compensation) May, 1993.

GOALTENDER

- 6-0 • 182 lbs.
- Catches Left
- Born: Winnipeg, MB
  March 27, 1972
- Last Amateur Club:
  Sault Ste. Marie Greyhounds (OHL)

Career vs. N.H.L.

Team	GP	MP	GA	SO	GAA	W	L	T
Anaheim	0	0	0	0	.00	0	0	0
Boston	1	60	1	0	1.00	1	0	0
Buffalo	0	0	0	0	.00	0	0	0
Calgary	0	0	0	0	.00	0	0	0
Chicago	3	178	4	1	1.35	1	1	1
Colorado	1	0	0	0	.00	0	0	0
Dallas	0	0	0	0	.00	0	0	0
Detroit	0	0	0	0	.00	0	0	0
Edmonton	0	0	0	0	.00	0	0	0
Florida	0	0	0	0	.00	0	0	0
Hartford	0	0	0	0	.00	0	0	0
Los Angeles	1	60	2	0	2.00	1	0	0
Montréal	0	0	0	0	.00	0	0	0
New Jersey	0	0	0	0	.00	0	0	0
NY Islanders	0	0	0	0	.00	0	0	0
NY Rangers	0	0	0	0	.00	0	0	0
Ottawa	0	0	0	0	.00	0	0	0
Philadelphia	0	0	0	0	.00	0	0	0
Phoenix	0	0	0	0	.00	0	0	0
Pittsburgh	1	28	1	0	2.14	0	0	0
San Jose	1	15	0	0	.00	0	0	0
St. Louis	0	0	0	0	.00	0	0	0
Tampa Bay	0	0	0	0	.00	0	0	0
Toronto	0	0	0	0	.00	0	0	0
Vancouver	1	56	3	0	3.21	0	1	0
Washington	1	60	0	1	.00	1	0	0

1996-97 SEASON — Was 2-2-1 in six games played including one shutout Dec. 4, 1996 (2-0) at Washington...Collected first career assist on power play goal Mar. 19 vs Boston in 4-1 win.

CAREER — Recorded first NHL shutout in first NHL start Jan. 6, 1996 with 2-0 victory (20 saves) vs. Chicago to become second Red Wing goalie to earn shutout in first regular season start, Dave Gatherum was first (4-0 shutout Oct. 11, 1953 vs. Toronto)...Played 28 minutes and allowed one goal Jan. 5, 1996 at Pittsburgh in NHL debut...Adirondack (AHL) Rookie of the Year in 1993-94....Went to three Memorial Cups with Sault Ste. Marie (OHL), won 1993 Memorial Cup and was named most valuable player....Led OHL in goals-against in all three seasons with Sault Ste. Marie.

PERSONAL — Was married during summer....Kevin and his wife reside in Sault Ste. Marie in off-season....Enjoys golf and fishing.

CAREER

Season	Club	League	GP	W	L	T	MP	GA	SO	AVG.	GP	W	L	MP	GA	SO	AVG.
			Regular Schedule								Playoffs						
1990-91	S. Ste. Marie	OHL	30	18	11	0	1638	88	2	3.22	10	9	1	600	28	0	2.87
1991-92	S. Ste. Marie	OHL	50	28	12	4	2722	151	0	3.33	18	12	6	1116	59	1	2.90
1992-93	S. Ste. Marie	OHL	26	18	5	2	1470	76	1	3.10	8	8	0	448	17	0	2.28
1993-94	Adirondack	AHL	37	20	10	4	2083	102	2	2.94	3	0	2	89	10	0	6.74
1994-95	Adirondack	AHL	51	19	22	8	2731	161	1	3.54	4	0	4	237	14	0	3.53
1995-96	Adirondack	AHL	32	13	13	2	1654	87	0	3.16	3	0	2	149	8	0	3.21
	DETROIT	NHL	4	2	0	0	163	3	1	1.10	–	–	–	–	–	–	–
1996-97	DETROIT	NHL	6	2	2	1	294	8	1	1.63	–	–	–	–	–	–	–
DETROIT and NHL Totals			**10**	**4**	**2**	**1**	**457**	**11**	**2**	**1.44**	–	–	–	–	–	–	–

Signed as a free agent by DETROIT May, 1993.

HOLMSTROM Tomas

BECAME RED WING: Ninth pick (257th overall) in 1994 Entry Draft

LEFT WING

- 6-0 • 210 lbs.
- Shoots Left
- Born: Pieta, Sweden
  January 23, 1973
- Last Amateur Club:
  Lulea (Sweden)

Career vs. N.H.L.

Team	GP	G	A	PTS
Anaheim	2	0	0	0
Boston	1	0	0	0
Buffalo	1	0	0	0
Calgary	2	0	0	0
Chicago	2	0	0	0
Colorado	3	0	0	0
Dallas	3	0	0	0
Detroit	0	0	0	0
Edmonton	1	0	0	0
Florida	2	0	1	1
Hartford	0	0	0	0
Los Angeles	3	2	0	2
Montréal	2	0	0	0
New Jersey	1	0	0	0
NY Islanders	1	0	0	0
NY Rangers	1	0	0	0
Ottawa	1	0	0	0
Philadelphia	2	1	1	2
Phoenix	3	0	0	0
Pittsburgh	2	0	0	0
San Jose	3	1	0	1
St. Louis	4	1	0	1
Tampa Bay	0	0	0	0
Toronto	4	0	1	1
Vancouver	3	1	0	1
Washington	0	0	0	0

1996-97 SEASON — Made NHL debut in season opener Oct. 6 at New Jersey....Collected first NHL point/goal on power play Nov. 16 vs. San Jose....Posted first career NHL assist (on power play) Nov. 27 vs. Toronto....Had two-game streak (0-2–2) Nov. 27-Dec. 1....Was assigned to Adirondack Dec. 30 where he collected three goals and one assist in six games before being recalled Jan. 13....Missed seven games with knee injury (Nov. 1-13)....2-2–4 home, 4-1–5 road....3-2–5 on power play....Played in first and only playoff game Apr. 16 vs. St. Louis....First Stanley Cup Championship.

CAREER — Spent two seasons with Lulea (Sweden) where he scored 26 goals, added 25 assists for 51 points in 74 games played.

PERSONAL — Returns to Sweden in off-season....Brought Stanley Cup to hometown during summer.

CAREER

			Regular Schedule					Playoffs				
Season	Club	League	GP	G	A	P	PM	GP	G	A	P	PM
1994-95	Lulea	Sweden	40	14	14	28	56	–	–	–	–	–
1995-96	Lulea	Sweden	34	12	11	23	78	11	6	2	8	22
1996-97	DETROIT	NHL	47	6	3	9	33	3	0	0	0	0
	Adirondack	AHL	6	3	1	4	7	–	–	–	–	–

Drafted by DETROIT in 1994 Entry Draft (9th choice, 257th overall).

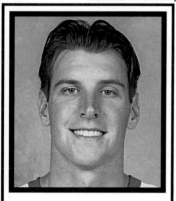

KNUBLE Mike

BECAME RED WING: Fourth pick (76th overall) in 1991 Entry Draft.

RIGHT WING

- •6-3 • 225 lbs.
- •Shoots Right
- •Born: Toronto, ON
  July 4, 1972
- •Last Amateur Club:
  University of Michigan (CCHA)

Career vs. N.H.L.

Team	GP	G	A	PTS
Anaheim	1	0	0	0
Boston	0	0	0	0
Buffalo	1	0	0	0
Calgary	1	0	0	0
Chicago	0	0	0	0
Colorado	1	0	0	0
Dallas	0	0	0	0
Detroit	0	0	0	0
Edmonton	1	0	0	0
Florida	0	0	0	0
Hartford	0	0	0	0
Los Angeles	0	0	0	0
Montréal	0	0	0	0
New Jersey	0	0	0	0
NY Islanders	0	0	0	0
NY Rangers	0	0	0	0
Ottawa	1	0	0	0
Philadelphia	0	0	0	0
Phoenix	0	0	0	0
Pittsburgh	0	0	0	0
San Jose	0	0	0	0
St. Louis	1	0	0	0
Tampa Bay	0	0	0	0
Toronto	1	1	0	1
Vancouver	0	0	0	0
Washington	0	0	0	0

1996-97 SEASON — Collected first career NHL goal and point Apr. 5 at Toronto....Played in first career NHL game Mar. 26 vs. Colorado....Spent most of season at Adirondack where he led club in goals, assists, points and game-winning goals before being called up to NHL....Had 28 goals, 35 assists for 63 points in 68 games with Adirondack.

CAREER — Posted 50 goals, 58 assists for 108 points with 113 penalty minutes in 148 games played in two seasons with Adirondack....Spent four seasons at University of Michigan....Was selected to CCHA Second All-Star Team (1994, 1995) and NCAA West Second All-American Team (1995).

PERSONAL — Single, spends part of off-season in Ann Arbor working hockey schools....Plays on Red Wings charity softball team....Enjoys golf.

CAREER

Season	Club	League	Regular Schedule					Playoffs				
			GP	G	A	P	PM	GP	G	A	P	PM
1991-92	Univ. of Michigan	CCHA	43	7	8	15	48	–	–	–	–	–
1992-93	Univ. of Michigan	CCHA	39	26	16	42	57	–	–	–	–	–
1993-94	Univ. of Michigan	CCHA	41	32	26	58	71	–	–	–	–	–
1994-95	Univ. of Michigan	CCHA	34	38	22	60	62	–	–	–	–	–
	Adirondack	AHL	3	0	0	0	0	–	–	–	–	–
1995-96	Adirondack	AHL	80	22	23	45	59	3	1	0	1	0
1996-97	Adirondack	AHL	68	28	35	63	54	–	–	–	–	–
	DETROIT	NHL	9	1	0	1	0	–	–	–	–	–
DETROIT and NHL Totals			**9**	**1**	**0**	**1**	**0**	–	–	–	–	–

Drafted by DETROIT in the 1991 NHL Entry Draft (4th choice, 76th overall, 4th round).

KOCUR Joe

BECAME RED WING: Signed as free agent December 28,1996
(Originally, Detroit's sixth pick, 88th overall, in 1983 Entry Draft)

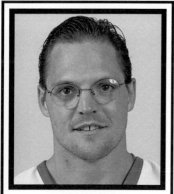

RIGHT WING

- 6-0 • 220 lbs.
- Shoots Right
- Born: Calgary, AB
  December 21, 1964
- Last Amateur Club:
  Saskatoon (WHL)

Career vs. N.H.L.

Team	GP	G	A	PTS
Anaheim	6	0	0	0
Boston	27	2	4	6
Buffalo	32	3	2	5
Calgary	24	4	1	5
Chicago	52	7	7	14
Colorado	29	3	1	4
Dallas	50	2	8	10
Detroit	8	3	0	3
Edmonton	19	3	3	6
Florida	10	1	0	1
Hartford	28	3	6	9
Los Angeles	27	1	2	3
Montréal	28	1	3	4
New Jersey	42	4	4	8
NY Islanders	32	3	1	4
NY Rangers	14	2	5	7
Ottawa	10	0	0	0
Philadelphia	32	3	2	5
Phoenix	23	1	2	3
Pittsburgh	34	1	2	3
San Jose	9	2	1	3
St. Louis	51	4	3	7
Tampa Bay	13	1	0	1
Toronto	60	12	10	22
Vancouver	22	3	2	5
Washington	37	3	3	6

1996-97 SEASON — Played first game of season (400th as Red Wing) Jan. 3 vs. Dallas after signing with Detroit as free agent Dec. 28....Scored first goal of year (first since Oct. 25, 1995 with New York) Feb. 6 vs. Vancouver....Netted game winner Mar. 15 at San Jose....Assisted on game-tying goal Apr. 1 vs. St. Louis....1-1–2 home, 1-0–1 road....Collected an assist in Conference Finals vs. Colorado....Scored first playoff goal of season May 31 in Game One of Finals at Philadelphia....Assisted on game winner June 3 at Philadelphia....Second Stanley Cup Championship (first in 1994 with New York).

CAREER — Before re-signing with Detroit, previously played five full seasons with club from 1985-86 to 1990-91 accumulating 111 points (56-55–111) and 1714 penalty minutes in 399 games played....Had been traded by Detroit (Mar. 5, 1991) along with Per Djoos to NY Rangers for Kevin Miller, Dennis Vial and Jim Cummins....Played five full seasons with Rangers before being traded to Vancouver (Mar. 20, 1996) by New York for Kay Whitmore....Career highs in goals (16), assists (20) and points (36) in 1989-90 with Detroit....In 1992-93, became 19th player in NHL history to surpass the 2,000 mark in penalty minutes Apr. 4, 1993 at Washington....Final goal in first stint with Red Wings came on a penalty shot Nov. 29 in Chicago....In 1986-87 and 1985-86, led Wings in penalty minutes and set a club record (and led NHL) in '85-86 with 377 PIM....Also, set a Detroit club record for PIM in a single game with 42 Nov. 2, 1985 vs. St. Louis....Recorded first NHL goal Mar. 9, 1985 vs. New Jersey....Made NHL debut Feb. 20, 1985....Entering 1997-98 season, ranked 13th among all-time penalty-minute leaders.

PERSONAL — Joe and his wife have one daughter....Spends off-season in suburban Detroit....Has hockey school in summer....Enjoys golf and fishing.

CAREER

Season	Club	League	Regular Schedule					Playoffs				
			GP	G	A	P	PM	GP	G	A	P	PM
1982-83	Saskatoon	WHL	62	23	17	40	289	6	2	3	5	25
1983-84	Saskatoon	WHL	69	40	41	81	258	–	–	–	–	–
	Adirondack	AHL	–	–	–	–	–	5	0	0	0	20
1984-85	DETROIT	NHL	17	1	0	1	64	3	1	0	1	5
	Adirondack	AHL	47	12	7	19	171	–	–	–	–	–
1985-86	DETROIT	NHL	59	9	6	15	*377	–	–	–	–	–
	Adirondack	AHL	9	6	2	8	34	–	–	–	–	–
1986-87	DETROIT	NHL	77	9	9	18	276	16	2	3	5	71
1987-88	DETROIT	NHL	63	7	7	14	263	10	0	1	1	13
1988-89	DETROIT	NHL	60	9	9	18	213	3	0	1	1	6
1989-90	DETROIT	NHL	71	16	20	36	268	–	–	–	–	–
1990-91	DETROIT	NHL	52	5	4	9	253	–	–	–	–	–
	NY Rangers	NHL	5	0	0	0	36	6	0	2	2	21
1991-92	NY Rangers	NHL	51	7	4	11	121	12	1	1	2	38
1992-93	NY Rangers	NHL	65	3	6	9	131	–	–	–	–	–
1993-94	NY Rangers	NHL	71	2	1	3	129	20	1	1	2	17
1994-95	NY Rangers	NHL	48	1	2	3	71	10	0	0	0	8
1995-96	NY Rangers	NHL	38	1	2	3	49	–	–	–	–	–
	Vancouver	NHL	7	0	1	1	19	1	0	0	0	0
1996-97	DETROIT	NHL	34	2	1	3	70	19	1	3	4	22
NHL Totals			**642**	**62**	**66**	**128**	**1899**	**97**	**5**	**12**	**17**	**196**

*-League-leading total.

KOZLOV Vyacheslav

BECAME RED WING: Second choice (45th overall, third round) in 1990 Entry Draft.

LEFT WING

- 5-10 • 185 lbs.
- Shoots Left
- Born: Voskresensk, Russia
  May 3, 1972
- Last Amateur Club:
  Central Red Army (Russia)

Career vs. N.H.L.

Team	GP	G	A	PTS
Anaheim	16	6	5	11
Boston	5	2	1	3
Buffalo	6	1	0	1
Calgary	17	5	7	12
Chicago	24	6	10	16
Colorado	9	0	4	4
Dallas	24	10	9	19
Detroit	0	0	0	0
Edmonton	16	5	10	15
Florida	6	3	2	5
Hartford	7	4	4	8
Los Angeles	15	8	11	19
Montréal	6	7	3	10
New Jersey	7	3	1	4
NY Islanders	7	5	3	8
NY Rangers	7	1	2	3
Ottawa	6	1	0	1
Philadelphia	5	1	0	1
Phoenix	22	10	10	20
Pittsburgh	6	3	2	5
San Jose	18	10	4	14
St. Louis	22	6	10	16
Tampa Bay	9	1	6	7
Toronto	21	6	9	15
Vancouver	17	5	8	13
Washington	6	1	0	1

1996-97 SEASON — Finished third on team in goals (23), tied for second with Darren McCarty in game winning goals, and seventh overall in points....Points in 34 of 75 games....Goals in 22 outings...12 multiple-point games (all twos)....9-13–22 home, 14-9–23 road....3-6–9 on power play goals....6-3–9 in game winning goals....Assisted on one game-tying goal....Scored game winner in OT Feb. 2 at Dallas....Did not dress Dec. 17 in Colorado ending a streak of 120 consecutive games played dating back to 1995 season....Tied for third in playoff scoring....Tied for second in playoff goals, led club in power play playoff goals....Scored game-winning, power play goal in triple OT May 4 vs. Anaheim (game 2, round 2)....Recorded two two-goal performances in playoffs....Had three two-game streaks in playoffs....Posted a three-point effort May 6 at Anaheim (round 2, game 3)....First Stanley Cup Championship.

CAREER — In 1995-96, tied for second on team in goals, tied for fourth in scoring...Tied career- high 73 points, best since 1993-94 season....Only Red Wing to play full 82-game schedule....Posted four straight two-point performances in four-game streak Jan. 27-Feb. 6....Had seven multiple-goal outings (one four- 12/2 at Montréal, six twos)....Scored two goals, added three assists Feb. 13 vs. Los Angeles for second career five-point effort....In 1995, tied for third on team in playoff goals....Sixth on team in goals, seventh in scoring in 1995....Shared club lead in goals, was third in 1995 NHL playoffs....Tied club playoff record with four GWGs in 1995 playoffs....Also in 1995 playoffs, clinched Western Conference title with GWG at 2:25 of second OT in Game 5 June 11 vs. Chicago (first career playoff OTG)....100th NHL point with goal Mar. 14, 1995 vs. Los Angeles....Third on team in goals, tied for fifth in scoring, second in GWGs (6), sixth with plus-27 in 93-94....First NHL hat trick in career-best 3-2–5 outing Jan. 6, 1994, at San Jose....Career-high eight-game streak (8-4–12) Nov. 20-Dec. 3, 1993....One regular-season OTG (Nov. 20, 1993, at New Jersey)....Two assists in NHL debut Mar. 12, 1992, at St. Louis (first on first shift when Sergei Fedorov scored at 1:37 of first period)....First NHL goal Oct. 8, 1992, at Los Angeles....Auto accident in November of '91 limited him to 11 games with Red Army....Rookie of Year in Soviet Elite League in 89-90....Starred in '89, '90 World Junior Championships....Helped Soviets win gold medal in '90 Goodwill Games at Seattle....World Championships in '91, '94....'91 Canada Cup....Participated in 1996 World Cup of Hockey with Team Russia.

PERSONAL — Single....Resides in suburban Detroit....Plays for Red Wings charity soft-ball team in off-season....Returned to Russia with Stanley Cup during summer and visited hometown of Voskresensk.

CAREER

Season	Club	League	Regular Schedule					Playoffs				
			GP	G	A	P	PM	GP	G	A	P	PM
1987-88	Khimik	Soviet	2	0	1	1	0	–	–	–	–	–
1988-89	Khimik	Soviet	13	0	1	1	2	–	–	–	–	–
1989-90	Khimik	Soviet	45	14	12	26	38	–	–	–	–	–
1990-91	Khimik	Soviet	45	11	13	24	46	–	–	–	–	–
1991-92	Khimik	Soviet	11	6	5	10	12	–	–	–	–	–
1991-92	DETROIT	NHL	7	0	2	2	2	–	–	–	–	–
1992-93	DETROIT	NHL	17	4	1	5	14	4	0	2	2	2
	Adirondack	AHL	45	23	36	59	54	4	1	1	2	4
1993-94	DETROIT	NHL	77	34	39	73	50	7	2	5	7	12
	Adirondack	AHL	3	0	1	1	0	–	–	–	–	–
1995	DETROIT	NHL	46	13	20	33	45	18	9	7	16	10
1995-96	DETROIT	NHL	82	36	37	73	70	19	5	7	12	10
1996-97	DETROIT	NHL	75	23	22	45	46	20	8	5	13	14
DETROIT and NHL Totals			**304**	**110**	**121**	**231**	**227**	**68**	**24**	**26**	**50**	**48**

Drafted by DETROIT in 1990 NHL Entry Draft (2nd choice, 45th overall, 3rd round).

1997-1998
RED WINGS

LAPOINTE Martin

BECAME RED WING: First choice (10th overall) in 1991 Entry Draft.

RIGHT WING

- 5-11 • 215 lbs.
- Shoots Right
- Born: Ville Ste-Pierre, PQ
  September 12, 1973
- Last Amateur Club:
  Laval Titan (QMJHL)

Career vs. N.H.L.

Team	GP	G	A	PTS
Anaheim	12	1	1	2
Boston	5	2	0	2
Buffalo	5	1	1	2
Calgary	13	0	1	1
Chicago	20	3	2	5
Colorado	9	3	0	3
Dallas	16	2	2	4
Detroit	0	0	0	0
Edmonton	11	2	1	3
Florida	2	0	0	0
Hartford	5	1	0	1
Los Angeles	13	1	2	3
Montréal	7	1	2	3
New Jersey	6	0	2	2
NY Islanders	5	1	1	2
NY Rangers	5	0	0	0
Ottawa	6	3	2	5
Philadelphia	5	0	2	2
Phoenix	17	1	3	4
Pittsburgh	3	0	0	0
San Jose	13	2	4	6
St. Louis	17	1	4	5
Tampa Bay	7	1	0	1
Toronto	15	5	1	6
Vancouver	11	3	4	7
Washington	4	0	0	0

1996-97 SEASON — Collected career-best 33 points; five of seven total goals came on power play....Posted career-high four-game goal streak Oct. 26-Nov. 2....Two other two-game goal streaks (Nov. 8-10; Apr. 9-11)....Registered first career two-goal game Mar. 26 vs. Colorado....Missed four games (Dec. 3-12) with fractured finger....In playoffs, tied for fifth in scoring, tied for third in assists....Scored first career game-winning OT goal May 2 vs. Anaheim (round 2, game 1)....Recorded first career two-goal playoff performance June 5 vs. Philadelphia in Finals....Posted three-assist effort (GWG, 2 PPG) May 22 vs. Colorado in Conference Finals....7-8–15 home, 9-9–18 road....5-4–9 on power play....Scored one shorthanded goal Oct. 30 vs. Montréal....1-3–4 on game-winning goals....First Stanley Cup Championship.

CAREER — NHL debut Oct. 5, 1992, at Toronto....First regular-season point with assist Dec. 3, 1992, vs. Calgary....First NHL goal Nov. 21, 1993, at St. Louis....Assist in NHL playoff debut Apr. 26, 1992, vs. Minnesota....Missed eight games with knee injury (Mar. 2-19, 1996)....Four seasons with Laval (QMJHL)....First All-Star Team in QMJHL in 89-90, Second Team in 90-91....Postseason action with Adirondack's Calder Cup champions in '92....Played in 1995 AHL All-Star Game, named Player of Game for U.S. club in loss to Canadian team.

PERSONAL — Martin, his wife and son spend off-season in hometown of Ville Ste-Pierre, PQ, near Montréal....Enjoys summer sports and weightlifting.

CAREER

Season	Club	League	Regular Schedule					Playoffs				
			GP	G	A	P	PM	GP	G	A	P	PM
1989-90a	Laval	QMJHL	65	42	54	96	77	–	–	–	–	–
1990-91b	Laval	QMJHL	64	44	54	98	66	13	7	14	21	26
1991-92	DETROIT	NHL	4	0	1	1	5	3	0	1	1	4
	Laval	QMJHL	31	25	30	55	81	10	4	10	14	32
1992-93	DETROIT	NHL	3	0	0	0	5	–	–	–	–	–
	Adirondack	AHL	8	1	2	3	9	–	–	–	–	–
	Laval	QMJHL	35	38	51	89	41	5	1	8	9	11
1993-94	DETROIT	NHL	50	8	8	16	55	4	0	0	0	0
	Adirondack	AHL	28	25	21	46	47	4	1	1	2	8
1995	DETROIT	NHL	39	4	6	10	73	2	0	1	1	8
1995-96	DETROIT	NHL	58	6	3	9	93	11	1	2	3	12
1996-97	DETROIT	NHL	78	16	17	33	167	20	4	8	12	60
DETROIT and NHL Totals			**232**	**34**	**35**	**69**	**393**	**40**	**5**	**12**	**17**	**90**

a-QMJHL First Team All-Star.
b-QMJHL Second Team All-Star.
Drafted by DETROIT in 1991 NHL Entry Draft (1st choice, 10th overall, 1st round).

LARIONOV IGOR

BECAME RED WING: Obtained October 24, 1995 from San Jose for Ray Sheppard.

CENTER

- 5-9 • 170 lbs.
- Shoots Left
- Born: Voskresensk, Russia
  December 3, 1960
- Last Amateur Club:
  Central Red Army (Russia)

Career vs. N.H.L.

Team	GP	G	A	PTS
Anaheim	16	2	15	17
Boston	13	3	6	9
Buffalo	13	4	9	13
Calgary	33	7	16	23
Chicago	24	6	9	15
Colorado	15	3	13	16
Dallas	25	7	13	20
Detroit	15	3	7	10
Edmonton	30	13	16	29
Florida	6	1	6	7
Hartford	10	3	6	9
Los Angeles	34	5	20	25
Montréal	14	3	11	14
New Jersey	11	0	4	4
NY Islanders	13	3	6	9
NY Rangers	12	3	8	11
Ottawa	3	0	1	1
Philadelphia	13	1	5	6
Phoenix	35	11	25	36
Pittsburgh	14	4	9	13
San Jose	15	6	6	12
St. Louis	24	7	11	18
Tampa Bay	5	1	0	1
Toronto	21	5	6	11
Vancouver	14	4	9	13
Washington	12	2	6	8

1996-97 SEASON — Finished fifth in scoring on club, tied for second in assists....Posted two season-high five-game streaks(1-8–9) Dec. 17-26 and (2-6–8) Feb. 19-Mar. 1....Recorded seven three-point outings including back to back (Dec. 22-26)....Three three-assist games....Also posted five two-point efforts....Scored shorthanded, game-winning goal Mar. 8 at Vancouver....Missed seven games to wrist injury (Nov. 1-13); four to groin injury (Oct. 17-23); three with lower back contusion (Apr. 9-13)....5-20–25 home....7-22–29 road....2-15–17 on power play....1-1–2 shorthanded....4-10–14 on game winners....Assisted on one game-tying goal....In playoffs, tied for fourth in team scoring, tied for second in power play goals....Scored two goals May 22 vs. Colorado in Conference Finals....Posted two other two-point playoff outings....First Stanley Cup Championship.

CAREER — In 1995-96, set career record for points (21-50–71)....Tied for fourth on club in scoring, assists, power play goals....Scored goal on which Paul Coffey earned his 1000th career assist Dec. 13 vs. Chicago....Was successful on first career penalty shot Nov. 22 against Arturs Irbe of San Jose.... Scored shorthanded goal in Red Wing debut Oct. 27, 1995....Finished fifth in team scoring in 1996 playoffs....Drafted by Vancouver (11th round, 214th overall) in 1985 and played for Canucks for three years....Played one season in Switzerland with Lugano before being acquired by San Jose in Waiver Draft on Oct. 4, 1992....First NHL game Oct. 5, 1989 vs. Edmonton (with Vancouver)....First NHL goal Oct. 11, 1989 vs. Edmonton (with Vancouver)....While with San Jose, tied as Sharks all-time career plus/minus leader at +17 in 1995....Was Sharks leading scorer in 1994 playoffs scoring 18 points in 14 contests....Earned Soviet Player of the Year honors in 1987-88 and was named to five all-star teams with Central Red Army....Accomplished veteran of various international competitions with Soviet National Team, including capturing gold medals at both the 1984 and 1988 Winter Olympics and a gold medal in 1983 World Championships....Centered famous KLM line with Vladimir Krutov and Sergei Makarov during the 1980s....Played for Team Russia in 1996 World Cup of Hockey.

PERSONAL — Igor and his wife have two daughters....Enjoys travel, tennis, soccer and has played in the Red Wings charity softball games in the off-season....Returned to Russia with Stanley Cup during summer including a stop in hometown of Voskresensk.

CAREER

Season	Club	League	GP	G	A	P	PM	GP	G	A	P	PM
			Regular Schedule					Playoffs				
1977-78	Khimik Voskresensk	Soviet	6	3	0	3	4	–	–	–	–	–
1978-79	Khimik Voskresensk	Soviet	25	3	4	7	12	–	–	–	–	–
1979-80	Khimik Voskresensk	Soviet	42	11	7	18	24	–	–	–	–	–
1980-81	Khimik Voskresensk	Soviet	56	22	23	45	36	–	–	–	–	–
1981-82	Central Red Army	Soviet	46	31	22	53	6	–	–	–	–	–
1982-83	Central Red Army	Soviet	44	20	19	39	20	–	–	–	–	–
1983-84	Central Red Army	Soviet	43	15	26	41	30	–	–	–	–	–
1984-85	Central Red Army	Soviet	40	18	28	46	20	–	–	–	–	–
1985-86	Central Red Army	Soviet	40	21	31	52	33	–	–	–	–	–
1986-87	Central Red Army	Soviet	39	20	26	46	34	–	–	–	–	–
1987-88	Central Red Army	Soviet	51	25	32	57	54	–	–	–	–	–
1988-89	Central Red Army	Soviet	31	15	12	27	22	–	–	–	–	–
1989-90	Vancouver	NHL	74	17	27	44	20	–	–	–	–	–
1990-91	Vancouver	NHL	64	13	21	34	14	6	1	0	1	6
1991-92	Vancouver	NHL	72	21	44	65	54	13	3	7	10	4
1992-93	Lugano	Switz.	32	13	34	47	44	–	–	–	–	–
1993-94	San Jose	NHL	60	18	38	56	40	14	5	13	18	10
1995	San Jose	NHL	33	4	20	24	14	11	1	8	9	2
1995-96	San Jose	NHL	4	1	1	2	0	–	–	–	–	–
	DETROIT	NHL	69	21	50	71	34	19	6	7	13	6
1996-97	DETROIT	NHL	64	12	42	54	26	20	4	8	12	8
DETROIT Totals			133	33	92	125	60	39	10	15	25	14
NHL Totals			440	107	243	350	202	83	20	43	63	36

Traded to DETROIT by San Jose for Ray Sheppard on Oct. 24, 1996.

LIDSTROM Nicklas

BECAME RED WING: Third choice (53rd overall) in 1989 Entry Draft.

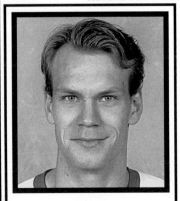

DEFENSE

- 6-2 • 190 lbs.
- Shoots Left
- Born: Vasteras, Sweden
  April 28, 1970
- Last Amateur Club:
  Vasteras (Sweden)

Career vs. N.H.L.

Team	GP	G	A	PTS
Anaheim	16	3	9	12
Boston	10	2	4	6
Buffalo	11	0	7	7
Calgary	23	3	13	16
Chicago	39	8	15	23
Colorado	15	5	5	10
Dallas	36	7	17	24
Detroit	0	0	0	0
Edmonton	22	3	13	16
Florida	6	1	2	3
Hartford	11	2	3	5
Los Angeles	23	1	11	12
Montréal	10	1	5	6
New Jersey	11	1	12	13
NY Islanders	11	2	4	6
NY Rangers	11	1	5	6
Ottawa	8	1	2	3
Philadelphia	11	1	0	1
Phoenix	27	3	13	16
Pittsburgh	11	1	5	6
San Jose	22	7	22	29
St. Louis	35	6	18	24
Tampa Bay	14	2	12	14
Toronto	34	4	22	26
Vancouver	22	4	11	15
Washington	12	1	7	8

1996-97 SEASON — Finished fourth in team scoring, second in assists, third in scoring among NHL defensemen....31 of 57 total points came on power play....Recorded career-best seven-game streak (2-7–9) Mar. 15-28 with eight of those nine points on power play....Posted back-to-back two-assist efforts (all on power play) Mar. 15-16 collecting 300th and 301st career points....Collected three assists Feb. 12 vs. San Jose....Had back-to-back two-point outings on three separate streaks....15 multiple-point efforts (1 three, 14 twos)....Had points in 41 of 79 games played....Was plus-11....8-23–30 home, 7-20–27 road....8-23–31 on power play goals....Assisted on one shorthanded goal....1-7–8 on game-winning goals....Was second on team in playoffs with plus-12....Assisted on three power play goals in Conference Finals vs. Colorado....Scored goal in Stanley Cup-clinching game vs. Philadelphia....First Stanley Cup Championship.

CAREER — In 1995-96, posted career-best 67 points to top rookie season (60 points)....Was fifth in overall points and assists, tied for sixth among NHL defensemen....37 of 67 total points came on power play....One two-goal game (one PPG Mar. 19 vs. Toronto)....Tied for second on team in playoff scoring....Played first career NHL All-Star Game in Boston in 1996....Second in 1995 playoff scoring among NHL, team defensemen after Paul Coffey....Also in '95 playoffs, tied club postseason record for assists by blueliner (with Coffey)....Scored game winner at 1:01 of OT June 1, 1995 in Game 1 vs. Chicago (first playoff overtime goal)....Missed five games Apr. 11-19, 1995 (back); never had missed game in NHL career (284 in a row; third longest streak among active players after Trevor Linden, Vincent Damphousse)....Third in NHL, second on team with career-high plus-43 in 93-94, when he was second in scoring among club defensemen....Career-best plus-7 outing Jan. 14, 1994, vs. Dallas....Career-high four-assist performance Jan. 6, 1994, at San Jose....One other four-pointer (2-2–4 Nov. 7, 1991, vs. St. Louis)....Runner-up to Pavel Bure for 91-92 Calder Trophy....NHL All-Rookie Team....Third in NHL, third on team at plus-36 in 91-92....Among NHL rookies, was first in plus-minus, first in assists, tied for third in scoring....Ninth in scoring among NHL defensemen, led team blueliners in 91-92....Third on team in assists in 91-92, setting club record for assists by rookie defenseman, tying Marcel Dionne's overall team freshman assist mark....Tied Reed Larson's rookie defenseman point mark....In 92-93, was third in scoring among club defensemen....NHL debut Oct. 3, 1991, at Chicago....First points with two assists Oct. 5, 1991, at Toronto....First goal was PPG Oct. 17, 1991, vs. St. Louis....Three seasons for Vasteras (Swedish Elite League)....With Sweden in '91 Canada Cup....'91, '94 World Championships, helping Sweden win '91 gold medal....Named one of Sweden's top three players in '90 World Junior Championships....Played for Team Sweden in inaugural World Cup of Hockey in summer of 1996.

PERSONAL — Nicklas, his wife and two sons spend off-season in Vasteras, Sweden....Enjoys tennis, golf....Brought Stanley Cup home to Sweden during summer.

CAREER

Season	Club	League	Regular Schedule					Playoffs				
			GP	G	A	P	PM	GP	G	A	P	PM
1988-89	Vasteras	Sweden	19	0	2	2	4	–	–	–	–	–
1989-90	Vasteras	Sweden	39	8	8	16	14	–	–	–	–	–
1990-91	Vasteras	Sweden	20	2	12	14	14	–	–	–	–	–
1991-92a	DETROIT	NHL	80	11	49	60	22	11	1	2	3	0
1992-93	DETROIT	NHL	84	7	34	41	28	7	1	0	1	0
1993-94	DETROIT	NHL	84	10	46	56	26	7	3	2	5	0
1995	DETROIT	NHL	43	10	16	26	6	18	4	12	16	8
1996-97	DETROIT	NHL	79	15	42	57	30	20	2	6	8	2
DETROIT and NHL Totals			451	70	237	307	132	82	16	31	47	20

a-Named to Upper Deck All-Rookie Team (1991-92).
Drafted by DETROIT in 1989 NHL Entry (3rd choice, 53rd overall, 3rd round).

1997-1998 RED WINGS

DETROIT 18

MALTBY Kirk

BECAME RED WING: Obtained March 20, 1996, from Edmonton for Dan McGillis.

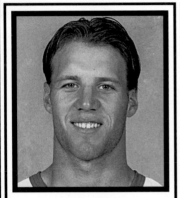

LEFT WING

- 6-0 • 200 lbs.
- Shoots Right
- Born: Guelph, ON
  December 22, 1972
- Last Amateur Club:
  Owen Sound (OHL)

Career vs. N.H.L.

Team	GP	G	A	PTS
Anaheim	16	3	3	6
Boston	3	0	0	0
Buffalo	6	0	0	0
Calgary	16	1	1	2
Chicago	13	0	0	0
Colorado	9	1	0	1
Dallas	15	0	0	0
Detroit	11	3	1	4
Edmonton	4	0	0	0
Florida	5	1	1	2
Hartford	4	0	1	1
Los Angeles	17	2	4	6
Montréal	3	0	1	1
New Jersey	6	1	0	1
NY Islanders	4	1	0	1
NY Rangers	5	0	0	0
Ottawa	5	0	1	1
Philadelphia	6	0	0	0
Phoenix	13	4	1	5
Pittsburgh	4	1	0	1
San Jose	15	3	0	3
St. Louis	16	1	0	1
Tampa Bay	5	0	0	0
Toronto	13	0	4	4
Vancouver	18	3	3	6
Washington	4	0	1	1

1996-97 SEASON — Scored five goals in playoffs to surpass mark of three scored during regular season....Assisted on one regular-season shorthanded goal and scored first playoff shorthanded tally May 31 at Philadelphia during Finals....3-0–3 home, 0-5–5 road during regular season....Total playoff output (5-2–7) nearly matched regular season (3-5–8)....First career NHL playoff goal Apr. 27 at St. Louis (round 1, game 6)....Recorded first career two-goal playoff game May 22 vs. Colorado in Conference Finals....First Stanley Cup Championship.

CAREER — Scored first goal as Red Wing Apr. 10, 1996 vs. Winnipeg....Red Wing debut Mar. 25, 1996 vs. Anaheim....In 1995-96, played 49 games with Edmonton (2-6–8) before missing 16 games recovering from a scratched cornea....With the Edmonton Oilers in 1994-95, finished 12th in scoring, eighth in goals, tied for first in SHGs (two)....Recorded his first career multiple-goal game with two goals (SHG, GWG) at Vancouver (with Edmonton) Apr. 13, 1995....Scored first NHL goal in NHL debut (with Edmonton) Oct. 8, 1993 vs. New York Islanders....Captured the AHL Calder Cup with the Cape Breton Oilers in 1992-93....Named Owen Sound's MVP in 1990-91 and 1991-92 and was the Rookie-of-the-Year in 1989-90....Was the Owen Sound Platers' team captain in his final season and played in the CHL East-West All-Star Challenge in 1991-92.

PERSONAL — Single, resides in Cambridge, Ontario in the off-season....Enjoys softball.

CAREER

Season	Club	League	Regular Schedule					Playoffs				
			GP	G	A	P	PM	GP	G	A	P	PM
1989-90	Owen Sound	OHL	61	12	15	27	90	12	1	6	7	15
1990-91	Owen Sound	OHL	66	34	32	66	100	–	–	–	–	–
1991-92	Owen Sound	OHL	64	50	41	91	99	5	3	3	6	18
1992-93	Cape Breton	AHL	73	22	23	45	130	16	3	3	6	45
1993-94	Edmonton	NHL	68	11	8	19	74	–	–	–	–	–
1995	Edmonton	NHL	47	8	3	11	49	–	–	–	–	–
1995-96	Edmonton	NHL	49	2	6	8	61	–	–	–	–	–
	DETROIT	NHL	6	1	0	1	6	8	0	1	1	4
1996-97	DETROIT	NHL	66	3	5	8	75	20	5	2	7	24
DETROIT Totals			72	4	5	9	81	28	5	3	8	28
NHL Totals			236	25	22	47	265	28	5	3	8	28

1997-1998 DETROIT RED WINGS 25

McCARTY Darren

BECAME RED WING: Second choice (46th overall) in 1992 Entry Draft.

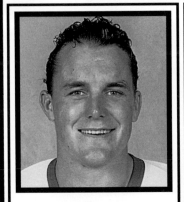

RIGHT WING
- 6-1 • 215 lbs.
- Shoots Right
- Born: Burnaby, BC
  April 1, 1972
- Last Amateur Club:
  Belleville Bulls (OHL)

Career vs. N.H.L.

Team	GP	G	A	PTS
Anaheim	15	5	3	8
Boston	6	1	6	7
Buffalo	6	1	0	1
Calgary	13	3	6	9
Chicago	17	2	2	4
Colorado	8	2	2	4
Dallas	18	3	5	8
Detroit	0	0	0	0
Edmonton	12	2	2	4
Florida	6	1	2	3
Hartford	6	1	2	3
Los Angeles	13	1	6	7
Montréal	5	1	2	3
New Jersey	4	0	1	1
NY Islanders	4	1	1	2
NY Rangers	5	1	4	5
Ottawa	5	1	2	3
Philadelphia	4	0	0	0
Phoenix	18	8	5	13
Pittsburgh	4	2	1	3
San Jose	14	4	9	13
St. Louis	13	3	1	4
Tampa Bay	4	0	1	1
Toronto	15	3	4	7
Vancouver	11	0	2	2
Washington	3	1	0	1

1996-97 SEASON — Posted career-high 49 points....Finished sixth in overall team scoring....Scored game-winning and Stanley Cup-clinching goal June 7 vs. Philadelphia....Had two career and season-best four-game scoring streaks (3-5–8) Nov. 15-23 and (3-5–8) Feb. 8-16....Was tied with for second in regular-season (6) and playoff (2) game-winning goals....Was fifth on club in goals (19)....Had one game-tying goal....Had two two-goal outings....Registered 16 multiple-point efforts (one three, 15 twos) including string of four consecutive two-point outings (3-5–8) Feb. 8-16....Recorded three assists (one on game winner, two power play) Nov. 21 at San Jose....Scored game-winning goal :39 into OT Mar. 26 vs. Colorado....8-14–22 home, 11-16–27 road....5-10–15 on power play....5-5–10 on game winners....Missed seven games due to hand injury Jan. 5-22, four games due to charley horse Feb. 1-6....First Stanley Cup Championship.

CAREER — Had first two-power play goal outing Mar. 12, 1996 vs. Winnipeg....First career two-goal game (FG and GTG) Oct. 17, 1995 vs. Calgary....In 1995-96 season, missed six games Dec. 5-15 (shoulder), seven Feb. 16-29 (hand)....First career OT goal (Feb. 12, 1994, at St. Louis)....NHL debut Oct. 5, 1993, at Dallas....First point with assist Oct. 8, 1993, at Los Angeles....First goal Oct. 21, 1993, vs. Winnipeg....Goal in NHL playoff debut Apr. 18, 1994, vs. San Jose....Two seasons at Belleville (OHL), leading league in goals in 91-92 while notching 55-72–127 in 65 outings.

PERSONAL — Darren and his wife and son reside in suburban Detroit....Born in Burnaby, BC, but raised in nearby Leamington, ON....Honored by Royal Canadian Mounted Police for helping juvenile drug prevention programs....Active with Make-a-Wish Foundation....Enjoys golf and participates in Red Wings charity softball games in the off-season....Played rugby in high school.

CAREER

			Regular Schedule					Playoffs				
Season	Club	League	GP	G	A	P	PM	GP	G	A	P	PM
1990-91	Belleville	OHL	60	30	37	67	151	6	2	2	4	13
1991-92	Belleville	OHL	65	55	72	127	177	5	1	4	5	13
1992-93	Adirondack	AHL	73	17	19	36	278	11	0	1	1	33
1993-94	DETROIT	NHL	67	9	17	26	181	7	2	2	4	8
1995	DETROIT	NHL	31	5	8	13	88	18	3	2	5	14
1995-96	DETROIT	NHL	63	15	14	29	158	19	3	2	5	20
1996-97	DETROIT	NHL	68	19	30	49	126	20	3	4	7	34
DETROIT and NHL Totals			**229**	**48**	**69**	**117**	**553**	**64**	**11**	**10**	**21**	**76**

Drafted by DETROIT in 1992 NHL Entry Draft (2nd choice, 46th overall, 2nd round).

1997-1998 DETROIT 55 RED WINGS

MURPHY Larry

BECAME RED WING: Obtained Mar. 18, 1997 from Toronto for future considerations.

Career vs. N.H.L.

Team	GP	G	A	PTS
Anaheim	11	0	7	7
Boston	55	7	36	43
Buffalo	55	14	27	41
Calgary	55	9	41	50
Chicago	58	11	40	51
Colorado	56	12	37	49
Dallas	45	8	31	39
Detroit	60	6	42	48
Edmonton	60	9	49	58
Florida	11	3	5	8
Hartford	50	12	29	41
Los Angeles	38	7	27	34
Montréal	51	12	14	26
New Jersey	92	17	53	70
NY Islanders	83	16	53	69
NY Rangers	86	15	39	54
Ottawa	18	6	4	10
Philadelphia	82	12	48	60
Phoenix	54	11	32	43
Pittsburgh	59	17	44	61
San Jose	14	5	11	16
St. Louis	62	13	38	51
Tampa Bay	13	3	9	12
Toronto	51	8	25	33
Vancouver	55	9	29	38
Washington	41	12	27	39

DEFENSE

- 6-2 • 218 lbs.
- Shoots Right
- Born: Scarborough, ON
  March 8, 1961
- Last Amateur Club:
  Peterborough (OHL)

1996-97 SEASON — Scored power play goal for first with Detroit in Red Wing debut Mar. 19 vs. Boston....Assisted on two goals Mar. 26 vs Colorado to pass Henri Richard on NHL's all-time point list....Scored game-winning OT goal Mar. 28 vs. Buffalo....Assisted on pair of power play goals Apr. 8 at Calgary....Had three-game streak (1-3-4) Mar. 12-16 (with Toronto)....In playoffs, finished tied for third in points among NHL defensemen....Was first on team/league in plus/minus (+16)....Second on team in assists....Six of nine total points came on game winners (1-5-6)....Scored two goals (one game winner, one power play) and collected three assists in first round vs. St. Louis....Assisted on two game-winning goals in second round vs. Anaheim....Had one assist in Conference Finals vs. Colorado....Notched three assists, was plus-ten in Stanley Cup Finals vs. Philadelphia....Third Stanley Cup Championship.

CAREER — Originally drafted by Los Angeles (1st pick, 4th overall) in 1980 Entry Draft....Was traded to Washington by Los Angeles for Ken Houston and Brian Engblom Oct. 18, 1983....Traded to Minnesota by Washington with Mike Gartner for Dino Ciccarelli and Bob Rouse Mar. 7, 1989....Traded to Pittsburgh by Minnesota with Peter Taglianetti for Chris Dahlquist and Jim Johnson Dec. 11, 1990....Traded to Toronto by Pittsburgh for Dmitri Mironov and Toronto's second round choice in 1996 Entry Draft July 8, 1995....Became just fourth defenseman and 45th player overall to reach 1000 career points Mar. 27, 1996....Trails only Paul Coffey, Ray Bourque, and Denis Potvin among career NHL defensemen point leaders (one point behind Potvin)....Playing in his 17th NHL season, had missed just one game since the start of the 1992-93 season while playing in 279 consecutive games, but record was snapped Feb. 15, 1997 at Calgary (with Toronto)....In 1995-96, led Leaf defensemen in power play goals (8), assists, and points....Tied for 10th among NHL defensemen in scoring....Was second on club with 49 assists and third with 61 points....Appeared in 1996 NHL All-Star Game....In 1994-95 with Pittsburgh, was named to NHL Second All-Star Team for third time in career (previously selected in 1986-87 and 1992-93)....Finished tied for fifth among NHL defensemen in scoring with 38 points....Led all defensemen with 13 playoff assists....His nine-game point streak and five-game assist streak were NHL's longest of the post-season Won two Stanley Cup championships with Pittsburgh (1991, 1992).

PERSONAL — Larry and his wife have three children: two daughters and one son....Spend off-season at cottage near Toronto.

CAREER

			Regular Schedule					Playoffs				
Season	Club	League	GP	G	A	P	PM	GP	G	A	P	PM
1978-79	Peterborough	OHL	66	6	21	27	82	19	1	9	10	42
1979-80	Peterborough	OHL	68	21	68	89	88	14	4	13	17	20
1980-81	LOS ANGELES	NHL	80	16	60	76	79	4	3	0	3	2
1981-82	LOS ANGELES	NHL	79	22	44	66	95	10	2	8	10	12
1982-83	LOS ANGELES	NHL	77	14	48	62	81	–	–	–	–	–
1983-84	LOS ANGELES	NHL	6	0	3	3	0	–	–	–	–	–
	WASHINGTON	NHL	72	13	33	46	50	8	0	3	3	6
1984-85	WASHINGTON	NHL	79	13	42	55	51	5	2	3	5	0
1985-86	WASHINGTON	NHL	78	21	44	65	50	9	1	5	6	6
1986-87	WASHINGTON	NHL	80	23	58	81	39	7	2	2	4	6
1987-88	WASHINGTON	NHL	79	8	53	61	72	13	4	4	8	33
1988-89	DETROIT	NHL	65	7	29	36	70	–	–	–	–	–
	MINNESOTA	NHL	13	4	6	10	12	5	0	2	2	8
1989-90	MINNESOTA	NHL	77	10	58	68	44	7	1	2	3	31
1990-91	MINNESOTA	NHL	31	4	11	15	38	–	–	–	–	–
	PITTSBURGH	NHL	44	5	23	28	30	23	5	18	23	44
1991-92	PITTSBURGH	NHL	77	21	56	77	48	21	6	10	16	19
1992-93	PITTSBURGH	NHL	83	22	63	85	73	12	2	11	13	10
1993-94	PITTSBURGH	NHL	84	17	56	73	44	6	0	5	5	0
1994-95	PITTSBURGH	NHL	48	13	25	38	18	12	2	13	15	0
1995-96	TORONTO	NHL	82	12	49	61	34	6	0	2	2	4
1996-97	DETROIT	NHL	81	9	36	45	20	20	2	9	11	8
NHL Totals			1315	254	916	1015	948	168	32	97	129	189

1997-1998 DETROIT RED WINGS

OSGOOD Chris

BECAME RED WING: Third choice (54th overall) in 1991 Entry Draft.

GOALTENDER

- 5-10 • 178 lbs.
- Catches Left
- Born: Peace River, AB
  November 26, 1972
- Last Amateur Club:
  Seattle Thunderbirds (WHL)

Career vs. N.H.L.

Team	GP	MP	GA	SO	GAA	W	L	T
Anaheim	5	285	17	0	3.58	3	0	2
Boston	4	242	9	0	2.23	4	0	0
Buffalo	3	179	7	0	2.35	1	2	0
Calgary	15	917	29	2	1.90	8	4	3
Chicago	9	515	16	0	1.86	6	2	1
Colorado	4	238	12	0	3.03	2	2	0
Dallas	14	796	29	1	2.19	11	1	1
Detroit	0	0	0	0	.00	0	0	0
Edmonton	10	604	17	3	1.69	7	2	1
Florida	5	304	13	0	2.57	4	1	0
Hartford	4	240	5	1	1.25	4	0	0
Los Angeles	8	490	21	2	2.57	5	1	2
Montréal	3	150	9	0	3.60	2	1	0
New Jersey	3	145	7	0	2.90	0	2	0
NY Islanders	2	120	3	0	1.50	2	0	0
NY Rangers	5	257	5	2	1.17	2	2	0
Ottawa	3	184	5	0	1.63	2	0	1
Philadelphia	2	120	6	0	3.00	2	0	0
Phoenix	12	702	34	0	2.91	6	4	1
Pittsburgh	4	212	13	1	3.68	2	2	0
San Jose	8	464	17	2	2.20	7	1	0
St. Louis	7	364	17	0	2.80	2	2	3
Tampa Bay	3	181	5	0	1.66	3	0	0
Toronto	14	790	35	0	2.66	8	2	3
Vancouver	6	309	16	0	3.11	3	1	1
Washington	4	188	11	0	3.51	3	0	0

1996-97 SEASON — Along with Vernon and Hodson, finished with second best combined goals-against average (2.35) in NHL....Season-best eight-game unbeaten streak (6-0–2) Feb. 12-Mar. 15....Earned career-best six shutouts including scoreless tie Dec. 10 vs. Edmonton... Credited with an assist (third career point vs. Hartford) in 5-1 victory Nov. 4....Missed five games due to hamstring injury Jan. 20-Feb. 1 which sidelined him from All-Star game despite second consecutive selection...First Stanley Cup Championship.

CAREER — In 1995-96, tied for first in NHL for best goals against average (2.17)....First in NHL in wins (39)....Tied for third in league in shutouts (5)....Earned Jennings Trophy (fewest goals against during regular-season) with teammate Mike Vernon....Career-best 21-game unbeaten streak Jan. 10-Mar. 27 set new club record for longest unbeaten streak (19-0-2), topping Mike Vernon's previous mark of 13-0–3, Feb. 12-Apr. 13, 1995....Career-best 13-game winning streak (Jan. 30-Mar. 20) also set new franchise record topping Terry Sawchuk's mark of nine, which he set twice, Mar. 3-21, 1951 & Feb. 27-Mar. 20, 1955....Scored goal in 4-2 win Mar. 6 in 100th career game at Hartford....Became second goaltender to be credited with scoring a goal....Earned an assist in 4-2 victory Mar. 27 vs. Buffalo....Became sixth Red Wing goalie to get 30 wins, first since Tim Cheveldae (38) in 1991-92 season....Three of six defeats were by one goal....Earned an assist in 4-2 victory Mar. 27 vs. Buffalo....Third best goals-against average (2.12) among playoff goal-tenders....Played in first career NHL All-Star Game in Boston in 1996....Selected to Second All-Star Team....In 1994-95, tied for second in NHL with .917 save percentage (41 goals, 496 shots) and fourth in league with 2.26 goals-against average....Also in '95, allowed two goals or less 13 times in 19 outings, all starts....Had .622 winning percentage as rookie in 93-94....First two NHL shutouts came in succession in '94: 3-0 Feb. 24 vs. Hartford at Richfield, OH, 2-0 Feb. 26 vs. San Jose (first consecutive shutouts by Detroit goalie since Tim Cheveldae Nov. 13-14, 1992, vs. Pittsburgh, Hartford)....NHL Rookie of Month in February of '94 (7-1–0, 2.30 average, two shutouts in nine outings)....4-0 shutout in NHL playoff debut Apr. 20, 1994, vs. San Jose (first Detroit rookie shutout since Terry Sawchuk in '51; second Red Wing to post shutout in playoff debut; Norm Smith was other in '36)....First NHL victory 8-3 (23 saves) Oct. 23, 1993, vs. Los Angeles....6-3 defeat Oct. 15, 1993, at Toronto in NHL debut....Three years in junior (WHL) with Medicine Hat, Brandon, Seattle....WHL East Second-Team All-Star with Brandon in 90-91....Seven shutouts as junior....92-93 season at Adirondack (AHL), recording first two pro shutouts.

PERSONAL — Brought Stanley Cup home to Medicine Hat, AB....Likes golf, fishing, camping....Belongs to paintball league back home in summer.

CAREER

			Regular Schedule							Playoffs						
Season	Club	League	GP	W	L	T	MP	GA	SO	AVG.	GP	W	L	MP	GA	SO AVG.
1989-90	Medicine Hat	WHL	57	24	28	2	3094	228	0	4.42	3	0	3	173	17	0 5.91
1990-91*a*	Medicine Hat	WHL	46	23	18	3	2630	173	2	3.95	12	7	5	712	42	0 3.54
1991-92	Medicine Hat	WHL	15	10	3	0	819	44	0	3.22	–	–	–	–	–	– –
	Brandon	WHL	16	3	10	1	890	60	1	4.04	–	–	–	–	–	– –
	Seattle	WHL	21	12	7	1	1217	65	1	3.20	15	9	6	904	51	0 3.30
1992-93	Adirondack	AHL	45	19	19	2	2438	159	0	3.91	1	0	1	59	2	0 2.03
1993-94	DETROIT	NHL	41	23	8	5	2206	105	2	2.86	6	3	2	307	12	1 2.35
	Adirondack	AHL	4	3	1	1	240	13	0	3.25	–	–	–	–	–	– –
1995	DETROIT	NHL	19	14	5	0	1087	41	1	2.26	2	0	0	68	2	0 1.76
1995-96	DETROIT	NHL	50	39	6	5	2933	106	5	2.17	15	8	7	936	33	2 2.12
1996-97	DETROIT	NHL	47	23	13	9	2769	106	6	2.30	2	0	0	47	2	0 2.55
DETROIT and NHL Totals			**157**	**99**	**32**	**19**	**8995**	**358**	**14**	**2.39**	**25**	**11**	**9**	**1358**	**49**	**9 2.16**

a-WHL East Second All-Star Team.
Drafted by DETROIT in 1991 (3rd choice, 54th overall, 3rd round).

PUSHOR Jamie

BECAME RED WING: Second choice (32nd overall, 2nd round) in 1991 Entry Draft.

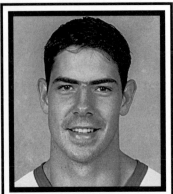

DEFENSE

- 6-3 • 225 lbs.
- Shoots Right
- Born: Lethbridge, AB
  February 11, 1973
- Last Amateur Club:
  Lethbridge Hurricanes (WHL)

Career vs. N.H.L.

Team	GP	G	A	PTS
Anaheim	2	0	0	0
Boston	2	0	0	0
Buffalo	2	0	1	1
Calgary	4	0	0	0
Chicago	6	0	1	1
Colorado	4	0	2	2
Dallas	8	0	1	1
Detroit	0	0	0	0
Edmonton	4	1	0	1
Florida	2	0	0	0
Hartford	2	0	0	0
Los Angeles	4	0	0	0
Montréal	2	0	0	0
New Jersey	2	0	0	0
NY Islanders	2	0	1	1
NY Rangers	1	0	0	0
Ottawa	1	0	0	0
Philadelphia	2	0	0	0
Phoenix	6	1	0	1
Pittsburgh	2	0	2	2
St. Louis	4	1	0	1
San Jose	4	0	0	0
Tampa Bay	2	0	0	0
Toronto	6	1	0	1
Vancouver	4	0	0	0
Washington	2	0	0	0

1996-97 SEASON — Assisted on game winner Oct. 12 at Buffalo for first point of season....Scored first NHL goal Nov. 2 at Toronto....Collected two assists Feb. 8 at Pittsburgh for first career two-point effort....Had two-game streak (1-1–2) Dec. 28-30....1-2–3 home, 3-5–8 road....Posted shorthanded assist Apr. 18 vs. St. Louis (first round) for first career NHL playoff game/point....First Stanley Cup Championship.

CAREER — NHL debut Oct. 8, 1995 at Edmonton...First NHL point was assist Nov. 4, 1995 at Dallas....1992-93, voted best defenseman for Lethbridge (WHL)....Also in Lethbridge, earned most valuable player honors in 92-93 (as voted by his teammates).

PERSONAL — Single, splits time in summer between upstate New York and home-town of Lethbridge, Alberta....Played in Red Wings charity softball team....In 1995-95, won Adirondack's Community Service Award....Voted 1992-93 Western Hockey League Humanitarian of the Year....In juniors, served as honorary chairman for Canadian Cancer Society....Enjoys fishing.

CAREER

			Regular Schedule					Playoffs				
Season	Club	League	GP	G	A	P	PM	GP	G	A	P	PM
1989-90	Lethbridge	WHL	10	0	2	2	0	–	–	–	–	–
1990-91	Lethbridge	WHL	71	1	13	14	193	–	–	–	–	–
1991-92	Lethbridge	WHL	49	2	15	17	232	5	0	0	0	33
1992-93	Lethbridge	WHL	72	6	22	28	200	4	0	1	1	9
1993-94	Adirondack	AHL	73	1	17	18	124	12	0	0	0	22
1994-95	Adirondack	AHL	58	2	11	13	129	4	0	1	1	0
1995-96	Adirondack	AHL	65	2	16	18	126	3	–	–	–	5
	DETROIT	NHL	5	0	1	1	17	–	–	–	–	–
1996-97	DETROIT	NHL	75	4	7	11	129	5	0	1	1	5
DETROIT and NHL Totals			**80**	**4**	**8**	**12**	**146**	**5**	**0**	**1**	**1**	**5**

Drafted by DETROIT in 1991 NHL Entry Draft (2nd choice, 32nd overall, 2nd round).

ROUSE Bob

BECAME RED WING: Signed as free agent (no compensation) August 5, 1994.

DEFENSE

- 6-2 • 220 lbs.
- Shoots Right
- Born: Surrey, BC
  June 18, 1964
- Last Amateur Club:
  Lethbridge Broncos (WHL)

Career vs. N.H.L.

Team	GP	G	A	PTS
Anaheim	13	1	4	5
Boston	30	2	3	5
Buffalo	23	0	5	5
Calgary	37	0	7	7
Chicago	78	4	7	11
Colorado	31	0	10	10
Dallas	40	1	9	10
Detroit	56	2	13	15
Edmonton	36	1	5	6
Florida	6	0	1	1
Hartford	25	0	2	2
Los Angeles	37	1	10	11
Montréal	33	2	6	8
New Jersey	34	1	5	6
NY Islanders	34	2	8	10
NY Rangers	34	2	8	10
Ottawa	8	0	0	0
Philadelphia	37	3	3	6
Phoenix	39	0	9	9
Pittsburgh	37	1	9	10
San Jose	20	1	3	4
St. Louis	77	9	11	20
Tampa Bay	12	0	2	2
Toronto	54	1	9	10
Vancouver	37	1	3	4
Washington	26	1	6	7

1996-97 SEASON — Recorded most productive season as Red Wing; 2-3–5 home, 2-6–8 road....2-1–3 on shorthanded goals... Assisted on one game-winning goal....Posted season-high three-game streak (1-3–4) Mar. 10-15 which included a shorthanded goal.... Collected two assists Mar. 10 at Los Angeles....Recorded shorthanded goal Dec. 12 vs. Chicago....Scored empty-net goal in home opener Oct. 9 vs. Edmonton.... Missed four games (Dec. 30-Jan. 8) with groin strain and two (Mar. 26-28) due to illness...Was tied for third on team in playoff plus/minus (+8)....First Stanley Cup Championship.

CAREER — In 1995, only Red Wing to appear in every game....Red Wings debut Jan. 20, 1995 vs. Chicago....First point as Red Wing with assist Feb. 4 at Los Angeles....En route to first appearance in Stanley Cup final, he made fourth trip to conference final (also '90 for Washington, '93, '94 with Toronto)....Career-best plus-15 for Minnesota is 85-86....Minnesota's third pick (80th overall) in '82 draft....Voted Minnesota's top rookie in 84-85....Dealt to Washington late in 88-89 season....Traded to Toronto midway through 90-91 season....Second among Maple Leafs' defensemen with plus-8 in 93-94....Played junior for Billings, Nanaimo, Lethbridge (WHL)....83-84 WHL East Division All-Star.

PERSONAL — Bob and his wife reside in suburban Detroit with their son and daughter....He enjoys computers, along with golf, fishing....Plays in Red Wings charity softball games in off-season.

CAREER

Season	Club	League	Regular Schedule					Playoffs				
			GP	G	A	P	PM	GP	G	A	P	PM
1987-88	Hamilton	OHL	47	6	6	12	69	11	0	2	2	2
1980-81	Billings	WHL	70	0	13	13	116	5	0	0	0	2
1981-82	Billings	WHL	71	7	22	29	209	5	0	2	2	10
1982-83	Nanaimo	WHL	29	7	20	27	86	–	–	–	–	–
	Lethbridge	WHL	42	8	30	38	82	20	2	13	15	55
1983-84	Minnesota	NHL	1	0	0	0	0	–	–	–	–	–
	Lethbridge	WHL	71	18	42	60	101	5	0	1	1	28
1984-85	Minnesota	NHL	63	2	9	11	113	–	–	–	–	–
	Springfield	AHL	8	0	3	3	6	–	–	–	–	–
1985-86	Minnesota	NHL	75	1	14	15	151	3	0	0	0	2
1986-87	Minnesota	NHL	72	2	10	12	179	–	–	–	–	–
1987-88	Minnesota	NHL	74	0	12	12	168	–	–	–	–	–
1988-89	Minnesota	NHL	66	4	13	17	124	–	–	–	–	–
	Washington	NHL	13	0	2	2	36	6	2	0	2	4
1989-90	Washington	NHL	70	4	16	20	123	15	2	3	5	47
1990-91	Washington	NHL	47	5	15	20	65	–	–	–	–	–
	Toronto	NHL	13	2	4	6	10	–	–	–	–	–
1991-92	Toronto	NHL	79	3	19	22	97	–	–	–	–	–
1992-93	Toronto	NHL	82	3	11	14	130	21	3	8	11	29
1993-94	Toronto	NHL	63	5	11	16	101	18	0	3	3	29
1995	DETROIT	NHL	48	1	7	8	36	18	0	3	3	8
1995-96	DETROIT	NHL	58	0	6	6	48	7	0	1	1	4
1996-97	DETROIT	NHL	70	4	9	13	58	20	0	0	0	55
DETROIT Totals			**176**	**5**	**22**	**27**	**142**	**45**	**0**	**4**	**4**	**67**
NHL Totals			**894**	**36**	**158**	**194**	**1439**	**108**	**7**	**18**	**25**	**176**

Drafted by Minnesota in 1982 Entry Draft (3rd choice, 80th overall, 4th Round).
Traded to Washington by Minnesota with Dino Ciccarelli for Mike Gartner and Larry Murphy, March 7, 1989.
Traded to Toronto by Washington with Peter Zezel for Al Iafrate, January 16, 1991.
Signed by DETROIT as a free agent August 5, 1994.

SHANAHAN Brendan

BECAME RED WING: Obtained Oct. 9, 1996 from Hartford for Keith Primeau, Paul Coffey, Brian Glynn and first round pick in 1997 Entry Draft.

LEFT WING
- 6-3 • 220 lbs.
- Shoots Right
- Born: Mimico, ON
  January 23, 1969
- Last Amateur Club:
  London (OHL)

Career vs. N.H.L.

Team	GP	G	A	PTS
Anaheim	14	6	7	13
Boston	26	12	13	25
Buffalo	23	11	9	20
Calgary	28	9	14	23
Chicago	40	24	19	43
Colorado	23	15	10	25
Dallas	47	26	20	46
Detroit	38	12	19	31
Edmonton	29	17	13	30
Florida	8	8	4	12
Hartford	21	11	8	19
Los Angeles	30	14	17	31
Montréal	24	9	14	23
New Jersey	11	6	4	10
NY Islanders	39	16	17	33
NY Rangers	38	15	15	30
Ottawa	9	10	9	19
Philadelphia	37	6	23	29
Phoenix	36	18	20	38
Pittsburgh	35	18	15	33
San Jose	19	15	15	30
St. Louis	17	6	8	14
Tampa Bay	13	9	5	14
Toronto	44	27	21	48
Vancouver	27	6	11	17
Washington	37	9	21	30

1996-97 SEASON — Finished first in overall team scoring, first in goals, second in assists, second in plus/minus, first in power play goals, first in power play goals, first in game-winning goals and first in shorthanded goals....Finished 10th in NHL scoring race, tied for first in power play goals....Made Red Wings debut Oct. 9 vs. Edmonton (after playing two games with Hartford before trade)....Collected first point as Red Wing with assist Oct. 12 at Buffalo for 600th career point....First goal(s) as Red Wing (first goal and game winner) Oct. 21 vs. Los Angeles....Scored two power play goals (club's first of season on power play) Oct. 23 vs. Dallas....Had natural hat trick (first with Detroit) which included 300th career goal (power play) and game winner and added an assist Nov. 27 vs. Toronto....Posted another natural hat trick and added an assist Feb. 12 vs. San Jose for second hat trick in as many games, making him first Red Wing to record back-to-back hat tricks since Vaclav Nedomansky Feb. 25 and 28, 1979....Registered two four-point efforts in three game span Nov. 23-27 and three more four-point outings over a span of eight games Feb. 8-24....Was NHL's Player of the Month for February after leading all scorers with 21 points (14-7–21)....Had three hat tricks, six two-goal performances....Had 28 multiple-point outings (5 fours, 3 threes, 21 twos)....Points in 46 of 81 games played....22-25–37 home, 24-27–51 road....20-16–36 on power play....Was one power play goal shy of tying club record for most power play goals in season (21) last reached by Dino Ciccarelli in 1992-93 and set by Mickey Redmond in 1973-74....2-2–4 on shorthanded goals....7-10–17 on game winners....2-1–3 on game-tying goals....Served one-game suspension Oct. 11 vs. Calgary for high sticking infraction from Oct. 9 game vs. Edmonton....Missed one game Nov. 1 with pulled groin....Was second in team in playoff points, tied for ninth among NHL scorers....Was first on club in playoff goals, tied for fifth in NHL....Tied for first on team in game winners, tied for fifth in NHL....Tied for third on club in plus/minus, tied for sixth in NHL....Played in 1997 NHL All-Star Game in San Jose....Scored game and series-winning goal at 17:03 of double OT May 8 at Anaheim to sweep series....Scored three goals and added three assists in first round vs. St. Louis....Had two goals and pair of assists in Conference Finals vs. Colorado....Netted three goals and collected an assist in Finals vs. Philadelphia....First Stanley Cup Championship.

CAREER — Began NHL career with New Jersey (first pick, 2nd overall, in 1987 Entry Draft) in 1987-88 before signing as free agent with St. Louis July 25, 1991....Traded to Hartford by St. Louis for Chris Pronger July 27, 1995....Played junior hockey with London (OHL) where he mostly played center....Played with Canadian National Junior Team in 1986 World Junior Championships in Czechoslovakia....First NHL game: Oct. 9, 1987 (with New Jersey) in which he collected his first career point with an assist....First career goal was game winner Nov. 10, 1987 vs. New York Rangers (second goal was also game winner)....Scored first career hat trick vs. Toronto Feb.13, 1989....In 1989-90, posted first 30-goal season....In 1990-91, tied for team lead (3-5–8) in New Jersey's seven-game playoff series loss to Pittsburgh in division semi-finals....In 1991-92, signed with St. Louis as free agent (New Jersey was awarded Scott Stevens in compensation)....In 1992-93, broke 50-goal mark for first time with 51....In 1993-94, registered career highs in goals (52), assists (50), points (102), and penalty minutes (211)....Was First Team NHL All-Star, played in 1994 All-Star Game, scoring two goals....Also in 1993-94, led NHL in hat tricks (4), shots (397) and shorthanded goals (7)....Was NHL Player of the Month for April of 1994....In 1995-96, led Whalers in goals (44), points (78), power play goals (17), was second in game-winning goals (6)....Had one hat trick and twice posted four-point outings....Was voted to start for Eastern Conference in the 1996 All-Star Game in Boston....Played for Team Canada in inaugural World Cup of Hockey in summer of 1996.

PERSONAL — Spent part of summer traveling in Europe....Brought Stanley Cup to Toronto....Was honorary chairman of the Detroit Red Wings First Annual Celebrity Softball Game to benefit the Michigan Alzheimer's Disease Research Center.

CAREER

Season	Club	League	Regular Schedule GP	G	A	P	PM	Playoffs GP	G	A	P	PM
1985-86	London	OHL	59	28	34	62	70	5	5	5	10	5
1986-87	London	OHL	56	39	53	92	92	–	–	–	–	–
1987-88	NEW JERSEY	NHL	65	7	19	26	131	12	2	1	3	44
1988-89	NEW JERSEY	NHL	68	22	28	50	115	–	–	–	–	–
1989-90	NEW JERSEY	NHL	73	30	42	72	137	6	3	3	6	20
1990-91	NEW JERSEY	NHL	75	29	37	66	141	7	3	5	8	12
1991-92	ST. LOUIS	NHL	80	33	36	69	171	6	2	3	5	14
1992-93	ST. LOUIS	NHL	71	51	43	94	174	11	4	3	7	18
1993-94a	ST. LOUIS	NHL	81	52	50	102	211	4	2	5	7	4
1994-95	Dusseldorf	Ger.	3	5	3	8	4	–	–	–	–	–
	ST. LOUIS	NHL	45	20	21	41	136	5	4	5	9	14
1995-96	HARTFORD	NHL	74	44	34	78	125	–	–	–	–	–
1996-97	DETROIT	NHL	81	47	41	88	131	20	9	8	17	43
NHL Totals			**713**	**335**	**351**	**686**	**1472**	**71**	**29**	**33**	**62**	**169**

a-NHL First All-Star Team

37
RED WINGS

TAYLOR Tim

BECAME RED WING: Signed as free agent July 28, 1993.

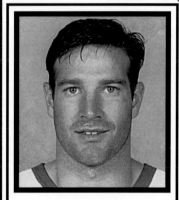

LEFT WING
- 6-1 • 190 lbs.
- Shoots Left
- Born: Stratford, ON
  February 6, 1969
- Last Amateur Club:
  London Knights (OHL)

Career vs. N.H.L.

Team	GP	G	A	PTS
Anaheim	7	1	1	2
Boston	2	0	0	0
Buffalo	4	1	1	2
Calgary	8	0	1	1
Chicago	12	1	0	1
Colorado	5	1	1	2
Dallas	11	2	2	4
Detroit	0	0	0	0
Edmonton	6	1	1	2
Florida	3	0	3	3
Hartford	2	0	1	1
Los Angeles	8	0	1	1
Montréal	3	0	1	1
New Jersey	2	0	0	0
NY Islanders	3	0	1	1
NY Rangers	2	0	0	0
Ottawa	2	1	0	1
Philadelphia	2	0	0	0
Phoenix	9	1	1	2
Pittsburgh	2	0	0	0
San Jose	8	1	2	3
St. Louis	12	2	2	4
Tampa Bay	3	0	0	0
Toronto	12	1	3	4
Vancouver	7	1	1	2
Washington	4	0	0	0

68

1996-97 SEASON — Posted back-to-back game-tying goals Apr. 1-3....Other two-game streak (0-2–2) came Nov. 27-Dec. 1....Scored shorthanded goal (second of career) and added an assist Oct. 12 at Buffalo for first two-point effort of season....Missed 16 games with shoulder injury (Oct. 17-Nov. 18)....2-3-5 home, 1-1–2 road....Assisted on one power play goal and one game-winning goal....First Stanley Cup Championship.

CAREER — In 1995-96, recorded career-best 25 points posting points in 22 of 72 games...."Plus" or "even" in 62 games....Three two-point outings....Four of his 11 goals were game winners and nine of his 25 total points have been on game winners....Scored first career shorthanded goal Apr. 2, 1996 at San Jose....Scored first career power play goal Mar. 22, 1996 vs. Colorado....Scored goal in NHL debut Dec. 18, 1993, at Montréal (lone outing for Detroit that season)....Led AHL in scoring in 93-94 with 36-81–117 while playing for Adirondack....AHL First-Team All-Star center in 93-94....Three years in junior ranks with London (OHL), notching 114 points in final season, 88-89, then leading all junior playoff scorers in goals (21), points (46)....Washington's second pick (36th overall) in '89 draft but never played for Capitals.

PERSONAL — Tim and his wife have a daughter and infant son....Spend off-season in hometown of Stratford, Ontario....He enjoys woodworking, especially making furniture....Also likes golf.

CAREER

Season	Club	League	Regular Schedule					Playoffs				
			GP	G	A	P	PM	GP	G	A	P	PM
1987-88	Hamilton	OHL	47	6	6	12	69	11	0	2	2	2
1986-87	London	OHL	34	7	9	16	11	–	–	–	–	–
1987-88	London	OHL	64	46	50	96	66	12	9	9	18	28
1988-89	London	OHL	61	34	80	114	93	21	21	25	46	58
1989-90	Baltimore	AHL	79	31	36	67	124	9	2	2	4	4
1990-91	Baltimore	AHL	79	25	42	67	75	5	0	1	1	4
1991-92	Baltimore	AHL	65	9	18	27	131	–	–	–	–	–
1992-93	Batimore	AHL	41	15	16	31	49	–	–	–	–	–
	Hamilton	AHL	36	15	22	37	37	–	–	–	–	–
1993-94	Adirondack	AHL	79	36	81	117	86	12	2	10	12	12
	DETROIT	NHL	1	1	0	1	0	–	–	–	–	–
1995	DETROIT	NHL	22	0	4	4	16	6	0	1	1	12
1995-96	DETROIT	NHL	72	11	14	25	39	18	0	4	4	4
1996-97	DETROIT	NHL	44	3	4	7	52	2	0	0	0	0
DETROIT and NHL Totals			**139**	**15**	**22**	**37**	**107**	**26**	**0**	**5**	**5**	**16**

Drafted by Washington in 1988 Entry Draft (2nd choice, 36th overall, 2nd Round).
Signed by DETROIT as a free agent, July 28, 1993.

WARD Aaron

BECAME RED WING: Obtained June 11, 1993, from Winnipeg (with Toronto's fourth choice in 1993 Entry Draft) for Paul Ysebaert and future considerations.

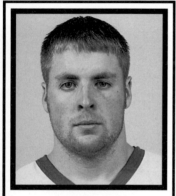

DEFENSE

- 6-2 • 225 lbs.
- Shoots Right
- Born: Windsor, ON
  January 17, 1973
- Last Amateur Club:
  University of Michigan (CCHA)

Career vs. N.H.L.

Team	GP	G	A	PTS
Anaheim	4	0	1	1
Boston	2	1	0	1
Buffalo	2	0	0	0
Calgary	1	0	0	0
Chicago	4	0	0	0
Colorado	3	0	0	0
Dallas	5	0	0	0
Detroit	0	0	0	0
Edmonton	3	0	0	0
Florida	1	0	0	0
Hartford	2	1	0	1
Los Angeles	2	0	1	1
Montréal	0	0	0	0
New Jersey	2	0	0	0
NY Islanders	0	0	0	0
NY Rangers	1	0	0	0
Ottawa	2	0	0	0
Philadelphia	0	0	0	0
Phoenix	4	0	1	1
Pittsburgh	2	0	1	1
San Jose	3	0	1	1
St. Louis	1	0	0	0
Tampa Bay	2	0	0	0
Toronto	4	0	0	0
Vancouver	4	0	2	2
Washington	1	0	0	0

1996-97 — First full season with Detroit after three years at Adirondack with two brief NHL recalls....Scored first goal of season Nov. 4 vs. Hartford for first NHL goal since Oct. 8, 1993 at Anaheim....First assist of season came on shorthanded goal Nov. 18 at Phoenix....Had three-game streak (three assists, including one shorthanded and one on power play) Nov. 18-23....Missed two games with acute bronchitis Dec. 26-28....2-1–3 home, 0-4–4 road....Assisted on one power play goal, one shorthanded goal....Made first playoff appearance of NHL career Apr. 18 vs. St. Louis.... First Stanley Cup Championship.

CAREER — Scored first career NHL goal Oct. 8, 1993 at Anaheim (first goal-against in Ducks' franchise history)....Collected 20 goals, 46 assists and 307 penalty minutes in 208 games played in three years with Adirondack....Spent three years at University of Michigan.

PERSONAL — Aaron and his wife spend off-season in suburban Detroit....Plays with Red Wings charity softball team....Police Athletic League (PAL) representative for team, put on a clinic for PAL youth hockey team with teammate Jamie Pushor last season....Visited Mott's Children's Hopital in Ann Arbor with Stanley Cup.

CAREER

Season	Club	League	Regular Schedule GP	G	A	P	PM	Playoffs GP	G	A	P	PM
1990-91	U.of Michigan	CCHA	46	8	11	19	126	–	–	–	–	–
1991-92	U.of Michigan	CCHA	42	7	12	19	64	–	–	–	–	–
1992-93	U.of Michigan	CCHA	30	5	8	13	73	–	–	–	–	–
	Cdn. National	–	4	0	0	0	8	–	–	–	–	–
1993-94	DETROIT	NHL	5	1	0	1	4	–	–	–	–	–
	Adirondack	AHL	58	4	12	16	87	9	2	6	8	6
1994-95	Adirondack	AHL	76	11	24	35	87	4	0	1	1	0
	DETROIT	NHL	1	0	1	1	2	–	–	–	–	–
1995-96	Adirondack	AHL	74	5	10	15	133	3	0	0	0	6
1996-97	DETROIT	NHL	49	2	5	7	52	19	0	0	0	17
NHL Totals			**55**	**3**	**6**	**9**	**58**	**19**	**0**	**0**	**0**	**17**

YZERMAN Steve

BECAME RED WING: First choice (fourth overall) in 1983 Entry Draft.

CENTER

- 5-11 • 185 lbs.
- Shoots Right
- Born: Cranbrook, BC May 9, 1965
- Last Amateur Club: Peterborough Petes (OHL)

Career vs. N.H.L.

Team	GP	G	A	PTS
Anaheim	15	8	9	17
Boston	32	19	20	39
Buffalo	34	24	37	61
Calgary	45	23	23	46
Chicago	98	45	74	119
Colorado	37	21	27	48
Dallas	93	40	81	121
Detroit	0	0	0	0
Edmonton	41	35	27	62
Florida	6	3	8	11
Hartford	31	11	22	33
Los Angeles	44	28	37	65
Montréal	32	17	22	39
New Jersey	33	10	31	41
NY Islanders	30	16	23	39
NY Rangers	31	16	21	37
Ottawa	6	2	3	5
Philadelphia	34	26	30	56
Phoenix	48	23	35	58
Pittsburgh	33	15	29	44
San Jose	21	8	21	29
St. Louis	93	39	64	103
Tampa Bay	14	12	19	31
Toronto	94	57	81	138
Vancouver	44	26	30	56
Washington	34	15	27	42

1996-97 SEASON — Second on club in points, first in assists, fourth in goals, tied for third in power play goals....Collected three assists in 1000th career game Feb. 19 vs. Calgary....Game-winning assist in OT marked 800th career assist Mar. 28 vs. Buffalo....Posted 1300th career point with goal Jan. 5 at Chicago....Three-point effort (1-2–3) Nov. 21 at San Jose edged Yzerman past Alex Delvecchio (1281 points) for second on all-time Red Wings point list....Had season-best nine-game streak (3-9–12) Oct. 19-Nov. 4....Other streaks: eight-game (5-13–18) Nov. 10-27, six-game (2-11–13) Feb. 8-19....Had 23 multiple-point efforts (2 fours, 5 threes, 16 twos) and two two-goal games, two three-assist games....8-30–38 home, 14-33–47 road....8-18–26 on power play goals....Two shorthanded assists....3-6–9 on game winners....Assisted on three game-tying tallies....Tied for second on team in playoff goals, tied for third in overall points....Credited with two playoff game winners....Played in 1997 All-Star Game in San Jose....First Stanley Cup Championship.

CAREER — 1995-96: Finished second on club in points, tied for second in goals, third in assists....Was 15th in NHL in scoring....First on team in power play goals, tied for second in shorthanded goals (2), and second in game winners (8)....Missed one game due to illness which snapped season-high streak at 16 games (10-16–26) Feb. 10-Mar. 12....Scored 30th and 31st goals of year Mar. 2 vs. Vancouver marking the 11th time Yzerman has scored 30 or more goals in a season, first since scoring 58 in 1992-93....Scored 500th career goal (PPG) Jan. 17 vs. Colorado making him only the 22nd NHL player to reach 500 goals....Had eight multiple-point performances over 12-game span Dec. 1-26....29....Tied for first in team playoff scoring, led club with eight goals including OT game-winning goal vs. St. Louis in Game 7 of second round, sending team to conference finals....**1992-93:** Recorded 1,000th point with assist Feb. 24, 1993, at Buffalo....Was fourth in league scoring, shared lead in short-handed goals (7)....Has led team in points eight times, goals, six, assists eight....Has topped 100-point mark six times (one of 13 in NHL history to do it six times in row)....50 or more goals five times, 60 twice....50-goal mark fewer games (55 in 88-89) than any Red Wing....18 regular-season hat tricks (recent Feb. 14, 1993, at Chicago); needs one to break tie with Gordie Howe for club record....Three "natural" hat tricks (recent Nov. 17, 1990, at Toronto)....146 career power play goals....Club-record 43 shorthanded goals....Won 1988-89 Lester B. Pearson Award as top performer in vote by Players' Association (third in Hart Trophy vote that year)....Club records in goals, assists, points in 88-89 (third in NHL in each)....One of four in NHL history to get 150 or more points, one of 17 to net at least 60 goals, one of six to score minimum of 60 two seasons in row....**1989-90:** Was second in NHL in goals, third in points....**1988-89:** Club record 28-game scoring streak (29-36–65) Nov. 1-Jan.4, 1988-89....Two six-pointers (2-4 Mar. 15, 1989, at Edmonton, 2-4 Feb. 16, 1990, vs. Philadelphia)....Club-record nine-game goal streak (12 total Nov. 18-Dec. 5, 1988, 14 Jan. 29-Feb. 12, 1992)....3-for-5 on penalty shots....Youngest captain (21) in team history in 86-87....Starting center for '93 Campbell Conference All Stars....Second to Tom Barrasso for 83-84 Calder Trophy, named top rookie by Sporting News....NHL All-Rookie Team....Club rookie records in goals, points....1-1–2 in NHL debut Oct. 5, 1983, at Winnipeg....Missed 26 games in 93-94 (herniated disc), last 16 regular-season games, first 13 playoff contests in '88 (torn posterior cruciate ligament in right knee Mar. 1 vs. Buffalo; same night he first scored 50th goal), final 29 in 85-86 (collarbone)....'84 Canada Cup....'85, '89, '90 World Championships....Played for Team Canada in inaugural World Cup of Hockey in summer of 1996.

PERSONAL — Steve and his wife reside in suburban Detroit with their daughter....Enjoys golf....Raised in Ottawa suburb of Nepean where he brought Stanley Cup during summer.

CAREER

Season	Club	League	Regular Schedule					Playoffs				
			GP	G	A	P	PM	GP	G	A	P	PM
1981-82	Peterborough	OHL	58	21	43	64	65	6	0	1	1	16
1982-83	Peterborough	OHL	56	42	49	91	33	4	1	4	5	0
1983-84	DETROIT	NHL	80	39	48	87	33	4	3	3	6	0
1984-85	DETROIT	NHL	80	30	59	89	58	3	2	1	3	2
1985-86	DETROIT	NHL	51	14	28	42	16	–	–	–	–	–
1986-87	DETROIT	NHL	80	31	59	90	43	16	5	13	18	8
1987-88	DETROIT	NHL	64	50	52	102	44	3	1	3	4	6
1988-89*a*	DETROIT	NHL	80	65	90	155	61	6	5	5	10	2
1989-90	DETROIT	NHL	79	62	65	127	79	–	–	–	–	–
1990-91	DETROIT	NHL	80	51	57	108	34	7	3	3	6	4
1991-92	DETROIT	NHL	79	45	58	103	64	11	3	5	8	12
1992-93	DETROIT	NHL	84	58	79	137	44	7	4	3	7	4
1993-94	DETROIT	NHL	58	24	58	82	36	3	1	3	4	0
1995	DETROIT	NHL	47	12	26	38	40	15	4	8	12	0
1995-96	DETROIT	NHL	80	36	59	95	64	18	8	12	20	4
1996-97	DETROIT	NHL	81	22	63	85	78	20	7	6	13	4
DETROIT and NHL Totals			**1023**	**559**	**801**	**1340**	**694**	**113**	**46**	**65**	**111**	**46**

a-Won the Lester B. Pearson Award.
Drafted by DETROIT in 1983 Entry Draft (1st choice, 4th overall, 1st round).

 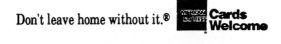

IN THE WINGS

PHILIPPE AUDET

LEFT WING **6-2 — 175 lbs. — SHOOTS LEFT**
BORN: OTTAWA, ONTARIO
JUNE 4, 1977

			Regular Schedule					Playoffs				
Season	Club	League	GP	G	A	P	PM	GP	G	A	P	PM
1994-95	Granby	QMJHL	62	19	17	36	93	13	2	5	7	10
1995-96*a*	Granby	QMJHL	67	40	43	83	162	21	12	18	30	32
1996-97	Granby	QMJHL	67	52	56	108	138	4	4	1	5	35
	Adirondack	AHL	3	1	1	2	0	1	1	0	1	0

a-Memorial Cup All-Star Team (1996).
Drafted by DETROIT in 1995 Entry Draft (2nd choice, 52nd overall).

SYLVAIN CLOUTIER

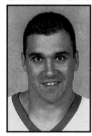

CENTER **6-0 — 191 lbs. — SHOOTS LEFT**
BORN: MONT-LAURIER, QUÉBEC
FEBRUARY 13, 1974

AMATEUR RECORD

			Regular Schedule					Playoffs				
Season	Club	League	GP	G	A	P	PM	GP	G	A	P	PM
1991-92	Guelph	OHL	62	35	31	66	74	–	–	–	–	–
1992-93	Guelph	OHL	44	26	29	55	78	5	0	5	5	14
1993-94	Guelph	OHL	66	45	71	116	127	9	7	9	16	32
	Adirondack	AHL	2	0	2	2	2	–	–	–	–	–
1994-95	Adirondack	AHL	71	7	26	33	144	–	–	–	–	–
1995-96	Adirondack	AHL	65	11	17	28	118	3	0	0	0	4
1996-97	Adirondack	AHL	77	13	36	49	190	4	0	2	2	4

Drafted by DETROIT in 1992 NHL Entry Draft (3rd choice, 70th overall, 3rd round).

PER EKLUND

LEFT WING   **5-11 — 196 lbs. — SHOOTS RIGHT**
BORN: STOCKHOLM, SWEDEN
JULY 9, 1970

(no picture available)

			Regular Schedule					Playoffs				
Season	Club	League	GP	G	A	P	PM	GP	G	A	P	PM
1991-92	Vasby	Swe.2	29	13	24	37	26	–	–	–	–	–
1992-93	Huddinge	Swe.2	36	22	23	45	14	–	–	–	–	–
1993-94	Huddinge	Swe.2	35	20	11	31	40	–	–	–	–	–
1994-95	Djurgarden	Sweden	40	19	10	29	20	3	1	1	2	4
1995-96	Djurgarden	Sweden	39	17	10	27	10	1	0	0	0	0
1996-97	Djurgarden	Sweden	50	20	16	36	14	4	1	0	1	0

Drafted by DETROIT in 1995 Entry Draft (8th choice, 182nd overall).

SEAN GILLAM

DEFENSE   **6-2 — 207 lbs. — SHOOTS RIGHT**
BORN: LETHBRIDGE, ALBERTA
MAY 7, 1976

			Regular Schedule					Playoffs				
Season	Club	League	GP	G	A	P	PM	GP	G	A	P	PM
1992-93	Spokane	WHL	70	6	37	33	131	10	0	2	2	10
1993-94	Spokane	WHL	70	7	17	24	106	3	0	0	0	6
1994-95*a*	Spokane	WHL	72	16	40	56	192	11	0	3	3	33
1995-96	Spokane	WHL	69	11	58	69	123	18	2	12	14	26
1996-97	Adirondack	AHL	64	1	7	8	50	–	–	–	–	–

a-WHL West Second All-Star Team (1995).
Drafted by DETROIT in 1994 Entry Draft (3rd choice, 75th overall).

YAN GOLUBOVSKY

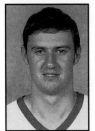

DEFENSE   6-4 — 204 lbs. — SHOOTS LEFT
BORN: NOVOSIBIRSK, RUSSIA
MARCH 9, 1976

Season	Club	League	Regular Schedule					Playoffs				
			GP	G	A	P	PM	GP	G	A	P	PM
1993-94	Moscow Dynamo	CIS	10	0	1	1	–	–	–	–	–	–
1994-95	Adirondack	AHL	57	4	2	6	39	–	–	–	–	–
1995-96	Adirondack	AHL	71	5	16	21	97	3	0	0	0	2
1996-97	Adirondack	AHL	62	2	11	13	67	4	0	0	0	0

Drafted by DETROIT in 1993 NHL Entry Draft (1st choice, 23rd overall, 1st round).

MAXIM KUZNETSOV

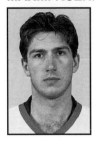

DEFENSE   6-5 — 198 lbs. — SHOOTS LEFT
BORN: PAVLODAR, RUSSIA
MARCH 24, 1977

Season	Club	League	Regular Schedule					Playoffs				
			GP	G	A	P	PM	GP	G	A	P	PM
1994-95	Moscow Dynamo	CIS	11	0	0	0	8	–	–	–	–	–
1995-96	Moscow Dynamo	CIS	9	1	1	2	22	4	0	0	0	0
1996-97	Moscow Dynamo	CIS	23	0	0	2	16	–	–	–	–	–
	Adirondack	AHL	2	0	1	1	6	2	0	0	0	0

Drafted by DETROIT in 1995 Entry Draft (1st choice, 26th overall).

DARRYL LAPLANTE

CENTER   6-0 — 185 lbs. — SHOOTS LEFT
BORN: CALGARY, ALBERTA
MARCH 28, 1977

Season	Club	League	Regular Schedule					Playoffs				
			GP	G	A	P	PM	GP	G	A	P	PM
1994-95	Moose Jaw	WHL	71	22	24	46	66	10	2	2	4	7
1995-96	Moose Jaw	WHL	72	42	40	82	76	–	–	–	–	–
1996-97	Moose Jaw	WHL	69	38	42	80	79	12	2	4	6	15

Drafted by DETROIT in 1995 Entry Draft (3rd choice, 58th overall).

NORM MARACLE

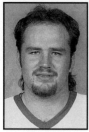

GOALTENDER **5-9 — 175 lbs. — CATCHES LEFT**
BORN: BELLEVILLE, ONTARIO
OCTOBER 2, 1974

AMATEUR RECORD

Season	Club	League	GP	W	L	T	MP	GA	SO	AVG.	GP	W	L	MP	GA	SO	AVG.
							Regular Schedule							Playoffs			
1991-92	Saskatoon	WHL	29	13	6	3	1529	87	1	3.41	15	9	5	860	37	0	3.38
1992-93a	Saskatoon	WHL	53	27	18	3	1939	160	1	3.27	9	4	5	569	33	0	3.48
1993-94	Saskatoon	WHL	56	41	13	1	3219	148	2	2.76	16	11	5	940	48	1	3.06
1994-95	Adirondack	AHL	39	12	15	2	1997	119	0	3.57	–	–	–	–	–	–	–
1995-96	Adirondack	AHL	54	24	18	6	2949	135	2	2.75	1	0	1	29	8	0	8.11
1996-97	Adirondack	AHL	68	34	22	9	3843	173	5	2.70	4	1	3	191	10	1	3.13

a-WHL East Second All-Star Team.
Drafted by DETROIT in 1993 (6th choice, 126th overall, 5th round).

STACY ROEST

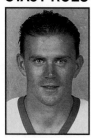

CENTER **5-9 — 192 lbs. — SHOOTS RIGHT**
BORN: LETHBRIDGE, ALBERTA
MARCH 15, 1974

PROFESSIONAL RECORD

Season	Club	League	GP	G	A	P	PM	GP	G	A	P	PM
				Regular Schedule					Playoffs			
1992-93	Medicine Hat	WHL	72	33	73	106	30	–	–	–	–	–
1993-94	Medicine Hat	WHL	72	48	72	120	48	–	–	–	–	–
1994-95	Medicine Hat	WHL	69	37	78	115	32	–	–	–	–	–
	Adirondack	AHL	3	0	0	0	0	–	–	–	–	–
1995-96	Adirondack	AHL	76	16	39	55	40	3	0	0	0	0
1996-97	Adirondack	AHL	78	25	41	66	30	4	1	1	2	0

FORWARDS

Player	Position	Hgt	Wgt	Birthplace	Birthdate
AUDET, Philippe	LW/L	6-2	175	Ottawa, Ontario	Jun. 4, 1977
BROWN, Doug	RW/R	5-10	188	Southborough, MA	June 12, 1964
CLOUTIER, Sylvain	C/L	6-0	195	Mont-Laurier, Québec	Feb.13, 1974
DANDENAULT, Mathieu	RW/R	6-1	200	Sherbrooke, Québec	Feb. 3, 1976
DRAPER, Kris	C/L	5-11	190	Toronto, Ontario	May 24, 1971
EKLUND, Per	LW/R	5-11	196	Stockholm, Sweden	July 9, 1970
FEDOROV, Sergei	C/L	6-1	200	Pskov, Russia	Dec. 13, 1969
GILCHRIST, Brent	LW/L	5-11	180	Moose Jaw, Sask.	Apr. 3, 1967
HOLMSTROM, Tomas	LW/L	6-0	210	Pitea, Sweden	Jan. 23, 1973
KNUBLE, Mike	RW/R	6-3	225	Toronto, Ontario	July 4, 1972
KOCUR, Joe	RW/R	6-0	220	Calgary, Alberta	Dec. 21, 1964
KOZLOV, Vyacheslav	LW/L	5-10	185	Voskresensk, Russia	May 3, 1972
LAPLANTE, Darryl	C/L	6-0	185	Calgary, Alberta	Mar. 28, 1977
LAPOINTE, Martin	RW/R	5-11	215	Ville Ste. Pierre, Québec	Sep. 12, 1973
LARIONOV, Igor	C/L	5-9	170	Voskresensk, Russia	Dec. 3, 1960
MALTBY, Kirk	RW/R	6-0	200	Guelph, Ontario	Dec. 22, 1972
McCARTY, Darren	RW/R	6-1	215	Burnaby, B.C.	Apr. 1, 1972
ROEST, Stacy	C/R	5-9	192	Lethbridge, Alberta	Mar. 15, 1974
SHANAHAN, Brendan	LW/R	6-3	220	Mimico, Ontario	Jan. 23, 1969
TAYLOR, Tim	C/L	6-1	190	Stratford, Ontario	Feb. 6, 1969
YZERMAN, Steve	C/R	5-11	185	Cranbrook, B.C.	May 9, 1965

DEFENSEMEN

Player	Position	Hgt	Wgt	Birthplace	Birthdate
ERIKSSON, Anders	Def/L	6-3	218	Bollnas, Sweden	Jan. 9, 1975
FETISOV, Viacheslav	Def/L	6-1	215	Moscow, Russia	Apr. 20, 1958
GILLAM, Sean	Def/R	6-1	187	Lethbridge, Alberta	May 7, 1976
GOLUBOVSKY, Yan	Def/R	6-3	183	Novosibirsk, Russia	Mar. 9, 1976
KUZNETSOV, Maxim	Def/L	6-5	198	Pavlodar, Russia	Mar. 24, 1977
LIDSTROM, Nicklas	Def/L	6-2	190	Vasteras, Sweden	Apr. 28, 1970
MURPHY, Larry	Def/R	6-2	218	Scarborough, Ontario	Mar. 8, 1961
PUSHOR, Jamie	Def/R	6-3	225	Lethbridge, Alberta	Feb. 11, 1973
ROUSE, Bob	Def/R	6-2	220	Surrey, B.C.	June 18, 1964
WARD, Aaron	Def/R	6-2	225	Windsor, Ontario	Jan. 17, 1973

GOALTENDERS

Players	Catch	Hgt	Wgt	Birthplace	Birthdate
HODSON, Kevin	L	6-0	182	Winnipeg, Manitoba	Mar. 27, 1972
MARACLE, Norm	L	5-9	175	Belleville, Ontario	Oct. 2, 1974
OSGOOD, Chris	L	5-11	178	Peace River, Alberta	Nov. 26, 1972

RED WINGS ROSTER

FORWARDS	Regular Season					Playoffs				
1996-97 Club/League	GP	G	A	P	PM	GP	G	A	P	PM
Granby (QMJHL)	67	52	56	108	138	4	4	1	5	35
Adirondack (AHL)	3	1	1	2	0	1	1	0	1	0
Detroit (NHL)	49	6	7	13	8	14	3	3	6	2
Adirondack (AHL)	77	13	36	49	190	4	0	2	6	4
Detroit (NHL)	65	3	9	12	28	–	–	–	–	–
Detroit (NHL)	76	8	5	13	73	20	2	4	6	12
Djurgarden Stockholm	50	20	16	36	14	4	1	0	1	0
Detroit (NHL)	74	30	33	63	30	20	8	12	20	12
Dallas (NHL)	67	10	20	30	24	6	2	2	4	2
Detroit (NHL)	47	6	3	9	33	1	0	0	0	0
Detroit (NHL)	9	1	0	1	0	–	–	–	–	–
Detroit (NHL)	34	2	1	3	70	19	1	3	4	22
Detroit (NHL)	75	23	22	45	46	20	8	5	13	14
Moose Jaw (WHL)	69	38	42	80	79	12	2	4	6	15
Detroit (NHL)	78	16	17	33	167	20	4	8	12	60
Detroit (NHL)	64	12	42	54	26	20	4	8	12	8
Detroit (NHL)	66	3	5	8	75	20	5	2	7	24
Detroit (NHL)	68	19	30	49	126	20	3	4	7	34
Adirondack (AHL)	78	25	41	66	30	4	1	1	2	0
Hartford (NHL)	2	1	0	1	0	–	–	–	–	–
Detroit (NHL)	79	46	41	87	131	20	9	8	17	43
Detroit (NHL)	44	3	4	7	52	2	0	0	0	0
Detroit (NHL)	81	22	63	85	78	20	7	6	13	4

DEFENSEMEN	Regular Season					Playoffs				
1996-97 Club/League	GP	G	A	P	PM	GP	G	A	P	PM
Adirondack (AHL)	44	3	25	28	36	4	0	1	1	4
Detroit (NHL)	64	5	23	28	76	20	0	4	4	42
Adirondack (AHL)	64	1	7	8	50	–	–	–	–	–
Adirondack (AHL)	62	2	11	13	67	4	0	0	0	0
Adirondack (AHL)	2	0	1	1	6	2	0	0	0	0
Detroit (NHL)	79	15	42	57	30	20	2	6	8	2
Toronto (NHL)	69	7	32	39	20	–	–	–	–	–
Detroit (NHL)	12	2	4	6	0	20	2	9	11	8
Detroit (NHL)	75	4	7	11	129	5	0	1	1	5
Detroit (NHL)	70	4	9	13	58	20	0	0	0	55
Detroit (NHL)	49	2	5	7	52	19	0	0	0	17

GOALTENDERS						
1995-96 Club/League	GP	Min	GA	SO	Avg.	(W-L-T)
Detroit (NHL)	6	294	8	1	1.63	2-2-1
Adirondack (AHL)	68	3843	173	5	2.70	34-22-9
PLAYOFFS	4	191	10	1	3.13	1-3
Detroit (NHL)	47	2769	106	6	2.30	23-13-9
PLAYOFFS	2	47	2	0	2.55	0-0

WESTERN CONFERENCE

CENTRAL DIVISION

	GP	W	L	T	GF	GA	PTS	PCTG.
DALLAS	82	48	26	8	252	198	104	.634
DETROIT	**82**	**38**	**26**	**18**	**253**	**197**	**94**	**.573**
PHOENIX	82	38	37	7	240	243	83	.506
ST. LOUIS	82	36	35	11	236	239	83	.506
CHICAGO	82	34	35	13	223	210	81	.494
TORONTO	82	30	44	8	230	273	68	.415

PACIFIC DIVISION

	GP	W	L	T	GF	GA	PTS	PCTG.
COLORADO	82	49	24	9	277	205	107	.652
ANAHEIM	82	36	33	13	245	233	85	.518
EDMONTON	82	36	37	9	252	247	81	.494
VANCOUVER	82	35	40	7	257	273	77	.470
CALGARY	82	32	41	9	214	239	73	.445
LOS ANGELES	82	28	43	11	214	268	67	.409
SAN JOSE	82	27	47	8	211	278	62	.378

EASTERN CONFERENCE

NORTHEAST DIVISION

	GP	W	L	T	GF	GA	PTS	PCTG.
BUFFALO	82	40	30	12	237	208	92	.561
PITTSBURGH	82	38	36	8	285	280	84	.512
OTTAWA	82	31	36	15	226	234	77	.470
MONTRÉAL	82	31	36	15	249	276	77	.470
HARTFORD	82	32	39	11	226	256	75	.457
BOSTON	82	26	47	9	234	300	61	.372

ATLANTIC DIVISION

	GP	W	L	T	GF	GA	PTS	PCTG.
NEW JERSEY	82	45	23	14	231	182	104	.634
PHILADELPHIA	82	45	24	13	274	217	103	.628
FLORIDA	82	35	28	19	221	201	89	.543
NY RANGERS	82	38	34	10	258	231	86	.524
WASHINGTON	82	33	40	9	214	231	75	.457
TAMPA BAY	82	32	40	10	217	247	74	.451
NY ISLANDERS	82	29	41	12	240	250	70	.427

1996-97 NHL SEASON SCORING LEADERS

		GP	G	A	PTS	+/-	PIM	PP	SH	GW	GT	S	PCT
Mario Lemieux	Pittsburgh	76	50	72	122	27	65	15	3	7	1	327	15.3
Teemu Selanne	Anaheim	78	51	58	109	28	34	11	1	8	2	273	18.7
Paul Kariya	Anaheim	69	44	55	99	36	6	15	3	10	0	340	12.9
John LeClair	Philadelphia	82	50	47	97	44	58	10	0	5	2	324	15.4
Wayne Gretzky	NY Rangers	82	25	72	97	12	28	6	0	2	1	286	8.7
Jaromir Jagr	Pittsburgh	63	47	48	95	22	40	11	2	6	1	234	20.1
Mats Sundin	Toronto	82	41	53	94	6	59	7	4	8	1	281	14.6
Zigmund Palffy	NY Islanders	80	48	42	90	21	43	6	4	6	1	292	16.4
Ron Francis	Pittsburgh	81	27	63	90	7	20	10	1	2	0	183	14.8
BRENDAN SHANAHAN	**HFD-DET**	81	47	41	88	32	131	20	3	7	2	336	**14.0**
Keith Tkachuk	Phoenix	81	52	34	86	1-	228	9	2	7	1	296	17.6
Peter Forsberg	Colorado	65	28	58	86	31	73	5	4	4	0	188	14.9
Pierre Turgeon	MTL-STL	78	26	59	85	8	14	5	0	7	1	216	12.0
STEVE YZERMAN	**DETROIT**	81	22	63	85	22	78	8	0	3	0	232	**9.5**
Mark Messier	NY Rangers	71	36	48	84	12	88	7	5	9	1	227	15.9
Mike Modano	Dallas	80	35	48	83	43	42	9	5	9	2	291	12.0
Brett Hull	St. Louis	77	42	40	82	9-	10	12	2	6	2	302	13.9
Adam Oates	BOS-WSH	80	22	60	82	5-	14	3	2	5	0	160	13.8
Doug Gilmour	TOR-NJ	81	22	60	82	2	68	4	1	1	1	143	15.4
Doug Weight	Edmonton	80	21	61	82	1	80	4	0	2	0	235	8.9
Vincent Damphousse	Montréal	82	27	54	81	6-	82	7	2	3	2	244	11.1
Mark Recchi	Montréal	82	34	46	80	1-	58	7	2	3	0	202	16.8
Eric Lindros	Philadelphia	52	32	47	79	31	136	9	0	7	2	198	16.2
Brian Leetch	NY Rangers	82	20	58	78	31	40	9	0	2	0	256	7.8
Peter Bondra	Washington	77	46	31	77	7	72	10	4	3	2	314	14.6
Tony Amonte	Chicago	81	41	36	77	35	64	9	2	4	2	266	15.4

1996-97 NHL SEASON GOALTENDING LEADERS
(Minimum 25 games played)

		GP	MINS	GA	SO	AVG	W-L-T
Martin Brodeur	New Jersey	67	3838	120	10	1.88	37-14-13
Andy Moog	Dallas	48	2738	98	3	2.15	28-13-5
Jeff Hackett	Chicago	41	2473	89	9	2.16	19-18-4
Dominik Hasek	Buffalo	67	4037	153	5	2.27	37-20-10
J. Vanbiesbrouck	Florida	57	3347	128	2	2.29	27-19-10
CHRIS OSGOOD	**DETROIT**	**47**	**2769**	**106**	**6**	**2.30**	**23-13-9**

1997 STANLEY CUP PLAYOFF RESULTS
(All Best-of-Seven Series)

CONFERENCE QUARTERFINALS

EASTERN CONFERENCE

SERIES 'A'

THU.	APR. 17	MONTRÉAL	2	AT	NEW JERSEY	5
SAT.	APR. 19	MONTRÉAL	1	AT	NEW JERSEY	4
TUE.	APR. 22	NEW JERSEY	6	AT	MONTRÉAL	4
THU.	APR. 24	NEW JERSEY	3	AT	MONTRÉAL	4*
SAT.	APR. 26	MONTRÉAL	0	AT	NEW JERSEY	4

*PATRICE BRISEBOIS SCORED AT 47:37 OF OVERTIME
(NEW JERSEY WON SERIES 4-1)

SERIES 'B'

THU.	APR. 17	OTTAWA	1	AT	BUFFALO	3
SAT.	APR. 19	OTTAWA	3	AT	BUFFALO	1
MON.	APR. 21	BUFFALO	3	AT	OTTAWA	2
WED.	APR. 23	BUFFALO	0	AT	OTTAWA	1*
FRI.	APR. 25	OTTAWA	4	AT	BUFFALO	1
SUN.	APR. 27	BUFFALO	3	AT	OTTAWA	0
TUE.	APR. 29	OTTAWA	2	AT	BUFFALO	3**

*DANIEL ALFREDSSON SCORED AT 2:34 OF OVERTIME
**DEREK PLANTE SCORED AT 5:24 OF OVERTIME
(BUFFALO WON SERIES 4-3)

SERIES 'C'

THU.	APR. 17	PITTSBURGH	1	AT	PHILADELPHIA	5
SAT.	APR. 19	PITTSBURGH	2	AT	PHILADELPHIA	3
MON.	APR. 21	PHILADELPHIA	5	AT	PITTSBURGH	3
WED.	APR. 23	PHILADELPHIA	1	AT	PITTSBURGH	4
SAT.	APR. 26	PITTSBURGH	3	AT	PHILADELPHIA	6

(PHILADELPHIA WON SERIES 4-1)

SERIES 'D'

THU.	APR. 17	NY RANGERS	0	AT	FLORIDA	3
SUN.	APR. 20	NY RANGERS	3	AT	FLORIDA	0
TUE.	APR. 22	FLORIDA	3	AT	NY RANGERS	4*
WED.	APR. 23	FLORIDA	2	AT	NY RANGERS	3
FRI.	APR. 25	NY RANGERS	3	AT	FLORIDA	2**

*ESA TIKKANEN SCORED AT 16:29 OF OVERTIME
**ESA TIKKANEN SCORED AT 12:02 OF OVERTIME
(NY RANGERS WON SERIES 4-1)

WESTERN CONFERENCE

SERIES 'E'

WED.	APR. 16	CHICAGO	0	AT	COLORADO	6
FRI.	APR. 18	CHICAGO	1	AT	COLORADO	3
SUN.	APR. 20	COLORADO	3	AT	CHICAGO	4*
TUE.	APR. 22	COLORADO	3	AT	CHICAGO	6
THU.	APR. 24	CHICAGO	0	AT	COLORADO	7
SAT.	APR. 26	COLORADO	6	AT	CHICAGO	3

*SERGEI KRIVOKRASOV SCORED AT 31:03 OF OVERTIME
(COLORADO WON SERIES 4-2)

SERIES 'F'

WED.	APR. 16	EDMONTON	3	AT	DALLAS	5
FRI.	APR. 18	EDMONTON	4	AT	DALLAS	0
SUN.	APR. 20	DALLAS	3	AT	EDMONTON	4*
TUE.	APR. 22	DALLAS	4	AT	EDMONTON	3
FRI.	APR. 25	EDMONTON	1	AT	DALLAS	0**
SUN.	APR. 27	DALLAS	3	AT	EDMONTON	2
TUE.	APR. 29	EDMONTON	4	AT	DALLAS	3***

*KELLY BUCHBERGER SCORED AT 9:15 OF OVERTIME
**RYAN SMYTH SCORED AT 20:22 OF OVERTIME
***TODD MARCHANT SCORED AT 12:26 OF OVERTIME
(EDMONTON WON SERIES 4-3)

SERIES 'G'

WED.	APR. 16	ST. LOUIS	2	AT	DETROIT	0
FRI.	APR. 18	ST. LOUIS	1	AT	DETROIT	2
SUN.	APR. 20	DETROIT	3	AT	ST. LOUIS	2
TUE.	APR. 22	DETROIT	0	AT	ST. LOUIS	4
FRI.	APR. 25	ST. LOUIS	2	AT	DETROIT	5
SUN.	APR. 27	DETROIT	3	AT	ST. LOUIS	1

(DETROIT WON SERIES 4-2)

SERIES 'H'

WED.	APR. 16	PHOENIX	2	AT	ANAHEIM	4
FRI.	APR. 18	PHOENIX	2	AT	ANAHEIM	4
SUN.	APR. 20	ANAHEIM	1	AT	PHOENIX	4
TUE.	APR. 22	ANAHEIM	0	AT	PHOENIX	2
THU.	APR. 24	PHOENIX	5	AT	ANAHEIM	2
SUN.	APR. 27	ANAHEIM	3	AT	PHOENIX	2*
TUE.	APR. 29	PHOENIX	0	AT	ANAHEIM	3

*PAUL KARIYA SCORED AT 7:29 OF OVERTIME
(ANAHEIM WON SERIES 4-3)

CONFERENCE SEMIFINALS

EASTERN CONFERENCE

SERIES 'I'

FRI.	MAY 2	NY RANGERS	0	AT	NEW JERSEY	2
SUN.	MAY 4	NY RANGERS	2	AT	NEW JERSEY	0
TUE.	MAY 6	NEW JERSEY	2	AT	NY RANGERS	3
THU.	MAY 8	NEW JERSEY	0	AT	NY RANGERS	3
SUN.	MAY 11	NY RANGERS	2	AT	NEW JERSEY	1*

*ADAM GRAVES SCORED AT 14:08 OF OVERTIME
(NY RANGERS WON SERIES 4-1)

SERIES 'J'

SAT.	MAY 3	PHILADELPHIA	5	AT	BUFFALO	3
MON.	MAY 5	PHILADELPHIA	2	AT	BUFFALO	1
WED.	MAY 7	BUFFALO	1	AT	PHILADELPHIA	4
FRI.	MAY 9	BUFFALO	5	AT	PHILADELPHIA	4*
SUN.	MAY 11	PHILADELPHIA	6	AT	BUFFALO	3

*ED RONAN SCORED AT 6:24 OF OVERTIME
(PHILADELPHIA WON SERIES 4-1)

WESTERN CONFERENCE

SERIES 'K'

FRI.	MAY 2	EDMONTON	1	AT	COLORADO	5
SUN.	MAY 4	EDMONTON	1	AT	COLORADO	4
WED.	MAY 7	COLORADO	3	AT	EDMONTON	4
FRI.	MAY 9	COLORADO	3	AT	EDMONTON	2*
SUN.	MAY 11	EDMONTON	3	AT	COLORADO	4

*CLAUDE LEMIEUX SCORED AT 8:35 OF OVERTIME
(COLORADO WON SERIES 4-1)

SERIES 'L'

FRI.	MAY 2	ANAHEIM	1	AT	DETROIT	2*
SUN.	MAY 4	ANAHEIM	1	AT	DETROIT	3**
TUE.	MAY 6	DETROIT	5	AT	ANAHEIM	3
THU.	MAY 8	DETROIT	3	AT	ANAHEIM	2***

*MARTIN LAPOINTE SCORED AT 0:59 OF OVERTIME
**VYACHESLAV KOZLOV SCORED AT 41:31 OF OVERTIME
***BRENDAN SHANAHAN SCORED AT 37:03 OF OVERTIME
(DETROIT WON SERIES 4-0)

CONFERENCE CHAMPIONSHIPS

EASTERN CONFERENCE

SERIES 'M'

FRI.	MAY 16	NY RANGERS	1	AT	PHILADELPHIA	3
SUN.	MAY 18	NY RANGERS	5	AT	PHILADELPHIA	4
TUE.	MAY 20	PHILADELPHIA	6	AT	NY RANGERS	3
FRI.	MAY 23	PHILADELPHIA	3	AT	NY RANGERS	2
SUN.	MAY 25	NY RANGERS	2	AT	PHILADELPHIA	4

(PHILADELPHIA WON SERIES 4-1)

WESTERN CONFERENCE

SERIES 'N'

THU.	MAY 15	DETROIT	1	AT	COLORADO	2
SAT.	MAY 17	DETROIT	4	AT	COLORADO	2
MON.	MAY 19	COLORADO	1	AT	DETROIT	2
THU.	MAY 22	COLORADO	0	AT	DETROIT	6
SAT.	MAY 24	DETROIT	0	AT	COLORADO	6
MON.	MAY 26	COLORADO	1	AT	DETROIT	3

(DETROIT WON SERIES 4-2)

STANLEY CUP CHAMPIONSHIP

SERIES 'O'

SAT.	MAY 31	DETROIT	4	AT	PHILADELPHIA	2
MON.	JUNE 3	DETROIT	4	AT	PHILADELPHIA	2
THU.	JUNE 5	PHILADELPHIA	1	AT	DETROIT	6
SAT.	JUNE 7	PHILADELPHIA	1	AT	DETROIT	2

(DETROIT WON SERIES 4-0)

1997 NHL PLAYOFF SCORING LEADERS

		GP	G	A	PTS	+/-	PIM	PP	SH	GW	OT	S	PCTG
Eric Lindros	Philadelphia	19	12	14	26	7	40	4	0	1	0	71	16.9
Joe Sakic	Colorado	17	8	17	25	5	14	3	0	0	0	50	16.0
Claude Lemieux	Colorado	17	13	10	23	7	32	4	0	4	1	73	17.8
Valeri Kamensky	Colorado	17	8	14	22	1-	16	5	0	2	0	49	16.3
Rod Brind'Amour	Philadelphia	19	13	8	21	9	10	4	2	1	0	65	20.0
John LeClair	Philadelphia	19	9	12	21	5	10	4	0	3	0	79	11.4
Wayne Gretzky	NY Rangers	15	10	10	20	5	2	3	0	2	0	44	22.7
SERGEI FEDOROV	**DETROIT**	**20**	**8**	**12**	**20**	**5**	**12**	**3**	**0**	**4**	**0**	**79**	**10.1**
BRENDAN SHANAHAN	**DETROIT**	**20**	**9**	**8**	**17**	**8**	**43**	**2**	**0**	**2**	**1**	**82**	**11.0**
Peter Forsberg	Colorado	14	5	12	17	6-	10	3	0	0	0	35	14.3
Sandis Ozolinsh	Colorado	17	4	13	17	1-	24	2	0	1	0	39	10.3
VYACHESLAV KOZLOV	**DETROIT**	**20**	**8**	**5**	**13**	**3**	**14**	**4**	**0**	**2**	**1**	**58**	**13.8**
Paul Kariya	Anaheim	11	7	6	13	2-	4	4	0	1	1	61	11.5
STEVE YZERMAN	**DETROIT**	**20**	**7**	**6**	**13**	**3**	**4**	**3**	**0**	**2**	**0**	**65**	**10.8**
Janne Niinimaa	Philadelphia	19	1	12	13	3	16	1	0	1	0	56	1.8
Esa Tikkanen	NY Rangers	15	9	3	12	2	26	3	1	3	2	45	20.0
IGOR LARIONOV	**DETROIT**	**20**	**4**	**8**	**12**	**8**	**8**	**3**	**0**	**1**	**0**	**29**	**13.8**
MARTIN LAPOINTE	**DETROIT**	**20**	**4**	**8**	**12**	**8**	**60**	**1**	**0**	**1**	**1**	**37**	**10.8**
Mark Messier	NY Rangers	15	3	9	12	2	6	0	0	1	0	43	7.0
Mikael Renberg	Philadelphia	18	5	6	11	1	4	2	0	0	0	35	14.3
Luc Robitaille	NY Rangers	15	4	7	11	7	4	0	0	0	0	43	9.3
Doug Weight	Edmonton	12	3	8	11	0	8	0	0	0	0	54	5.6
LARRY MURPHY	**DETROIT**	**20**	**2**	**9**	**11**	**16**	**8**	**1**	**0**	**1**	**0**	**51**	**3.9**
Dmitri Mironov	Anaheim	11	1	10	11	0	10	1	0	0	0	36	2.8

1997 NHL PLAYOFF GOALTENDING LEADERS
(Minimum 420 minutes)

		GP	MINS	GA	SO	AVG	W-L
Martin Brodeur	New Jersey	10	659	19	2	1.73	5-5
Mike Vernon	Detroit	20	1229	36	1	1.76	16-4
Guy Hebert	Anaheim	9	534	18	1	2.02	4-4
Mike Richter	NY Rangers	15	939	33	3	2.11	9-6
Patrick Roy	Colorado	17	1034	38	3	2.21	10-7

1996-97 NHL ALL-STARS

FIRST TEAM	POS	SECOND TEAM
DOMINIK HASEK Buffalo	G	MARTIN BRODEUR New Jersey
SANDIS OZOLINSH Colorado	D	SCOTT STEVENS New Jersey
BRIAN LEETCH NY Rangers	D	CHRIS CHELIOS Chicago
MARIO LEMIEUX Pittsburgh	C	WAYNE GRETZKY NY Rangers
PAUL KARIYA Anaheim	LW	JOHN LECLAIR Philadelphia
TEEMU SELANNE Anaheim	RW	JAROMIR JAGR Pittsburgh

NHL TROPHY WINNERS

NORRIS
(Defenseman)
BRIAN LEETCH
NY Rangers

ROSS
(Top Scorer)
MARIO LEMIEUX
Pittsburgh

SELKE
(Defensive Forward)
MICHAEL PECA
Buffalo

HART
(MVP)
DOMINIK HASEK
Buffalo

LESTER B. PEARSON
(NHLPA Top Player)
DOMINIK HASEK
Buffalo

VEZINA
(Goalie)
DOMINIK HASEK
Buffalo

JENNINGS
(Team GAA)
MARTIN BRODEUR
(Co-winner)
New Jersey

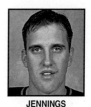

JENNINGS
(Team GAA)
MIKE DUNHAM
(Co-winner)
New Jersey

CALDER
(Rookie)
BRYAN BERARD
NY Islanders

JACK ADAMS
(Coach)
TED NOLAN
Buffalo

CONN SMYTHE
(Playoff MVP)
MIKE VERNON
Detroit

LADY BYNG
(Sportsmanship)
PAUL KARIYA
Anaheim

CLANCY
(Humanitarian Efforts)
TREVOR LINDEN
Vancouver

MASTERTON
(Perseverance)
TONY GRANATO
San Jose

(82 Games, Oct. 5 – Apr. 13)

	GP	G	A	PTS	+/-	PIM	PP	SH	GW	GT	S	PCT.
B. Shanahan HFD	2	1	0	1	1	0	0	1	0	0	13	7.7
DET	79	46	41	87	31	131	20	2	7	2	323	14.2
TOT	81	47	41	88	32	131	20	3	7	2	336	14.0
Steve Yzerman	81	22	63	85	22	78	8	0	3	0	232	9.5
Sergei Fedorov	74	30	33	63	29	30	9	2	4	0	273	11.0
Nicklas Lidstrom	79	15	42	57	11	30	8	0	1	0	214	7.0
Igor Larionov	64	12	42	54	31	26	2	1	4	0	95	12.6
Darren McCarty	68	19	30	49	14	126	5	0	6	1	171	11.1
Vyacheslav Kozlov	75	23	22	45	21	46	3	0	6	0	211	10.9
Larry Murphy TOR	69	7	32	39	1	20	4	0	0	1	137	5.1
DET	12	2	4	6	2	0	1	0	1	0	21	9.5
TOT	81	9	36	45	3	20	5	0	1	1	158	5.7
+T. Sandstrom PIT	40	9	15	24	4	33	1	1	0	0	73	12.3
DET	34	9	9	18	2	36	0	1	2	1	66	13.6
TOT	74	18	24	42	6	69	1	2	2	1	139	12.9
Vlad. Konstantinov	77	5	33	38	38	151	0	0	0	0	141	3.5
Martin Lapointe	78	16	17	33	14-	167	5	1	1	0	149	10.7
Viacheslav Fetisov	64	5	23	28	26	76	0	0	1	0	95	5.3
+Greg Johnson	43	6	10	16	5-	12	0	0	0	0	56	10.7
Kris Draper	76	8	5	13	11-	73	1	0	1	0	85	9.4
Doug Brown	49	6	7	13	3-	8	1	0	0	0	69	8.7
Bob Rouse	70	4	9	13	8	58	0	2	0	0	70	5.7
Mathieu Dandenault	65	3	9	12	10-	28	0	0	0	0	81	3.7
* Jamie Pushor	75	4	7	11	1	129	0	0	0	0	63	6.3
* Tomas Holmstrom	47	6	3	9	10-	33	3	0	0	0	53	11.3
Kirk Maltby	66	3	5	8	3	75	0	0	0	0	62	4.8
Tim Taylor	44	3	4	7	6-	52	0	1	0	2	44	6.8
* Aaron Ward	49	2	5	7	9-	52	0	0	0	0	40	5.0
* Anders Eriksson	23	0	6	6	5	10	0	0	0	0	27	.0
Joe Kocur	34	2	1	3	7-	70	0	0	1	0	38	5.3
+Bob Errey	36	1	2	3	3-	27	0	0	0	0	34	2.9
Chris Osgood	47	0	2	2	0	6	0	0	0	0	0	.0
* Mike Knuble	9	1	0	1	1-	0	0	0	0	0	10	10.0
* Kevin Hodson	6	0	1	1	0	0	0	0	0	0	0	.0
Mike Ramsey	2	0	0	0	0	0	0	0	0	0	3	.0
Mark Major	2	0	0	0	0	5	0	0	0	0	0	.0
+Mike Vernon	33	0	0	0	0	35	0	0	0	0	0	.0
BENCH	–	–	–	–	–	12	–	–	–	–	–	–
DETROIT TOTALS	**82**	**253**	**435**	**688**	**–**	**1582**	**66**	**10**	**38**	**6**	**2636**	**9.6**

GOALTENDERS	GP	MIN	GAA	W	L	T	EN	SO	GA	SA	SPCT.
* Kevin Hodson	6	294	1.63	2	2	1	0	1	8	114	.930
Chris Osgood	47	2769	2.30	23	13	9	3	6	106	1175	.910
+Mike Vernon	33	1952	2.43	13	11	8	1	0	79	782	.899
TOTALS	**82**	**@5031**	**2.35**	**38**	**26**	**18**	**4**	**7**	**197**	**2075**	**.905**

@-Includes minutes goalie out of net.

*-Rookie

+ -Traded

1997 DETROIT RED WINGS' PLAYOFF STATISTICS
(20 Games, Apr. 16 – June 7)

	GP	G	A	PTS	+/-	PIM	PP	SH	GW	OT	S	PCT.
Sergei Fedorov	20	8	12	20	5	12	3	0	4	1	79	10.1
Brendan Shanahan	20	9	8	17	8	43	2	0	2	1	82	11.0
Vyacheslav Kozlov	20	8	5	13	3	14	4	0	2	1	58	13.8
Steve Yzerman	20	7	6	13	3	4	3	0	2	0	65	10.8
Igor Larionov	20	4	8	12	8	8	3	0	1	0	29	13.8
Martin Lapointe	20	4	8	12	8	60	1	0	1	1	37	10.8
Larry Murphy	20	2	9	11	16	8	1	0	1	0	51	3.9
Nicklas Lidstrom	20	2	6	8	12	2	0	0	0	0	79	2.5
Kirk Maltby	20	5	2	7	6	24	0	1	1	0	35	14.3
Darren McCarty	20	3	4	7	1	34	0	0	2	0	34	8.8
Doug Brown	14	3	3	6	4	2	0	0	0	0	23	13.0
Kris Draper	20	2	4	6	5	12	0	1	0	0	30	6.7
Joe Kocur	19	1	3	4	5	22	0	0	0	0	16	6.3
Viacheslav Fetisov	20	0	4	4	2	42	0	0	0	0	27	.0
+Tomas Sandstrom	20	0	4	4	3-	24	0	0	0	0	36	.0
Vlad. Konstantinov	20	0	4	4	1-	29	0	0	0	0	29	.0
* Jamie Pushor	5	0	1	1	1-	5	0	0	0	0	3	.0
+Mike Vernon	20	0	1	1	0	12	0	0	0	0	0	.0
* Tomas Holmstrom	1	0	0	0	1-	0	0	0	0	0	0	.0
Tim Taylor	2	0	0	0	1-	0	0	0	0	0	0	.0
Chris Osgood	2	0	0	0	0	2	0	0	0	0	0	.0
* Aaron Ward	19	0	0	0	1	17	0	0	0	0	9	.0
Bob Rouse	20	0	0	0	8	55	0	0	0	0	14	.0
TOTALS	**20**	**58**	**92**	**150**	**–**	**431**	**17**	**2**	**16**	**3**	**736**	

GOALTENDERS		GP	MIN	GAA	W	L	EN	SO	GA	SA	SPCT.
+ Mike Vernon		20	1229	1.76	16	4	0	1	36	494	.927
Chris Osgood		2	47	2.55	0	0	0	0	2	21	.905
TOTALS		**20**	**@1280**	**1.78**	**16**	**4**	**0**	**1**	**@38**	**@515**	**.926**

@-Includes minutes goalie out of net, empty net goals, shots.
*-Rookie
+ -Traded

Game	Date	Opposition	W-L-T	Score	Record
1	10-5-96	@ New Jersey	L	1-3	0-1-0
2	10-9-96	Edmonton	W	2-0	1-1-0
3	10-11-96	Calgary	L	1-2	1-2-0
4	10-12-96	@ Buffalo	W	6-1	2-2-0
5	10-15-96	@ Dallas	L	1-3	2-3-0
6	10-17-96	@ Chicago	L	1-2	2-4-0
7	10-19-96	NY Islanders	W	4-2	3-4-0
8	10-21-96	Los Angeles	W	3-0	4-4-0
9	10-23-96	Dallas	W	4-1	5-4-0
10	10-25-96	Chicago	T	2-2	5-4-1
11	10-26-96	@ Boston	W	2-1	6-4-1
12	10-30-96	Montréal	W	5-3	7-4-1
13	11-1-96	@ Ottawa	T	2-2	7-4-2
14	11-2-96	@ Toronto	L	2-6	7-5-2
15	11-4-96	Hartford	W	5-1	8-5-2
16	11-6-96	New Jersey	L	0-2	8-6-2
17	11-8-96	@ Hartford	W	4-1	9-6-2
18	11-10-96	Tampa Bay	W	4-2	10-6-2
19	11-13-96	Colorado	L	1-4	10-7-2
20	11-15-96	San Jose	W	5-1	11-7-2
21	11-18-96	@ Phoenix	T	2-2	11-7-3
22	11-21-96	@ San Jose	W	6-1	12-7-3
23	11-23-96	@ Los Angeles	W	6-0	13-7-3
24	11-24-96	@ Anaheim	L	1-3	13-8-3
25	11-27-96	Toronto	W	5-2	14-8-3
26	12-1-96	Florida*	L	2-4	14-9-3
27	12-3-96	Vancouver	T	2-2	14-9-4
28	12-4-96	@ Washington	W	2-0	15-9-4
29	12-10-96	Edmonton	T	0-0	15-9-5
30	12-12-96	Chicago	W	6-2	16-9-5
31	12-15-96	Toronto	W	3-1	17-9-5
32	12-17-96	@ Colorado	L	3-4	17-10-5
33	12-18-96	@ Calgary	T	3-3	17-10-6
34	12-20-96	@ Vancouver	L	2-3	17-11-6
35	12-22-96	@ Edmonton	W	6-2	18-11-6
36	12-26-96	Washington	W	5-4	19-11-6
37	12-28-96	@ NY Islanders	W	7-1	20-11-6
38	12-30-96	Phoenix	L	3-5	20-12-6
39	1-3-97	Dallas	L	1-2	20-13-6
40	1-5-97	@ Chicago	T	5-5	20-13-7
41	1-8-97	@ Dallas	L	3-6	20-14-7
42	1-9-97	@ Phoenix	W	5-4	21-14-7
43	1-11-97	Chicago	L	1-3	21-15-7
44	1-14-97	Los Angeles	T	3-3	21-15-8

GAME-BY-GAME RESULTS

Pts	GF	GA	Goalie	Deciding Goal
0	1	3	Osgood	Thomas
2	3	3	OSGOOD	KOZLOV
2	4	5	Osgood	Reichel
4	10	6	VERNON	YZERMAN
4	11	9	Vernon	Zubov
4	12	11	Osgood	Chelios
6	16	13	VERNON	FETISOV
8	19	13	OSGOOD	SHANAHAN
10	23	14	OSGOOD	DRAPER
11	25	16	HODSON	SHANAHAN
13	27	17	OSGOOD	SHANAHAN
15	32	20	OSGOOD	FEDOROV
16	34	22	OSGOOD	Daigle
16	36	28	Vernon	Schneider
18	41	29	OSGOOD	FEDOROV
18	41	31	Osgood	MacLean
20	45	32	VERNON	LAPOINTE
22	49	34	OSGOOD	KOZLOV
22	50	38	Osgood	Forsberg
24	55	39	VERNON	McCARTY
25	57	41	OSGOOD	McCARTY
27	63	42	VERNON	LIDSTROM
29	69	42	OSGOOD	YZERMAN
29	70	45	Vernon	Valk
31	75	47	OSGOOD	SHANAHAN
31	77	51	Osgood	Skrudland
32	79	53	Osgood	Shanahan
34	81	53	HODSON	McCARTY
35	81	53	OSGOOD	
37	87	55	OSGOOD	LARIONOV
39	90	56	OSGOOD	McCARTY
39	93	60	Vernon	Lacroix
40	96	63	OSGOOD	Simpson
40	98	66	Hodson	Gelinas
42	104	68	OSGOOD	KOZLOV
44	109	72	OSGOOD	FEDOROV
46	116	73	VERNON	KOZLOV
46	119	78	Osgood	Ronning
46	120	80	Vernon	Modano
47	125	85	VERNON	Suter
47	128	91	Osgood	Harvey
49	133	95	OSGOOD	LARIONOV
49	134	98	Osgood	Probert
50	137	101	Osgood	Stevens

Game	Date	Opposition	W-L-T	Score	Record
45	1-20-97	@ Montréal	L	1-4	21-16-8
46	1-22-97	Philadelphia	T	2-2	21-16-9
47	1-25-97	@ Philadelphia*	W	4-1	22-16-9
48	1-29-97	Phoenix	L	0-3	22-17-9
49	2-1-97	@ St. Louis*	W	4-1	23-17-9
50	2-2-97	Dallas	W	4-3	24-17-9
51	2-4-97	St. Louis	T	1-1	24-17-10
52	2-6-97	Vancouver	L	4-7	24-18-10
53	2-8-97	@ Pittsburgh*	W	6-5	25-18-10
54	2-12-97	San Jose	W	7-1	26-18-10
55	2-14-97	@ Dallas	L	3-4	26-19-10
56	2-16-97	@ Florida	W	4-2	27-19-10
57	2-17-97	@ Tampa Bay	T	3-3	27-19-11
58	2-19-97	Calgary	W	4-0	28-19-11
59	2-22-97	@ St. Louis*	T	2-2	28-19-12
60	2-24-97	@ Phoenix	W	5-3	29-19-12
61	2-27-97	Pittsburgh	W	4-1	30-19-12
62	3-1-97	NY Rangers*	W	3-0	31-19-12
63	3-2-97	Anaheim	T	1-1	31-19-13
64	3-5-97	@ Toronto	T	4-4	31-19-14
65	3-8-96	@ Vancouver	W	5-3	32-19-14
66	3-10-97	@ Los Angeles	T	3-3	32-19-15
67	3-12-97	@ Anaheim	L	1-2	32-20-15
68	3-15-97	@ San Jose	W	7-4	33-20-15
69	3-16-97	@ Colorado	L	2-4	33-21-15
70	3-19-97	Boston	W	4-1	34-21-15
71	3-21-97	@ NY Rangers	L	1-3	34-22-15
72	3-23-97	@ Chicago*	L	3-5	34-23-15
73	3-26-97	Colorado	W	6-5	35-23-15
74	3-28-97	Buffalo+	W	2-1	36-23-15
75	3-30-97	Anaheim*	L	0-1	36-24-15
76	4-1-97	St. Louis	T	1-1	36-24-16
77	4-3-97	Toronto	T	2-2	36-24-17
78	4-5-97	@ Toronto	W	4-2	37-24-17
79	4-8-97	@ Calgary	W	3-2	38-24-17
80	4-9-97	@ Edmonton	T	3-3	38-24-18
81	4-11-97	Ottawa	L	2-3	38-25-18
82	4-13-97	St. Louis*	L	1-3	38-26-18

*-Matinee
+-Clinched playoff berth, Red Wings victory over Buffalo
a-Hodson replaced Vernon at 7:19 of 1st period

Pts	GF	GA	Goalie	Deciding Goal
50	138	105	Vernon	Tucker
51	140	107	Vernon	LeClair
53	144	108	VERNON	SHANAHAN
53	144	111	Vernon	Shannon
55	148	112	VERNON	SHANAHAN
57	152	115	OSGOOD	KOZLOV
58	153	116	Vernon	Campbell
58	157	123	Osgood	Gelinas
60	163	128	VERNON	SHANAHAN
62	170	129	OSGOOD	SHANAHAN
62	173	133	Vernon	Kennedy
64	177	135	OSGOOD	McCARTY
65	180	138	Vernon	Langkow
67	184	138	OSGOOD	SANDSTROM
68	186	140	Vernon	Turgeon
70	191	143	OSGOOD	KOZLOV
72	195	144	VERNON	FEDOROV
74	198	144	OSGOOD	McCARTY
75	199	145	Vernon	Drury
76	203	149	Osgood	Sundin
78	208	152	VERNON	LARIONOV
79	211	155	Osgood	Ferraro
79	212	157	Vernon	Kurri
81	219	161	OSGOOD	KOCUR
81	221	165	Osgood	Jones
83	225	166	HODSON	LARIONOV
83	226	169	Osgood	Courtnall
83	229	174	*a*-Hodson/ Vernon	Krivokrasov
85	235	179	VERNON	McCARTY
87	237	180	VERNON	MURPHY
87	237	181	Vernon	Rucchin
88	238	182	Vernon	TAYLOR
89	240	184	Osgood	TAYLOR
91	244	186	OSGOOD	YZERMAN
93	247	188	OSGOOD	SANDSTROM
94	250	191	Vernon	Sandstrom
94	252	194	Vernon	Redden
94	253	197	Osgood	Demitra

You can tell they've got the blues.

Having the Blues is great. Blue Cross Blue Shield of Michigan, that is.
You can choose from our many plans to find the one that's just right
for you. And whether you have Blue Managed Traditional, the most
accepted coverage around; Blue Care Network HMO; Blue Choice POS;
or our newest product, Community Blue PPO, you get the backing of
Blue Cross Blue Shield of Michigan. And that makes people with the
Blues very happy. To find out more about getting the Blues, contact a
Blue Cross Blue Shield and Blue Care Network authorized independent
insurance agent.

GAME	DAY	DATE	OPPONENT	SCORE	RESULT	W-L-T	ATTENDANCE
1	Wed.	Oct. 9	Edmonton	2-0	W	1-0-0	19,983
2	Fri.	Oct. 11	Calgary	1-2	L	1-1-0	19,983
3	Sat.	Oct. 19	NY Islanders	4-2	W	2-1-0	19,983
4	Mon.	Oct. 21	Los Angeles	3-0	W	3-1-0	19,849
5	Wed.	Oct. 23	Dallas	4-1	W	4-1-0	19,983
6	Fri.	Oct. 25	Chicago	2-2 OT	T	4-1-1	19,983
7	Wed.	Oct. 30	Montréal	5-3	W	5-1-1	19,983
8	Mon.	Nov. 4	Hartford	5-1	W	6-1-1	19,983
9	Wed.	Nov. 6	New Jersey	0-2	L	6-2-1	19,983
10	Sun.	Nov.10	Tampa Bay	4-2	W	7-2-1	19,983
11	Wed.	Nov. 13	Colorado	1-4	L	7-3-1	19,983
12	Fri.	Nov. 15	San Jose	5-1	W	8-3-1	19,983
13	Wed.	Nov. 27	Toronto	5-2	W	9-3-1	19,983
14	Sun.	Dec. 1	Florida	2-4	L	9-4-1	19,983
15	Tue.	Dec. 3	Vancouver	2-2 OT	T	9-4-2	19,921
16	Tue.	Dec. 10	Edmonton	0-0 OT	T	9-4-3	19,983
17	Thu.	Dec. 12	Chicago	6-2	W	10-4-3	19,983
18	Sun.	Dec. 15	Toronto	3-1	W	11-4-3	19,983
19	Thu.	Dec. 26	Washington	5-4	W	12-4-3	19,983
20	Mon.	Dec. 30	Phoenix	3-5	L	12-5-3	19,983
21	Fri.	Jan. 3	Dallas	1-2	L	12-6-3	19,983
22	Sat.	Jan. 11	Chicago	1-3	L	12-7-3	19,983
23	Tue.	Jan. 14	Los Angeles	3-3 OT	T	12-7-4	19,983
24	Wed.	Jan. 22	Philadelphia	2-2 OT	T	12-7-5	19,983
25	Wed.	Jan. 29	Phoenix	0-3	L	12-8-5	19,983
26	Sun.	Feb. 2	Dallas	4-3	W	13-8-5	19,983
27	Tue.	Feb. 4	St. Louis	1-1 OT	T	13-8-6	19,983
28	Thu.	Feb. 6	Vancouver	4-7	L	13-9-6	19,983
29	Wed.	Feb. 12	San Jose	7-1	W	14-9-6	19,983
30	Wed.	Feb. 19	Calgary	4-0	W	15-9-6	19,983
31	Thu.	Feb. 27	Pittsburgh	4-1	W	16-9-6	19,983
32	Sat. .	Mar. 1	N.Y. Rangers	3-0	W	17-9-6	19,983
33	Sun	Mar. 2	Anaheim	1-1 OT	T	17-9-7	19,983
34	Wed..	Mar. 19	Boston	4-1	W	18-9-7	19,983
35	Wed.	Mar. 26	Colorado	6-5 OT	W	19-9-7	19,983
36	Fri.	Mar. 28	Buffalo	2-1 OT	W	20-9-7	19,983
37	Sun.	Mar. 30	Anaheim	0-1 OT	L	20-10-7	19,983
38	Tue.	Apr. 1	St. Louis	1-1 OT	T	20-10-8	19,983
39	Thu.	Apr. 3	Toronto	2-2 OT	T	20-10-9	19,983
40	Fri.	Apr. 11	Ottawa	2-3	L	20-11-9	19,983
41	Sun.	Apr. 13	St. Louis	1-3	L	20-12-9	19,983

Home Record: 20-12-9
Home Attendance: 819,107
Average: 19,978

1996-97 GAME-BY-GAME ROAD RESULTS

GAME	DAY	DATE	OPPONENT	SCORE	RESULT	W-L-T	ATTENDANCE
1	Sat.	Oct. 5	New Jersey	1-3	L	0-1-0	18,622
2	Sat.	Oct. 12	Buffalo	6-1	W	1-1-0	18,595
3	Tue.	Oct. 15	Dallas	1-3	L	1-2-0	15,983
4	Thu.	Oct. 17	Chicago	1-2	L	1-3-0	18,261
5	Sat.	Oct. 26	Boston	2-1	W	2-3-0	17,012
6	Fri.	Nov. 1	Ottawa	2-2 OT	T	2-3-1	14,158
7	Sat.	Nov. 2	Toronto	2-6	L	2-4-1	15,726
8	Fri.	Nov. 8	Hartford	4-1	W	3-4-1	14,660
9	Mon.	Nov. 18	Phoenix	2-2 OT	T	3-4-2	15,436
10	Thu.	Nov. 21	San Jose	6-1	W	4-4-2	17,442
11	Sat.	Nov. 23	Los Angeles	6-0	W	5-4-2	16,005
12	Sun.	Nov. 24	Anaheim	1-3	L	5-5-2	17,174
13	Wed.	Dec. 4	Washington	2-0	W	6-5-2	16,117
14	Tue.	Dec. 17	Colorado	3-4	L	6-6-2	16,061
15	Wed.	Dec. 18	Calgary	3-3 OT	T	6-6-3	16,237
16	Fri.	Dec. 20	Vancouver	2-3	L	6-7-3	18,422
17	Sun.	Dec. 22	Edmonton	6-2	W	7-7-3	16,724
18	Sat.	Dec. 28	NY Islanders	7-1	W	8-7-3	16,297
19	Sun.	Jan. 5	Chicago	5-5 OT	T	8-7-4	21,914
20	Wed.	Jan. 8	Dallas	3-6	L	8-8-4	15,326
21	Thu.	Jan. 9	Phoenix	5-4 OT	W	9-8-4	16,210
22	Mon.	Jan. 20	Montréal	1-4	L	9-9-4	21,273
23	Sat.	Jan. 25	Philadelphia	4-1	W	10-9-4	19,711
24	Sat.	Feb. 1	St. Louis	4-1	W	11-9-4	20,330
25	Sat.	Feb. 8	Pittsburgh	6-5 OT	W	12-9-4	17,355
26	Fri.	Feb. 14	Dallas	3-4	L	12-10-4	16,924
27	Sun.	Feb. 16	Florida	4-2	W	13-10-4	14,703
28	Mon.	Feb. 17	Tampa Bay	3-3 OT	T	13-10-5	19,579
29	Sat.	Feb. 22	St. Louis	2-2 OT	T	13-10-6	20,371
30	Mon.	Feb. 24	Phoenix	5-3	W	14-10-6	16,210
31	Wed.	Mar. 5	Toronto	4-4 OT	T	14-10-7	15,726
32	Sat.	Mar. 8	Vancouver	5-3	W	15-10-7	18,422
33	Mon.	Mar. 10	Los Angeles	3-3 OT	T	15-10-8	10,663
34	Wed.	Mar. 12	Anaheim	2-1	L	15-11-8	17,174
35	Sat.	Mar. 15	San Jose	7-4	W	16-11-8	17,442
36	Sun.	Mar. 16	Colorado	2-4	L	16-12-8	16,061
37	Fri.	Mar. 21	NY Rangers	1-3	L	16-13-8	18,200
38	Sun.	Mar. 23	Chicago	3-5	L	16-14-8	22,422
39	Sat.	Apr. 5	Toronto	4-2	W	17-14-8	15,726
40	Tue.	Apr. 8	Calgary	3-2 OT	W	18-14-8	17,841
41	Wed.	Apr. 9	Edmonton	3-3 OT	T	18-14-9	17,099

Road Record: 18-14-9
Road Attendance: 539,158
Average: 13,150

DETROIT VS. ANAHEIM 1996-97 SEASON

TEAM	W	L	T	P	GF	GA	PPG	SHG	PM
Anaheim	3	0	1	7	7	3	1	0	26
Detroit	0	3	1	1	3	7	0	0	32

at Anaheim (0-2-0)
Nov. 24, 1996 – Anaheim 3, DETROIT 1
March 12, 1997 – Anaheim 2, DETROIT 1
Totals – Anaheim 5, DETROIT 2

at Detroit (0-1-1)
March 2, 1997 – DETROIT 1, Anaheim 1
March 30, 1997 – Anaheim 1, DETROIT 0
Totals – Anaheim 2, DETROIT 1

ANAHEIM MIGHTY DUCKS

PLAYER	GP	G	A	P	PM	+/-
Selanne	3	2	0	2	2	–
Drury	4	1	1	2	2	1
Van Impe	4	1	1	2	4	–
Todd	3	0	2	2	0	1
Kariya	4	0	2	2	0	1
Valk	1	1	0	1	0	1
Kurri	4	1	0	1	0	–
Rucchin	4	1	0	1	0	1
Daigneault	1	0	1	1	0	1
Jomphe	2	0	1	1	0	1
Baumgartner	3	0	1	1	0	1
Dollas	4	0	1	1	0	1
Mironov	4	0	1	1	4	1
Rychel	4	0	1	1	0	1
Janssens	1	0	0	0	0	–
LeClerc	1	0	0	0	0	–
Park	1	0	0	0	0	–
Salei	1	0	0	0	0	–
Tsulygin	1	0	0	0	0	-1
Leboutillier	2	0	0	0	0	–
Trebil	2	0	0	0	0	–
Karpa	3	0	0	0	4	4
Pronger	3	0	0	0	0	–
Bellows	4	0	0	0	4	1
Marshall	4	0	0	0	4	–
Sacco	4	0	0	0	2	–
Totals	**4**	**7**	**12**	**19**	**26**	**–**

DETROIT RED WINGS

PLAYER	GP	G	A	P	PM	+/-
Fedorov	4	1	1	2	0	–
Lidstrom	4	1	0	1	2	-1
Maltby	4	1	0	1	0	1
Brown	3	0	1	1	0	–
Fetisov	3	0	1	1	0	–
Rouse	3	0	1	1	2	1
Yzerman	4	0	1	1	14	1
Knuble	1	0	0	0	0	–
Murphy	1	0	0	0	0	–
Ramsey	1	0	0	0	0	–
Holmstrom	2	0	0	0	0	-1
Kocur	2	0	0	0	0	–
Pushor	2	0	0	0	0	-2
Taylor	2	0	0	0	0	-1
Dandenault	3	0	0	0	0	–
Draper	3	0	0	0	0	-1
Sandstrom	3	0	0	0	4	–
Ward	3	0	0	0	0	-2
Konstantinov	4	0	0	0	4	-2
Kozlov	4	0	0	0	2	-2
Lapointe	4	0	0	0	0	-3
Larionov	4	0	0	0	0	-2
McCarty	4	0	0	0	2	-1
Shanahan	4	0	0	0	2	–
Totals	**4**	**3**	**5**	**8**	**32**	**–**

GOALIE:	GP	MP	GA	ENG	SO	AVG
Herbert (2-0-1)	3	185	3	0	0	.97
Shtalenkov (1-0-0)	1	64	0	0	1	.00
Totals (3-0-1)	**4**	**249**	**3**	**0**	**1**	**.72**

GOALIE:	GP	MP	GA	ENG	SO	AVG
Vernon (0-3-1)	4	246	7	0	0	1.71
Totals (0-3-1)	**4**	**246**	**7**	**0**	**0**	**1.71**

DETROIT VS. BOSTON 1996-97 SEASON

TEAM	W	L	T	P	GF	GA	PPG	SHG	PM
Boston	0	2	0	0	2	6	1	0	22
DETROIT	2	0	0	4	6	2	2	0	18

at Boston (1-0-0)
Oct. 26, 1996 – DETROIT 2, Boston 1
Totals – DETROIT 2, Boston 1

at DETROIT (1-0-0)
March 19, 1997 – DETROIT 4, Boston 1
Totals – DETROIT 4, Boston 1

BOSTON BRUINS

PLAYER	GP	G	A	P	PM	+/-
Stumpel	2	0	2	2	2	–
Roy	1	1	0	1	0	–
Sweeney	2	1	0	1	0	-1
Allison	1	0	1	1	0	–
Beddoes	1	0	0	0	0	–
Carter	1	0	0	0	0	-1
Chynoweth	1	0	0	0	0	-1
Donato	1	0	0	0	0	–
Elik	1	0	0	0	0	–
Harkins	1	0	0	0	0	-2
Heinze	1	0	0	0	0	–
Kennedy	1	0	0	0	2	-2
Malkoc	1	0	0	0	0	-1
Mallette	1	0	0	0	0	-1
McCleary	1	0	0	0	0	–
Oates	1	0	0	0	0	–
Payne	1	0	0	0	0	–
Richter	1	0	0	0	0	–
Rohloff	1	0	0	0	0	-1
Staios	1	0	0	0	0	-1
Stewart	1	0	0	0	0	–
Timander	1	0	0	0	2	–
Tocchet	1	0	0	0	8	–
Wilson	1	0	0	0	6	–
Beers	2	0	0	0	0	–
DiMaio	2	0	0	0	0	-2
McLaren	2	0	0	0	0	-1
Odgers	2	0	0	0	0	-1
Sweeney	2	0	0	0	2	–
Totals	**2**	**2**	**3**	**5**	**22**	**–**

DETROIT RED WINGS

PLAYER	GP	G	A	P	PM	+/-
McCarty	2	0	4	4	4	4
Larionov	2	2	1	3	0	3
Konstantinov	2	0	2	2	2	2
Murphy	1	1	0	1	0	1
Lapointe	2	1	0	1	0	-1
Shanahan	2	1	0	1	0	4
Ward	2	1	0	1	4	1
Hodson	1	0	1	1	0	–
Kozlov	1	0	1	1	0	–
Lidstrom	2	0	1	1	0	–
Yzerman	2	0	1	1	0	1
Dandenault	1	0	0	0	0	-1
Eriksson	1	0	0	0	0	–
Errey	1	0	0	0	0	–
Holmstrom	1	0	0	0	2	–
Johnson	1	0	0	0	0	–
Kocur	1	0	0	0	0	–
Maltby	1	0	0	0	0	–
Osgood	1	0	0	0	2	–
Sandstrom	1	0	0	0	2	–
Brown	2	0	0	0	2	–
Draper	2	0	0	0	0	-1
Fedorov	2	0	0	0	0	–
Pushor	2	0	0	0	0	2
Rouse	2	0	0	0	0	–
Totals	**2**	**6**	**11**	**17**	**18**	**–**

GOALIE:	GP	MP	GA	ENG	SO	AVG
Ranford (0-1-0)	1	59	2	0	0	2.03
Carey (0-1-0)	1	60	4	0	0	4.00
Totals (0-2-0)	**2**	**119**	**6**	**0**	**0**	**3.03**

GOALIE:	GP	MP	GA	ENG	SO	AVG
Osgood (1-0-0)	1	60	1	0	0	1.00
Hodson (1-0-0)	1	60	1	0	0	1.00
Totals (2-0-0)	**2**	**120**	**2**	**0**	**0**	**1.00**

DETROIT VS. BUFFALO 1996-97 SEASON

TEAM	W	L	T	P	GF	GA	PPG	SHG	PM
Buffalo	0	2	0	0	2	8	0	0	23
DETROIT	2	0	0	4	8	2	1	1	36

at Buffalo (1-0-0)	**at DETROIT (1-0-0)**
Oct. 12, 1996 – DETROIT 6, Buffalo 1	March 28, 1997 – DETROIT 2, Buffalo 1
Totals – DETROIT 6, Buffalo 1	Totals – DETROIT 2, Buffalo 1

BUFFALO SABRES

PLAYER	GP	G	A	P	PM	+/-
Barnaby	1	1	0	1	4	1
Peca	2	1	0	1	4	-2
Dawe	2	0	1	1	0	-2
Galley	2	0	1	1	0	-3
Grosek	2	0	1	1	0	1
Plante	2	0	1	1	0	-2
Boughner	1	0	0	0	4	–
Brown	1	0	0	0	0	-2
Burridge	1	0	0	0	0	-2
LaFontaine	1	0	0	0	0	-2
May	1	0	0	0	0	-1
McKee	1	0	0	0	0	-2
Satan	1	0	0	0	2	–
Audette	2	0	0	0	2	-2
Holzinger	2	0	0	0	0	-1
Primeau	2	0	0	0	0	–
Ray	2	0	0	0	7	–
Shannon	2	0	0	0	0	-1
Smehlik	2	0	0	0	0	-1
Ward	2	0	0	0	0	-2
Wilson	2	0	0	0	0	-1
Zhitnik	2	0	0	0	0	-1
Totals		**2**	**2**	**4**	**6**	**23**	**–**

DETROIT RED WINGS

PLAYER	GP	G	A	P	PM	+/-
Yzerman	2	2	3	5	0	5
Larionov	2	1	2	3	0	3
Lidstrom	2	0	3	3	0	2
Lapointe	2	1	1	2	2	–
Taylor	2	1	1	2	0	–
Fedorov	2	0	2	2	0	2
Kozlov	1	1	0	1	0	3
Murphy	1	1	0	1	0	1
Dandenault	2	1	0	1	0	1
Johnson	1	0	1	1	0	1
Pushor	2	0	1	1	0	1
Shanahan	2	0	1	1	0	1
Brown	1	0	0	0	2	–
Draper	1	0	0	0	2	-1
Eriksson	1	0	0	0	0	1
Holmstrom	1	0	0	0	0	–
Knuble	1	0	0	0	0	–
Kocur	1	0	0	0	4	–
Maltby	1	0	0	0	15	–
Rouse	1	0	0	0	0	2
Sandstrom	1	0	0	0	0	–
Konstantinov	2	0	0	0	2	2
McCarty	2	0	0	0	9	–
Ward	2	0	0	0	0	–
Totals		**2**	**8**	**15**	**23**	**36**	**–**

GOALIE:	GP	MP	GA	ENG	SO	AVG
Hasek (0-1-0)	1	60	6	0	0	6.00
Shields (0-1-0)	1	63	2	0	0	1.90
Totals (0-1-0)	**2**	**123**	**8**	**0**	**0**	**3.90**

GOALIE:	GP	MP	GA	ENG	SO	AVG
Vernon (2-0-0)	2	123	2	0	0	.98
Totals (2-0-0)	**2**	**123**	**2**	**0**	**0**	**.98**

DETROIT VS. CALGARY 1996-97 SEASON

TEAM	W	L	T	P	GF	GA	PPG	SHG	PM
Calgary	1	2	1	3	7	11	3	0	83
DETROIT	2	1	1	5	11	7	5	0	74

at Calgary (1-0-1)
Dec. 18, 1996 – DETROIT 3, Calgary 3
April 8, 1997 – DETROIT 3, Calgary 2
Totals – DETROIT 6, Calgary 5

at DETROIT (1-1-0)
Oct. 11, 1996 – Calgary 2, DETROIT 1
Feb. 19, 1996 – DETROIT 4, Calgary 0
Totals – DETROIT 5, Calgary 2

CALGARY FLAMES

PLAYER	GP	G	A	P	PM	+/-
Reichel	3	2	0	2	0	–
Hoglund	4	1	1	2	0	1
Iginla	4	1	1	2	0	–
Millen	4	1	1	2	2	-2
O'Sullivan	1	0	2	2	0	1
Simpson	4	1	0	1	13	–
Stern	4	1	0	1	8	–
McInnis	1	0	1	1	0	1
Ward	2	0	1	1	0	–
Racine	3	0	1	1	0	–
Stillman	3	0	1	1	0	-1
Fleury	4	0	1	1	6	-2
Gagner	4	0	1	1	8	-1
Hulse	4	0	1	1	2	-1
Allison	1	0	0	0	2	–
Chiasson	1	0	0	0	0	–
Featherstone	1	0	0	0	2	–
Gavey	1	0	0	0	0	-1
Huscroft	1	0	0	0	5	–
Kruse	1	0	0	0	5	–
Patrick	1	0	0	0	0	–
Hlushko	2	0	0	0	2	–
Lakovic	2	0	0	0	4	1
McCarthy	2	0	0	0	12	–
Albelin	3	0	0	0	0	-2
Kidd	3	0	0	0	10	–
Sullivan	3	0	0	0	0	–
Bouchard	4	0	0	0	2	-2
Titov	4	0	0	0	0	-1
Totals	**4**	**7**	**12**	**19**	**83**	**–**

DETROIT RED WINGS

PLAYER	GP	G	A	P	PM	+/-
Yzerman	4	2	4	6	0	2
Kozlov	4	1	3	4	2	2
Sandstrom	2	3	0	3	0	3
Lidstrom	4	1	2	3	2	4
Larionov	4	0	3	3	0	2
Shanahan	3	1	1	2	2	1
Murphy	1	0	2	2	0	-2
Fedorov	4	0	2	2	0	-2
Brown	1	1	0	1	2	1
Fetisov	2	1	0	1	2	–
McCarty	3	1	0	1	12	-1
Eriksson	1	0	1	1	0	1
Johnson	2	0	1	1	2	1
Rouse	4	0	1	1	2	2
Knuble	1	0	0	0	0	-1
Ward	1	0	0	0	0	-1
Errey	2	0	0	0	7	–
Holmstrom	2	0	0	0	0	-1
Kocur	2	0	0	0	2	-1
Dandenault	3	0	0	0	0	-1
Maltby	3	0	0	0	0	-1
Taylor	3	0	0	0	2	1
Draper	4	0	0	0	4	-1
Konstantinov	4	0	0	0	21	3
Lapointe	4	0	0	0	6	-2
Pushor	4	0	0	0	6	–
Totals	**4**	**11**	**20**	**31**	**74**	**–**

GOALIE:	GP	MP	GA	ENG	SO	AVG
Kidd (1-1-1)	3	185	8	0	0	2.59
Roloson (0-1-0)	1	65	3	0	0	2.77
Totals (1-2-1)	**4**	**250**	**11**	**0**	**0**	**2.64**

GOALIE:	GP	MP	GA	ENG	SO	AVG
Osgood (2-1-1)	4	249	7	0	1	1.69
Totals (2-1-1)	**4**	**249**	**7**	**0**	**1**	**1.69**

DETROIT VS. CHICAGO 1996-97 SEASON

TEAM	W	L	T	P	GF	GA	PPG	SHG	PM
Chicago	3	1	2	8	19	18	4	0	180
DETROIT	1	3	2	4	18	19	5	1	144

at Chicago (0-2-1)	at DETROIT (1-1-1)
Oct. 17, 1996 – Chicago 2, DETROIT 1	Oct. 25, 1996 – DETROIT 2, Chicago 2
Jan. 5, 1997 – DETROIT 5, Chicago 5	Dec. 12, 1996 – DETROIT 6, Chicago 2
March 23, 1997 – Chicago 5, DETROIT 3	Jan. 11, 1997 — Chicago 3, DETROIT 1
Totals – Chicago 12, DETROIT 9	Totals – DETROIT 9, Chicago 7

CHICAGO BLACKHAWKS

PLAYER	GP	G	A	P	PM	+/-
Craven	6	0	6	6	0	-2
Amonte	6	2	3	5	8	2
Chelios	6	2	3	5	20	4
Suter	6	2	3	5	8	2
Daze	5	3	0	3	2	–
Cummins	4	2	1	3	9	3
Krivokrasov	4	2	1	3	2	1
Zhamnov	5	2	1	3	0	–
Black	5	1	2	3	2	–
Savard	5	0	3	3	0	2
Weinrich	6	0	3	3	6	-1
Miller	4	1	1	2	12	-3
Probert	6	1	1	2	55	-1
Moreau	6	0	2	2	18	5
Shantz	6	0	2	2	4	2
Russell	4	1	0	1	5	-4
Creighton	1	0	1	1	0	-1
Dahlen	1	0	1	1	0	1
Sykora	1	0	1	1	0	-1
Dubinsky	1	0	0	0	0	–
McRae	1	0	0	0	0	–
Prokopec	1	0	0	0	2	–
Chyzowski	2	0	0	0	2	–
Gronman	2	0	0	0	2	1
Sutter	3	0	0	0	2	-1
Belfour	4	0	0	0	4	–
Ciccone	5	0	0	0	9	-1
Carney	6	0	0	0	8	3
Totals	**6**	**19**	**35**	**54**	**180**	**–**

DETROIT RED WINGS

PLAYER	GP	G	A	P	PM	+/-
Shanahan	6	4	3	7	9	1
Yzerman	6	3	4	7	4	1
Lidstrom	6	0	5	5	2	-3
Fedorov	5	2	2	4	2	2
Kozlov	5	2	2	4	4	3
Fetisov	6	2	2	4	8	4
Draper	6	2	1	3	4	1
Larionov	5	1	1	2	0	4
McCarty	4	0	2	2	9	-1
Konstantinov	6	0	2	2	12	4
Lapointe	5	1	0	1	32	-3
Rouse	5	1	0	1	2	-2
Sandstrom	1	0	1	1	0	–
Dandenault	5	0	1	1	2	-2
Johnson	5	0	1	1	4	-6
Pushor	5	0	1	1	12	-5
Murphy	1	0	0	0	0	1
Eriksson	2	0	0	0	0	–
Holmstrom	2	0	0	0	4	1-
Vernon	2	0	0	0	2	–
Errey	3	0	0	0	0	1
Kocur	3	0	0	0	12	-2
Ward	3	0	0	0	4	-1
Maltby	4	0	0	0	2	–
Taylor	4	0	0	0	14	-6
Brown	5	0	0	0	0	-2
Totals	**6**	**18**	**28**	**46**	**144**	**–**

GOALIE:	GP	MP	GA	ENG	SO	AVG
Belfour (2-1-1)	4	245	13	0	0	3.18
Waite (0-0-1)	1	65	2	0	0	1.85
Terreri (1-0-0)	1	60	3	0	0	3.00
Totals (3-1-2)	**6**	**370**	**18**	**0**	**0**	**2.92**

GOALIE:	GP	MP	GA	ENG	SO	AVG
Osgood (1-2-0)	3	179	7	0	0	2.35
Hodson (0-1-1)	2	118	4	0	0	2.03
Vernon (0-0-1)	2	72	8	0	0	6.67
Totals (1-3-2)	**6**	**369**	**19**	**0**	**0**	**3.09**

DETROIT VS. COLORADO 1996-97 SEASON

TEAM	W	L	T	P	GF	GA	PPG	SHG	PM
Colorado	3	1	0	6	17	12	8	2	143
DETROIT	1	3	0	2	12	17	4	0	190

<table>
<tr><td>at Colorado (0-2-0)</td><td>at DETROIT (1-1-0)</td></tr>
<tr><td>Dec. 17, 1996 – Colorado 4, DETROIT 3</td><td>Nov. 13, 1996 – Colorado 4, DETROIT 1</td></tr>
<tr><td>March 16, 1997 – Colorado 4, DETROIT 2</td><td>March 26, 1997 – DETROIT 6, Colorado 5</td></tr>
<tr><td>Totals – Colorado 8, DETROIT 5</td><td>Totals – Colorado 9, DETROIT 7</td></tr>
</table>

COLORADO AVALANCHE

PLAYER	GP	G	A	P	PM	+/-
Deadmarsh	4	5	3	8	23	3
Kamensky	4	3	3	6	0	–
Forsberg	3	2	4	6	13	4
Ozolinsh	4	2	3	5	8	–
Sakic	4	0	5	5	8	–
Jones	4	1	2	3	2	–
Young	4	1	2	3	4	-3
Lacroix	4	1	1	2	0	1
Yelle	3	0	2	2	0	1
Klemm	3	1	0	1	0	1
Corbet	4	1	0	1	9	–
Lemieux	2	0	1	1	12	–
Miller	3	0	1	1	0	3
Lefebvre	4	0	1	1	2	4
Marha	1	0	0	0	0	-1
Messier	1	0	0	0	0	–
Ricci	2	0	0	0	4	-2
Sarault	2	0	0	0	0	–
Severyn	2	0	0	0	20	–
Gusarov	3	0	0	0	0	-5
Krupp	3	0	0	0	7	1
Foote	4	0	0	0	19	-1
Keane	4	0	0	0	5	-1
Roy	4	0	0	0	7	–
Totals	**4**	**17**	**28**	**45**	**143**	**–**

DETROIT RED WINGS

PLAYER	GP	G	A	P	PM	+/-
Fedorov	4	3	2	5	0	–
Shanahan	4	2	3	5	11	-1
Larionov	3	1	3	4	2	1
Yzerman	4	1	3	4	2	-1
Lidstrom	4	1	2	3	0	-1
Lapointe	4	2	0	2	35	-1
McCarty	4	1	1	2	13	-1
Murphy	1	0	2	2	0	1
Kozlov	3	0	2	2	0	1
Pushor	4	0	2	2	14	–
Johnson	2	1	0	1	0	1
Brown	1	0	0	0	0	–
Eriksson	1	0	0	0	0	–
Knuble	1	0	0	0	0	–
Kocur	1	0	0	0	2	–
Taylor	1	0	0	0	0	-1
Errey	2	0	0	0	12	-1
Osgood	2	0	0	0	2	–
Rouse	2	0	0	0	4	-1
Sandstrom	2	0	0	0	2	1
Vernon	2	0	0	0	7	–
Dandenault	3	0	0	0	0	1
Fetisov	3	0	0	0	16	1
Holmstrom	3	0	0	0	7	-2
Ward	3	0	0	0	17	-2
Draper	4	0	0	0	18	-2
Konstantinov	4	0	0	0	9	–
Maltby	4	0	0	0	17	-1
Totals	**4**	**12**	**20**	**32**	**190**	**–**

GOALIE:	GP	MP	GA	ENG	SO	AVG
Roy (3-1-0)	4	239	12	0	0	3.01
Billington (0-0-0)	1	1	0	0	0	.00
Totals (3-1-0)	**4**	**240**	**12**	**0**	**0**	**3.00**

GOALIE:	GP	MP	GA	ENG	SO	AVG
Osgood (0-2-0)	2	118	7	1	0	3.56
Vernon (1-1-0)	2	119	9	0	0	4.54
Hodson (0-0-0)	10	0	0	0		.00
Totals (1-3-0)	**4**	**237**	**16**	**1**	**0**	**4.05**

DETROIT VS. DALLAS 1996-97 SEASON

TEAM	W	L	T	P	GF	GA	PPG	SHG	PM
Dallas	4	2	0	8	19	16	4	0	106
Detroit	2	4	0	4	16	19	8	0	82

at Dallas (0-3-0)
Oct. 15, 1996 – Dallas 3, DETROIT 1
Jan. 8, 1997 – Dallas 6, DETROIT 3
Feb. 14, 1997 – Dallas 4, DETROIT 3
Totals – Dallas 13, DETROIT 7

at Detroit (2-1-0)
Oct. 23, 1996 – DETROIT 4, Dallas 1
Jan. 3, 1997 – Dallas 2, DETROIT 1
Feb. 2, 1997 – DETROIT 4, Dallas 3
Totals – DETROIT 9, Dallas 6

DALLAS STARS

PLAYER	GP	G	A	P	PM	+/-
Nieuwendyk	4	5	1	6	0	4
Sydor	6	0	6	6	2	7
Reid	6	3	2	5	2	5
Zubov	6	2	2	4	0	3
Harvey	5	1	3	4	4	5
Langenbrunner	5	1	3	4	6	3
Modano	6	1	3	4	20	2
Lehtinen	4	1	2	3	0	-1
Kennedy	3	1	1	2	0	1
Bassen	4	1	1	2	0	1
Carbonneau	6	1	1	2	4	4
Verbeek	5	0	2	2	18	-1
Gilchrist	5	1	0	1	2	-4
Hogue	6	1	0	1	8	–
Adams	2	0	1	1	0	1
Broten	2	0	1	1	0	1
Ledyard	3	0	1	1	0	4
Hatcher	4	0	1	1	2	–
Labelle	1	0	0	0	7	–
Huard	3	0	0	0	7	–
Lalor	5	0	0	0	4	2
Marshall	5	0	0	0	8	–
Ludwig	6	0	0	0	8	-1
Matvichuk	6	0	0	0	4	–
Totals	**6**	**19**	**31**	**50**	**106**	**–**

DETROIT RED WINGS

PLAYER	GP	G	A	P	PM	+/-
Shanahan	6	5	1	6	2	-2
Yzerman	6	1	4	5	0	-3
Larionov	5	2	2	4	4	-1
Kozlov	6	2	2	4	6	–
Brown	4	1	2	3	0	-2
McCarty	4	1	2	3	0	-2
Fedorov	5	1	2	3	6	–
Lidstrom	6	0	3	3	2	-4
Johnson	3	1	1	2	0	1
Lapointe	6	1	1	2	6	-6
Sandstrom	2	0	2	2	4	–
Fetisov	5	0	2	2	2	2
Konstantinov	6	0	2	2	6	-2
Draper	6	1	0	1	4	-2
Dandenault	4	0	1	1	0	-4
Errey	3	0	0	0	2	-1
Holmstrom	3	0	0	0	0	–
Kocur	3	0	0	0	7	-1
Taylor	3	0	0	0	0	-1
Vernon	3	0	0	0	10	–
Eriksson	4	0	0	0	2	–
Maltby	4	0	0	0	4	–
Rouse	4	0	0	0	4	–
Ward	4	0	0	0	2	-3
Pushor	6	0	0	0	9	-4
Totals	**6**	**16**	**27**	**43**	**82**	**–**

GOALIE:	GP	MP	GA	ENG	SO	AVG
Irbe (2-1-0)	3	182	8	0	0	2.64
Turek (2-0-0)	2	114	4	0	0	2.11
Moog (0-1-0)	2	67	4	0	0	3.58
Totals (4-2-0)	**6**	**363**	**16**	**0**	**0**	**2.65**

GOALIE:	GP	MP	GA	ENG	SO	AVG
Vernon (0-3-0)	3	180	9	0	0	3.00
Osgood (2-1-0)	3	181	10	0	0	3.31
Totals (2-4-0)	**6**	**361**	**19**	**0**	**0**	**3.16**

DETROIT VS. EDMONTON 1996-97 SEASON

TEAM	W	L	T	P	GF	GA	PPG	SHG	PM
Edmonton	0	2	2	2	5	11	0	0	64
DETROIT	2	0	2	6	11	5	2	1	74

at Edmonton (1-0-1)
Dec. 22, 1996 – DETROIT 6, Edmonton 2
April 9, 1997 – DETROIT 3, Edmonton 3
Totals – DETROIT 9, Edmonton 5

at DETROIT (1-0-1)
Oct. 9, 1996 – DETROIT 2, Edmonton 0
Dec. 10, 1996 – DETROIT 0, Edmonton 0
Totals – DETROIT 2, Edmonton 0

EDMONTON OILERS

PLAYER	GP	G	A	P	PM	+/-
Mironov	3	1	1	2	10	-2
Kovalenko	4	1	1	2	2	-1
Arnott	4	0	2	2	0	-3
Norton	3	1	0	1	0	-1
Smyth	4	1	0	1	8	-2
Weight	4	1	0	1	4	-1
Buchberger	4	0	1	1	15	–
Marchant	4	0	1	1	4	1
Marchment	4	0	1	1	0	1
Belanger	1	0	0	0	0	–
Dufresne	1	0	0	0	0	–
Intranuovo	1	0	0	0	0	–
Kelly	1	0	0	0	0	–
De Vries	2	0	0	0	5	-1
McAmmond	2	0	0	0	2	-1
McGillis	2	0	0	0	0	–
Oliver	2	0	0	0	0	-2
Petit	2	0	0	0	2	-1
Satan	2	0	0	0	2	–
Lindgren	3	0	0	0	0	-1
Lowe	3	0	0	0	0	–
Czerkawski	4	0	0	0	0	-1
Grier	4	0	0	0	8	-2
Murray	4	0	0	0	2	-2
Richardson	4	0	0	0	0	-2
Totals	**4**	**5**	**7**	**12**	**64**	**–**

DETROIT RED WINGS

PLAYER	GP	G	A	P	PM	+/-
Konstantinov	3	1	3	4	2	3
Larionov	3	0	4	4	0	3
Kozlov	4	2	1	3	4	3
Sandstrom	1	1	1	2	0	1
Fedorov	4	1	1	2	2	3
Shanahan	4	1	1	2	7	–
Lidstrom	4	0	2	2	2	3
Errey	3	1	0	1	6	1
Lapointe	3	1	0	1	0	-2
Pushor	3	1	0	1	13	2
Rouse	4	1	0	1	8	1
Yzerman	4	1	0	1	0	1
Johnson	3	0	1	1	0	–
Taylor	3	0	1	1	2	–
Eriksson	1	0	0	0	0	–
Holmstrom	1	0	0	0	0	–
Knuble	1	0	0	0	0	–
Murphy	1	0	0	0	0	–
Vernon	1	0	0	0	12	–
Brown	2	0	0	0	0	–
Draper	3	0	0	0	4	2
Fetisov	3	0	0	0	2	-1
McCarty	3	0	0	0	0	-1
Ward	3	0	0	0	4	–
Dandenault	4	0	0	0	4	-1
Maltby	4	0	0	0	2	1
Totals	**4**	**11**	**15**	**26**	**74**	**–**

GOALIE:	GP	MP	GA	ENG	SO	AVG
Essensa (0-1-0)	2	71	1	1	0	.85
Joseph (0-1-2)	3	178	9	0	1	3.03
Totals (0-2-2)	**4**	**249**	**10**	**1**	**1**	**2.41**

GOALIE:	GP	MP	GA	ENG	SO	AVG
Osgood (2-0-1)	3	185	2	0	2	.65
Vernon (0-0-1)	1	65	3	0	0	2.77
Totals (2-0-2)	**4**	**250**	**5**	**0**	**0**	**1.20**

DETROIT VS. FLORIDA

1996-97 SEASON

TEAM	W	L	T	P	GF	GA	PPG	SHG	PM
Florida	1	1	0	2	6	6	2	0	25
DETROIT	1	1	0	2	6	6	3	0	39

at Florida (1-0-0)
Feb. 16, 1997 – DETROIT 4, Florida 2
Totals – DETROIT 4, Florida 2

at DETROIT (0-1-0)
Dec.1, 1996 – Florida 4, DETROIT 2
Totals – Florida 4, DETROIT 2

FLORIDA PANTHERS

PLAYER	GP	G	A	P	PM	+/-
Svehla	2	3	0	3	2	–
Fitzgerald	2	1	1	2	0	–
Gustafsson	1	0	2	2	0	–
Carkner	2	0	2	2	6	-1
Skrudland	1	1	0	1	2	2
Dvorak	2	1	0	1	0	-1
Niedermayer	1	0	1	1	0	–
Mellanby	2	0	1	1	2	–
Straka	2	0	1	1	0	1
Ferguson	1	0	0	0	0	–
Garpenlov	1	0	0	0	2	-1
Hough	1	0	0	0	0	2
Jovanovski	1	0	0	0	5	1
Lowry	1	0	0	0	2	1
Nemirovsky	1	0	0	0	0	–
Sheppard	1	0	0	0	0	1
Hull	2	0	0	0	2	–
Laus	2	0	0	0	0	–
Lindsay	2	0	0	0	0	-2
Murphy	2	0	0	0	0	1
Podollan	2	0	0	0	0	–
Warrener	2	0	0	0	0	1
Wells	2	0	0	0	2	–
Totals	**2**	**6**	**8**	**14**	**25**	**–**

DETROIT RED WINGS

PLAYER	GP	G	A	P	PM	+/-
Larionov	2	0	4	4	2	2
Yzerman	2	1	2	3	0	-2
Lidstrom	2	1	1	2	0	-2
McCarty	2	1	1	2	4	-1
Fedorov	2	1	0	1	4	–
Kozlov	2	1	0	1	0	2
Shanahan	2	1	0	1	2	-2
Sandstrom	1	0	1	1	0	–
Taylor	1	0	1	1	0	-1
Holmstrom	2	0	1	1	2	–
Konstantinov	2	0	1	1	0	–
Dandenault	1	0	0	0	0	-3
Johnson	1	0	0	0	0	-1
Kocur	1	0	0	0	2	–
Ward	1	0	0	0	4	–
Draper	2	0	0	0	0	–
Fetisov	2	0	0	0	12	2
Lapointe	2	0	0	0	5	–
Maltby	2	0	0	0	0	–
Pushor	2	0	0	0	2	–
Rouse	2	0	0	0	0	–
Totals	**2**	**6**	**12**	**18**	**39**	**–**

GOALIE:	GP	MP	GA	ENG	SO	AVG
Fitzpatrick (1-0-0)	1	60	2	0	0	2.00
Vanbiesbrouck (0-1-0)	1	60	4	0	0	4.00
Totals (1-1-0)	**2**	**120**	**6**	**0**	**0**	**3.00**

GOALIE:	GP	MP	GA	ENG	SO	AVG
Osgood (1-1-0)	2	120	5	1	0	2.50
Totals (1-1-0)	**2**	**120**	**5**	**1**	**0**	**2.50**

TEAM	W	L	T	P	GF	GA	PPG	SHG	PM
Hartford	0	2	0	0	2	9	0	0	26
DETROIT	2	0	0	2	9	2	1	0	12

at Hartford (1-0-0)
Nov. 8, 1996 – DETROIT 4, Hartford 1
Totals – DETROIT 4, Hartford 1

at DETROIT (1-0-0)
Nov. 4, 1996 – DETROIT 5, Hartford 1
Totals – DETROIT 5, Hartford 1

HARTFORD WHALERS

PLAYER	GP	G	A	P	PM	+/-
Cassels	2	1	1	2	0	-1
Sanderson	2	1	1	2	0	-1
Godynyuk	2	0	1	1	2	-3
Coffey	1	0	0	0	0	-1
Diduck	1	0	0	0	0	-1
Emerson	1	0	0	0	0	–
Malik	1	0	0	0	0	-1
O'Neill	1	0	0	0	2	–
Pratt	1	0	0	0	0	–
Burt	2	0	0	0	4	-4
Dineen	2	0	0	0	12	-1
Featherstone	2	0	0	0	2	-1
Grimson	2	0	0	0	2	–
Janssens	2	0	0	0	2	–
Kapanen	2	0	0	0	0	-2
Kron	2	0	0	0	0	-3
Nikolishin	2	0	0	0	0	-3
Primeau	2	0	0	0	0	-3
Ranheim	2	0	0	0	0	-2
Rice	2	0	0	0	0	-3
Wesley	2	0	0	0	0	-1
Totals	**2**	**2**	**3**	**5**	**26**	**–**

DETROIT RED WINGS

PLAYER	GP	G	A	P	PM	+/-
Brown	2	3	2	5	0	5
Fedorov	2	1	2	3	0	5
Fetisov	2	0	3	3	2	3
Kozlov	2	1	1	2	2	5
McCarty	2	1	1	2	0	1
Draper	2	1	0	1	0	1
Lapointe	2	1	0	1	0	-1
Ward	2	1	0	1	0	–
Eriksson	1	0	1	1	0	3
Osgood	1	0	1	1	0	–
Johnson	2	0	1	1	0	-1
Lidstrom	2	0	1	1	0	4
Maltby	2	0	1	1	2	1
Rouse	2	0	1	1	2	1
Yzerman	2	0	1	1	2	1
Konstantinov	1	0	0	0	2	2
Dandenault	2	0	0	0	0	-1
Errey	2	0	0	0	0	1
Pushor	2	0	0	0	0	-1
Shanahan	2	0	0	0	0	1
Totals	**2**	**9**	**16**	**25**	**12**	**–**

GOALIE:	GP	MP	GA	ENG	SO	AVG
Burke (0-1-0)	1	60	5	0	0	5.00
Muzzatti (0-1-0)	1	59	3	1	0	3.05
Totals (0-2-0)	**2**	**119**	**8**	**1**	**0**	**4.03**

GOALIE:	GP	MP	GA	ENG	SO	AVG
Osgood (1-0-0)	1	60	1	0	0	1.00
Vernon (1-0-0)	1	60	1	0	0	1.00
Totals (2-0-0)	**2**	**120**	**2**	**0**	**0**	**1.00**

DETROIT VS. LOS ANGELES 1996-97 SEASON

TEAM	W	L	T	P	GF	GA	PPG	SHG	PM
Los Angeles	0	2	2	2	6	15	0	0	100
DETROIT	2	0	2	6	15	6	3	0	58

at Los Angeles (1-0-1)
Nov. 23, 1996 – DETROIT 6, Los Angeles 0
March 10, 1997 – DETROIT 3, Los Angeles 3
Totals – DETROIT 9, Los Angeles 3

at DETROIT (1-0-1)
Oct. 21, 1996 – DETROIT 3, Los Angeles 0
Jan. 14, 1997 – DETROIT 3, Los Angeles 3
Totals – DETROIT 6, Los Angeles 3

LOS ANGELES KINGS

PLAYER	GP	G	A	P	PM	+/-
Stevens	4	1	3	4	10	–
Ferraro	4	2	0	2	6	-1
Boucher	3	0	2	2	2	1
O'Donnell	1	1	0	1	4	1
Khristich	4	1	0	1	0	-3
Olczyk	4	1	0	1	2	–
Tsyplakov	3	0	1	1	0	–
Laperriere	4	0	1	1	7	-2
Nurminen	4	0	1	1	0	–
Broten	1	0	0	0	0	-1
Klima	1	0	0	0	0	-2
Modry	1	0	0	0	0	–
Potomski	1	0	0	0	0	–
Vopat, R	1	0	0	0	5	–
Finn	2	0	0	0	2	-3
Grieve	2	0	0	0	0	-1
Johnson, M	2	0	0	0	12	–
Slaney	2	0	0	0	0	-4
Vopat, J	2	0	0	0	2	-1
Berg	3	0	0	0	0	1
Blake	3	0	0	0	8	-2
Johnson, C	3	0	0	0	2	-3
Perreault	3	0	0	0	0	1
Yachmenev	3	0	0	0	2	-3
Zmolek	3	0	0	0	22	-1
Bylsma	4	0	0	0	2	-2
Norstrom	4	0	0	0	12	-5
Totals	**4**	**6**	**8**	**14**	**100**	**–**

DETROIT RED WINGS

PLAYER	GP	G	A	P	PM	+/-
Shanahan	4	5	2	7	8	7
Yzerman	4	3	4	7	0	8
Johnson	3	1	3	4	2	3
Holmstrom	3	2	0	2	8	1
Sandstrom	1	1	1	2	0	1
McCarty	3	1	1	2	7	3
Kozlov	4	1	1	2	0	–
Eriksson	2	0	2	2	0	3
Konstantinov	4	0	2	2	4	2
Lapointe	4	0	2	2	4	–
Rouse	4	0	2	2	0	–
Draper	4	1	0	1	0	-2
Fetisov	2	0	1	1	0	-1
Ward	2	0	1	1	0	2
Fedorov	3	0	1	1	0	-1
Larionov	3	0	1	1	2	–
Dandenault	4	0	1	1	2	3
Lidstrom	4	0	1	1	0	4
Maltby	4	0	1	1	5	1
Brown	3	0	0	0	0	-2
Taylor	3	0	0	0	5	-1
Pushor	4	0	0	0	11	-1
Totals		**4**	**15**	**27**	**42**	**58**	**–**

GOALIE:	GP	MP	GA	ENG	SO	AVG
Fiset (0-2-1)	3	185	12	0	0	3.89
Dafoe (0-0-1)	1	65	3	0	0	2.77
Totals (0-2-2)	**4**	**250**	**15**	**0**	**0**	**3.60**

GOALIE:	GP	MP	GA	ENG	SO	AVG
Osgood (2-0-2)	4	250	6	0	2	1.44
Totals (2-0-2)	**4**	**250**	**6**	**0**	**2**	**1.44**

TEAM	W	L	T	P	GF	GA	PPG	SHG	PM
Montréal	1	1	0	2	7	6	1	0	41
DETROIT	1	1	0	2	6	7	0	1	38

at Montréal (0-1-0)	at DETROIT (1-0-0)
Jan. 20, 1997 – Montréal 4, DETROIT 1	Oct. 30, 1996 – DETROIT 5, Montréal 3
Totals – Montréal 4, DETROIT 1	Totals – DETROIT 5, Montréal 3

MONTRÉAL CANADIENS

PLAYER	GP	G	A	P	PM	+/-
Recchi	2	2	1	3	2	1
Savage	2	1	2	3	0	–
Damphousse	2	0	3	3	0	-1
Stevenson	1	0	2	2	17	1
Malakhov	1	1	0	1	0	–
Tucker	1	1	0	1	0	1
Quintal	2	1	0	1	0	–
Thornton	2	1	0	1	2	–
Koivu	1	0	1	1	2	–
Baron	2	0	1	1	4	-1
Popovic	2	0	1	1	2	2
Bordeleau	1	0	0	0	0	–
Brashear	1	0	0	0	0	–
Brisebois	1	0	0	0	0	–
Brown	1	0	0	0	6	-1
Bure	1	0	0	0	0	–
Bureau	1	0	0	0	2	–
Cullimore	1	0	0	0	0	1
Rivet	1	0	0	0	0	–
Rucinsky	1	0	0	0	0	-2
Wilkie	1	0	0	0	0	–
Brunet	2	0	0	0	0	-2
Corson	2	0	0	0	2	–
Murray	2	0	0	0	0	–
Richer	2	0	0	0	2	–
Totals	**2**	**7**	**11**	**18**	**41**	**–**

DETROIT RED WINGS

PLAYER	GP	G	A	P	PM	+/-
McCarty	1	1	1	2	0	1
Draper	2	1	1	2	0	–
Fedorov	2	1	1	2	4	2
Kozlov	2	1	1	2	0	–
Yzerman	2	1	1	2	0	-1
Lapointe	2	1	0	1	2	-3
Lidstrom	1	0	1	1	0	–
Dandenault	2	0	1	1	0	1
Errey	2	0	1	1	0	2
Fetisov	2	0	1	1	0	1
Konstantinov	2	0	1	1	2	1
Rouse	2	0	1	1	0	–
Brown	1	0	0	0	0	–
Taylor	1	0	0	0	0	–
Vernon	1	0	0	0	2	–
Eriksson	2	0	0	0	2	–
Holmstrom	2	0	0	0	2	-2
Johnson	2	0	0	0	0	-2
Larionov	2	0	0	0	0	-1
Pushor	2	0	0	0	4	–
Shanahan	2	0	0	0	20	–
Totals	**2**	**6**	**11**	**17**	**38**	**–**

GOALIE:	GP	MP	GA	ENG	SO	AVG
Jablonski (0-1-0)	1	60	5	0	0	5.00
Thibault (1-0-0)	1	60	1	0	0	1.00
Totals (1-1-0)	**2**	**120**	**6**	**0**	**0**	**3.00**

GOALIE:	GP	MP	GA	ENG	SO	AVG
Osgood (1-0-0)	1	60	3	0	0	3.00
Vernon (0-1-0)	1	59	3	1	0	3.0
Totals (1-1-0)	**2**	**119**	**6**	**1**	**0**	**3.03**

TEAM	W	L	T	P	GF	GA	PPG	SHG	PM
New Jersey	2	0	0	4	5	1	0	1	45
DETROIT	0	2	0	0	1	5	0	0	47

at New Jersey (0-1-0)
Oct. 5, 1996 – New Jersey 3, DETROIT 1
Totals – New Jersey 3, DETROIT 1

at DETROIT (0-1-0)
Nov. 6, 1996 – New Jersey 2, DETROIT 0
Totals – New Jersey 2, DETROIT 0

NEW JERSEY DEVILS

PLAYER	GP	G	A	P	PM	+/-
Zelepukin	2	0	2	2	0	3
Guerin	2	1	0	1	0	1
Holik	2	1	0	1	4	2
MacLean	2	1	0	1	4	–
Rolston	2	1	0	1	4	–
Thomas	2	1	0	1	0	1
Broten	1	0	1	1	0	1
Daneyko	2	0	1	1	2	2
Niedermayer	2	0	1	1	0	3
Brylin	1	0	0	0	2	–
Pederson	1	0	0	0	0	–
Sullivan	1	0	0	0	2	–
Andreychuk	2	0	0	0	2	1
Carpenter	2	0	0	0	0	–
Chambers	2	0	0	0	2	–
McKay	2	0	0	0	5	–
Odelein	2	0	0	0	2	1
Peluso	2	0	0	0	0	–
Smith	2	0	0	0	5	1
Stevens	2	0	0	0	11	2
Totals		**2**	**5**	**5**	**10**	**45**	**–**

GOALIE:	GP	MP	GA	ENG	SO	AVG
Brodeur (2-0-0)	2	120	1	0	1	.50
Totals (2-0-0)	**2**	**120**	**1**	**0**	**1**	**.50**

DETROIT RED WINGS

PLAYER	GP	G	A	P	PM	+/-
Fedorov	2	1	0	1	0	-1
Lapointe	2	0	1	1	11	–
Yzerman	2	0	1	1	0	-1
Brown	1	0	0	0	0	-1
Eriksson	1	0	0	0	0	-1
Fetisov	1	0	0	0	4	-1
Grimson	1	0	0	0	0	-1
Holmstrom	1	0	0	0	2	-1
Konstantinov	1	0	0	0	2	-1
Larionov	1	0	0	0	2	–
Shanahan	1	0	0	0	0	-1
Dandenault	2	0	0	0	2	-1
Draper	2	0	0	0	2	-2
Errey	2	0	0	0	0	–
Johnson	2	0	0	0	0	-1
Kozlov	2	0	0	0	0	-2
Lidstrom	2	0	0	0	0	-1
Maltby	2	0	0	0	0	-1
McCarty	2	0	0	0	4	–
Pushor	2	0	0	0	7	-1
Rouse	2	0	0	0	2	-1
Ward	2	0	0	0	9	–
Totals	**2**	**1**	**2**	**3**	**47**	**–**

GOALIE:	GP	MP	GA	ENG	SO	AVG
Osgood (0-2-0)	2	118	5	0	0	2.54
Totals (2-0-0)	**2**	**120**	**5**	**0**	**0**	**2.54**

DETROIT VS. NEW YORK ISLANDERS 1996-97 SEASON

TEAM	W	L	T	P	GF	GA	PPG	SHG	PM
New York	0	2	0	0	3	11	0	0	30
DETROIT	2	0	0	4	11	3	0	0	32

at New York (1-0-0)
Dec. 28, 1996 – DETROIT 7, New York 1
Totals – DETROIT 7, New York 1

at DETROIT (1-0-0)
Oct. 19, 1996 – DETROIT 4, New York 2
Totals – DETROIT 4, New York 2

NEW YORK ISLANDERS

PLAYER	GP	G	A	P	PM	+/-
Andersson	2	0	2	2	2	-2
Green	2	1	0	1	0	1
McInnis	2	1	0	1	0	-2
Palffy	2	1	0	1	0	-1
Kasparaitis	1	0	1	1	0	-2
Lachance	2	0	1	1	0	-3
McCabe	2	0	1	1	5	–
Archibald	1	0	0	0	0	-2
Donnelly	1	0	0	0	2	–
Foster	1	0	0	0	0	–
Houda	1	0	0	0	2	-1
Hughes	1	0	0	0	0	-3
Johansson	1	0	0	0	0	-1
Kruse	1	0	0	0	0	-1
Lapointe	1	0	0	0	2	-3
Pilon	1	0	0	0	0	-4
Smolinski	1	0	0	0	0	-4
Vukota	1	0	0	0	0	–
Armstrong	2	0	0	0	2	-1
Berard	2	0	0	0	2	-1
Jonsson	2	0	0	0	2	-4
King	2	0	0	0	2	-3
Plante	2	0	0	0	5	-1
Wood	2	0	0	0	4	-4
Totals	**2**	**3**	**5**	**8**	**30**	**–**

DETRO!T RED WINGS

PLAYER	GP	G	A	P	PM	+/-
Kozlov	2	3	1	4	4	5
Fedorov	2	1	3	4	2	6
Fetisov	2	1	3	4	0	5
Yzerman	2	1	2	3	0	3
Konstantinov	2	0	3	3	7	5
Johnson	2	2	0	2	2	2
Lidstrom	2	1	1	2	0	1
McCarty	2	1	1	2	2	5
Brown	2	1	0	1	0	1
Draper	2	0	1	1	0	1
Lapointe	2	0	1	1	2	–
Pushor	2	0	1	1	0	2
Rouse	2	0	1	1	0	2
Shanahan	2	0	1	1	5	–
Holmstrom	1	0	0	0	2	–
Larionov	1	0	0	0	4	3
Maltby	1	0	0	0	2	–
Taylor	1	0	0	0	0	-1
Dandenault	2	0	0	0	0	1
Errey	2	0	0	0	0	1
Totals		**2**	**11**	**19**	**30**	**32**	**–**

GOALIE:	GP	MP	GA	ENG	SO	AVG
Salo (0-2-0)	2	119	10	1	0	5.04
Totals (0-2-0)	**2**	**119**	**10**	**1**	**0**	**5.04**

GOALIE:	GP	MP	GA	ENG	SO	AVG
Vernon (2-0-0)	2	120	3	0	0	1.50
Totals (2-0-0)	**2**	**120**	**3**	**0**	**0**	**1.50**

DETROIT VS. NEW YORK RANGERS 1996-97 SEASON

TEAM	W	L	T	P	GF	GA	PPG	SHG	PM
New York	1	1	0	2	3	4	0	1	34
DETROIT	1	1	0	2	4	3	1	0	18

at New York (0-1-0)
March 21, 1997 – New York 3, DETROIT 1
Totals – New York 3, DETROIT 1

at DETROIT (1-0-0)
March 1, 1997 – DETROIT 3, New York 0
Totals – DETROIT 3, New York 0

NEW YORK RANGERS

PLAYER	GP	G	A	P	PM	+/-
Courtnall	1	1	0	1	0	2
Messier	1	1	0	1	0	1
Gretzky	2	1	0	1	10	–
Tikkanen	1	0	1	1	0	1
Eastwood	2	0	1	1	0	–
Graves	2	0	1	1	4	-1
Leetch	2	0	1	1	0	–
Noonan	1	0	0	0	0	-1
Oliver	1	0	0	0	0	-1
Robitaille	1	0	0	0	2	-1
Berg	2	0	0	0	0	-1
Beukeboom	2	0	0	0	6	2
Churla	2	0	0	0	2	–
Driver	2	0	0	0	0	–
Ferraro	2	0	0	0	0	–
Flatley	2	0	0	0	0	-1
Karpovtsev	2	0	0	0	2	-2
Langdon	2	0	0	0	2	-1
Lidster	2	0	0	0	2	–
Samuelsson	2	0	0	0	4	–
Sundstrom	2	0	0	0	0	1
Totals	**2**	**3**	**4**	**7**	**34**	**–**

DETROIT RED WINGS

PLAYER	GP	G	A	P	PM	+/-
McCarty	2	1	2	2	0	1
Shanahan	2	1	1	2	2	–
Lidstrom	2	1	0	1	0	–
Sandstrom	2	1	0	1	2	–
Larionov	1	0	1	1	0	2
Fetisov	2	0	1	1	0	–
Konstantinov	2	0	1	1	4	2
Kozlov	2	0	1	1	4	-1
Yzerman	2	0	1	1	0	-1
Dandenault	1	0	0	0	0	-1
Holmstrom	1	0	0	0	2	–
Kocur	1	0	0	0	2	-1
Murphy	1	0	0	0	0	-1
Pushor	1	0	0	0	0	–
Taylor	1	0	0	0	0	–
Ward	1	0	0	0	0	–
Brown	2	0	0	0	0	–
Draper	2	0	0	0	0	–
Fedorov	2	0	0	0	0	–
Lapointe	2	0	0	0	0	–
Maltby	2	0	0	0	0	–
Rouse	2	0	0	0	2	–
Totals	**2**	**4**	**8**	**12**	**18**	**–**

GOALIE:	GP	MP	GA	ENG	SO	AVG.
Richter (0-1-0)	1	59	2	1	0	2.03
Healy (1-0-0)	1	60	1	0	0	1.00
Totals (1-1-0)	**2**	**119**	**3**	**0**	**0**	**1.51**

GOALIE:	GP	MP	GA	ENG	SO	AVG.
Osgood (1-1-0)	2	120	3	0	1	1.50
Totals (1-1-0)	**2**	**120**	**3**	**0**	**1**	**1.50**

DETROIT VS. OTTAWA 1996-97 SEASON

TEAM	W	L	T	P	GF	GA	PPG	SHG	PM
Ottawa	1	0	1	3	5	4	0	0	10
DETROIT	0	1	1	1	4	5	0	0	8

at Ottawa (0-0-1)
Nov.1, 1996 – DETROIT 2, Ottawa 2
Totals – DETROIT 2, Ottawa 2

at DETROIT (0-1-0)
April 11, 1997 – Ottawa 3, DETROIT 2
Totals – Ottawa 3, DETROIT 2

OTTAWA SENATORS

PLAYER	GP	G	A	P	PM	+/-
Bonk	2	1	1	2	2	1
Daigle	2	1	0	1	0	–
Lambert	2	1	0	1	0	1
Redden	2	1	0	1	0	–
Yashin	2	1	0	1	0	-1
Bicanek	1	0	1	1	0	1
Zholtok	1	0	1	1	0	1
Alfredsson	2	0	1	1	0	–
Duchesne	2	0	1	1	0	1
McEachern	2	0	1	1	0	–
York	2	0	1	1	4	2
Chasse	1	0	0	0	0	–
Chorske	1	0	0	0	0	1
Hannan	1	0	0	0	0	–
Musil	1	0	0	0	0	–
Cunneyworth	2	0	0	0	0	-1
Dackell	2	0	0	0	0	1
Gardiner	2	0	0	0	0	–
Laukkanen	2	0	0	0	4	–
Pitlick	2	0	0	0	0	-2
Van Allen	2	0	0	0	0	–
Totals	**2**	**5**	**7**	**12**	**10**	**–**

DETROIT RED WINGS

PLAYER	GP	G	A	P	PM	+/-
Lapointe	2	2	0	2	2	2
Dandenault	2	1	0	1	2	–
Fedorov	2	1	0	1	0	-1
Errey	1	0	1	1	0	1
McCarty	1	0	1	1	0	–
Yzerman	1	0	1	1	0	1
Brown	2	0	1	1	0	-2
Konstantinov	2	0	1	1	0	-2
Maltby	2	0	1	1	0	–
Eriksson	1	0	0	0	2	1
Holmstrom	1	0	0	0	0	–
Johnson	1	0	0	0	0	-1
Knuble	1	0	0	0	0	–
Major	1	0	0	0	0	–
Murphy	1	0	0	0	0	1
Pushor	1	0	0	0	0	–
Sandstrom	1	0	0	0	0	–
Shanahan	1	0	0	0	0	-1
Draper	2	0	0	0	0	–
Fetisov	2	0	0	0	0	-2
Kozlov	2	0	0	0	2	-1
Lidstrom	2	0	0	0	0	1
Rouse	2	0	0	0	0	-1
Ward	2	0	0	0	0	-1
Totals	**2**	**4**	**6**	**10**	**8**	**–**

GOALIE:	GP	MP	GA	ENG	SO	AVG
Rhodes (0-0-1)	1	65	2	0	0	1.85
Tugnutt (1-0-0)	1	60	2	0	0	2.00
Totals (1-0-1)	**2**	**125**	**4**	**0**	**0**	**1.92**

GOALIE:	GP	MP	GA	ENG	SO	AVG
Osgood (0-0-1)	1	65	2	0	0	1.85
Vernon (0-1-0)	1	59	3	0	0	3.05
Totals (0-1-1)	**2**	**124**	**5**	**0**	**0**	**2.42**

DETROIT VS. PHILADELPHIA 1996-97 SEASON

TEAM	W	L	T	P	GF	GA	PPG	SHG	PM
Philadelphia	0	1	1	1	3	6	1	0	45
DETROIT	1	0	1	3	6	3	2	0	61

at Philadelphia (1-0-0)	**at DETROIT (0-0-1)**
Jan. 25, 1997 – DETROIT 4, Philadelphia 1	Jan. 22, 1997 – DETROIT 2, Philadelphia 2
Totals – DETROIT 4, Philadelphia 1	Totals – DETROIT 2, Philadelphia 2

PHILADELPHIA FLYERS

PLAYER	GP	G	A	P	PM	+/-
Brind'Amour	2	1	0	1	4	–
Klatt	2	1	0	1	0	–
LeClair	2	1	0	1	4	-2
Desjardins	2	0	1	1	0	-1
Hawerchuk	2	0	1	1	0	2
Lindros	2	0	1	1	12	-2
Niinimaa	2	0	1	1	4	-2
Druce	1	0	0	0	0	–
Dykhuis	1	0	0	0	0	–
Kordic	1	0	0	0	0	–
Petit	1	0	0	0	2	–
Snow	1	0	0	0	2	–
Coffey	2	0	0	0	2	-1
Daniels	2	0	0	0	4	-1
Lacroix	2	0	0	0	2	–
Otto	2	0	0	0	0	–
Podein	2	0	0	0	0	–
Renberg	2	0	0	0	0	-2
Svoboda	2	0	0	0	5	-1
Therien	2	0	0	0	2	–
Zubrus	2	0	0	0	2	–
Totals	**2**	**3**	**4**	**7**	**45**	**–**

DETROIT RED WINGS

PLAYER	GP	G	A	P	PM	+/-
Yzerman	2	1	3	4	0	2
Shanahan	2	1	2	3	14	2
Holmstrom	2	1	1	2	0	-1
Lapointe	2	0	2	2	20	2
Draper	2	1	0	1	5	1
Konstantinov	2	1	0	1	4	1
Lidstrom	2	1	0	1	0	2
Larionov	2	0	1	1	0	-1
Johnson	1	0	0	0	0	–
McCarty	1	0	0	0	0	–
Brown	2	0	0	0	0	-1
Dandenault	2	0	0	0	0	-1
Errey	2	0	0	0	0	–
Fetisov	2	0	0	0	8	-1
Kocur	2	0	0	0	2	–
Maltby	2	0	0	0	4	1
Pushor	2	0	0	0	2	1
Rouse	2	0	0	0	2	2
Taylor	2	0	0	0	0	1
Totals	**2**	**6**	**9**	**15**	**61**	**–**

GOALIE:	GP	MP	GA	ENG	SO	AVG
Hestall (0-1-1)	2	93	6	0	0	3.87
Snow (0-0-0)	1	32	0	0	0	.00
Totals (1-1-0)	**2**	**120**	**5**	**1**	**0**	**2.50**

GOALIE:	GP	MP	GA	ENG	SO	AVG
Vernon (1-0-1)	2	125	3	0	O	1.44
Totals (1-0-1)	**2**	**125**	**3**	**0**	**0**	**1.44**

TEAM	W	L	T	P	GF	GA	PPG	SHG	PM
Phoenix	2	2	1	5	17	15	4	0	144
DETROIT	2	2	1	5	15	17	3	1	137

at Phoenix (2-0-1)
Nov. 18, 1996 – DETROIT 2, Phoenix 2
Jan. 9, 1997 – DETROIT 5, Phoenix 4
Feb. 24, 1997 – DETROIT 5, Phoenix 3
Totals – DETROIT 12, Phoenix 9

at DETROIT (0-2-0)
Dec. 30, 1996 – Phoenix 5, DETROIT 3
Jan. 29, 1997 – Phoenix 3, DETROIT 0

Totals – Phoenix 8, DETROIT 3

PHOENIX COYOTES

PLAYER	GP	G	A	P	PM	+/-
Tkachuk	5	3	6	9	21	1
Roenick	5	5	3	8	43	1
Tverdovsky	5	0	5	5	0	1
Corkum	5	1	2	3	6	3
Gartner	5	1	2	3	2	-2
Ronning	5	1	2	3	2	–
Drake	4	2	0	2	2	-2
Doan	2	1	1	2	0	2
Korolev	4	0	2	2	16	–
Janney	5	0	2	2	0	1
Kilger	1	1	0	1	0	1
MacIver	3	1	0	1	6	–
Shannon	5	1	0	1	6	–
Quint	2	0	1	1	0	-2
Finley	5	0	1	1	0	1
Khabibulin	5	0	1	1	4	–
Eakins	1	0	0	0	0	–
Eastwood	1	0	0	0	0	–
Hansen	1	0	0	0	0	–
Hudson	1	0	0	0	0	–
McCrimmon	1	0	0	0	0	–
More	1	0	0	0	0	–
McKenzie	2	0	0	0	2	-1
Johnson	3	0	0	0	2	1
Manson	4	0	0	0	4	1
Stapleton	4	0	0	0	14	-1
King	5	0	0	0	14	–
Numminen	5	0	0	0	0	–
Totals	**5**	**17**	**28**	**45**	**144**	**–**

DETROIT RED WINGS

PLAYER	GP	G	A	P	PM	+/-
Shanahan	5	6	5	11	8	5
Larionov	4	1	5	6	4	1
Yzerman	5	0	5	5	6	-2
McCarty	4	3	1	4	2	2
Lidstrom	5	1	2	3	0	1
Fedorov	4	0	3	3	2	–
Kozlov	4	2	0	2	8	-2
Lapointe	5	0	2	2	19	-1
Johnson	3	1	0	1	0	–
Pushor	5	1	0	1	12	-1
Eriksson	1	0	1	1	0	1
Sandstrom	2	0	1	1	0	-1
Ward	3	0	1	1	0	1
Osgood	4	0	1	1	0	–
Maltby	2	0	0	0	4	–
Taylor	2	0	0	0	0	–
Holmstrom	3	0	0	0	0	-2
Kocur	3	0	0	0	19	-2
Rouse	3	0	0	0	20	-2
Brown	4	0	0	0	0	-1
Dandenault	4	0	0	0	0	–
Errey	4	0	0	0	0	-2
Draper	5	0	0	0	18	-1
Fetisov	5	0	0	0	2	-1
Konstantinov	5	0	0	0	13	–
Totals	**6**	**15**	**27**	**42**	**137**	**–**

GOALIE:	GP	MP	GA	ENG	SO	AVG
Khabibulin (2-2-1)	5	305	15	0	1	2.95
Totals (2-2-1)	**5**	**305**	**15**	**0**	**1**	**2.95**

GOALIE:	GP	MP	GA	ENG	SO	AVG
Osgood (2-1-1)	4	245	13	1	0	3.18
Vernon (0-1-0)	1	60	3	0	0	3.00
Totals (2-2-1)	**5**	**305**	**16**	**1**	**0**	**3.15**

DETROIT VS. PITTSBURGH 1996-97 SEASON

TEAM	W	L	T	P	GF	GA	PPG	SHG	PM
Pittsburgh	0	2	0	0	6	10	1	1	14
DETROIT	2	0	0	4	10	6	3	0	18

at Pittsburgh (1-0-0)
Feb. 8, 1997 – DETROIT 6, Pittsburgh 5
Totals – DETROIT 6, Pittsburgh 5

at DETROIT (1-0-0)
Feb. 27, 1997 – DETROIT 4, Pittsburgh 1
Totals – DETROIT 4, Pittsburgh 1

PITTSBURGH PENGUINS

PLAYER	GP	G	A	P	PM	+/-
Jagr	2	0	3	3	0	-1
Lemieux	2	2	0	2	0	-1
Johnson	2	1	1	2	0	–
Francis	2	0	2	2	2	1
Woolley	2	0	2	2	2	2
Roche	1	1	0	1	0	–
Barnes	2	1	0	1	0	-2
Nedved	2	1	0	1	0	1
Muni	1	0	1	1	0	–
Valk	1	0	1	1	0	1
Kasparaitis	2	0	1	1	0	-1
Murray	2	0	1	1	0	–
Christian	1	0	0	0	0	-1
Daigneault	1	0	0	0	2	-2
Hatcher	1	0	0	0	2	1
Hicks	1	0	0	0	0	–
Johansson	1	0	0	0	0	-1
Leroux	1	0	0	0	0	-1
Moran	1	0	0	0	0	1
Mullen	1	0	0	0	0	-1
Olausson	1	0	0	0	0	–
Stojanov	1	0	0	0	0	-1
Tamer	1	0	0	0	2	-2
Wilkinson	1	0	0	0	2	-2
Wright	1	0	0	0	2	-2
Dziedzic	2	0	0	0	0	–
Totals	**2**	**6**	**12**	**18**	**14**	–

DETROIT RED WINGS

PLAYER	GP	G	A	P	PM	+/-
Shanahan	2	3	3	6	0	4
Larionov	2	1	3	4	2	4
McCarty	2	2	1	3	0	5
Konstantinov	2	1	2	3	2	-1
Yzerman	2	1	2	3	0	1
Fedorov	2	1	1	2	2	–
Pushor	2	0	2	2	0	4
Sandstrom	2	0	2	2	0	-2
Lidstrom	2	1	0	1	0	2
Rouse	2	0	1	1	2	–
Ward	2	0	1	1	0	1
Dandenault	1	0	0	0	2	–
Fetisov	1	0	0	0	0	-1
Draper	2	0	0	0	4	-1
Holmstrom	2	0	0	0	2	-1
Kocur	2	0	0	0	0	-1
Kozlov	2	0	0	0	0	-2
Lapointe	2	0	0	0	2	–
Maltby	2	0	0	0	0	-1
Totals		**2**	**10**	**18**	**28**	**18**	–

GOALIE:	GP	MP	GA	ENG	SO	AVG
Lalime (0-1-0)	1	62	6	0	0	5.81
Wregget (0-1-0)	1	60	4	0	0	4.00
Totals (0-2-0)	**2**	**122**	**10**	**0**	**0**	**4.92**

GOALIE:	GP	MP	GA	ENG	SO	AVG
Vernon (2-0-0)	2	122	6	0	0	2.95
Totals (2-0-0)	**2**	**122**	**6**	**0**	**0**	**2.95**

DETROIT VS. SAN JOSE 1996-97 SEASON

TEAM	W	L	T	P	GF	GA	PPG	SHG	PM
San Jose	0	4	0	0	7	25	5	0	111
DETROIT	4	0	0	8	25	7	10	1	111

<table>
<tr><td>at San Jose (2-0-0)</td><td>at DETROIT (2-0-0)</td></tr>
<tr><td>Nov. 21, 1996 – DETROIT 6, San Jose 1</td><td>Nov. 15, 1996 – DETROIT 5, San Jose 1</td></tr>
<tr><td>March 15, 1997 – DETROIT 7, San Jose 4</td><td>Feb. 12, 1997 – DETROIT 7, San Jose 1</td></tr>
<tr><td>Totals – DETROIT 13, San Jose 5</td><td>Totals – DETROIT 12, San Jose 2</td></tr>
</table>

SAN JOSE SHARKS

PLAYER	GP	G	A	P	PM	+/-
Friesen	4	2	1	3	6	-5
Turcotte	3	1	1	2	0	-1
Hawgood	4	1	1	2	2	-3
Kozlov	4	1	1	2	0	-5
Granato	3	0	2	2	0	-2
Tancill	1	1	0	1	2	-1
Guolla	2	1	0	1	2	-3
Kroupa	2	0	1	1	0	-2
McSorley	3	0	1	1	15	-2
Nazarov	3	0	1	1	10	-5
Bodger	4	0	1	1	4	-6
Hunter	1	0	0	0	0	–
Rathje	1	0	0	0	0	–
Widmer	1	0	0	0	0	–
Wood	1	0	0	0	9	-1
Dahlen	2	0	0	0	0	–
Errey	2	0	0	0	0	–
Sykora	2	0	0	0	2	-1
Ewen	3	0	0	0	20	–
Nicholls	3	0	0	0	4	-2
Peltonen	3	0	0	0	0	–
Donovan	4	0	0	0	4	-3
Gill	4	0	0	0	15	-7
Nolan	4	0	0	0	10	-6
Ragnarsson	4	0	0	0	2	-5
Sutter	4	0	0	0	4	-2
Totals	**4**	**7**	**10**	**17**	**111**	**–**

DETROIT RED WINGS

PLAYER	GP	G	A	P	PM	+/-
Shanahan	4	5	5	10	15	7
McCarty	4	2	7	9	25	6
Yzerman	4	2	7	9	16	8
Lidstrom	4	2	6	8	0	4
Fedorov	4	4	3	7	2	7
Konstantinov	4	2	5	7	8	8
Larionov	4	1	3	4	2	4
Kozlov	4	2	1	3	4	3
Lapointe	4	0	3	3	12	1
Kocur	2	1	0	1	4	–
Rouse	2	1	0	1	0	1
Sandstrom	2	1	0	1	2	2
Holmstrom	3	1	0	1	0	-1
Pushor	4	1	0	1	7	4
Johnson	2	0	1	1	0	-1
Dandenault	3	0	1	1	0	3
Fetisov	3	0	1	1	6	4
Ward	3	0	1	1	0	1
Draper	4	0	1	1	4	–
Ramsey	1	0	0	0	0	–
Brown	2	0	0	0	0	–
Taylor	2	0	0	0	0	–
Maltby	3	0	0	0	4	–
Totals		**4**	**25**	**45**	**70**	**111**	**–**

GOALIE:	GP	MP	GA	ENG	SO	AVG
Hrudey (0-2-0)	2	69	8	0	0	6.96
Terreri (0-0-0)	1	51	3	0	0	3.53
Flaherty (0-1-0)	1	60	7	0	0	7.00
Belfour (0-1-0)	1	60	7	0	0	7.00
Totals (0-4-0)	**4**	**240**	**25**	**0**	**0**	**6.25**

GOALIE:	GP	MP	GA	ENG	SO	AVG
Vernon (2-0-0)	2	120	2	0	0	1.00
Osgood (2-0-0)	2	120	5	0	0	2.50
Totals (4-0-0)	**4**	**240**	**7**	**0**	**0**	**1.75**

DETROIT VS. ST. LOUIS 1996-97 SEASON

TEAM	W	L	T	P	GF	GA	PPG	SHG	PM
St. Louis	1	1	3	5	8	9	2	1	92
DETROIT	1	1	3	5	9	8	2	1	94

at St. Louis (1-0-1)
Feb. 1, 1997 – DETROIT 4, St. Louis 1
Feb. 22, 1997 – DETROIT 2, St. Louis 2

Totals – DETROIT 6, St. Louis 3

at DETROIT (0-1-2)
Feb. 4, 1997 – DETROIT 1, St. Louis 1
April 1, 1997 – DETROIT 1, St. Loiuis 1
April 13, 1997 – St. Louis 3, DETROIT 1
Totals – St. Louis 5, DETROIT 3

ST. LOUIS BLUES

PLAYER	GP	G	A	P	PM	+/-
Turgeon	5	2	2	4	0	-1
Campbell	4	2	1	3	0	1
Hull	3	1	1	2	0	-1
Murphy	4	1	1	2	0	-1
Matteau	5	1	1	2	7	2
Demitra	2	1	0	1	2	–
Momesso	3	0	1	1	0	–
MacInnis	4	0	1	1	9	-4
Petrovicky	4	0	1	1	0	–
Kravchuk	5	0	1	1	0	2
Pronger	5	0	1	1	6	3
MacTavish	1	0	0	0	7	–
Rivers	1	0	0	0	0	-1
Yawney	1	0	0	0	2	–
Zabransky	1	0	0	0	2	–
Leach	2	0	0	0	0	1
McAlpine	2	0	0	0	14	0
Twist	4	0	0	0	2	–
York	4	0	0	0	2	-2
Bergevin	5	0	0	0	0	-1
Conroy	5	0	0	0	4	1
Courtnall	5	0	0	0	10	-1
Fuhr	5	0	0	0	2	–
Pellerin	5	0	0	0	6	-2
Peluso	5	0	0	0	9	-1
Persson	5	0	0	0	8	-1
Totals	**5**	**8**	**11**	**19**	**92**	**–**

DETROIT RED WINGS

PLAYER	GP	G	A	P	PM	+/-
Shanahan	5	2	0	2	2	2
Larionov	4	1	1	2	0	2
Kozlov	5	1	1	2	0	1
Lidstrom	5	1	1	2	6	-4
Lapointe	5	0	2	2	2	-1
Holmstrom	4	1	0	1	0	2
Taylor	4	1	0	1	21	1
Maltby	5	1	0	1	2	1
Rouse	5	1	0	1	2	1
Kocur	4	0	1	1	4	1
Konstantinov	5	0	1	1	9	1
Yzerman	5	0	1	1	16	–
Errey	1	0	0	0	0	–
Knuble	1	0	0	0	0	-1
Dandenault	2	0	0	0	2	–
Eriksson	2	0	0	0	0	–
Murphy	2	0	0	0	0	-1
Brown	3	0	0	0	0	–
Fedorov	3	0	0	0	0	-1
McCarty	3	0	0	0	9	-2
Draper	4	0	0	0	0	-2
Fetisov	4	0	0	0	6	3
Pushor	4	0	0	0	9	2
Vernon	4	0	0	0	2	–
Sandstrom	5	0	0	0	2	-1
Totals	**5**	**9**	**8**	**17**	**94**	**–**

GOALIE:	GP	MP	GA	ENG	SO	AVG
Fuhr (1-1-3)	5	315	9	0	0	1.71
Totals (1-1-3)	**5**	**315**	**9**	**0**	**0**	**1.71**

GOALIE:	GP	MP	GA	ENG	SO	AVG
Vernon (1-0-3)	4	255	5	0	0	1.18
Osgood (0-1-0)	1	60	3	0	0	3.00
Totals (1-1-3)	**5**	**315**	**8**	**0**	**0**	**1.52**

TEAM	W	L	T	P	GF	GA	PPG	SHG	PM
Tampa Bay	0	1	1	1	5	7	0	1	43
DETROIT	1	0	1	3	7	5	2	0	37

at Tampa Bay (0-0-1)
Feb. 17, 1997 – DETROIT 3, Tampa Bay 3
Totals – DETROIT 3, Tampa Bay 3

at DETROIT (1-0-0)
Nov. 10, 1996 – DETROIT 4, Tampa Bay 2
Totals – DETROIT 4, Tampa Bay 2

TAMPA BAY LIGHTNING

PLAYER	GP	G	A	P	PM	+/-
Langkow	2	1	1	2	0	1
Peterson	1	1	0	1	0	1
Poulin	2	1	0	1	0	1
Shaw	2	1	0	1	4	–
Zamuner	2	1	0	1	0	–
Gavey	1	0	1	1	0	2
Andersson	2	0	1	1	0	–
Burr	2	0	1	1	0	–
Ciccarelli	2	0	1	1	2	-1
Gratton	2	0	1	1	4	-3
Selivanov	2	0	1	1	14	-1
Houlder	1	0	0	0	2	-1
Myhres	1	0	0	0	0	–
Poeschek	1	0	0	0	0	–
Tabaracci	1	0	0	0	2	–
Toms	1	0	0	0	0	–
Ulanov	1	0	0	0	0	1
Wells	1	0	0	0	2	2
Bannister	2	0	0	0	7	2
Cross	2	0	0	0	0	-2
Cullen	2	0	0	0	2	-2
Hamrlik	2	0	0	0	0	–
Wiemer	2	0	0	0	4	-1
Totals	**2**	**5**	**7**	**12**	**43**	**–**

GOALIE:	GP	MP	GA	ENG	SO	AVG
Wilkinson (0-1-0)	1	59	3	1	0	3.05
Tabaracci (0-0-1)	1	64	3	0	0	2.81
Totals (0-1-1)	**2**	**123**	**6**	**1**	**0**	**2.93**

DETROIT RED WINGS

PLAYER	GP	G	A	P	PM	+/-
Lidstrom	2	1	3	4	2	2
Yzerman	2	0	4	4	2	2
Fedorov	2	2	1	3	0	-1
Kozlov	2	1	1	2	0	–
Shanahan	2	1	1	2	6	–
Fetisov	1	0	2	2	0	2
Sandstrom	1	1	0	1	0	-1
Lapointe	2	1	0	1	5	2
Draper	1	0	0	0	0	–
Errey	1	0	0	0	0	–
Johnson	1	0	0	0	0	–
Kocur	1	0	0	0	0	–
Larionov	1	0	0	0	0	-1
Taylor	1	0	0	0	0	–
Brown	2	0	0	0	2	–
Dandenault	2	0	0	0	0	-1
Konstantinov	2	0	0	0	4	3
Maltby	2	0	0	0	2	–
McCarty	2	0	0	0	2	-1
Pushor	2	0	0	0	2	-3
Rouse	2	0	0	0	2	-1
Ward	2	0	0	0	6	-2
Totals	**2**	**7**	**12**	**19**	**37**	**–**

GOALIE:	GP	MP	GA	ENG	SO	AVG
Osgood (1-0-0)	1	60	2	0	0	2.00
Vernon (0-0-1)	1	65	3	0	0	2.77
Totals (1-0-1)	**2**	**125**	**5**	**0**	**0**	**2.40**

TEAM	W	L	T	P	GF	GA	PPG	SHG	PM
Toronto	1	3	2	4	17	20	5	0	70
DETROIT	3	1	2	8	20	17	4	1	70

at Toronto (1-1-1)
Nov. 2, 1996 – Toronto 6, DETROIT 2
March 5, 1997 – DETROIT 4, Toronto 4
April 5, 1997 – DETROIT 4, Toronto 2
Totals – Toronto 12, DETROIT 10

at DETROIT (2-0-1)
Nov. 27 , 1996 – DETROIT 5, Toronto 2
Dec. 15, 1996 – DETROIT 3, Toronto 1
April 3, 1997 – DETROIT 2, Toronto 2
Totals – DETROIT 10, Toronto 5

TORONTO MAPLE LEAFS

PLAYER	GP	G	A	P	PM	+/-
Sundin	6	3	4	7	6	-3
Warriner	5	0	4	4	0	3
Berezin	6	3	0	3	2	-1
Muller	4	2	1	3	6	1
Heward	3	1	2	3	2	2
Clark	4	2	0	2	0	-2
Yushkevich	5	2	0	2	6	1
Baker	4	1	1	2	2	2
Domi	4	1	1	2	12	–
Convery	4	0	2	2	4	2
Macoun	5	0	2	2	0	2
Schneider	2	1	0	1	6	2
Kypreos	4	1	0	1	0	1
Ellett	3	0	1	1	2	-2
Gilmour	3	0	1	1	2	-1
Sullivan	3	0	1	1	2	-1
Zettler	3	0	1	1	0	–
Murphy	4	0	1	1	0	-1
Cooper	1	0	0	0	0	–
Dempsey	1	0	0	0	0	–
Nedved	1	0	0	0	0	–
Pederson	1	0	0	0	0	-2
Tremblay	1	0	0	0	0	-1
Wiseman	1	0	0	0	0	–
Wolanin	1	0	0	0	0	-1
Fairchild	2	0	0	0	0	–
Johnson	2	0	0	0	0	-3
Podollan	2	0	0	0	0	4
Smith	2	0	0	0	2	-3
Craig	3	0	0	0	0	-1
Smith	3	0	0	0	4	-2
Martin	4	0	0	0	2	-2
Hendrickson	5	0	0	0	2	-4
Modin	6	0	0	0	2	-6
Potvin	6	0	0	0	2	–
Totals	**6**	**17**	**22**	**39**	**70**	**–**

DETROIT RED WINGS

PLAYER	GP	G	A	P	PM	+/-
Shanahan	6	5	6	11	2	4
Lidstrom	4	1	5	6	0	3
Yzerman	5	1	5	6	6	4
McCarty	6	2	3	5	5	1
Lapointe	6	3	1	4	0	4
Dandenault	5	1	3	4	0	1
Fedorov	6	1	3	4	4	1
Kozlov	6	1	2	3	0	–
Taylor	4	1	1	2	6	3
Fetisov	5	0	2	2	2	-1
Knuble	2	1	0	1	0	1
Sandstrom	2	1	0	1	4	–
Draper	6	1	0	1	2	–
Pushor	6	1	0	1	2	3
Brown	2	0	1	1	0	1
Larionov	3	0	1	1	2	-2
Holmstrom	4	0	1	1	0	1
Konstantinov	4	0	1	1	12	-2
Maltby	5	0	1	1	2	1
Rouse	6	0	1	1	0	5
Eriksson	1	0	0	0	2	-3
Errey	1	0	0	0	0	-4
Major	1	0	0	0	5	–
Murphy	1	0	0	0	0	1
Johnson	3	0	0	0	2	-1
Kocur	3	0	0	0	10	1
Ward	4	0	0	0	0	-3
Osgood	6	0	0	0	2	–
Totals	**6**	**20**	**37**	**57**	**70**	**–**

GOALIE:	GP	MP	GA	ENG	SO	AVG
Potvin (1-3-2)	6	369	20	0	0	3.25
Totals (1-3-2)	**6**	**369**	**20**	**0**	**0**	**3.25**

GOALIE:	GP	MP	GA	ENG	SO	AVG
Vernon (0-1-0)	1	41	6	0	0	8.78
Osgood (3-0-2)	6	329	11	0	0	2.01
Totals (3-1-2)	**6**	**370**	**17**	**0**	**0**	**2.76**

DETROIT VS. VANCOUVER 1996-97 SEASON

TEAM	W	L	T	P	GF	GA	PPG	SHG	PM
Vancouver	2	1	1	5	15	13	4	1	70
DETROIT	1	2	1	3	13	15	4	1	71

at Vancouver (1-1-0)
Dec. 20, 1996 – Vancouver 3, DETROIT 2
March 8, 1997 – DETROIT 5, Vancouver 3
Totals – DETROIT 7, Vancouver 6

at DETROIT (0-1-1)
Dec. 3, 1996 – DETROIT 2, Vancouver 2
Feb. 6, 1997 – Vancouver 7, DETROIT 4
Totals – Vancouver 9, DETROIT 6

VANCOUVER CANUCKS

PLAYER	GP	G	A	P	PM	+/-
Gelinas	4	4	3	7	2	5
Bure	3	0	5	5	2	3
Linden	2	0	4	4	0	2
Mogilny	3	1	2	3	2	–
Aucoin	4	1	2	3	2	–
Lumme	4	1	2	3	2	2
Ridley	4	1	2	3	0	–
Courtnall	3	0	3	3	0	-1
Naslund	3	2	0	2	0	-1
Babych	4	1	1	2	2	-2
Bohonos	1	1	0	1	0	2
Joseph	3	1	0	1	2	–
Walker	3	1	0	1	18	1
Tikkanen	4	1	0	1	0	-2
Murzyn	3	0	1	1	17	2
Hedican	4	0	1	1	2	1
Odjick	4	0	1	1	17	–
Courville	1	0	0	0	0	–
Semak	2	0	0	0	0	–
Wotton	2	0	0	0	2	1
Roberts	3	0	0	0	0	–
Brashear	4	0	0	0	0	-2
Sillinger	4	0	0	0	0	-2
Totals	**4**	**15**	**27**	**42**	**70**	**–**

DETROIT RED WINGS

PLAYER	GP	G	A	P	PM	+/-
Fedorov	4	2	3	5	0	3
Shanahan	4	2	3	5	4	-2
Fetisov	4	1	3	4	2	4
Larionov	4	1	3	4	0	3
Yzerman	4	1	3	4	0	-6
Lapointe	3	1	1	2	0	1
Kozlov	4	1	1	2	2	1
Lidstrom	4	1	1	2	0	-4
Konstantinov	4	0	2	2	16	4
Kocur	2	1	0	1	0	-1
Holmstrom	3	1	0	1	0	-1
Maltby	3	1	0	1	6	–
Eriksson	1	0	1	1	2	-1
Dandenault	3	0	1	1	2	-2
McCarty	3	0	1	1	2	-3
Ward	3	0	1	1	2	-1
Draper	4	0	1	1	2	-1
Brown	1	0	0	0	0	–
Johnson	1	0	0	0	0	–
Errey	2	0	0	0	0	-1
Sandstrom	2	0	0	0	14	-1
Taylor	2	0	0	0	0	-1
Rouse	3	0	0	0	2	-1
Pushor	4	0	0	0	15	-1
Totals	**4**	**13**	**25**	**38**	**71**	**–**

GOALIE:	GP	MP	GA	ENG	SO	AVG
Hirsch (1-1-1)	3	184	9	0	0	2.93
McLean (1-0-0)	1	60	4	0	0	4.00
Totals (1-3-0)	**4**	**244**	**13**	**0**	**0**	**3.20**

GOALIE:	GP	MP	GA	ENG	SO	AVG
Osgood (0-1-1)	3	128	9	0	0	4.22
Hodson (0-1-0)	1	56	3	0	0	3.21
Vernon (1-0-0)	1	60	3	0	0	3.00
Totals (1-2-1)	**4**	**244**	**15**	**0**	**0**	**3.69**

DETROIT VS. WASHINGTON 1996-97 SEASON

TEAM	W	L	T	P	GF	GA	PPG	SHG	PM
Washington	0	2	0	0	4	7	0	0	73
DETROIT	2	0	0	4	7	4	1	1	69

at Washington (1-0-0)
Dec. 4, 1996 – DETROIT 2, Washington 0
Totals – DETROIT 2, Washington 0

at DETROIT (1-0-0)
Dec. 26, 1996 – DETROIT 5, Washington 4
Totals – DETROIT 5, Washington 4

WASHINGTON CAPITALS

PLAYER	GP	G	A	P	PM	+/-
Bondra	2	2	0	2	2	1
Hunter	2	1	0	1	14	2
Nikolishin	2	1	0	1	0	1
Johansson	1	0	1	1	0	-1
Pivonka	1	0	1	1	0	1
Cote	2	0	1	1	0	-2
Gonchar	2	0	1	1	2	–
Klee	2	0	1	1	10	1
Konowalchuk	2	0	1	1	0	-1
Miller	2	0	1	1	0	-1
Reekie	2	0	1	1	2	1
Carter	1	0	0	0	0	–
Juneau	1	0	0	0	0	-3
Kaminski	1	0	0	0	0	–
Krygier	1	0	0	0	2	-1
Allison	2	0	0	0	0	-1
Berube	2	0	0	0	10	-1
Eagles	2	0	0	0	2	-1
Housley	2	0	0	0	0	-2
Simon	2	0	0	0	19	-3
Tinordi	2	0	0	0	10	–
Totals	**2**	**4**	**8**	**12**	**73**	**–**

GOALIE:	GP	MP	GA	ENG	SO	AVG
Carey (0-2-0)	2	123	7	0	0	3.41
Totals (0-2-0)	**2**	**123**	**7**	**0**	**0**	**3.41**

DETROIT RED WINGS

PLAYER	GP	G	A	P	PM	+/-
Fedorov	2	6	0	6	0	5
Konstantinov	2	0	4	4	4	5
Larionov	2	0	3	3	0	2
Shanahan	2	0	2	2	10	1
McCarty	2	1	0	1	15	-1
Fetisov	2	0	1	1	2	4
Lidstrom	2	0	1	1	12	-2
Maltby	2	0	1	1	2	–
Brown	1	0	0	0	0	–
Draper	1	0	0	0	0	–
Lapointe	1	0	0	0	0	-2
Ward	1	0	0	0	0	1
Dandenault	2	0	0	0	10	-2
Errey	2	0	0	0	0	-1
Johnson	2	0	0	0	0	–
Kozlov	2	0	0	0	0	2
Pushor	2	0	0	0	2	-1
Rouse	2	0	0	0	0	-1
Taylor	2	0	0	0	2	1
Yzerman	2	0	0	0	10	-2
Totals	**2**	**7**	**12**	**19**	**69**	**–**

GOALIE:	GP	MP	GA	ENG	SO	AVG
Hodson (1-0-0)	1	60	0	0	1	.00
Osgood (1-0-0)	1	63	4	0	0	3.81
Totals (2-0-0)	**2**	**123**	**4**	**0**	**0**	**1.95**

DETROIT VS. ST. LOUIS 1997 PLAYOFFS

TEAM	W	L	GF	GA	PPG	SHG	PM
St. Louis	2	4	12	13	5	0	198
DETROIT	4	2	13	12	6	1	149

GAME	DATE	VENUE	RESULT	SCORE	GOALIE	WINNING GOAL
1	April 16	Detroit	L	0-2	Vernon	Courtnall
2	April 18	Detroit	W	2-1	VERNON	MURPHY
3	April 20	St. Louis	W	3-2	VERNON	YZERMAN
4	April 22	St. Louis	L	0-4	Vernon/ Osgood	Courtnall
5	April 25	Detroit	W	5-2	VERNON	McCARTY
6	April 27	St. Louis	W	3-1	VERNON	SHANAHAN

ST. LOUIS BLUES

PLAYER	GP	G	A	P	PM	+/-
Hull	6	2	7	9	2	4
Courtnall	6	3	1	4	23	–
DeMitra	6	1	3	4	6	3
MacInnis	6	1	2	3	4	-1
Turgeon	5	1	1	2	2	–
Murphy	6	1	1	2	10	-2
Pronger	6	1	1	2	22	–
Campbell	4	1	0	1	6	-1
Bergevin	6	1	0	1	8	2
McAlpine	4	0	1	1	0	1
MacTavish	1	0	0	0	2	-1
Kravchuk	2	0	0	0	2	-1
Petrovicky	2	0	0	0	0	1
Momesso	3	0	0	0	6	–
Matteau	5	0	0	0	0	–
Peluso	5	0	0	0	25	-1
York	5	0	0	0	2	-1
Conroy	6	0	0	0	8	-1
Fuhr	6	0	0	0	4	–
Leach	6	0	0	0	33	-2
Pellerin	6	0	0	0	6	-1
Persson	6	0	0	0	27	-1
Twist	6	0	0	0	0	–
Totals	**6**	**12**	**17**	**29**	**198**	**–**

DETROIT RED WINGS

PLAYER	GP	G	A	P	PM	+/-
Shanahan	6	3	3	6	12	2
Murphy	6	2	3	5	4	1
Larionov	6	0	5	5	2	-1
Draper	6	2	1	3	8	3
Yzerman	6	2	1	3	4	–
Kozlov	6	2	0	2	8	-2
Maltby	6	1	1	2	6	2
McCarty	6	1	1	2	10	1
Fedorov	6	0	2	2	10	-2
Lapointe	6	0	2	2	21	1
Lidstrom	6	0	2	2	0	1
Pushor	5	0	1	1	5	-1
Kocur	6	0	1	1	2	1
Sandstrom	6	0	1	1	14	-4
Holmstrom	1	0	0	0	0	-1
Osgood	1	0	0	0	2	–
Taylor	1	0	0	0	0	–
Ward	5	0	0	0	2	1
Fetisov	6	0	0	0	2	–
Konstantinov	6	0	0	0	8	-3
Rouse	6	0	0	0	29	2
Totals	**6**	**13**	**24**	**37**	**149**	**–**

GOALIE:	GP	MP	GA	ENG	SO	AVG
Fuhr (2-4)	6	357	13	0	2	2.18
Totals (2-4)	**6**	**357**	**13**	**0**	**2**	**2.18**

GOALIE:	GP	MP	GA	ENG	SO	AVG
Vernon (4-2)	6	348	12	0	0	2.07
Osgood (0-0)	1	10	0	0	0	.00
Totals (4-2)	**6**	**358**	**12**	**0**	**0**	**2.01**

DETROIT VS. ANAHEIM   1997 PLAYOFFS

TEAM	W	L	GF	GA	PPG	SHG	PM
Anaheim	0	4	8	8	4	0	60
DETROIT	4	0	13	13	3	0	56

GAME	DATE	VENUE	RESULT	SCORE	GOALIE	WINNING GOAL
1	May 2	Detroit	W	2-1	VERNON	LAPOINTE
2	May 4	Detroit	W	3-2	VERNON	KOZLOV
3	May 6	Anaheim	W	5-3	VERNON	FEDOROV
4	May 8	Anaheim	W	3-2	VERNON	SHANAHAN

MIGHTY DUCKS of ANAHEIM

PLAYER	GP	G	A	P	PM	+/-
Kariya	4	2	2	4	2	-4
Mironov	4	0	4	4	6	-3
Selanne	4	2	0	2	2	-3
Bellows	4	1	1	2	2	-4
Daigneault	4	0	2	2	8	-4
Drury	3	1	0	1	0	–
Kurri	4	1	0	1	2	-2
Sacco	4	1	0	1	2	-2
Pronger	3	0	1	1	0	1
Baumgartner	4	0	1	1	0	1
Park	4	0	1	1	0	1
Rucchin	4	0	1	1	10	–
Rychel	4	0	1	1	6	-1
Van Impe	4	0	1	1	4	-4
Karpa	1	0	0	0	2	–
LeClerc	1	0	0	0	0	–
Todd	1	0	0	0	0	–
Marshall	3	0	0	0	2	1
Shtalenkov	3	0	0	0	2	–
Dollas	4	0	0	0	2	-2
Janssens	4	0	0	0	6	-4
Trebil	4	0	0	0	2	–
Totals	4	8	15	23	60	–

DETROIT RED WINGS

PLAYER	GP	G	A	P	PM	+/-
Fedorov	4	2	3	5	0	5
Kozlov	4	3	1	4	2	1
Konstantinov	4	0	4	4	6	2
Brown	4	3	0	3	0	1
Shanahan	4	1	2	3	2	2
Yzerman	4	1	2	3	0	1
Lapointe	4	1	1	2	0	2
Larionov	4	1	1	2	0	4
Lidstrom	4	1	1	2	2	3
Fetisov	4	0	2	2	14	4
Murphy	4	0	2	2	0	4
Sandstrom	4	0	2	2	2	1
Draper	4	0	1	1	0	–
McCarty	4	0	1	1	8	–
Taylor	1	0	0	0	0	-1
Kocur	3	0	0	0	0	–
Maltby	4	0	0	0	2	1
Rouse	4	0	0	0	6	–
Vernon	4	0	0	0	12	–
Ward	4	0	0	0	0	-1
Totals	4	13	23	36	56	–

GOALIE:	GP	MP	GA	ENG	SO	AVG
Hebert (0-1)	2	108	3	0	0	1.67
Shtalenkov (0-3)	3	211	10	0	0	2.84
Totals (0-4)	4	319	13	0	0	2.45

GOALIE:	GP	MP	GA	ENG	SO	AVG
Vernon (4-0)	4	320	8	0	0	1.50
Totals (4-0)	4	320	8	0	0	1.50

DETROIT VS. COLORADO 1997 PLAYOFFS

TEAM	W	L	GF	GA	PPG	SHG	PM
Colorado	2	4	12	16	2	0	196
DETROIT	4	2	16	12	4	0	186

GAME	DATE	VENUE	RESULT	SCORE	GOALIE	WINNING GOAL
1	May 15	Colorado	L	1-2	Vernon	Ricci
2	May 17	Colorado	W	4-2	VERNON	YZERMAN
3	May 19	Detroit	W	2-1	VERNON	KOZLOV
4	May 22	Detroit	W	6-0	VERNON	LARIONOV
5	May 24	Colorado	L	0-6	Vernon/ Osgood	Lemieux
6	May 26	Detroit	W	3-1	VERNON	FEDOROV

COLORADO AVALANCHE

PLAYER	GP	G	A	P	PM	+/-
Sakic	6	4	2	6	4	–
Kamensky	6	0	5	5	6	1
Lemieux	6	3	1	4	14	2
Young	6	3	1	4	0	1
Ozolinsh	6	0	3	3	8	–
Ricci	6	1	1	2	6	-1
Deadmarsh	6	0	2	2	16	-2
Yelle	3	1	0	1	0	1
Forsberg	5	0	1	1	10	-2
Foote	6	0	1	1	35	-3
Keane	6	0	1	1	14	-1
Lacroix	6	0	1	1	17	–
Miller	6	0	1	1	4	1
Sarault	3	0	0	0	2	–
Severyn	3	0	0	0	0	1
Messier	4	0	0	0	4	-1
Corbet	6	0	0	0	17	-3
Gusarov	6	0	0	0	6	1
Klemm	6	0	0	0	2	-3
Lefebvre	6	0	0	0	21	-4
Roy	6	0	0	0	10	–
Totals	**6**	**12**	**20**	**32**	**196**	**–**

DETROIT RED WINGS

PLAYER	GP	G	A	P	PM	+/-
Fedorov	6	3	4	7	0	–
Kozlov	6	3	2	5	4	3
Larionov	6	3	2	5	2	2
Lapointe	6	1	4	5	33	2
Shanahan	6	2	2	4	29	1
Yzerman	6	1	2	3	0	-1
Lidstrom	6	0	3	3	0	2
Maltby	6	2	0	2	14	1
Brown	6	0	2	2	0	2
McCarty	6	1	0	1	12	-4
Draper	6	0	1	1	2	-1
Kocur	6	0	1	1	18	1
Murphy	6	0	1	1	4	1
Fetisov	6	0	0	0	16	-2
Konstantinov	6	0	0	0	13	1
Rouse	6	0	0	0	20	3
Sandstrom	6	0	0	0	4	-2
Ward	6	0	0	0	15	–
Totals		**6**	**16**	**24**	**40**	**186**	**–**

GOALIE:	GP	MP	GA	ENG	SO	AVG
Roy (2-4)	6	337	14	1	1	2.49
Billington (0-0)	1	20	1	0	0	3.00
Totals (2-4)	**6**	**357**	**15**	**1**	**1**	**2.52**

GOALIE:	GP	MP	GA	ENG	SO	AVG
Vernon (4-2)	6	321	10	0	1	1.87
Osgood (0-0)	1	37	2	0	0	3.24
Totals (4-2)	**6**	**358**	**12**	**0**	**1**	**2.01**

DETROIT VS. PHILADELPHIA   1997 PLAYOFFS

TEAM	W	L	GF	GA	PPG	SHG	PM
Philadelphia	0	4	6	16	4	0	40
DETROIT	4	0	16	6	4	1	40

GAME	DATE	VENUE	RESULT	SCORE	GOALIE	WINNING GOAL
1	May 31	Philadelphia	W	4-2	VERNON	FEDOROV
2	June 3	Philadelphia	W	4-2	VERNON	MALTBY
3	June 5	Detroit	W	6-1	VERNON	FEDOROV
4	June 7	Detroit	W	2-1	VERNON	McCARTY

PHILADELPHIA FLYERS

PLAYER	GP	G	A	P	PM	+/-
Brind'Amour	4	3	1	4	0	–
LeClair	4	2	1	3	4	-5
Lindros	4	1	2	3	8	-5
Niinimaa	4	0	3	3	0	-5
Desjardins	4	0	2	2	2	-1
Renberg	4	0	1	1	0	-2
Kordic	1	0	0	0	0	–
Svoboda	1	0	0	0	2	–
Coffey	2	0	0	0	6	-5
Lacroix	2	0	0	0	2	–
Petit	2	0	0	0	2	-1
Dykhuis	3	0	0	0	2	-3
Falloon	3	0	0	0	2	-1
Forbes	3	0	0	0	0	–
Hawerchuk	3	0	0	0	0	-3
Druce	4	0	0	0	0	–
Klatt	4	0	0	0	6	-3
Otto	4	0	0	0	0	-3
Podein	4	0	0	0	2	-3
Samuelsson	4	0	0	0	2	-3
Therien	4	0	0	0	0	-2
Zubrus	4	0	0	0	0	-4
Totals	**4**	**6**	**10**	**16**	**40**	**–**

DETROIT RED WINGS

PLAYER	GP	G	A	P	PM	+/-
Fedorov	4	3	3	6	2	2
Shanahan	4	3	1	4	0	3
Yzerman	4	3	1	4	0	3
Lapointe	4	2	1	3	6	3
Maltby	4	2	1	3	2	2
McCarty	4	1	2	3	4	4
Murphy	4	0	3	3	0	10
Kocur	4	1	1	2	2	3
Fetisov	4	0	2	2	10	–
Kozlov	4	0	2	2	0	1
Lidstrom	4	1	0	1	0	6
Brown	4	0	1	1	2	1
Draper	4	0	1	1	2	3
Sandstrom	4	0	1	1	4	2
Vernon	4	0	1	1	0	–
Konstantinov	4	0	0	0	2	-1
Larionov	4	0	0	0	4	3
Rouse	4	0	0	0	0	3
Ward	4	0	0	0	0	1
Totals		**4**	**16**	**21**	**37**	**40**	**–**

GOALIE:	GP	MP	GA	ENG	SO	AVG
Hextall (0-3)	3	178	12	0	0	4.04
Snow (0-1)	1	58	4	0	0	4.14
Totals (0-4)	**4**	**236**	**16**	**0**	**0**	**4.07**

GOALIE:	GP	MP	GA	ENG	SO	AVG
Vernon (4-0)	4	240	6	0	0	1.50
Totals (4-0)	**4**	**240**	**6**	**0**	**0**	**1.50**

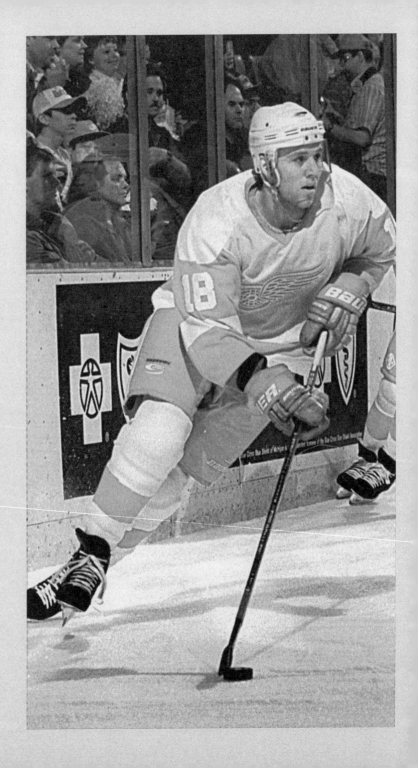

1996-97 RECORD BY MONTHS

	OVERALL				
MONTH	GP	W	L	T	P
October	12	7	4	1	15
November	13	7	4	2	16
December	13	6	4	3	15
January	10	2	5	3	7
February	13	8	2	3	19
March	14	6	5	3	15
April	7	2	2	3	7

	HOME						ROAD				
MONTH	GP	W	L	T	P		GP	W	L	T	P
October	7	5	1	1	11		5	2	3	0	4
November	6	4	2	0	8		7	3	2	2	8
December	7	3	2	2	8		6	3	2	1	7
January	5	0	3	2	2		5	2	2	1	5
February	6	4	1	1	9		7	4	1	2	10
March	6	4	1	1	9		8	2	4	2	6
April	4	0	2	2	2		3	2	0	1	5

1996-97 RECORD BY DAYS

	OVERALL				
DAY	GP	W	L	T	P
Sunday	13	5	6	2	12
Monday	8	3	2	3	9
Tuesday	8	1	2	5	7
Wednesday	18	9	5	4	22
Thursday	8	5	2	1	11
Friday	11	3	6	2	8
Saturday	16	12	3	1	25

	HOME						ROAD				
DAY	GP	W	L	T	P		GP	W	L	T	P
Sunday	7	3	3	1	7		6	2	3	1	5
Monday	3	2	1	0	4		5	1	1	3	5
Tuesday	5	0	0	5	5		3	1	2	0	2
Wednesday	12	8	3	1	17		6	1	2	3	5
Thursday	5	3	1	1	7		3	2	1	0	4
Friday	6	2	3	1	5		5	1	3	1	3
Saturday	3	2	1	0	4		13	10	2	1	21

1996-97 RECORD ON SUCCESSIVE DAYS

1st Game:	6-3-3, 15 points
2nd Game:	5-3-4, 14 points

1996-97 RECORD VS. DIVISIONS

Central:	8-11-8, 24 points;	H: 5-5-4,	R: 3-6-4
Pacific:	13-9-7, 33 points;	H: 6-4-4,	R: 7-5-3
Atlantic:	8-4-2, 18 points;	H: 4-2-1,	R: 4-2-1
Northeast	9-2-1, 19 points;	H: 5-1-0,	R: 4-1-1

1996-97 SHOTS BY PERIODS

	1st	2nd	3rd	OT	Total	Avg.	Pctg.
Detroit	925	868	880	53	2726	33.2	9.3
Opponents	656	743	641	35	2075	25.3	9.5

1996-97 GOALS BY PERIODS

	1st	2nd	3rd	OT	Total	Avg.
Detroit	82	90	74	7	253	3.1
Opponents	65	61	69	2	197	2.4

1996-97 FIRST GOAL

Scoring First:	27-8-7, 61 points
Opposition Scoring First:	11-18-10, 32 points

1996-97 HOLDING LEAD

Leading After One Period:	27-5-7, 61 points
Trailing After One Period:	6-13-8, 20 points
Tied After One Period:	5-9-3, 13 points
Leading After Two Periods:	33-4-9, 75 points
Trailing After Two Periods:	2-19-3, 7 points
Tied After Two Periods:	3-3-6, 12 points

1996-97 CLOSE DECISIONS

One-Goal Games:	8-9, 16 points
Two-Goal Games:	9-11, 18 points

1996-97 GOAL MARGINS

Scoring 0 Goals:	0-3-1, 1 point
Scoring 1 Goal:	0-12-3, 3 points
Scoring 2 Goals:	4-5-7, 15 points
Scoring 3 Goals:	4-5-5, 13 points
Scoring 4 Goals:	12-1-1, 25 points
Scoring 5 Goals:	8-0-1, 17 points
Scoring 6 Goals:	7-0-0, 14 points
Scoring 7 Goals:	3-0-0, 6 points
Scoring 8 Goals:	0-0-0, 0 points
Scoring 9 Goals:	0-0-0, 0 points
Scoring 10 Goals:	0-0-0, 0 points
Allowing 0 Goals:	6-0-1,13 points
Allowing 1 Goal:	15-1-3, 33 points
Allowing 2 Goals:	8-5-7, 23 points
Allowing 3 Goals:	4-9-5, 13 points
Allowing 4 Goals:	3-6-1, 7 points
Allowing 5 Goals:	2-3-1, 5 points
Allowing 6 Goals:	0-1-0, 0 points
Allowing 7 Goals:	0-1-0, 0 points
Allowing 8 Goals:	0-0-0, 0 points
Allowing 9 Goals:	0-0-0, 0 points
Allowing 10 Goals:	0-0-0, 0 points

—1996-97 POWER-PLAY GOALS & PENALTY KILLING—

Red Wings had 66 in 368 attempts,
Power-play percentage, 17.9,
7th in NHL

Opponents had 46 in 346 attempts,
Penalty killing percentage 88.3,
4th in NHL

vs. ANAHEIM MIGHTY DUCKS
RED WINGS (0-13)

MIGHTY DUCKS (1-11) – Selanne

vs. BOSTON BRUINS
RED WINGS (2-6) – Lapointe, Murphy

BRUINS (1-4) — J. Y. Roy

vs. BUFFALO SABRES
RED WINGS (1-6) – Yzerman

SABRES (0-7)

vs. CALGARY FLAMES
RED WINGS (5-17) – Yzerman (2), Kozlov, McCarty,
 Shanahan

FLAMES (3-18) – Iginla, Hogland,
 Reichel

vs. CHICAGO BLACKHAWKS
RED WINGS (5-31) – Shanahan (2), Yzerman,
 Fedorov, Lapointe

BLACKHAWKS (4-29) – Krivokrasov,
 Probert, Suter, Daze

vs. COLORADO AVALANCHE
RED WINGS (4-19) – Yzerman, Lidstrom,
 Fedorov, Shanahan

AVALANCHE (8-28) – Deadmarsh (2),
 Ozolinsh (2), Forsberg, Kamensky,
 Jones, Young

vs. DALLAS STARS
RED WINGS (8-31) – Shanahan(4), Lapointe,
 Fedorov, Larionov, Brown

STARS (4-23) – Nieuwendyk (2),
 Gilchrist, Modano

vs. EDMONTON OILERS
RED WINGS (2-19) – Shanahan, Fedorov

OILERS (0-19)

vs. FLORIDA PANTHERS
RED WINGS (3-9) – Lidstrom, Shanahan, McCarty

PANTHERS (2-11) – Svehla (2)

vs. HARTFORD WHALERS
RED WINGS (1-6) – Lapointe

WHALERS (0-4)

vs. LOS ANGELES KINGS
RED WINGS (3-21) – Holmstrom, Shanahan, Draper

KINGS (0-14)

vs. MONTRÉAL CANADIENS
RED WINGS (0-10)

CANADIENS (1-9) – Thornton

vs. NEW JERSEY DEVILS
RED WINGS (0-9)

DEVILS (0-11)

vs. NEW YORK ISLANDERS
RED WINGS (0-9)

ISLANDERS (0-9)

vs. NEW YORK RANGERS
RED WINGS (1-8) – Lidstrom

RANGERS (0-5)

vs. OTTAWA SENATORS
RED WINGS (0-5)

SENATORS (0-4)

vs. PHILADELPHIA FLYERS
RED WINGS (2-14) – Holmstrom, Yzerman

FLYERS (1-14) – Brind'Amour

vs. PHOENIX COYOTES
RED WINGS (3-22) – Shanahan (2), McCarty

COYOTES (4-23) – Roenick (3), Tkachuk

vs. PITTSBURGH PENGUINS
RED WINGS (3-7) – Shanahan, Fedorov, Lidstrom   PENGUINS (1-9) – Roche

vs. SAN JOSE SHARKS
RED WINGS (10-24) – Fedorov (3), Shanahan (2),   SHARKS (5-24) – Turcotte (2), Kozlov,
Lidstrom (2), Kozlov, Holmstrom, McCarty   Tancill, Friesen

vs. ST. LOUIS BLUES
RED WINGS (2-24) – Lidstrom, Larionov   BLUES (2-20) – Turgeon, Demitra

vs. TAMPA BAY LIGHTNING
RED WINGS (2-9) – Kozlov, Shanahan   LIGHTNING (0-9)

vs. TORONTO MAPLE LEAFS
RED WINGS (4-23) – Shanahan (2),   MAPLE LEAFS (5-22) – Clark (2), Muller,
Yzerman, Lapointe   Sundin, Yuskevich

vs. VANCOUVER CANUCKS
RED WINGS (4-14) – Fedorov, Shanahan,   CANUCKS (4-14) – Joseph, Lumme,
Yzerman, Lidstrom   Naslund, Ridley

vs. WASHINGTON CAPITALS
RED WINGS (1-9) – McCarty   CAPITALS (0-7)

——1996-97 RED WINGS' RECORDS BY QUARTERS——

OVERALL WON-LOST-TIED
1st 20 Games: 11-7-2 24 points
2nd 20 Games: 9-6-5 23 points
3rd 20 Games: 9-6-5 23 points
4th 22 Games: 9-7-6 24 points
Total: 38-26-18, 94 points

HOME WON-LOST-TIED
1st 20 Games: 8-3-1 17 points
2nd 20 Games: 4-3-2 10 points
3rd 20 Games: 3-3-3 9 points
4th 22 Games: 5-3-3 13 points
Total: 20-12-9, 49 points

ROAD WON-LOST-TIED
1st 20 Games: 3-4-1 7 points
2nd 20 Games: 5-3-3 13 points
3rd 20 Games: 6-3-2 14 points
4th 22 Games: 4-4-3 11 points
Total: 18-14-9, 45 points

GOALS FOR
1st 20 Games: 55
2nd 20 Games: 70
3rd 20 Games: 66
4th 22 Games: 62
Total: 253

GOALS AGAINST
1st 20 Games: 39
2nd 21 Games: 46
3rd 21 Games: 58
4th 20 Games: 54
Total: 197

POWER PLAY
1st 20 Games: 9-for-85 10.6 percent
2nd 20 Games: 18-for-88 20.5 percent
3rd 20 Games: 21-for-94 22.3 percent
4th 22 Games: 17-for-102 16.7 percent
Total: 65-for-369 17.6 percent

PENALTY KILLING
1st 20 Games: 7 ppga, 77 short,
               90.9 percent
2nd 20 Games: 11 ppga, 75 short,
               85.3 percent
3rd 20 Games: 14 ppga, 99 short,
               85.9 percent
4th 22 Games: 14 ppga, 93 short,
               84.9 percent
Total: 46 ppga, 344 short,
               86.6 percent

SHORTHANDED GOALS FOR
1st 20 Games: 2
2nd 20 Games: 4
3rd 20 Games: 0
4th 22 Games: 3
Total: 9

SHORTHANDED GOALS AGAINST
1st 20 Games: 2
2nd 20 Games: 0
3rd 20 Games: 1
4th 22 Games: 5
Total: 8

1996-97 THREE-GOAL OR MORE GAMES

By DETROIT – 4

PLAYER	DATE	OPPONENT	CAREER TOTALS
Shanahan	November 27	Toronto	8
Fedorov (5)	December 26	Washington	3
Shanahan	February 8	Pittsburgh	9
Shanahan	February 12	San Jose	10

By Opponents – 3

Reid	January 8	Dallas	2
Gelinas	February 6	Vancouver	2
Kamensky	March 26	Colorado	3

1996-97 TWO-GOAL GAMES

By DETROIT – 19

Shanahan	6	Brown	1
Yzerman	2	Lidstrom	1
McCarty	2	Kozlov	1
Johnson	1	Konstantinov	1
Sandstrom	1	Fedorov	1
Larionov	1	Lapointe	1

By Opponents – 16

Deadmarsh, Colorado	2	Berezan, Toronto	1
Nieuwendyk, Dallas	2	Forsberg, Colorado	1
Bondra, Washington	1	Ozolinsh, Colorado	1
Recchi, Montréal	1	Lemieux, Colorado	1
Svehla, Florida	1	Roenick, Phoenix	1
Sundin, Toronto	1	Friesen, San Jose	1
Turcotte, San Jose	1	Krivokrasov, Chicago	1

1996-97 SHORTHANDED GOALS

By DETROIT – (10)	By Opponents – (8)	
Shanahan 2 – Phoenix, St. Louis	Rolston, New Jersey	1
Fedorov 2 – Washington, Toronto	Poulin, Tampa Bay	1
Rouse 2 – Chicago, San Jose	Nedved, Pittsburgh	1
Taylor 1 – Buffalo	Tikkanen, Vancouver	1
Lapointe 1 – Montréal	Klemm, Colorado	1
Larionov 1 – Vancouver	Deadmarsh, Colorado	1
Sandstrom 1 – Edmonton	Courtnall, NY Rangers	1
	Matteau, St. Louis	1

PLAYER	*WIN	INS	G-1	D-1	D-0	TIE	LEAD	TOTAL
Shanahan	7(9)	13	4	10	1	11	8	46
Fedorov	4(2)	7	4	12	2	9	7	30
Kozlov	6(2)	4	5	8	0	2	9	23
Yzerman	3(8)	5	3	6	1	3	6	22
McCarty	6(4)	5	5	6	1	3	8	19
Lapointe	1(4)	4	3	5	0	4	5	16
Lidstrom	1(7)	2	3	6	3	3	3	15
Larionov	4(7)	2	0	1	1	0	4	12
Sandstrom	2(3)	1	1	1	0	1	3	9
Draper	1(1)	3	2	2	1	0	3	8
Brown	0(1)	0	2	3	1	0	2	6
Johnson	0(2)	2	0	1	0	1	1	6
Holmstrom	0(0)	1	3	3	0	0	3	6
Fetisov	1(3)	1	1	2	1	1	2	5
Konstantinov	0(5)	0	1	1	0	0	2	5
Rouse	0(1)	2	1	2	0	0	1	4
Pushor	0(1)	1	1	2	0	1	1	4
Maltby	0(0)	0	1	2	1	0	2	3
Dandenault	0(1)	0	1	2	0	1	1	3
Taylor	0(1)	0	0	1	1	2	0	3
Murphy	1(0)	0	0	1	0	1	1	2
Kocur	1(0)	0	0	0	0	0	1	2
Ward	0(0)	2	0	0	0	0	0	2
Errey	0(0)	0	0	0	0	0	0	1
Knuble	0(0)	0	0	0	0	0	1	1
Eriksson	0(1)	0	0	0	0	0	0	0

WIN–Winning Goal   INS–Insurance Goal   G-1–Game's First Goal   D-1–Detroit's First Goal
D-0–Detroit's Only Goal   TIE–Tying Goal   LEAD–Detroit's Go-Ahead Goal
★-Figure in parentheses denotes assists on winning goals.

PLAYER	1st	2nd	3rd	OT	HOME	AWAY	MID-YEAR	TOTAL
Shanahan	14	17	14	1	22	24	20	46
Fedorov	8	12	9	1	17	13	19	30
Kozlov	9	7	6	1	9	14	14	23
Yzerman	8	9	5	0	8	14	12	22
McCarty	7	6	5	1	3	11	10	19
Lapointe	5	5	6	0	7	9	9	16
Lidstrom	5	7	3	0	9	6	7	15
Larionov	1	5	5	1	5	7	6	12
Sandstrom	1	2	5	1	4	5	0	9
Draper	3	3	2	0	1	7	3	8
Brown	2	4	0	0	3	3	6	6
Johnson	1	2	3	0	2	4	4	6
Holmstrom	4	1	1	0	2	4	2	6
Fetisov	2	2	1	0	2	3	5	5
Konstantinov	2	1	2	0	4	1	1	5
Rouse	2	1	1	0	2	2	2	4
Pushor	1	2	1	0	1	3	4	4
Maltby	1	1	1	0	3	0	0	3
Dandenault	2	0	1	0	0	3	2	3
Taylor	0	1	2	0	2	1	1	3
Murphy	0	1	0	1	2	0	0	2
Kocur	0	1	1	0	1	1	0	2
Ward	1	0	1	0	2	0	2	2
Errey	0	0	1	0	0	1	1	1
Knuble	1	0	0	0	0	1	0	1

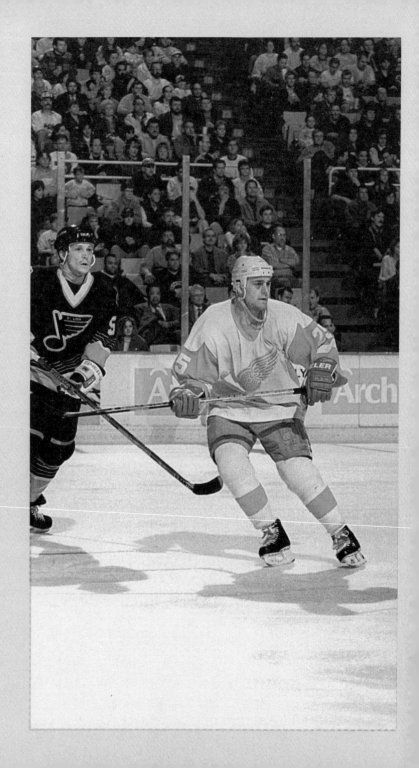

TEAM HISTORY

DETROIT NEWS

Ted Lindsay celebrates a Stanley Cup victory.

RED WINGS' HISTORY IN HOCKEYTOWN

The Detroit Red Wings concluded the 1996-97 season by capturing the club's eighth Stanley Cup championship in the franchise's history, the first since 1955. The hockey club enters its 72nd season in defense of the title and hoping to build another Cup-winning dynasty like the teams of the '50s.

While the 1996-97 team won the Cup, the 1995-96 campaign will be remembered as a season of remarkable individual and team accomplishments. The Red Wings finished atop the league with a franchise-best 131 points, shattering the previous club record of 103 set in 1992-93, and capturing the Presidents' Trophy for the second straight year. That mark also set a new NHL record for most wins in the regular season with 62 victories. In addition, the club clinched their third consecutive Western Conference regular-season title and their third straight Central Division title. One secret to the club's success was its commitment to defensive responsibility, boasting the fewest goals against in the league. Although Detroit was eliminated from the Western Conference Finals in six games by the eventual Stanley Cup winners, Colorado Avalanche, this team had an otherwise outstanding year.

The 70th anniversary season was also one for individual milestones such as Scotty Bowman setting a new league record (Dec. 29, 1995 at Dallas) for most games coached (1607) passing the legendary Al Arbour. Fans had even more to celebrate as their captain, Steve Yzerman, recorded his 500th career goal (Jan. 22, 1996 vs. Colorado) making him only the 22nd NHL player to hit the 500-goal milestone.

In that same year, several Red Wings were also honored with NHL postseason award recognition. Scotty Bowman won his second career Jack Adams Award (Coach of the year), Sergei Fedorov collected his second Selke Trophy (best defensive forward), and goaltenders Chris Osgood and Mike Vernon earned the Jennings Trophy (fewest goals against). Also, Chris Osgood and Vladimir Konstantinov were named to the Second All-Star Team.

Detroit fans continued to flock to Joe Louis Arena. The club drew 819,107 in 41 home games for an average of 19,978. Entering this season, including regular season and playoffs, the Red Wings have drawn more than 19,000 for 460 of their last 462 games, including 348 in a row.

One of the most important dates in club history was June 22, 1982, when Mike and Marian Ilitch purchased a struggling franchise and transformed it into one of the NHL's best. In the

Ilitchs' 15 years as owners, the club has won six division titles (87-88, 88-89, 91-92, 93-94, '95, 95-96) and made the playoffs in that stretch, including ten of the past eleven years.

Detroit's love affair with hockey goes back to the last 1920's and has continued to the present at Joe Louis Arena, which opened for hockey Dec. 27, 1979. The area has some of North America's finest youth programs, producing future players and cultivating life-long fans.

Pro hockey arrived in Detroit Sept. 25, 1926, when a group of Detroit businessmen purchased an NHL franchise and stocked it with players from the Victoria Cougars of the Western Hockey League. The club was called the Detroit Cougars but played its inaugural season across the Detroit River in Canada at Windsor's Border Cities Arena.

The Cougars' first NHL game was Nov. 18, 1926, in which they dropped a 2-0 decision to the Boston Bruins. Detroit won the next game, 4-2 against the New York Americans, but finished last with a 12-28-4 record.

The Cougars moved into legendary Olympia Stadium on Grand River Avenue for their second season and played the first game there Nov. 22, 1927. Detroit's Johnny Sheppard scored the first goal, but the Cougars suffered a 2-1 loss to the defending champion Ottawa Senators. Detroit registered its first home victory and shutout Nov. 27 as goaltender "Hap" Holmes posted a 2-0 decision over the Montréal Canadiens.

Arriving in 1927-28 was the club's new general manager Jack Adams, whose 35-year career with the club left an indelible mark on hockey in Detroit and earned him a spot in the Hockey Hall of Fame.

In 1928-29, Detroit finished third and made the first of 44 playoff appearances in 69 seasons. The team changed its name to Falcons in 1930 when some Detroit media members thought a change might bring some luck to a club that had missed the playoffs the previous season. No luck, however, as Detroit again missed the playoffs, although the Falcons did gain a berth in 1931-32.

In the summer of 1932, American industrialist James Norris bought the franchise and renamed it Red Wings. He imported the name from Canada, where he had played hockey for a club called the Winged Wheelers in the Montréal Athletic Association. That team's insignia — a winged wheel — struck Norris as a natural for a club representing the Motor City. The logo became an automobile tire with a flying wing attached and has remained the same except for minor artistic variations.

The Red Wings became an NHL power under Norris and Adams. In 1933-34, they won the first of 14 regular-season NHL titles and reached the Stanley Cup final for the first time before bowing to the Chicago Blackhawks, three games to one, in a best-of-five series.

The Red Wings dominated the NHL in 1935-36 and 36-37, winning a pair of regular-season championships and their first two Stanley Cup titles — a prize the club has now won eight times. Detroit won its third championship in 1943, but the best was yet to come.

Adams assembled a team in the late '40s that ranks among the NHL's greatest dynasties. Between the 1948-49 and 54-55 seasons, the Red Wings won seven consecutive regular-season titles — still a league record — and four Stanley Cup championships.

Detroit remained strong through the late 1950s and into the 60s, winning two more regular-season titles but bowing four times in the Cup final during that span.

The Norris family retained ownership of the team for 50 years. The elder Norris served as club president until his death in 1952 and was succeeded by his daughter, Marguerite. Norris' son, Bruce, took over as president in 1955 and remained until selling the club to Mike and Marian Ilitch in '82.

The Red Wings have featured some of the game's brightest stars — including the greatest of them all, Gordie Howe — and continue to showcase some of the world's most talented players. Forty-six people associated with the club are in the Hockey Hall of Fame. Detroit players have been voted to postseason NHL All-Star teams 94 times, and club players, coaches and executives have won 54 individual league trophies.

Season	GP	W	L	T	PTS	GF	GA	Position	Coach
1926-27	44	12	28	4	28	76	105	5th ×	Art Duncan/ Duke Keats*
1927-28	44	19	19	6	44	88	79	4th ×	Jack Adams
1928-29	44	19	16	9	47	72	63	3rd	Adams
1929-30	44	14	24	6	34	117	133	4th ×	Adams
1930-31	44	16	21	7	39	102	105	4th ×	Adams
1931-32	48	18	20	10	46	95	108	3rd	Adams
1932-33	48	25	15	8	58	111	93	2nd	Adams
1933-34	48	24	14	10	58	113	98	1st	Adams
1934-35	48	19	22	7	45	127	114	4th ×	Adams
1935-36	48	24	16	8	56	124	103	1st-**SC**	Adams
1936-37	48	25	14	9	59	128	102	1st-**SC**	Adams
1937-38	48	12	25	11	35	99	133	4th ×	Adams
1938-39	48	18	24	6	42	107	128	5th	Adams
1939-40	48	16	26	6	38	90	126	5th	Adams
1940-41	48	21	16	11	53	112	102	3rd	Adams
1941-42	48	19	25	4	42	140	147	5th	Adams
1942-43	50	25	14	11	61	169	124	1st-**SC**	Adams
1943-44	50	26	18	6	58	214	177	2nd	Adams
1944-45	50	31	14	5	67	218	161	2nd	Adams
1945-46	50	20	20	10	50	146	159	4th	Adams
1946-47	60	22	27	11	55	190	193	4th	Adams
1947-48	60	30	18	12	72	187	148	2nd	Tom Ivan
1948-49	60	34	19	7	75	195	145	1st	Ivan
1949-50	70	37	19	14	88	229	164	1st-**SC**	Ivan
1950-51	70	44	13	13	101	236	139	1st	Ivan
1951-52	70	44	14	12	100	215	133	1st-**SC**	Ivan
1952-53	70	36	16	18	90	222	133	1st	Ivan
1953-54	70	37	19	14	88	191	132	1st-**SC**	Ivan
1954-55	70	42	17	11	95	204	134	1st-**SC**	Jimmy Skinner
1955-56	70	30	24	16	76	183	148	2nd	Skinner
1956-57	70	38	20	12	88	198	157	1st	Skinner
1957-58	70	29	29	12	70	176	207	3rd	Skinner/ Sid Abel
1958-59	70	25	37	8	58	167	218	6th ×	Abel
1959-60	70	26	29	15	67	186	197	4th	Abel
1960-61	70	25	29	16	66	195	215	4th	Abel
1961-62	70	23	33	14	60	184	219	5th ×	Abel
1962-63	70	32	25	13	77	200	194	4th	Abel
1963-64	70	30	29	11	71	191	204	4th	Abel
1964-65	70	40	23	7	87	224	175	1st	Abel
1965-66	70	31	27	12	74	221	194	4th	Abel
1966-67	70	27	39	4	58	212	241	5th ×	Abel
1967-68	74	27	35	12	66	245	257	6th ×	Abel
1968-69	76	33	31	12	78	239	221	5th ×	Bill Gadsby
1969-70	76	40	21	15	95	246	199	3rd	Gadsby/ Abel
1970-71	78	22	45	11	55	209	308	7th ×	Ned Harkness/ Doug Barkley
1971-72	78	33	35	10	76	261	262	5th ×	Barkley/ JohnnyWilson
1972-73	78	37	29	12	86	265	243	5th ×	Wilson

Season	GP	W	L	T	PTS	GF	GA	Position	Coach
1973-74	78	29	39	10	68	255	319	6th ×	Ted Garvin/ Alex Delvecchio
1974-75	80	23	45	12	58	259	335	4th ×	Delvecchio
1975-76	80	26	44	10	62	226	300	4th ×	Barkley/ Delvecchio/ Billy Dea*
1976-77	80	16	55	9	41	'183	309	5th ×	Dea*/ Larry Wilson
1977-78	80	32	34	14	78	252	266	2nd	Bobby Kromm
1978-79	80	23	41	16	62	252	295	5th ×	Kromm
1979-80	80	26	43	11	63	268	306	5th ×	Kromm/ Marcel Pronovost*
1980-81	80	19	43	18	56	252	339	5th ×	Ted Lindsay/ Wayne Maxner
1981-82	80	21	47	12	54	270	351	6th ×	Maxner/ Dea
1982-83	80	21	44	15	57	263	344	5th ×	Nick Polano
1983-84	80	31	42	7	69	298	323	3rd	Polano
1984-85	80	27	41	12	66	313	357	3rd	Polano
1985-86	80	17	57	6	40	266	415	5th ×	Harry Neale/ Brad Park
1986-87	80	34	36	10	78	260	274	2nd	Jacques Demers
1987-88	80	41	28	11	93	322	269	1st	Demers
1988-89	80	34	34	12	80	313	316	1st	Demers
1989-90	80	28	38	14	70	288	323	5th ×	Demers
1990-91	80	34	38	8	76	273	298	3rd	Bryan Murray
1991-92	80	43	25	12	98	320	256	1st	Murray
1992-93	84	47	28	9	103	369	280	2nd	Murray
1993-94	84	46	30	8	100	356	275	1st	Scotty Bowman
1995	48	33	11	4	70	180	117	1st	Bowman
1995-96	82	62	13	7	131	325	181	1st	Bowman
1996-97	82	38	26	18	94	253	197	3rd -SC	Bowman
TOTALS	4664	1966	1962	736	4668	14410	14404		

×-Out of playoffs
SC-Won Stanley Cup
*-Interim coach

1st-19   2nd-8   3rd-8   4th-14   5th-16   6th-4   7th-1

──RED WINGS' ALL-TIME HOME-AWAY RECORDS──

	HOME						AWAY		
Won	Lost	Tied	Pts	Season	Games	Won	Lost	Tied	Pts
6	16	0	12	1926-27	44	6	12	4	16
9	10	3	21	1927-28	44	10	9	3	23
11	6	5	27	1928-29	44	8	10	4	20
9	10	3	21	1929-30	44	5	14	3	13
10	7	5	25	1930-31	44	6	14	2	14
15	3	6	36	1931-32	48	3	17	4	10
17	3	4	38	1932-33	48	8	12	4	20
15	5	4	34	1933-34	48	9	9	6	24
11	8	5	27	1934-35	48	8	14	2	18
14	5	5	33	1935-46	48	10	11	3	23
14	5	5	33	1936-37	48	11	9	4	26
8	10	6	22	1937-38	48	4	15	5	13
14	8	2	30	1938-39	48	4	16	4	12
11	10	3	25	1939-40	48	5	16	3	13
14	5	5	33	1940-41	48	7	11	6	20
14	7	3	31	1941-42	48	5	18	1	11
16	4	5	37	1942-43	50	9	10	6	24
18	5	2	38	1943-44	50	8	13	4	20
19	5	1	39	1944-45	50	12	9	4	28
16	5	4	36	1945-46	50	4	15	6	14
14	10	6	34	1946-47	60	8	17	5	21
16	9	5	37	1947-48	60	14	9	7	35
21	6	3	45	1948-49	60	13	13	4	30
19	9	7	45	1949-50	70	18	10	7	43
25	3	7	57	1950-51	70	19	10	6	44
24	7	4	52	1951-52	70	20	7	8	48
20	5	10	50	1952-51	70	19	11	8	40
24	4	7	55	1953-54	70	13	15	7	33
25	5	5	55	1954-55	70	17	12	6	40
21	6	8	50	1955-56	70	9	18	8	26
23	7	5	51	1956-57	70	15	13	7	37
16	11	8	40	1957-58	70	12	18	4	30
13	17	5	31	1958-59	70	12	20	3	27
18	14	3	39	1959-60	70	8	15	12	28
15	13	7	37	1960-61	70	10	16	9	29
17	11	7	41	1961-62	70	6	22	7	19
19	10	6	44	1962-63	70	13	15	7	33
23	9	3	49	1963-64	70	7	20	8	22
25	7	3	53	1964-65	70	15	16	4	34
20	8	7	47	1965-66	70	11	19	5	27
21	11	3	45	1966-67	70	6	28	1	13
18	15	4	40	1967-68	74	9	20	8	26
23	8	7	53	1968-69	76	10	23	5	25

HOME						AWAY			
Won	Lost	Tied	Pts	Season	Games	Won	Lost	Tied	Pts
20	11	7	47	1969-70	76	20	10	8	48
17	15	7	41	1970-71	78	5	30	4	14
25	11	3	53	1971-72	78	8	24	7	23
22	12	5	49	1972-73	78	15	17	7	37
21	12	6	48	1973-74	78	8	27	4	20
17	17	6	40	1974-75	80	6	28	6	18
17	15	8	42	1975-76	80	9	29	2	20
12	22	6	30	1976-77	80	4	33	3	11
22	11	7	51	1977-78	80	10	23	7	27
15	17	8	38	1978-79	80	8	24	8	24
14	21	5	33	1979-80	80	12	22	6	30
16	15	9	41	1980-81	80	3	28	9	15
15	19	6	36	1981-82	80	6	28	6	18
14	19	7	35	1982-83	80	7	25	8	22
18	20	2	38	1983-84	80	13	22	5	31
19	14	7	45	1984-85	80	8	27	5	21
10	26	4	24	1985-86	80	7	31	2	16
20	14	6	46	1986-87	80	14	22	4	32
24	10	6	54	1987-88	80	17	18	5	39
20	14	6	46	1988-89	80	14	20	6	34
20	14	6	46	1989-90	80	8	24	8	24
26	14	0	52	1990-91	80	8	24	8	24
24	12	4	52	1991-92	80	19	13	8	46
25	14	3	53	1992-93	84	22	14	6	50
23	13	6	52	1993-94	84	23	17	2	48
17	4	3	37	1995	48	16	7	1	33
36	3	2	74	1995-96	82	26	10	5	57
20	12	9	49	1996-97	82	18	14	9	45

Detroit Red Wings®

—DETROIT RED WINGS VS. ALL NHL TEAMS—

SINCE 1926-27 SEASON

Detroit Red Wings vs.	GP	W	L	T	PTS
Chicago Blackhawks	635	317	239	79	713
Toronto Maple Leafs	618	264	263	91	619
New York Rangers	558	247	208	103	597
Boston Bruins	561	239	227	95	573
Montréal Canadiens	552	190	266	96	476
+ Dallas Stars	183	77	79	27	181
St. Louis Blues	181	64	87	30	158
Pittsburgh Penguins	119	53	51	15	121
Vancouver Canucks	103	49	40	14	112
Los Angeles Kings	131	46	62	23	115
Philadelphia Flyers	107	38	48	21	97
★ Calgary Flames	91	37	40	14	88
Washington Capitals	82	34	33	15	83
Buffalo Sabres	96	34	50	12	80
New York Islanders	79	37	38	4	78
# New Jersey Devils	69	29	30	10	68
✗ Phoenix Coyotes	70	30	26	14	74
☆ Colorado Avalanche	53	24	25	4	52
Edmonton Oilers	60	25	27	8	58
Hartford Whalers	49	21	21	7	49
San Jose Sharks	23	20	2	1	41
Tampa Bay Lightning	14	11	2	1	23
Anaheim Mighty Ducks	16	9	3	4	22
Ottawa Senators	8	4	3	1	9
Florida Panthers	6	4	2	0	8
(a) Defunct Teams	282	125	103	54	304
TOTALS	**4646**	**2028**	**1975**	**743**	**4799**

HOME

Detroit Red Wings vs.	GP	W	L	T	PTS
Chicago Blackhawks	317	195	93	29	419
Toronto Maple Leafs	310	163	101	46	372
New York Rangers	280	160	75	45	365
Boston Bruins	280	152	76	52	356
Montréal Canadiens	276	127	96	53	307
+ Dallas Stars	91	47	31	13	107
Pittsburgh Penguins	60	38	11	11	87
St. Louis Blues	89	37	38	15	89
Vancouver Canucks	52	30	15	7	67
Los Angeles Kings	65	28	27	10	66
Philadelphia Flyers	53	25	18	10	60
Buffalo Sabres	49	26	18	5	57
★ Calgary Flames	45	23	14	8	54
Washington Capitals	42	18	13	11	47
New York Islanders	39	21	16	2	44
# New Jersey Devils	34	19	13	2	40

HOME, cont'd.

Detroit Red Wings vs.	GP	W	L	T	PTS
✗ Phoenix Coyotes	36	19	13	4	42
Hartford Whalers	25	12	7	6	30
☆ Colorado Avalanche	26	15	10	1	31
Edmonton Oilers	30	14	13	3	31
San Jose Sharks	11	11	0	0	22
Anaheim Mighty Ducks	8	5	1	2	12
Tampa Bay Lightning	6	5	1	0	10
Ottawa Senators	4	2	2	0	4
Florida Panthers	3	2	1	0	4
(a) Defunct Teams	141	76	40	25	177
TOTALS	**2372**	**1270**	**743**	**360**	**2900**

ROAD

Detroit Red Wings vs.	GP	W	L	T	PTS
Chicago Blackhawks	318	122	146	50	294
Toronto Maple Leafs	309	101	162	45	247
New York Rangers	278	87	133	58	232
Boston Bruins	281	87	151	43	217
Montréal Canadiens	276	63	170	43	169
+ Dallas Stars	92	30	48	14	74
St. Louis Blues	91	27	49	15	69
Los Angeles Kings	66	18	35	13	49
Vancouver Canucks	51	19	25	7	45
Philadelphia Flyers	54	13	30	11	37
Washington Capitals	40	16	20	4	36
Pittsburgh Penguins	59	15	40	4	34
New York Islanders	40	16	22	2	34
# New Jersey Devils	35	10	17	8	28
★ Calgary Flames	46	14	26	6	34
✗ Phoenix Coyotes	32	11	13	9	31
Buffalo Sabres	47	8	32	7	23
Edmonton Oilers	30	11	14	5	27
☆ Colorado Avalanche	27	10	14	3	21
Hartford Whalers	24	9	14	1	19
San Jose Sharks	12	9	2	1	19
Tampa Bay Lightning	8	6	1	1	13
Anaheim Mighty Ducks	8	4	2	2	10
Ottawa Senators	4	2	1	1	5
Florida Panthers	3	2	1	0	4
(a) Defunct Teams	141	48	63	30	126
TOTALS	**2372**	**758**	**1231**	**383**	**1899**

+- Formerly Minnesota North Stars.
★ - Formerly Atlanta Flames.
\# - Formerly Kansas City Scouts, Colorado Rockies.
☆ - Formerly Québec Nordiques.
✗ - Formerly Winnipeg Jets.
(a)- Includes records vs. Montréal Maroons, New York Americans, Ottawa
      Senators (1917-31), Pittsburgh Pirates, Philadelphia Quakers, St. Louis
      Eagles, California Golden Seals and Cleveland Barons.

RED WINGS' ALL-TIME COACHING RECORDS

	GC	W	L	T
ART DUNCAN, 1926-27 (First 33 games)	33	10	21	2
* DUKE KEATS, 1926-27 (Final 11 games)	11	2	7	2
JACK ADAMS, 1927-28 through 1946-47	964	413	390	161
TOMMY IVAN, 1947-48 through 1953-54	470	262	118	90
JIMMY SKINNER, 1954-55 to 1957-58 (First 38 games)	248	123	79	46
SID ABEL, 1957-58 (Final 32 games) through 1967-68& 1969-70 (Final 74 games)	810	340	338	132
BILL GADSBY, 1968-69 to1969-70 (First 2 games)	78	35	31	12
NED HARKNESS, 1970-71 (First 38 games)	38	12	22	4
DOUG BARKLEY, 1970-71 (Final 40 games), 1971-72 (First 11 games) & 1975-76 (First 26 games)	77	20	46	11
JOHNNY WILSON, 1971-72 (Final 67 games) through 1972-73	145	67	56	22
TED GARVIN, 1973-74 (First 11 games)	11	2	8	1
ALEX DELVECCHIO, 1973-74 (Final 67 games) through 1974-75 & 1975-76 (9 games)	156	53	82	21
**BILLY DEA, 1975-76 (Final 45 games), 1976-77 (First 44 games) & 1981-82 (Final 11 games)	100	32	57	11
LARRY WILSON, 1976-77 (Final 36 games)	36	3	29	4
BOBBY KROMM, 1977-78 through 1978-79, & 1979-80 (First 71 games)	231	79	111	41
***MARCEL PRONOVOST, 1979-80 (Final 9 games)	9	2	7	0
TED LINDSAY, 1980-81 (First 20 games)	20	3	14	3
WAYNE MAXNER, 1980-81 (Final 20 games) & 1981-82 (First 69 games)	129	34	68	27
NICK POLANO, 1982-83 through 1984-85	240	79	127	34
HARRY NEALE, 1985-86 (First 35 games)	35	8	23	4
BRAD PARK, 1985-86 (45 games)	45	9	36	2
JACQUES DEMERS, 1986-87 to 1989-90	320	137	136	47
BRYAN MURRAY, 1990-91 to 1992-93	244	124	91	29
SCOTTY BOWMAN, 1993-94 to present	296	179	80	37
TOTALS	**4726**	**1979**	**1975**	**751**

*-Art Duncan remained general manager/player but gave coaching duties to Duke Keats.

**-Alex Delvecchio officially was head coach late in 75-76 season and early 76-77, but Billy Dea worked behind bench. In 81-82, Dea replaced the fired Wayne Maxner late in season.

***-Ted Lindsay officially was head coach but Marcel Pronovost worked behind bench.

——RED WINGS' ALL-TIME GENERAL MANAGERS——

ART DUNCAN, 1926-27
JACK ADAMS, 1927-28 through 1962-63
SID ABEL, 1963-64 to 1970-71 (First 38 games)
NED HARKNESS, 1970-71 (Final 40 games) through 1973-74
ALEX DELVECCHIO, 1974-75 to 1976-77 (First 70 games)
TED LINDSAY, 1976-77 (Final 10 games) through 1979-80
JIMMY SKINNER, 1980-81 through 1981-82
JIM DEVELLANO, 1982-83 to 1989-90
BRYAN MURRAY, 1990-91 to 1993-94
JIM DEVELLANO, 1994-95 to 1996-97 (Senior Vice-President/Hockey Operations)
KEN HOLLAND, 1997-98 to present

———RED WINGS' ALL-TIME TEAM CAPTAINS———

1926-27 — Art Duncan	1963-64 — Alex Delvecchio
1927-28 — Reg Noble	1964-65 — Alex Delvecchio
1928-29 — Reg Noble	1965-66 — Alex Delvecchio
1929-30 — Reg Noble	1966-67 — Alex Delvecchio
1930-31 — George Hay	1967-68 — Alex Delvecchio
1931-32 — Carson Cooper	1968-69 — Alex Delvecchio
1932-33 — Larry Aurie	1969-70 — Alex Delvecchio
1933-34 — Herbie Lewis	1970-71 — Alex Delvecchio
1934-35 — Ebbie Goodfellow	1971-72 — Alex Delvecchio
1935-36 — Doug Young	1972-73 — Alex Delvecchio
1936-37 — Doug Young	1973-74 — Alex Delvecchio, Nick Libett,
1937-38 — Doug Young	Red Berenson, Gary Bergman,
1938-39 — Ebbie Goodfellow	Ted Harris, Mickey Redmond,
1939-40 — Ebbie Goodfellow	Larry Johnston
1940-41 — Ebbie Goodfellow	1974-75 — Marcel Dionne
1941-42 — Ebbie Goodfellow, Syd Howe	1975-76 — Danny Grant, Terry Harper
1942-43 — Sid Abel	1976-77 — Danny Grant, Dennis Polonich
1943-44 — Mud Bruneteau, Bill Hollett	1977-78 — Dan Maloney, Dennis Hextall
1944-45 — Bill Hollett	1978-79 — Dennis Hextall, Nick Libett,
1945-46 — Bill Hollett, Sid Abel	Paul Woods
1946-47 — Sid Abel	1979-80 — Dale McCourt
1947-48 — Sid Abel	1980-81 — Errol Thompson, Reed Larson
1948-49 — Sid Abel	1981-82 — Reed Larson
1949-50 — Sid Abel	1982-83 — Danny Gare
1950-51 — Sid Abel	1983-84 — Danny Gare
1951-52 — Sid Abel	1984-85 — Danny Gare
1952-53 — Ted Lindsay	1985-86 — Danny Gare
1953-54 — Ted Lindsay	1986-87 — Steve Yzerman
1954-55 — Ted Lindsay	1987-88 — Steve Yzerman
1955-56 — Ted Lindsay	1988-89 — Steve Yzerman
1956-57 — Red Kelly	1989-90 — Steve Yzerman
1957-58 — Red Kelly	1990-91 — Steve Yzerman
1958-59 — Gordie Howe	1991-92 — Steve Yzerman
1959-60 — Gordie Howe	1992-93 — Steve Yzerman
1960-61 — Gordie Howe	1993-94 — Steve Yzerman
1961-62 — Gordie Howe	1995 — Steve Yzerman
1962-63 — Alex Delvecchio	1995-96 — Steve Yzerman
	1996-97 — Steve Yzerman

SEASON

MOST POINTS – 131 – 1995-96
FEWEST POINTS – 28 – 1926-27
MOST WINS – 62 – 1995-96
FEWEST WINS – 12 – 1926-27, 37-38
MOST DEFEATS – 57 – 1985-86
FEWEST DEFEATS – 11 – 1995
MOST TIES – 18 – 1952-53, 80-81, 96-97
FEWEST TIES – 4 – 1926-27, 66-67, 95
MOST WINS, HOME – 36 – 1995-96
MOST DEFEATS, HOME – 26 – 1985-86
MOST TIES, HOME – 10 – 1952-53
MOST WINS, ROAD – 26 – 1995-96
MOST DEFEATS, ROAD – 33 – 1976-77
MOST GOALS FOR – 369 – 1992-93
MOST GOALS AGAINST – 415 – 1985-86
FEWEST GOALS FOR – 72 – 1928-29
FEWEST GOALS AGAINST – 63 – 1928-29
MOST POWER-PLAY GOALS FOR – 113 – 1992-93
MOST POWER-PLAY GOALS AGAINST – 111 – 1985-86
MOST SHORTHANDED GOALS FOR – 22 – 1993-94
MOST SHORTHANDED GOALS AGAINST – 15 – 1984-85
MOST PENALTY MINUTES – 2393 – 1985-86
MOST SHUTOUTS – 13 – 1953-54
FEWEST SHUTOUTS – 0 – 1980-81, 81-82, 84-85
LONGEST UNBEATEN STREAK – 15 games (8 wins, 7 ties) – Nov. 27-Dec. 28, 1952
LONGEST WINNING STREAK – 9 games (four times)
  – Mar. 3-21, 1951; Feb. 27-Mar. 20, 1955;
  – Dec. 12-31, 1995; Mar. 3-22, 1996
LONGEST UNBEATEN STREAK, HOME – 18 games (twice)
  – (13 wins, 5 ties) Nov. 19, 1931-Feb. 28, 1932;
  – (13 wins, 5 ties) Dec. 26-Mar. 20, 1955
LONGEST WINNING STREAK, HOME – 14 games – Jan. 21-Mar. 25, 1965
LONGEST UNBEATEN STREAK, ROAD – 15 games (10 wins, 5 ties)
  – Oct. 18-Dec. 20, 1951
LONGEST WINNING STREAK, ROAD – 7 games (twice)
  – Mar. 25-Apr. 14, 1995;
  – Feb. 18-Mar. 20, 1996
LONGEST UNBEATEN STREAK, START OF SEASON – 10 games (8 wins, 2 ties)
  – Oct. 11-Nov. 4, 1962
LONGEST WINNING STREAK, START OF SEASON – 6 games
  – Oct. 7-22, 1972
LONGEST HOME UNBEATEN STREAK, START OF SEASON – 17 games (13 wins, 4 ties)
  – Oct. 11-Dec. 25, 1956
LONGEST HOME WINNING STREAK, START OF SEASON – 6 games (twice)
  – Oct. 14-Nov. 4, 1962;
  – Oct. 10-26, 1990
LONGEST ROAD UNBEATEN STREAK, START OF SEASON – 15 games (11 wins, 4 ties)
  – Oct. 18-Dec. 20, 1951
LONGEST ROAD WINNING STREAK, START OF SEASON – 4 games (twice)
  – Oct. 27-Nov. 12, 1949;
  – Oct. 18-Nov. 3, 1951
LONGEST WINLESS STREAK – 19 games (18 losses, 1 tie) – Feb. 26-Apr. 3, 1977
LONGEST LOSING STREAK – 14 games – Feb. 24-Mar. 25, 1982
LONGEST WINNING STREAK, HOME – 10 games (9 losses, 1 tie)
  – Dec. 11, 1985-Jan. 18, 1986
LONGEST LOSING STREAK, HOME – 7 games – Feb. 20-Mar. 25, 1982
LONGEST WINLESS STREAK, ROAD – 26 games (23 losses, 3 ties)
  – Dec. 15, 1976-Apr. 3, 1977
LONGEST LOSING STREAK, ROAD – 14 games – Oct. 19-Dec. 21, 1966

LONGEST WINLESS STREAK, START OF SEASON – 10 games (7 losses, 3 ties)
   – Oct. 8-26, 1975
LONGEST LOSING STREAK, START OF SEASON – 5 games – Oct. 10-18, 1980
LONGEST HOME WINLESS STREAK, START OF SEASON – 5 games (twice)
   – Oct. 8-25, 1975 (2 losses, 3 ties);
   – Oct. 10-23, 1985 (1 loss, 4 ties)
LONGEST HOME LOSING STREAK, START OF SEASON – 3 games (four times)
   – Nov. 14-26, 1929; Nov. 6-13, 1938; Oct. 10-17, 1957; Oct. 6-20, 1982
LONGEST ROAD WINLESS STREAK, START OF SEASON – 19 games (18 losses, 1 tie)
   – Oct. 19, 1966-Jan. 14, 1967
LONGEST ROAD LOSING STREAK, START OF SEASON – 14 games
   – Oct. 19-Dec. 21, 1966
MOST PLAYERS – 45 – 1990-91

GAME

MOST GOALS FOR – 15
   – vs. N.Y. Rangers at Detroit, Jan. 23, 1944; Detroit 15, Rangers 0
MOST GOALS AGAINST – 13
   – by Toronto at Toronto, Jan. 2, 1971; Toronto 13, Detroit 0
MOST POINTS – 37 vs. N.Y. Rangers at Detroit, Jan. 23, 1944
MOST GOALS, ONE PERIOD – 8 vs. N.Y. Rangers at Detroit, Jan. 23, 1944
MOST POINTS, ONE PERIOD – 22 vs. N.Y. Rangers at Detroit, Jan. 23, 1944
FASTEST TWO GOALS, START OF GAME – 37 seconds apart
   – Dec. 4, 1987 vs. Chicago (Tim Higgins, STEVE YZERMAN)
FASTEST TWO GOALS – 7 seconds apart
   – Nov. 5, 1936 vs. Toronto (Syd Howe, Larry Aurie);
   – Nov. 25, 1987 vs. Winnipeg (Jeff Sharples, Brent Ashton)
FASTEST THREE GOALS – 28 seconds apart
   – Nov. 15, 1944 vs. Toronto (Hal Jackson, Steve Wochy, Don Grosso)
FASTEST FOUR GOALS – 2:25 apart
   – Nov. 7, 1991 vs. St. Louis
      (Shawn Burr, Jimmy Carson, NICKLAS LIDSTROM, Paul Ysebaert)
FASTEST FIVE GOALS – 4:54 apart
   – Nov. 25, 1987 vs. Winnipeg
      (Gerard Gallant, Adam Oates, Mel Bridgman, Jeff Sharples, Brent Ashton)
MOST POWER-PLAY GOALS – 6 vs N.Y. Rangers, Nov. 5, 1942; Detroit 12, Rangers 5
MOST POWER-PLAY GOALS, ONE PERIOD – 4
   – vs. N.Y. Rangers, Nov. 5, 1942; Detroit 12, Rangers 5
MOST POWER-PLAY GOALS AGAINST – 5 (four times) –
   – vs. Buffalo, Feb. 1, 1987, Buffalo 6, Detroit 1;
   – vs. Chicago, Nov. 11, 1987, Chicago 6, Detroit 3;
   – vs. St. Louis, Jan. 25, 1991, St. Louis 9, Detroit 4;
   – vs. Toronto, Dec. 9, 1992, Toronto 5, Detroit 3
MOST POWER-PLAY GOALS AGAINST, ONE PERIOD – 3 (several times)
   – Last time vs. St. Louis, Nov. 25, 1992, Detroit 11, St. Louis 6
MOST SHORTHANDED GOALS – 3 (four times)
   – vs. Minnesota, Jan. 9, 1990 (Shawn Burr 2, STEVE YZERMAN), Detroit 9, Minnesota 0;
   – vs. Minnesota, Apr. 14, 1992
      (STEVE YZERMAN 2, SERGEI FEDOROV), Detroit 7, Minnesota 4;
   – vs. Philadelphia, Feb. 11, 1994
      (SERGEI FEDOROV, VYACHESLAV KOZLOV, STEVE YZERMAN), Detroit 6, Phila. 3;
   – vs. Colorado, Mar. 22, 1996
      (STEVE YZERMAN, Keith Primeau, VIACHESLAV FETISOV)
MOST SHORTHANDED GOALS, ONE PERIOD – 2 (several times)
   – Last time vs. Colorado, Mar. 22, 1996
      (Keith Primeau, VIACHESLAV FETISOV), Detroit 7, Colorado 0
MOST SHORTHANDED GOALS AGAINST – 2 (several times)
   – Last time vs. NY Rangers, Feb. 9, 1992, Detroit 5, NY Rangers 5
MOST SHORTHANDED GOALS AGAINST, ONE PERIOD – 2 (several times)
   – Last time vs. NY Rangers, Feb. 9, 1992, Detroit 5, NY Rangers 5

ACTIVE PLAYERS IN CAPITALS

CAREER

MOST GAMES – 1687 – Gordie Howe (25 seasons)

MOST GAMES BY GOALIE – 734 – Terry Sawchuk

MOST CONSECUTIVE GAMES – 548 – Alex Delvecchio

MOST GOALS – 786 – Gordie Howe (25 seasons)

MOST ASSISTS – 1023 – Gordie Howe (25 seasons)

MOST POINTS – 1809 – Gordie Howe (25 seasons)

MOST PENALTY MINUTES – 2090 – Bob Probert

MOST SHUTOUTS – 85 – Terry Sawchuk

MOST POWER-PLAY GOALS – 211 – Gordie Howe

MOST POWER-PLAY GOALS BY DEFENSEMAN – 68 – Reed Larson

MOST SEASONS LEADING TEAM IN POWER-PLAY GOALS – 13 – Gordie Howe

MOST SHORTHANDED GOALS – 41 – STEVE YZERMAN

MOST 3-GOAL OR MORE GAMES – 18 – Gordie Howe, STEVE YZERMAN

MOST WINNING GOALS – 121 – Gordie Howe

MOST SEASONS LEADING TEAM IN WINNING GOALS – 12 – Gordie Howe

MOST ASSISTS BY GOALIE – 15 – Tim Cheveldae

SEASON

MOST GOALS – 65 – STEVE YZERMAN (1988-89)

MOST ASSISTS – 90 – STEVE YZERMAN (1988-89)

MOST POINTS – 155 – STEVE YZERMAN (1988-89)

MOST GOALS BY LINE – 140 (1988-89)
(STEVE YZERMAN, 65; Gerard Gallant, 39; Paul MacLean, 36)

MOST POINTS BY LINE – 319 (1988-89)
(STEVE YZERMAN, 155; Gerard Gallant, 93; Paul MacLean, 71)

MOST GOALS BY CENTER – 65 – STEVE YZERMAN (1988-89)

MOST GOALS BY RIGHT WING – 52
– Mickey Redmond (1972-73);
– Ray Sheppard (1993-94)

MOST GOALS BY LEFT WING – 55 – John Ogrodnick (1984-85)

MOST GOALS BY DEFENSEMAN – 27 – Reed Larson (1980-81)

MOST GOALS BY ROOKIE – 39 – STEVE YZERMAN (1983-84)

MOST GOALS BY ROOKIE DEFENSEMAN – 19 – Reed Larson (1977-78)

MOST ASSISTS BY CENTER – 90 – STEVE YZERMAN (1988-89)

MOST ASSISTS BY RIGHT WING – 59 – Gordie Howe (1968-69)

MOST ASSISTS BY LEFT WING – 55 – Ted Lindsay (1949-50, 56-57)

MOST ASSISTS BY DEFENSEMAN – 63 – Paul Coffey (1993-94)

MOST ASSISTS BY GOALTENDER – 5 – Tim Cheveldae (1990-91)

MOST ASSISTS BY ROOKIE – 49
– Marcel Dionne (1971-72);
– NICKLAS LIDSTROM (1991-92)

MOST ASSISTS BY ROOKIE DEFENSEMAN – 49 – NICKLAS LIDSTROM (1991-92)

MOST POINTS BY CENTER – 155 – STEVE YZERMAN (1988-89)

MOST POINTS BY RIGHT WING – 103 – Gordie Howe (1968-69)

MOST POINTS BY LEFT WING – 105 – John Ogrodnick (1984-85)

MOST POINTS BY DEFENSEMAN – 77 – Paul Coffey (1993-94)

MOST POINTS BY ROOKIE – 87 – STEVE YZERMAN (1983-84)

MOST POINTS BY ROOKIE DEFENSEMAN – 60
 – Reed Larson (1977-78);
 – NICKLAS LIDSTROM (1991-92)

MOST POWER-PLAY GOALS – 21
 – Mickey Redmond (1973-74);
 – Dino Ciccarelli (1992-93)

MOST POWER-PLAY GOALS BY DEFENSEMAN – 11 – Reed Larson (1985-86)

MOST POWER-PLAY GOALS BY ROOKIE – 13 – STEVE YZERMAN (1983-84)

MOST SHORTHANDED GOALS – 10 – Marcel Dionne (1974-75)

MOST WINNING GOALS – 11 – SERGEI FEDOROV (1995-96)

MOST WINNING GOALS BY DEFENSEMAN – 5
 – Red Kelly (1949-50);
 – Reed Larson (1983-84)

MOST WINNING GOALS BY ROOKIE – 6 – Alex Delvecchio (1951-52)

LONGEST GOAL STREAK – 9 games
 – STEVE YZERMAN (12 goals, Nov. 18-Dec. 5, 1988; 14 goals, Jan. 29-Feb. 12, 1992)

LONGEST GOAL STREAK, START OF SEASON – 6 games
 – STEVE YZERMAN (6 goals, Oct. 6-18, 1988)

LONGEST POINT STREAK – 28 games
 – STEVE YZERMAN (29 goals, 36 assists, 65 points, Nov. 1-Jan. 4, 1988-89)

MOST SHOTS ON GOAL – 388 – STEVE YZERMAN (1988-89)

MOST PENALTY MINUTES – 398 – Bob Probert (1987-88)

MOST GAMES BY GOALIE – 72 – Tim Cheveldae (1991-92)

MOST MINUTES PLAYED BY GOALIE – 4236 – Tim Cheveldae (1991-92)

MOST WINS BY GOALIE – 44 – Terry Sawchuk (1950-51, 51-52)

LONGEST WINNING STREAK BY GOALIE – 13
 – CHRIS OSGOOD (Jan. 30-Mar. 20, 1996)

LONGEST UNBEATEN STREAK BY GOALIE – 21
 – CHRIS OSGOOD (19 wins, 2 ties, Jan. 10-Mar. 27, 1996)

BEST GOALS-AGAINST AVERAGE BY GOALIE – 1.43 – Dolly Dolson (1928-29)

MOST SHUTOUTS BY GOALIE – 12
 – Terry Sawchuk (1951-52, 53-54, 54-55);
 – Glenn Hall (1955-56)

MOST CONSECUTIVE SHUTOUTS BY GOALIE – 3
 – Terry Sawchuk
   (1954 – 1-0 Nov. 7 vs. N.Y. Rangers, 1-0 Nov. 11 vs. Toronto, 1-0 Nov. 13 at Toronto);
 – Glenn Hall
   (1955 – 2-0 Dec. 11 vs. N.Y. Rangers, 4-0 Dec. 15 vs. Toronto, 2-0 Dec. 18 vs. Montréal);
 – Jim Rutherford
   (1975-76 – 4-0 Dec. 31 vs. Washington, 1-0 Jan. 3 at Toronto, 5-0 Jan. 8 vs. Minnesota)

MOST GAMES BY ROOKIE GOALIE – 70
 – Terry Sawchuk (1950-51);
 – Glenn Hall (1955-56);
 – Roger Crozier (1964-75)

MOST VICTORIES BY ROOKIE GOALIE – 44 – Terry Sawchuk (1950-51)

MOST MINUTES PLAYED BY ROOKIE GOALIE – 4200
 – Terry Sawchuk (1950-51);
 – Glenn Hall (1955-56)

BEST GOALS-AGAINST AVERAGE BY ROOKIE GOALIE – 1.43 – Dolly Dolson (1928-29)

MOST SHUTOUTS BY ROOKIE GOALIE – 11 – Terry Sawchuk (1950-51)

GAME

MOST GOALS – 6 – Syd Howe (Feb. 3, 1944; Detroit 12, N.Y. Rangers 2 at Detroit)

MOST ASSISTS – #7 – Billy Taylor (Mar. 16, 1947; Detroit 10, Chicago 6 at Chicago)

MOST POINTS – 7
  – Carl Liscombe (3 goals, 4 assists) vs. N.Y. Rangers at Detroit, Nov. 5, 1942, Detroit 12, N.Y. 5;
  – Don Grosso (1 goal, 6 assists) vs. N.Y. Rangers at Detroit, Feb. 3, 1944, Detroit 12, N.Y. 2;
  – Billy Taylor (7 assists) at Chicago, March 16, 1947, Detroit 10, Chicago 6.

MOST GOALS, ONE PERIOD – 3 (Several Players)
Active Red Wings:
  – STEVE YZERMAN (Mar. 30, 1985, Detroit 6, Vancouver 5);
  – YZERMAN (Jan. 3, 1988, Detroit 4, Winnipeg 4);
  – YZERMAN (Nov. 17, 1990, Detroit 8, Toronto 4)
  – BRENDAN SHANAHAN (Feb. 12, 1997, Detroit 7, San Jose 1)

MOST POWER-PLAY GOALS – 3
  – Ted Lindsay (vs. Montréal, Mar. 20, 1955, Detroit 6, Montréal 0);
  – Jimmy Carson (vs. Toronto, Dec. 27, 1989, Detroit 7, Toronto 7)

MOST POWER-PLAY GOALS, ONE PERIOD – 3
  – Jimmy Carson (Dec. 27, 1989; Detroit 7, Toronto 7)

MOST SHORTHANDED GOALS – 2
  – Shawn Burr (Jan. 9, 1990; Detroit 9, Minnesota 0);
  – STEVE YZERMAN (Apr. 14, 1992; Detroit 7, Minnesota 4);
  – YZERMAN (Apr. 8, 1993; Detroit 9, Tampa Bay 1)

MOST SHORTHANDED GOALS, ONE PERIOD – 2
  – Shawn Burr (Jan. 9, 1990; Detroit 9, Minnesota 0)

MOST ASSISTS, ONE PERIOD – 4
  – Joe Carveth (Jan. 23, 1944; Detroit 15, N.Y. Rangers 0)

MOST POINTS, ONE PERIOD – 4
  – Joe Carveth (Jan. 23, 1944; Detroit 15, N.Y. Rangers 0);
  – Mickey Redmond (Oct. 21, 1973; Detroit 11, California 2);
  – John Ogrodnick (Dec. 4, 1984; Detroit 7, Toronto 6);
  – STEVE YZERMAN (Nov. 17, 1990; Detroit 8, Toronto 4);
  – SERGEI FEDOROV (Jan. 21, 1992; Detroit 7, Philadelphia 3)

FASTEST GOAL, START OF GAME & PERIOD – 6 seconds
  – Henry Boucha (Jan. 28, 1973; Detroit 4, Montréal 2)

FASTEST TWO GOALS – 8 seconds apart
  – Don Grosso (Mar. 19, 1942; Detroit 6, Chicago 4)

FASTEST THREE GOALS – 1:52 apart
  – Carl Liscombe (Mar. 13, 1938; Detroit 5, Chicago 1)

MOST GOALS BY ROOKIE, FIRST NHL GAME – 2
  – Chris Cichocki (Oct. 10, 1985; Detroit 6, Minnesota 6)

MOST ASSISTS BY ROOKIE, FIRST NHL GAME – 4#
  – Earl Reibel (Oct. 8, 1953; Detroit 4, N.Y. Rangers 1)

MOST POINTS BY ROOKIE, FIRST NHL GAME – 4
  – Earl Reibel (Oct. 8, 1953; Detroit 4, N.Y. Rangers 1)

MOST PENALTY MINUTES – 42
  – JOE KOCUR (Nov. 2, 1985; Detroit 5, St. Louis 5)

MOST PENALTIES – 8
  – Dennis Polonich (Mar. 24, 1976; Detroit 7, Washington 3);
  – Bob Probert (Dec. 23, 1987; Buffalo 5, Detroit 2)

MOST PENALTY MINUTES, ONE PERIOD – 37
  – JOE KOCUR (Nov. 2, 1985; Detroit 5, St. Louis 5)

MOST PENALTIES, ONE PERIOD – 6
  – JOE KOCUR (Nov. 2, 1985; Detroit 5, St. Louis 5)

#-Shares NHL record
ACTIVE PLAYERS IN CAPITALS

RANK	PLAYER	YEARS	GP	G	A	PTS
1.	Gordie Howe	25	1687	786	1023	1809
2.	**STEVE YZERMAN**	**14**	**1023**	**539**	**801**	**1340**
3.	Alex Delvecchio	24	1549	456	825	1281
4.	Norm Ullman	13	875	324	434	758
5.	Ted Lindsay	14	862	335	393	728
6.	**SERGEI FEDOROV**	**7**	**506**	**242**	**350**	**592**
7.	Reed Larson	10	708	188	382	570
8.	John Ogrodnick	9	558	265	281	546
9.	Gerard Gallant	9	563	207	260	468
10.	Nick Libett	12	861	217	250	467
11.	Sid Abel	10	571	184	279	463
12.	Red Kelly	13	846	154	297	451
13.	Syd Howe	11	793	202	231	433
14.	Marcel Dionne	4	309	139	227	366
15.	Shawn Burr	11	659	148	214	362
16.	Dale McCourt	5	341	134	203	337
17.	Bruce MacGregor	11	673	151	184	335
18.	Ebbie Goodfellow	14	575	134	190	324
19.	Herbie Lewis	11	481	148	161	309
	Mickey Redmond	6	317	177	132	309
21.	**NICKLAS LIDSTROM**	**6**	**451**	**70**	**237**	**307**
22.	Gary Bergman	11	706	60	243	303
23.	Marcel Pronovost	15	983	80	217	297
24.	Mud Bruneteau	11	399	139	138	277
	Carl Liscombe	9	378	137	140	277
26.	Larry Aurie	12	490	147	129	276
27.	Steve Chiasson	8	471	67	200	267
28.	Ray Sheppard	5	244	152	113	265
29.	Bob Probert	9	474	114	145	259
30.	Walt McKechnie	5	321	89	167	256
31.	Marty Pavelich	10	634	93	159	252
32.	Vaclav Nedomansky	5	364	108	139	247
33.	Dino Ciccarelli	4	254	107	133	240
34.	Paul Coffey	4	231	46	193	239
35.	Joe Carveth	8	325	105	133	238
36.	**VYACHESLAV KOZLOV**	**5**	**304**	**110**	**121**	**231**
37.	Keith Primeau	6	363	97	132	229
38.	Petr Klima	5	293	129	93	222
39.	Ron Duguay	3	227	90	127	217
40.	Parker McDonald	7	361	94	122	216
41.	Floyd Smith	6	347	93	122	215
	Dutch Reibel	5	306	74	141	215
43.	Metro Prystai	8	433	91	123	214
44.	Willie Huber	5	372	88	140	208
45.	Red Berenson	5	231	111	91	202
	Jimmy Carson	3	240	100	102	202
47.	Adam Oates	4	246	54	145	199
48.	Kelly Kisio	4	236	68	129	197
49.	Frank Mahovlich	4	198	108	88	196
	Paul Woods	7	501	72	124	196
51.	Danny Gare	5	306	86	95	181

52.	Johnny Wilson	6	349	79	100	179
53.	**VLADIMIR KONSTANTINOV**	**6**	**446**	**47**	**128**	**175**
54.	John Sorrell	7	347	93	79	172
55.	Don Grosso	7	234	71	99	170
	Paul Ysebaert	3	210	84	86	170
57.	Ivan Boldirev	3	183	67	95	162
58.	Dave Barr	4	223	64	96	160
	Mike Foligno	3	186	77	83	160
60.	Marty Berry	4	192	60	94	154
61.	Garry Unger	4	216	84	58	152
62.	Dean Prentice	4	230	60	89	149
63.	Paul Henderson	6	269	67	79	146
64.	Bill Hogaboam	6	221	61	84	145
65.	Jim McFadden	4	253	64	78	142
66.	Dennis Polonich	8	390	59	82	141
67.	Guy Charron	5	265	61	78	139
68.	Dan Maloney	3	177	56	81	137
69.	Vic Stasiuk	7	330	52	84	136
70.	Errol Thompson	4	200	76	58	134
	Eddie Wares	6	216	50	84	134
72.	Bill Collins	4	239	54	77	131
73.	Bill Quackenbush	6	313	40	89	129
	Greg Smith	5	352	24	105	129
75.	Danny Grant	4	174	64	62	126
76.	Bill Lochead	5	296	65	60	125
	IGOR LARIONOV	**2**	**133**	**33**	**92**	**125**
78.	Yves Racine	4	231	22	102	124
79.	Glen Skov	5	301	62	61	123
	Andre St.Laurent	3	172	50	73	123
81.	Lee Norwood	4	238	33	89	122
82.	Dennis Hextall	4	193	39	82	121
83.	Tim Ecclestone	4	191	40	80	120
84.	John Chabot	3	199	24	94	118
85.	**DARREN McCARTY**	**4**	**229**	**48**	**69**	**117**
86.	Carson Cooper	5	222	68	48	116
87.	**JOE KOCUR**	**8**	**433**	**58**	**56**	**114**
	Pete Stemkowski	4	170	51	63	114
89.	George Hay	5	204	60	52	112
	Bill Gadsby	5	323	18	94	112
91.	Michel Bergeron	4	174	64	46	110
	Dwight Foster	4	215	48	62	110
	Mark Osborne	2	160	45	65	110
94.	Jack Stewart	10	503	30	79	109
95.	Gary Couture	6	266	61	46	107
96.	Dan Labraaten	3	198	52	54	106
97.	Mike Blaisdell	3	192	44	61	105
98.	Doug Barkley	4	247	24	80	104
99.	Darren Veitch	3	153	20	83	103
	Bob Goldham	6	406	11	92	103
101.	Adam Brown	4	148	58	43	101
	Brad Park	2	147	18	83	101
103.	Tony Leswick	5	291	41	59	100
	Warren Godfrey	12	528	23	77	100

ACTIVE PLAYERS IN BOLD CAPITALS

—**RED WINGS' ALL-TIME SEASON LEADERS**—

Season	GOALS Player	Total	ASSISTS Player	Total	POINTS Player	G	A	TP	PENALTIES Player	TPM
1926-27	Sheppard	13	Sheppard	8	Sheppard	13	8	21	Sheppard	60
1927-28	Hay	22	Hay	13	Hay	22	13	35	Traub	78
1928-29	Cooper	18	Cooper	9	Cooper	18	9	27	Connors	68
1929-30	Lewis	20	Cooper	18	Cooper	18	18	36	Rockburn	97
1930-31	Goodfellow	25	Goodfellow	23	Goodfellow	25	23	48	Rockburn	118*
1931-32	Goodfellow	14	Goodfellow	16	Goodfellow	14	16	30	Noble	72
1932-33	Lewis	20	Lewis	14	Lewis	20	14	34	Evans	74
1933-34	Sorrell	21	Aurie	19	Aurie	16	19	35	Emms	51
1934-35	S. Howe	22	Aurie	29	S. Howe	22	25	47	Goodfellow	44
1935-36	Barry	21	Lewis	23	Barry	21	19	40	Goodfellow	69
1936-37	Aurie	23*	Barry	27	Barry	17	27	44	Goodfellow	43
1937-38	Liscombe	14	Barry	20	Lewis	13	18	31	Barry	34
1938-39	S. Howe	16	Barry	28	Barry	13	28	41	Conacher	39
1939-40	S. Howe	14	S. Howe	23	S. Howe	14	23	37	Orlando	54
1940-41	S. Howe	20	S. Howe	24	S. Howe	20	24	44	Orlando	99*
1941-42	Grosso	23	Abel	31	Grosso	23	30	53	Orlando	111*
1942-43	Bruneteau	23	S. Howe	35	S. Howe	20	35	55	Orlando	99*
1943-44	Liscombe	36	Liscombe	37	Liscombe	36	37	73	Jackson	76
1944-45	Carveth	26	S. Howe	36	Carveth	26	28	54	Jackson	45
1945-46	Brown	20	Carveth / Armstrong	18 / 18	Carveth	17	18	35	Stewart	73*
1946-47	Conacher	30	Taylor	46*	Taylor	17	46	63	Stewart	83
1947-48	Lindsay	33*	Abel	30	Lindsay	33	19	52	Lindsay	95
1948-49	Abel	28*	Lindsay	28	Abel / Lindsay	28 / 26	26 / 28	54 / 54	Lindsay	97
1949-50	G. Howe	35	Lindsay	55*	Lindsay	23	55	78*	Lindsay	141
1950-51	G. Howe	43*	G. Howe	43*	G. Howe	43	43	86*	Lindsay	110
1951-52	G. Howe	47*	G. Howe	39*	G. Howe	47	39	86*	Lindsay	123
1952-53	G. Howe	49*	G. Howe	46*	G. Howe	49	46	95*	Lindsay	111
1953-54	G. Howe	33	G. Howe	48*	G. Howe	33	48	81*	Lindsay	112
1954-55	G. Howe	29	Reibel	41	Reibel	25	41	66	Leswick	137
1955-56	G. Howe	38	G. Howe	41	G. Howe	38	41	79	Lindsay	161
1956-57	G. Howe	44*	Lindsay	55*	G. Howe	44	45	89*	Lindsay / Godfrey	103 / 103
1957-58	G. Howe	33	G. Howe	44	G. Howe	33	44	77	Kennedy	135
1958-59	G. Howe	32	G. Howe	46	G. Howe	32	46	78	Goegan	111
1959-60	G. Howe	28	G. Howe	45	G. Howe	28	45	73	Morrison	62
1960-61	Ullman	28	G. Howe	49	G. Howe	23	49	72	Young	108
1961-62	G. Howe	33	G. Howe	44	G. Howe	33	44	77	Gadsby	88
1962-63	G. Howe	38*	G. Howe	48	G. Howe	38	48	86*	Young	273*
1963-64	G. Howe	26	G. Howe	47	G. Howe	26	47	73	Barkley	115
1964-65	Ullman	42	G. Howe	47	Ullman	42	41	83	Lindsay	173
1965-66	Ullman / Delvecchio	31 / 31	G. Howe	46	G. Howe	29	46	75	Watson	133
1966-67	MacGregor	28	Ullman	44	Ullman	26	44	70	Bergman	129
1967-68	G. Howe	39	Delvecchio	48	G. Howe	39	43	82	Douglas	126
1968-69	F. Mahovlich	49	G. Howe	59	G. Howe	44	59	103	Baun	121

Season	GOALS Player	Total	ASSISTS Player	Total	POINTS Player	G	A	TP	PENALTIES Player	TPM
1969-70	Unger	42	Delvecchio	47	G. Howe	31	40	71	Bergman	122
1970-71	Webster	30	Webster	37	Webster	30	37	67	Bergman	149
1971-72	Redmond	42	Dionne	49	Dionne	28	49	77	Bergman	138
1972-73	Redmond	52	Delvecchio	53	Redmond	52	41	93	Johnston	169
1973-74	Redmond	51	Dionne	54	Dionne	24	53	78	Johnston	139
1974-75	Grant	50	Dionne	74	Dionne	47	74	121	Watson	238
1975-76	Bergeron	32	McKechnie	56	McKechnie	26	56	82	Watson	322
1976-77	McKechnie	25	McKechnie	34	McKechnie	24	34	59	Polonich	274
1977-78	McCourt	33	Larson	41	McCourt	33	39	72	Polonich	254
1978-79	Nedomansky	38	Larson	49	Nedomansky	38	35	73	Polonich	208
1979-80	Foligno	36	McCourt	51	McCourt	30	51	81	Huber	164
1980-81	Ogrodnick	35	McCourt	56	McCourt	30	56	86	Korn	246
1981-82	Ogrodnick	28	Osborne	41	Osborne	26	41	67	Larson	112
1982-83	Ogrodnick	41	Larson	52	Ogrodnick	41	44	85	Gare	107
1983-84	Ogrodnick	42	Park	53	Yzerman	39	48	87	Paterson	148
1984-85	Ogrodnick	55	Yzerman	59	Ogrodnick	55	50	105	Gare	163
1985-86	Ogrodnick	38	Kisio	48	Shedden	34	37	71	Kocur	377*
1986-87	Ashton	40	Yzerman	59	Yzerman	31	59	90	Kocur	276
1987-88	Yzerman	50	Yzerman	52	Yzerman	50	52	102	Probert	398*
1988-89	Yzerman	65	Yzerman	90	Yzerman	65	90	155	Gallant	230
1989-90	Yzerman	62	Yzerman	65	Yzerman	62	65	127	Kocur	268
1990-91	Yzerman	51	Yzerman	57	Yzerman	51	57	108	Probert	315
1991-92	Yzerman	45	Yzerman	58	Yzerman	45	58	103	Probert	276
1992-93	Yzerman	58	Yzerman	79	Yzerman	58	79	137	Probert	292
1992-93	Yzerman	58	Yzerman	79	Yzerman	58	79	137	Probert	292
1993-94	Fedorov	56	Fedorov	64	Fedorov	56	64	120	Probert	275
1995	Sheppard	30	Coffey	44	Coffey	14	44	58	Grimson	147
1995-96	Fedorov	39	Fedorov	68	Fedorov	39	68	107	Primeau	168
1996-97	Shanahan	47	Yzerman	63	Shanahan	47	41	88	Lapointe	167

*-League leader

GOALS

Total	Player	Season	Total	Player	Season
65	**STEVE YZERMAN**	**88-89**	35	Mud Bruneteau	43-44
62	**STEVE YZERMAN**	**89-90**		Gordie Howe	49-50
58	**STEVE YZERMAN**	**92-93**		Vaclav Nedomansky	79-80
56	**SERGEI FEDOROV**	**93-94**		John Ogrodnick	80-81
55	John Ogrodnick	84-85		Ivan Boldirev	83-84
52	Mickey Redmond	72-73		Errol Thompson	79-80
	Ray Sheppard	93-94		Paul Ysebaert	91-92
51	Mickey Redmond	73-74	34	Gerard Gallant	87-88
	STEVE YZERMAN	**90-91**		Jim Carson	91-92
50	Danny Grant	74-75		Paul Ysebaert	92-93
	STEVE YZERMAN	**87-88**		**VYACHESLAV KOZLOV**	**93-94**
49	Gordie Howe	52-53	33	Ted Lindsay	47-48
	Frank Mahovlich	68-69		Gordie Howe (3)	53-54
47	Gordie Howe	51-52			57-58
	Marcel Dionne	74-75			61-62
	BRENDAN SHANAHAN	**96-97**		Parker MacDonald	62-63
45	**STEVE YZERMAN**	**91-92**		Dale McCourt	77-78
44	Gordie Howe (2)	56-57		Ron Duguay	83-84
		68-69	32	Syd Howe	43-44
43	Gordie Howe	50-51		Ted Lindsay	52-53
42	Norm Ullman	64-65		Gordie Howe	58-59
	Garry Unger	69-70		Michel Bergeron	75-76
	Mickey Redmond	71-72		Petr Klima	85-86
	John Ogrodnick	83-84		**SERGEI FEDOROV**	**91-92**
41	John Ogrodnick	82-83		Ray Sheppard	92-93
	Dino Ciccarelli	92-93	31	Norm Ullman	65-66
40	Marcel Dionne	72-73		Alex Delvecchio	65-66
39	Gordie Howe	67-68		Gordie Howe	69-70
	STEVE YZERMAN	**83-84**		Nick Libbett	71-72
	Gerard Gallant	88-89		Andre St. Laurent	77-78
	SERGEI FEDOROV	**95-96**		**STEVE YZERMAN**	**86-87**
38	Gordie Howe (2)	55-56		**SERGEI FEDOROV**	**90-91**
		66-63		Keith Primeau	93-94
	Frank Mahovlich	69-70	30	Roy Conacher	46-47
	Vaclav Nedomansky	78-79		Ted Lindsay (2)	51-52
	Ron Duguay	84-85			56-57
	John Ogrodnick	85-86		Norm Ullman	67-68
	Gerard Gallant	86-87		Tom Webster	70-71
37	Petr Klima	87-88		Dale McCourt	79-80
36	Carl Liscombe	43-44		Dan Labraaten	79-80
	Mike Foligno	79-80		Dale McCourt	80-81
	Paul MacLean	88-89		**STEVE YZERMAN**	**84-85**
	Gerard Gallant	89-90		Petr Klima	86-87
	Ray Sheppard	91-92		Ray Sheppard	95
	STEVE YZERMAN	**95-96**		**SERGEI FEDOROV**	**96-97**
	VYACHESLAV KOZLOV	**96-96**			

ACTIVE PLAYERS IN BOLD CAPITALS

ASSISTS

Total	Player	Season
90	**STEVE YZERMAN**	**88-89**
79	**STEVE YZERMAN**	**92-93**
74	Marcel Dionne	74-75
68	**SERGEI FEDOROV**	**95-96**
65	**STEVE YZERMAN**	**89-90**
64	**SERGEI FEDOROV**	**93-94**
63	Paul Coffey	93-94
	STEVE YZERMAN	**96-97**
62	Adam Oates	88-89
60	Paul Coffey	95-96
59	Gordie Howe	68-69
	STEVE YZERMAN (3)	**84-85**
		86-87
		95-96
58	Alex Delvecchio	68-69
	STEVE YZERMAN	**91-92**
		93-94
57	**STEVE YZERMAN**	**90-91**
56	Walt McKechnie	75-76
	Dale McCourt	80-81
	Dino Ciccarelli	92-93
55	Ted Lindsay (2)	49-50
		56-57
54	Marcel Dionne	73-74
	Gerard Gallant	88-89
	SERGEI FEDOROV	**91-92**
53	Alex Delvecchio	72-73
	Brad Park	83-84
	SERGEI FEDOROV	**92-93**
52	Reed Larson	82-83
	STEVE YZERMAN	**87-88**
51	Dale McCourt	79-89
	Ron Duguay	84-85
	IGOR LARIONOV	**95-96**
50	Marcel Dionne	72-73
	John Ogrodnick	84-85
	Steve Chiasson	92-93
	NICKLAS LIDSTROM	**95-96**
49	Gordie Howe	60-61
	Marcel Dionne	71-72
	Reed Larson	78-79
	Peter Mahovlich	79-80
	NICKLAS LIDSTROM	**91-92**
48	Gordie Howe (2)	53-54
		62-63
	Alex Delvecchio	67-68
	STEVE YZERMAN	**83-84**
	Ivan Boldirev	83-84
	Kelly Kisio	85-86
	SERGEI FEDOROV	**90-91**

Total	Player	Season
47	Gordie Howe (2)	63-64
		64-65
	Alex Delvecchio	69-70
	Ron Duguay	83-84
	Alex Delvecchio	69-70
46	Billy Taylor	46-47
	Gordie Howe (3)	52-53
		58-59
		65-66
	NICKLAS LIDSTROM	**93-94**
45	Gordie Howe (2)	56-57
		59-60
	Alex Delvecchio	71-72
	Reed Larson	84-85
	Darren Veitch	86-87
44	Gordie Howe (2)	57-58
		61-62
	Alex Delvecchio	62-63
	Norm Ullman	66-67
	Reed Larson	79-80
	John Ogrondick	82-83
	John Chabot	87-88
	Gerard Gallant	89-90
	Paul Coffey	95
43	Gordie Howe (2)	50-51
		67-68
	Alex Delvecchio (2)	52-53
		61-62
	Dale McCourt	78-79
	Mickey Redmond	72-73
	Red Berenson	71-72
	Reed Larson	77-78
	Mark Osborne	81-82
	Kelly Kisio	84-85
42	Norm Ullman	60-61
	Alex Delvecchio	64-65
	Red Berenson	73-74
	Keith Primeau	93-94
	IGOR LARIONOV	**96-97**
	NICKLAS LIDSTROM	**96-97**
41	Dutch Reibel	54-55
	Gordie Howe	55-56
	Norm Ullman (2)	60-61
		65-66
	Ray Sheppard	93-94
	BRENDAN SHANAHAN	**96-97**
40	Gordie Howe (2)	66-67
		69-70
	Adam Oates	87-88
	Bernie Federko	89-90
	John Chabot	89-90
	Yves Racine	90-91
	Paul Ysebaert	91-92

ACTIVE PLAYERS IN BOLD CAPITALS

POINTS

Total	Player	Season	Total	Player	Season
155	**STEVE YZERMAN**	**88-89**	77	Gordie Howe (2)	57-58
137	**STEVE YZERMAN**	**92-93**			61-62
127	**STEVE YZERMAN**	**89-90**		Marcel Dionne	71-72
120	**SERGEI FEDOROV**	**93-94**		Mickey Redmond	73-74
121	Marcel Dionne	74-75		Paul Coffey	93-94
108	**STEVE YZERMAN**	**90-91**	76	Gordie Howe	64-65
107	**SERGEI FEDOROV**	**95-96**	75	Gordie Howe	65-66
105	John Ogrodnick	84-85		Paul Ysebaert	91-92
103	Gordie Howe	68-69	74	Vaclav Nedomansky	79-80
	STEVE YZERMAN	**91-92**		Reed Larson	82-83
102	**STEVE YZERMAN**	**87-88**		Paul Coffey	95-96
97	Dino Ciccarelli	92-93	73	Carl Liscombe	43-44
95	Gordie Howe	52-53		Gordie Howe (2)	59-60
	STEVE YZERMAN	**95-96**			63-64
93	Mickey Redmond	72-73		Vaclav Nedomansky	78-79
	Gerard Gallant	88-89		Gerard Gallant	87-88
	Ray Sheppard	93-94		**VYACHESLAV KOZLOV**	**93-94**
90	Marcel Dionne	72-73		Keith Primeau	93-94
	STEVE YZERMAN	**86-87**		**VYACHESLAV KOZLOV**	**95-96**
89	Gordie Howe	56-57		**IGOR LARIONOV**	**95-96**
	Ron Duguay	84-85	72	Gordie Howe	60-61
	STEVE YZERMAN	**84-85**		Norm Ullman	65-66
88	**BRENDAN SHANAHAN**	**96-97**		Dale McCourt	77-78
87	**STEVE YZERMAN**	**83-84**		Gerard Gallant	86-87
	SERGEI FEDOROV	**92-93**	71	Ted Lindsay	52-53
86	Gordie Howe (3)	50-51		Gordie Howe	69-70
		51-52		Mickey Redmond	71-72
		62-63		Alex Delvecchio	72-73
	Danny Grant	74-75		Dale McCourt	78-79
	Dale McCourt	80-81		Mike Foligno	79-80
	SERGEI FEDOROV	**91-92**		Paul MacLean	88-89
85	Ted Lindsay	56-57	70	Norm Ullman (2)	60-61
	John Ogrodnick	82-83			66-67
	STEVE YZERMAN	**96-97**		Alex Delvecchio	67-68
83	Norm Ullman	64-65		Frank Mahovlich	69-70
	Alex Delvecchio	68-69		Andre St. Laurent	77-78
	Ivan Boldirev	83-84		John Ogrodnick (2)	80-81
82	Gordie Howe	67-68			85-86
	Walt McKechnie	75-76			
	STEVE YZERMAN	**93-94**			
81	Gordie Howe	53-54			
	Dale McCourt	79-80			
80	Ron Duguay	83-84			
	Gerard Gallant	89-90			
79	Gordie Howe	55-56			
	SERGEI FEDOROV	**90-91**			
78	Ted Lindsay	49-50			
	Gordie Howe	58-59			
	Frank Mahovlich	68-69			
	Marcel Dionne	73-74			
	John Ogrodnick	83-84			
	Adam Oates	88-89			

ACTIVE PLAYERS IN BOLD CAPITALS

DETROIT RED WINGS
GOALTENDERS' ALL-TIME RECORDS

PLAYER	YRS	GP	WON	LOST	TIED	GA	SO	AVG
Terry Sawchuk	14	734	352	244	130	1782	85	2.46
Harry Lumley	7	324	163	107	54	885	26	2.73
Roger Crozier	7	310	130	119	43	853	20	2.94
Tim Cheveldae	6	264	128	93	30	851	9	3.39
Greg Stefan	9	299	115	127	30	1068	5	3.92
CHRIS OSGOOD	**4**	**157**	**99**	**32**	**19**	**358**	**14**	**2.39**
Jim Rutherford	10	314	97	165	43	1112	10	3.68
Roy Edwards	6	221	95	74	34	601	14	2.94
Norm Smith	7	178	76	68	34	417	17	2.34
Glenn Hall	4	148	74	45	29	317	17	2.14
John Mowers	4	152	65	61	26	399	13	2.63
Glen Hanlon	5	186	65	71	26	569	7	3.47
Mike Vernon	3	95	53	24	14	225	4	2.40
John Ross Roach	3	89	41	37	11	201	11	2.26
Clarence Dolson	3	93	35	41	17	192	17	2.06
Hank Bassen	6	99	34	39	19	274	3	2.99
Cecil Thompson	2	85	32	41	12	225	7	2.65
Harry Holmes	2	85	30	46	9	179	17	2.11
Rogie Vachon	2	109	30	57	19	398	4	3.74
Corrado Micalef	5	113	26	59	15	409	2	4.23
Connie Dion	2	38	23	11	4	119	1	3.13
Eddie Giacomin	3	71	23	37	7	234	6	3.47
Gilles Gilbert	3	95	21	48	16	365	0	4.18
Alex Connell	1	48	18	20	10	108	6	2.25
Al Smith	1	43	18	20	4	135	4	3.24
Doug Grant	3	46	17	22	2	182	1	4.33
Vince Riendeau	3	32	17	8	2	89	0	3.28
Wilf Cude	1	29	15	6	8	47	4	1.62
Bill Beveridge	1	39	14	20	5	109	2	2.79
Joe Daly	1	29	11	10	5	85	0	3.15
Bob Sauve	1	41	11	25	4	165	0	4.19
Ed Mio	3	49	10	20	5	205	1	5.00
Ron Low	1	32	9	12	9	102	1	3.37
Denis Dejordy	2	25	8	12	3	87	1	3.86
George Gardner	3	24	7	7	3	69	0	3.59
Jim Franks	2	18	7	8	3	72	1	4.00
Andy Brown	2	17	6	6	3	57	0	3.80
Mark Laforest	2	33	6	??	0	126	1	4.71
Larry Lozinski	1	30	6	11	7	105	0	4.32
Sam St. Laurent	4	30	5	11	4	79	0	3.76
Dennis Riggin	2	18	5	9	2	54	1	3.27
Bill McKenzie	2	26	5	13	6	101	1	4.16
Bob Essensa	1	13	4	7	2	34	1	2.62
Terry Richardson	4	19	3	10	0	75	0	5.31
Don McLeod	1	14	3	7	0	60	0	5.15
Greg Millen	1	10	3	2	3	22	0	2.71
KEVIN HODSON	**2**	**10**	**4**	**2**	**1**	**11**	**2**	**1.44**
Dave Gatherum	1	3	2	1	0	3	1	1.00
Bob Perrault	1	3	2	1	0	9	1	3.00
Harvey Teno	1	5	2	3	0	15	0	3.00
Herb Stuart	1	3	1	2	0	5	0	1.60
Gerry Gray	1	7	1	4	1	30	0	4.73
Peter Ing	1	3	1	2	0	15	0	5.29
Abbie Cox	1	1	0	0	1	4	0	4.00
Joe Turner	1	1	0	0	1	3	0	3.00
Ralph Almas	2	2	0	1	1	8	0	4.00
Ken Holland	1	3	0	1	1	11	0	4.11

Claude Legris	2	4	0	1	1	4	0	2.66
Pete McDuffe	1	4	0	3	1	22	0	5.50
Allan Bester	2	4	0	3	0	15	0	4.31
Darren Eliot	1	3	0	0	1	9	0	5.57
Alain Chevrier	1	3	0	3	0	11	0	6.11
Carl Wetzel	1	2	0	1	0	4	0	8.00
Claude Bourque	1	1	0	1	0	3	0	3.00
Alf Moore	1	1	0	1	0	3	0	3.00
Pat Rupp	1	1	0	1	0	4	0	4.00
Harrison Gray	1	1	0	1	0	5	0	7.50
Al Jensen	1	1	0	1	0	7	0	7.00
Gillies Boisvert	1	3	0	3	0	9	0	3.00
Dave Gagnon	1	2	0	1	0	6	0	10.29
Scott King	2	2	0	0	0	3	0	2.95
Chris Pusey	1	1	0	0	0	3	0	4.50
Tom McGratton	1	1	0	0	0	1	0	7.50
Lefty Wilson	1	1	0	0	0	0	0	0.00

ACTIVE PLAYERS IN BOLD CAPITALS

DETROIT NHL GOALTENDING LEADERS

REGULAR SEASON
(Minimum 30 Wins)

SHUTOUTS

T. Sawchuk – 12 ......51-52, 53-54, 54-55
G. Hall – 12 55-56
H. Holmes – 11 27-28
T. Sawchuk – 11 50-51
J.R. Roach – 10 32-33
C. Dolson – 10 28-29
T. Sawchuk – 9 52-53
H. Lumley – 7 ....47-48, 49-50
R. Crozier – 7 65-66
H. Holmes – 6 26-27
C. Dolson – 6 30-31
A. Connell – 6 31-32
N. Smith – 6 ....35-36, *36-37
H. Lumley – 6 48-49
R. Crozier – 6 64-65
R. Edwards – 6 ....*72-73
C. Osgood – 5 95-96
G. Hanlon – 4 ....*87-88
T. Cheveldae – 4 92-93

WINS

T. Sawchuk – 44 ....50-51, 51-52
T. Sawchuk – 40............................54-55
R. Crozier – 40...............................64-65
+C. Osgood – 39 95-96
G. Hall – 38...................................56-57
T. Cheveldae – 38 91-92
T. Sawchuk – 35............................53-54
H. Lumley – 34...............................48-49
H. Lumley – 33...............................49-50
T. Sawchuk – 32............................52-53
H. Lumley – 30 47-48
G. Hall – 30...................................55-56

*-Shared lead
+-1st in NHL

GOAL

Coach	No. Times Selected	Season and Team
John Ross Roach	1	1933 (1st Team)
Normie Smith	1	1937 (1st)
John Mowers	1	1943 (1st)
Glenn Hall	2	1956 (2nd), 1957 (1st)
Terry Sawchuk	7	1951 (1st), 1952 (1st), 1953 (1st), 1954 (2nd), 1955 (2nd), 1959 (2nd), 1963 (2nd)
Roger Crozier	1	1965 (1st)
CHRIS OSGOOD	**1**	**1996 (2nd)**

DEFENSE

Coach	No. Times Selected	Season and Team
Ebbie Goodfellow	3	1936 (2nd), 1937 (1st), 1940 (1st)
Jack Stewart	5	1943 (1st), 1946 (2nd), 1947 (2nd), 1948 (1st), 1949 (1st)
Flash Hollett	1	1945 (1st)
Bill Quackenbush	3	1947 (2nd), 1948 (1st), 1949 (1st)
Leo Reise	2	1950 (2nd), 1951 (2nd)
Bob Goldham	1	1955 (2nd)
Red Kelly	8	1950 (2nd), 1951 (1st), 1952 (1st), 1953 (1st), 1954 (1st), 1955 (1st), 1956 (2nd), 1957 (1st)
Marcel Pronovost	4	1958 (2nd), 1959 (2nd), 1960 (1st), 1961 (1st)
Bill Gadsby	1	1965 (2nd)
Carl Brewer	1	1970 (2nd)
Paul Coffey	1	1995 (1st)
VLADIMIR KONSTANTINOV	**1**	**1996 (2nd)**

LEFT WING

Coach	No. Times Selected	Season and Team
Sid Abel	1	1942 (2nd)
Syd Howe	1	1945 (2nd)
Ted Lindsay	9	1948 (1st), 1949 (2nd), 1950 (1st), 1951 (1st), 1952 (1st), 1953 (1st), 1954 (1st), 1956 (1st), 1957 (1st)
Alex Delvecchio	1	1959 (2nd)
Frank Mahovlich	2	1969 (2nd), 1970 (2nd)
John Ogrodnick	1	1985 (1st)
Gerard Gallant	1	1989 (2nd)

CENTER

Coach	No. Times Selected	Season and Team
Cooney Weiland	1	1935 (2nd)
Marty Barry	1	1937 (1st)
Sid Abel	3	1949 (1st), 1950 (1st), 1951 (2nd)
Alex Delvecchio	1	1953 (2nd)
Norm Ullman	2	1965 (1st), 1967 (2nd)
SERGEI FEDOROV	**1**	**1994 (1st)**

RIGHT WING

Coach	No. Times Selected	Season and Team
Larry Aurie	1	1937 (1st)
Gordie Howe	*21	1949 (2nd), 1950 (2nd), 1951 (1st), 1952 (1st), 1953 (1st), 1954 (1st), 1956 (2nd), 1957 (1st), 1958 (1st), 1959 (2nd), 1960 (1st), 1961 (2nd), 1962 (2nd), 1962 (2nd), 1963 (1st), 1964 (2nd), 1965 (2nd), 1966 (1st), 1967 (2nd), 1968 (1st), 1969 (1st), 1970 (1st)
Mickey Redmond	2	1973 (1st), 1974 (2nd)

COACH

Coach	No. Times Selected	Season and Team
Jack Adams	3	1937 (1st), 1943 (1st), 1945 (2nd)
Bobby Kromm	1	Jack Adams Trophy 1978
Jacques Demers	2	Jack Adams Trophy 1987, 1988
SCOTTY BOWMAN		**Jack Adams Trophy 1996**

*-NHL Record

ACTIVE PLAYERS IN BOLD CAPITALS

RED WINGS' NHL TROPHY WINNERS

ART ROSS TROPHY
(Leading Point-scorer)

Ted Lindsay	1949-50
Gordie Howe	1950-51
Gordie Howe	1951-52
Gordie Howe	1952-53
Gordie Howe	1953-54
Gordie Howe	1956-57
Gordie Howe	1962-63

HART TROPHY
(Most Valuable Player)

Ebbie Goodfellow	1939-40
Sid Abel	1948-49
Gordie Howe	1951-52
Gordie Howe	1952-53
Gordie Howe	1956-57
Gordie Howe	1957-58
Gordie Howe	1959-60
Gordie Howe	1962-63
SERGEI FEDOROV	**1993-94**

VEZINA TROPHY
(Best Goalie)

Norm Smith	1936-37
John Mowers	1942-43
Terry Sawchuk	1951-52
Terry Sawchuk	1952-53
Terry Sawchuk	1954-55

NORRIS TROPHY
(Best Defenseman)

Red Kelly	1953-54
Paul Coffey	1995

CALDER TROPHY
(Rookie of the Year)

Carl Voss	1932-33
Jim McFadden	1947-48
Terry Sawchuk	1950-51
Glenn Hall	1955-56
Roger Crozier	1964-65

FRANK J. SELKE TROPHY
(Best Defensive Forward)

SERGEI FEDOROV	**1993-94**
SERGEI FEDOROV	**1995-96**

WILLIAM M. JENNINGS TROPHY
(Goaltenders on Team with Fewest
Regular Season Goals Against)

CHRIS OSGOOD & Mike Vernon ....
1995-96

LADY BYNG TROPHY
(Sportsmanship & Ability)

Marty Barry	1936-37
Bill Quackenbush	1948-49
Red Kelly	1950-51
Red Kelly	1952-53
Red Kelly	1953-54
Dutch Reibel	1955-56
Alex Delvecchio	1958-59
Alex Delvecchio	1965-66
Alex Delvecchio	1968-69
Marcel Dionne	1974-75

LESTER B. PEARSON AWARD
(Oustanding Performer
Selected by Players' Assn.)

STEVE YZERMAN	**1988-89**
SERGEI FEDOROV	**1993-94**

PLUS-MINUS AWARD
(Plus-Minus Leader)

Paul Ysebaert	1991-92
VLADIMIR KONSTANTINOV	**1995-96**

CONN SMYTHE TROPHY
(Playoff MVP)

Roger Crozier	1966
Mike Vernon	1997

JACK ADAMS AWARD
(Coach of the Year)

Bobby Kromm	1977-78
Jacques Demers	1986-87
Jacques Demers	1987-88
SCOTTY BOWMAN	**1995-96**

BILL MASTERTON TROPHY
(Perseverance, Sportsmanship and
Dedication to Hockey)

Brad Park	1983-84

LESTER PATRICK TROPHY
(Outstanding Service
to U.S. Hockey)

Jack Adams	1965-66
Gordie Howe	1966-67
Alex Delvecchio	1973-74
Bruce A. Norris	1974-75
MIKE ILITCH	**1990-91**

ACTIVE PLAYER/OWNER IN BOLD CAPITALS

RED WINGS IN HOCKEY HALL OF FAME

Sid Abel 1969
Jack Adams 1959
Al Arbour 1996
Marty Barry 1965
Andy Bathgate 1978
Leo Boivin 1986
Scotty Bowman 1991
John Bucyk 1981
Charlie Conacher 1961
Alex Connell 1958
Alex Delvecchio 1977
Marcel Dionne 1992
Frank Fosyton 1958
Frank Frederickson 1958
Bill Gadsby 1970
Ed Giacomin 1987
Ebbie Goodfellow 1963
Glenn Hall 1975
Doug Harvey 1973
George Hay 1958
Hap Holmes 1972
Gordie Howe 1972
Syd Howe 1965
Tommy Ivan 1974
Duke Keats 1958
Red Kelly 1969

Herbie Lewis 1989
Ted Lindsay 1966
Harry Lumley 1980
Budd Lynch 1985
Frank Mahovlich 1981
Bruce Martyn 1991
Reg Noble 1962
Bruce A. Norris 1969
James Norris 1958
James D. Norris 1962
Brad Park 1988
Bud Poile 1990
Marcel Pronovost 1978
Bill Quackenbush 1976
Borje Salming 1996
Terry Sawchuk 1971
Earl Seibert 1964
Darryl Sittler 1989
Jack Stewart 1964
Cecil "Tiny" Thompson 1959
Norm Ullman 1982
Carl Voss 1974
Jack Walker 1960
Harry Watson 1994
Cooney Weiland 1971
John A. Ziegler Jr. 1987

MEMBERS OF RED WINGS HALL OF FAME

Sid Abel 1944
Jack Adams 1945
Larry Aurie 1944
Marty Barry 1944
Mud Bruneteau 1944
Joe Carveth 1978
Carson Cooper 1949
Alex Delvecchio 1978
Bill Gadsby 1978
Ebbie Goodfellow 1944
Don Grosso 1947
George Hay 1944
Gordie Howe 1985
Syd Howe 1944
Tommy Ivan 1977
Red Kelly 1978
Herb Lewis 1944
Ted Lindsay 1962

Carl Liscombe 1964
Carl Mattson 1978
Bucko McDonald 1961
John Mowers 1946
Reg Noble 1944
Bruce A. Norris 1968
James Norris 1959
James D. Norris 1968
Jimmy Orlando 1962
Marcel Pronovost 1978
Bill Quackenbush 1961
Marguerite Norris 1977
Terry Sawchuk 1971
Jimmy Skinner 1977
Norm Smith 1963
Jack Stewart 1944
Frank "Honey" Walker 1954
Doug Young 1951

RED WINGS' BIGGEST VICTORIES
(Scoring 10 Goals or More)

SEASON	DATE	OPPONENT	SCORE
1930-31	Dec. 25	Toronto	10-1
1934-35	Dec. 13	at St. Louis	11-2
1941-42	Jan. 4	Montréal	10-0
1942-43	Nov. 5	NY Rangers	12-5
1943-44	Jan. 23	NY Rangers	15-0
1943-44	Feb. 3	NY Rangers	12-2
1943-44	Mar. 16	Boston	10-9
1944-45	Nov. 2	NY Rangers	10-3
1944-45	Dec. 27	NY Rangers	11-3
1944-45	Mar. 4	Boston	10-4
1946-47	Mar. 16	at Chicago	10-6
1948-49	Dec. 29	Boston	10-2
1950-51	Feb. 7	Chicago	11-3
1952-53	Nov. 22	Chicago	10-1
1952-53	Dec. 11	at Boston	10-1
1952-53	Mar. 2	Boston	10-2
1964-65	Mar. 18	Boston	10-3
1965-66	Dec. 2	Boston	10-2
1973-74	Oct. 21	California	11-2
1977-78	Nov. 16	St. Louis	10-1
1981-82	Oct. 29	Calgary	12-4
1981-82	Nov. 5	Los Angeles	10-2
1984-85	Feb. 27	Vancouver	11-5
1987-88	Nov. 25	Winnipeg	10-8
1987-88	Dec. 4	Chicago	12-0
1991-92	Nov. 7	St. Louis	10-3
1991-92	Feb. 15	San Jose	11-1
1992-93	Nov. 23	Tampa Bay	10-5
1992-93	Nov. 25	St. Louis	11-6
1993-94	Nov. 27	Dallas	10-4
1993-94	Jan. 6	at San Jose	10-3
1995-96	Dec. 2	at Montréal	11-1

RED WINGS' BIGGEST DEFEATS
(Allowing 10 Goals or More)

SEASON	DATE	OPPONENT	SCORE
1939-40	Feb. 13	at Boston	10-3
1941-42	Jan. 25	at NY Rangers	11-2
1945-46	Mar. 17	Toronto	11-7
1958-59	Mar. 7	at Montréal	10-2
1964-65	Dec. 5	at Toronto	10-2
1966-67	Apr. 1	at NY Rangers	10-5
1970-71	Jan. 2	at Toronto	13-0
1970-71	Mar. 16	Boston	11-4
1973-74	Feb. 2	at Philadelphia	12-2
1974-75	Oct. 23	at Atlanta	10-1
1979-80	Mar. 27	at Buffalo	10-1
1980-81	Jan. 15	at Calgary	10-0
1980-81	Jan. 20	at Los Angeles	11-4
1984-85	Dec. 1	at St. Louis	10-5
1985-86	Oct. 17	at Minnesota	10-1
1985-86	Nov. 30	at Montréal	10-1
1985-86	Dec. 11	Minnesota	10-2
1985-86	Dec. 23	at NY Rangers	10-2
1987-88	Feb. 23	Philadelphia	11-6
1988-89	Jan. 20	at Pittsburgh	10-5
1989-90	Oct. 5	at Calgary	10-7
1992-93	Feb. 24	at Buffalo	10-7
1993-94	Oct. 9	at Los Angeles	10-3

RED WINGS' HISTORY OF SCORELESS TIES

SEASON	DATE	OPPONENT SITE	GOALIES DETROIT	OPPONENT
1927-28	Nov. 26	at Chicago	Hap Holmes	Chuck Gardiner
	Feb. 23	OTTAWA	Hap Holmes	Alex Connell
	Feb. 26	NY Rangers	Hap Holmes	Lorne Chabot
1928-29	Feb. 23	CHICAGO	Dolly Dolson	Chuck Gardiner
1931-32	Jan. 7	BOSTON	Alex Connell	Tiny Thompson
	Feb. 18	BOSTON	Alex Connelll	Tiny Thompson
1934-35	Dec. 30	NY Americans	John Ross Roach	Roy Worters
	Jan. 26	at Toronto	John Ross Roach	George Hainsworth
1935-36	Nov. 14	CHICAGO	Normie Smith	Mike Karakas
	Nov. 28	MONTRÉAL	Normie Smith	Wilf Cude
1936-37	Feb. 28	MONTRÉAL	Normie Smith	Wilf Cude
1939-40	Dec. 17	NY RANGERS	Tiny Thompson	Dave Kerr
1946-47	Dec. 4	at Chicago	Harry Lumley	Paul Bibeault
1947-48	Mar. 17	at Boston	Harry Lumley	Frank Brimsek
1948-49	Oct. 23	at Montréal	Harry Lumley	Bill Durnan
1050-51	Jan. 21	TORONTO	Terry Sawchuk	Turk Broda
1951-52	Nov. 6	at Boston	Terry Sawchuk	Jim Henry
1952-53	Dec. 14	MONTRÉAL	Terry Sawchuk	Gerry McNeil
	Mar. 15	at Chicago	Terry Sawchuk	Al Rollins
1953-54	Jan. 3	TORONTO	Terry Sawchuk	Harry Lumley
	Feb. 17	at Toronto	Terry Sawchuk	Harry Lumley
1955-56	Oct. 22	BOSTON	Glenn Hall	Terry Sawchuk
	Nov. 13	at Boston	Glenn Hall	Terry Sawchuk
1962-63	Oct. 13	at Chicago	Terry Sawchuk	Glenn Hall
1976-77	Nov. 7	ATLANTA	Eddie Giacomin	Phil Myre
1996-97	Dec 10	EDMONTON	Chris Osgood	Curtis Joseph

PENALTY SHOTS INVOLVING RED WINGS
(RULE INSTITUTED IN 1934-35) (GOOD UNLESS NG)

DATE	PLAYER	TEAM	GOALIE	TEAM
Nov. 15, 1934	Ebbie Goodfellow–NG	at DETROIT	Percy Jackson	NY Rangers
Nov. 22, 1934	Bill Cook–NG	at NY Rangers	Norm Smith	DETROIT
Nov. 22, 1934	Ebbie Goodfellow–NG	DETROIT	Andy Aitkenhead	at NY Rangers
Nov. 24, 1934	Bill Thomas–NG	at Toronto	Norm Smith	DETROIT
Dec. 13, 1934	Ebbie Goodfellow	DETROIT	Bill Beveridge	at St. Louis
Dec. 20, 1934	Ebbie Goodfellow–NG	at DETROIT	Alex Connell	Mon. Maroons
Feb. 10, 1935	Ebbie Goodfellow–NG	at DETROIT	Alex Connell	Mon. Marrons
Feb. 17, 1935	Ebbie Goodfellow–NG	at DETROIT	Dave Kerr	NY Rangers
Feb. 21, 1935	Earl Robinson–NG	Mon. Maroons	John Roach	at DETROIT
Mar. 3, 1935	Charlie McVeigh–NG	NY Americans	Norm Smith	at DETROIT
Mar. 9, 1935	Armand Mondou–NG	at Mon. Canadiens	Norm Smith	DETROIT
Nov.14, 1935	Art Coulter–NG	NY Rangers	Norm Smith	DETROIT
Nov. 24, 1935	Ebbie Goodfellow–NG	at DETROIT	George Hainsworth	Toronto
Dec. 19, 1935	Dave Schriner–NG	at NY Americans	Norm Smith	DETROIT
Dec. 29, 1935	Ebbie Goodfellow–NG	at DETROIT	Cecil Thompson	Boston
Jan. 1, 1936	Paul Thompson	at Chicago	Norm Smith	DETROIT
Nov. 22, 1936	King Clancy–NG	Toronto	Norm Smith	at DETROIT
Dec. 3, 1936	Neil Colvilli–NG	NY Rangers	Norm Smith	at DETROIT
Dec. 25, 1936	John Sorrell–NG	at DETROIT	Mike Karakas	Chicago
Dec. 31, 1936	Mud Bruneteau–NG	at DETROIT	Roy Wortors	NY Americans
Jan. 7, 1937	Hap Emms–NG	at NY Americans	Norm Smith	DETROIT
Feb. 7, 1937	John Sorrell	at DETROIT	Cecil Thompson	Boston
Mar. 4, 1937*	John Sorrell–NG	at DETROIT	Dave Kerr	NY Rangers
Mar. 4, 1937*	Alex Shibicky–NG	NY Rangers	Norm Smith	at DETROIT
Dec. 25, 1937	George Parsons–NG	at Toronto	Norm Smith	DETROIT
Nov. 6, 1938	Charlie Conacher–NG	at DETROIT	Frank Brimsek	Boston
Nov. 24, 1938	Mud Bruneteau–NG	at DETROIT	Mike Karakas	Chicago
Jan. 22, 1939	Woody Dumart	Boston	Cecil Thompson	at DETROIT
Jan. 28, 1939	Nick Metz–NG	at Toronto	Cecil Thompson	DETROIT
Dec. 17, 1939	Ebbie Goodfellow–NG	at DETROIT	Dave Kerr	NY Rangers
Feb. 13, 1940	Ebbie Goodfellow	DETROIT	Frank Brimsek	at Boston
Feb. 29, 1940	Syd Howe–NG	DETROIT	Turk Broda	at Toronto
Mar. 3, 1940	Mud Bruneteau	at DETROIT	Frank Brimsek	Boston
Nov. 19, 1940	Roy Conacher–NG	at Boston	John Mowers	DETROIT
Dec. 5, 1940	Earl Siebert–NG	at Chicago	John Mowers	DETROIT
Dec. 17, 1940	Archie Wilder–NG	DETROIT	Earl Robertson	at NY Americans
Jan. 24, 1941	Charlie Conacher	NY Americans	John Mowers	at DETROIT
Dec. 4, 1941	Don Grosso–NG	at DETROIT	Charlie Rayner	NY Americans
Dec. 25, 1941	Jack Stewart–NG	at DETROIT	Charlie Rayner	NY Americans
Jan. 3, 1942	Sid Abel–NG	DETROIT	Paul Bibeault	Mon. Canadiens
Feb. 22, 1942	Eddie Bush–NG	at DETROIT	Turk Broda	Toronto
Feb. 25, 1942	Sid Abel	DETROIT	Jim Henry	at NY Rangers
Mar. 24, 1942*	Charlie Sands–NG	at Mon. Canadiens	John Mowers	DETROIT
Nov. 21, 1943	Syd Howe	at DETROIT	Hec Highton	Chicago
Jan. 18, 1945	Fred Thurier	NY Rangers	Harry Lumley	at DETROIT
Jan. 21, 1945	Ray Getliffe	Mon. Canadiens	Harry Lumley	at DETROIT
Nov. 25, 1945	Alex Shibicky	NY Rangers	Harry Lumley	at DETROIT
Jan. 12, 1946	Carl Liscombe–NG	DETROIT	Frank McCool	at Toronto
Mar. 9, 1947	Pat Lundy–NG	DETROIT	Frank Brimsek	at Boston
Nov. 19, 1947	Buddy O'Connell–NG	NY Rangers	Harry Lumley	at DETROIT
Mar. 5, 1953	Gordie Howe	at DETROIT	Gump Worsley	NY Rangers
Dec. 31, 1961	Gordie Howe	at DETROIT	John Bower	Toronto
Jan. 31, 1962	Bruce MacGregor–NG	DETROIT	Glenn Hall	at Chicago
Feb. 4, 1962	Alex Delvecchio–NG	DETROIT	Bruce Gamble	at Boston
Mar. 14, 1962	Andy Bathgate	NY Rangers	Hank Bassen	at DETROIT
Nov. 20, 1963	Doug Barkley	DETROIT	Glenn Hall	at Chicago
Nov. 27, 1963	Rod Gilbert	at NY Rangers	Terry Sawchuk	DETROIT
Dec. 8, 1963	Claude LaForge	at DETROIT	Don Simmons	Toronto
Jan. 5, 1967	Norm Ullman	DETROIT	Glenn Hall	Chicago
Feb. 8, 1967	Pete Stemkowski–NG	at Toronto	Roger Crozier	DETROIT
Jan. 28, 1968	Wayne Connelly–NG	at Minnesota	Roger Crozier	DETROIT
Mar. 9, 1968	Mike Walton	at Toronto	Roger Crozier	DETROIT
Oct. 28, 1968	Claude Provost–NG	Montréal	Roger Crozier	at DETROIT

DATE	PLAYER	TEAM	GOALIE	TEAM
Dec. 6, 1969	Andre Boudrias–NG	at St. Louis	Roger Crozier	DETROIT
Jan. 14, 1971	Jean Pronovost	Pittsburgh	Roy Edwards	at DETROIT
Feb. 29, 1972	Guy Charron–NG	at DETROIT	Ed Dyke	Vancouver
Jan. 10, 1973	Ron Schock–NG	at Pittsburgh	Roy Edwards	DETROIT
Jan. 28, 1973	Jacques Lemaire–NG	at Montréal	Denis DeJordy	DETROIT
Mar. 7, 1974	Bill Clement	at Philadelphia	Jim Rutherford	DETROIT
Jan. 23, 1975	Pierre Jarry–NG	DETROIT	Roger Crozier	at Buffalo
Feb. 1, 1975	Lorne Henning	NY Islanders	Jim Rutherford	DETROIT
Dec. 4, 1976	Dennis Polonich–NG	DETROIT	Rogatien Vachon	at Los Angeles
Dec. 12, 1976	Bill Lochead–NG	DETROIT	Gilles Gilbert	at Boston
Jan. 6, 1977	Dean Talafous–NG	Minnesota	Ed Giacomin	at DETROIT
Mar. 12, 1977	Lanny McDonald–NG	Toronto	Jim Rutherford	at DETROIT
Nov. 5, 1977	Reed Larson–NG	at DETROIT	Gilles Meloche	Cleveland
Mar. 5, 1978	Andre St. Laurent–NG	at DETROIT	Gary Smith	Minnesota
Nov. 22, 1978	Dale McCourt–NG	DETROIT	Mario Lessard	at Los Angeles
Jan. 30,1980	Mike Foligno	DETROIT	Paul Harrison	at Toronto
Mar. 26, 1980	Mike Foligno–NG	at DETROIT	Ron Low	Edmonton
Mar. 14, 1981	Bernie Federko	at St. Louis	Larry Lozinski	DETROIT
Feb. 11, 1982	Tom Gradin	at DETROIT	Gilles Gilbert	Vancouver
Feb. 11, 1982	Ivan Hlinka	at DETROIT	Gilles Gilbert	Vancouver
Dec. 8, 1982	Clark Gillies–NG	NY Islanders	Corrado Miclaef	at DETROIT
Dec. 10, 1983	Alain Lemieux	at St. Louis	Greg Stefan	DETROIT
Jan. 9, 1984	Ron Duguay–NG	at DETROIT	Grant Fuhr	Edmonton
Jan. 14, 1984	Brent Peterson	Buffalo	Greg Stefan	at DETROIT
Feb. 1, 1984	Bob Crawford	Hartford	Ken Holland	at DETROIT
Feb. 7, 1985	Dwight Foster	at DETROIT	Rick Wamsley	St. Louis
Oct. 8, 1985	Bo Berglund	Minnesota	Corrado Micalef	at DETROIT
Oct. 16, 1985	Gerard Gallant	at DETROIT	Brian Hayward	Winnipeg
Dec. 15, 1985	Denis Savard	at Chicago	Greg Stefan	DETROIT
Feb. 16, 1986	Pierre LaRouche–NG	at NY Rangers	Corrado Micalef	DETROIT
Feb. 16, 1986	Mike Ridley–NG	at NY Rangers	Corrado Micalef	DETROIT
Feb. 17, 1987	Petr Klima–NG	DETROIT	John Vanbiesbrouck	at NY Rangers
Mar. 5, 1987	Bob Probert	at DETROIT	Kari Takko	Minnesota
Mar. 25, 1987	Mel Bridgman	at DETROIT	Roland Melanson	Los Angeles
Nov. 22, 1987	Steve Yzerman–NG	at DETROIT	Doug Kerns	Boston
Feb. 3, 1988	Denis Savard–NG	at Chicago	Glen Hanlon	DETROIT
Apr. 9, 1988*	Petr Klima	DETROIT	Alan Bester	at Toronto
Oct. 28, 1988	Miroslav Frycer–NG	at DETROIT	Don Beaupre	Minnesota
Feb. 13, 1989	Steve Yzerman	at DETROIT	Bob Essensa	Winnipeg
Feb. 19, 1989	Mike Foligno–NG	at Buffalo	Glen Hanlon	DETROIT
Mar. 20, 1989	Petr Klima–NG	at DETROIT	Jon Casey	Minnesota
Nov. 3, 1989	Jimmy Carson–NG	at DETROIT	Mike Liut	Hartford
Feb. 19, 1990	Russ Courtnall	Montréal	Tim Cheveldae	at DETROIT
Nov. 23, 1990	Rich Sutter–NG	St. Louis	Tim Cheveldae	at DETROIT
Nov. 29, 1990	Joe Kocur	at DETROIT	Jacques Cloutier	at Chicago
Jan. 9, 1991	Ken Linseman–NG	Edmonton	Tim Cheveldae	at DETROIT
Jan. 25, 1991	Brent Fedyk–NG	at DETROIT	Vince Riendeau	St. Louis
Oct. 30, 1991	Kevin Miller	at DETROIT	Patrick Roy	Montréal
Nov. 2, 1991	Wes Walz–NG	at Boston	Tim Cheveldae	DETROIT
Jan. 3, 1992	Steve Yzerman	at DETROIT	Grant Fuhr	Toronto
Jan. 29, 1992	Steve Yzerman	at DETROIT	Darren Puppa	Buffalo
Nov. 27, 1992	Paul Ysebaert	at DETROIT	Rob Stauber	Los Angeles
Mar. 18, 1993	Steve Yzerman–NG	at DETROIT	Darcy Wakaluk	Minnesota
Dec. 27, 1993	Sergei Fedorov	DETROIT	Andy Moog	at Dallas
Mar. 4, 1994	Peter Zezel–NG	Toronto	Chris Osgood	at DETROIT
Mar. 22, 1994	Mark Howe–NG	at DETROIT	Ed Belfour	Chicago
Feb. 12, 1995	Sergei Fedorov–NG	at DETROIT	Kelly Hrudey	Los Angeles
Mar. 22, 1995	Bob Errey–NG	at DETROIT	Nikolai Khabibulin	Winnipeg
Apr. 1, 1995	Dave Gagner–NG	at Dallas	Chris Osgood	DETROIT
Nov. 2, 1995	Steve Yzerman–NG	DETROIT	Blaine Lacher	at Boston
Nov. 22, 1995	Igor Larionov	DETROIT	Arturs Irbe	at San Jose
Nov. 18, 1996	Mike Hudson–NG	Phoenix	Chris Osgood	at Phoenix

*-Playoffs

DETROIT RED WINGS
ALL-TIME DETROIT HAT TRICKS
(Regular Season and Playoffs)

1926-27 — Duke Keats vs. Pittsburgh, March 10, 1927.

1927-28 — Larry Aurie vs. N.Y. Rangers, Jan. 3, 1928
George Hay vs. Chicago, March 6, 1928

1928-29 — NONE

1929-30 — Carson Cooper vs. Montréal Maroons, Nov. 28, 1929
Herbie Lewis (4) vs. Pittsburgh, Feb. 10, 1930

1930-31 — Larry Aurie vs. N.Y. Americans, Dec. 21, 1930
Ebbie Goodfellow (4) vs. Toronto, Dec. 25, 1930

1931-32 — NONE

1932-33 — Johnny Sorrell vs. N.Y. Americans, Nov. 15, 1932

1933-34 — Johnny Sorrell (4) vs. N.Y. Americans, Nov. 13, 1933

1934-35 — Cooney Weiland vs. St. Louis, Dec. 13, 1934

1935-36 — Marty Barry vs. Canadiens, Jan. 5, 1936
Syd Howe vs. N.Y. Americans, March 22, 1936

1936-37 — Larry Aurie vs. N.Y. Rangers, Feb. 2, 1937
Johnny Sorrell vs. Boston, Feb. 7, 1937
Syd Howe vs. Chicago, Feb. 21, 1937
Marty Barry vs. Montréal Maroons, March 2, 1937

1937-38 — Herbie Lewis vs. Boston, March 6, 1938
Carl Liscombe vs. Chicago, March 13, 1938

1938-39 — Gus Geisbrecht vs. N.Y. Americans, Feb. 5, 1939
Syd Howe vs. N.Y. Americans, March 2, 1939
*Syd Howe vs. Canadiens, March 23, 1939

1939-40 — Syd Howe vs. Canadiens, Dec. 25, 1939

1940-41 — Mud Bruneteau (4) vs. N.Y. Americans, March 6, 1941

1941-42 — NONE

1942-43 — Carl Liscombe vs. N.Y. Rangers, Nov. 5, 1942
Syd Howe vs. Toronto, Dec. 12, 1942
Carl Liscombe vs. N.Y. Rangers, Jan. 24, 1943
*Mud Bruneteau vs. Boston, April 1, 1943
*Don Grosso vs. Boston, April 7, 1943

1943-44 — Mud Bruneteau (4) vs. Boston, Nov. 7, 1943
Mud Bruneteau vs. Chicago, Nov. 21, 1943
Syd Howe vs. N.Y. Rangers, Jan. 23, 1944
Syd Howe (6) vs. N.Y. Rangers, Feb. 3, 1944
Joe Carveth vs. N.Y. Rangers, Feb. 10, 1944
Adam Brown vs. N.Y. Rangers, March 2, 1944
Mud Bruneteau vs. Toronto, March 12, 1944
Carl Liscombe vs. Boston, March 16, 1944

1944-45 — Jud McAtee vs. N.Y. Rangers, Nov. 2, 1944
Flash Hollett vs. N.Y. Rangers, Dec. 21, 1944
Joe Carveth vs. Boston, March 4, 1945
*Carl Liscombe (4) vs. Boston, April 3, 1945

1945-46 — Adam Brown vs. Boston, Oct. 28, 1945

1946-47 — Pete Horeck (4) vs. Chicago, Jan. 23, 1947
Roy Conacher vs. Canadiens, Feb. 22, 1947
Roy Conacher (4) vs. Chicago, March 16, 1947
Ted Lindsay vs. Chicago, March 16, 1947

1947-48 — Jim McFadden vs. Chicago, Nov. 22, 1947

1948-49 — Gerry Couture vs. Chicago, Nov. 28, 1948
Ted Lindsay vs. Chicago, Feb. 2, 1949

1949-50 — Sid Abel vs. Boston, Nov. 2, 1949
Gerry Couture (4) vs. Boston, Feb. 11, 1950
Gordie Howe vs. Boston, Feb. 11, 1950
Gordie Howe vs. Toronto, March 19, 1950

1950-51 — Gordie Howe vs. Chicago, Jan. 16, 1951
Gordie Howe vs. Chicago, Jan. 23, 1951
George Gee vs. Chicago, March 11, 1951
Gordie Howe vs. Chicago, March 17, 1951

1951-52 — Gordie Howe vs. Canadiens, Dec. 31, 1951
Gordie Howe vs. Canadiens, March 23, 1952

1952-53 — Gordie Howe vs. Toronto, Jan. 11, 1953
Gordie Howe vs. Toronto, Jan. 29, 1953
Ted Lindsay (4) vs. Boston, March 2, 1953

1953-54 — NONE

1954-55 — Red Kelly vs. Boston, Oct. 21, 1954
Dutch Reibel vs. Chicago, Jan. 9, 1955
Dutch Reibel vs. Toronto, March 13, 1955
Ted Lindsay vs. Montréal, March 20, 1955
*Ted Lindsay (4) vs. Montréal, April 5, 1955
*Gordie Howe vs. Montréal, April 10, 1955

1955-56 — Gordie Howe vs. Boston, Jan. 19, 1956

1956-57 — Ted Lindsay vs. Montréal, Nov. 18, 1956
Gordie Howe vs. N.Y. Rangers, Dec. 25, 1956
Lorne Ferguson vs. N.Y. Rangers, Feb. 2, 1957

1957-58 — Jack McIntyre vs. Boston, Feb. 22, 1958

1958-59 — Alex Delvecchio vs. Chicago, Oct. 18, 1958
Johnny Wilson vs. Boston, Nov. 18, 1958

1959-60 — Norm Ullman vs. Boston, Jan. 21, 1960

1960-61 — Howie Glover vs. Toronto, Jan. 4, 1961
Norm Ullman (4) vs. N.Y. Rangers, March 14, 1961

1961-62 — Vic Stasiuk vs. Boston, Oct. 19, 1961
Norm Ullman vs. Toronto, Dec. 3, 1961
Gordie Howe vs. Toronto, Dec. 31, 1961

1962-63 — Norm Ullman vs. N.Y. Rangers, March 14, 1963

1963-64 — Norm Ullman vs. Boston, March 8, 1964
Floyd Smith vs. Chicago, March 15, 1964
*Norm Ullman vs. Chicago, March 29, 1964
*Norm Ullman vs. Chicago, April 7, 1964

1964-65 — Norm Ullman vs. Montréal, Feb. 28, 1965
Norm Ullman vs. N.Y. Rangers, March 19, 1965
Gordie Howe vs. Chicago, March 21, 1965
Alex Delvecchio vs. N.Y. Rangers, March 25, 1965
*Norm Ullman vs. Chicago, April 11, 1965

1965-66 — Norm Ullman vs. Boston, Dec. 2, 1965
Gordie Howe vs. Boston, Dec. 12, 1965
Bruce MacGregor vs. Chicago, Dec. 19, 1965
Norm Ullman vs. Toronto, Jan. 16, 1966

1966-67 — Paul Henderson (4) vs. N.Y. Rangers, Oct. 27, 1966
Dean Prentice vs. N.Y. Rangers, Jan. 22, 1967
Norm Ullman vs. Toronto, Feb. 8, 1967

1967-68 — Norm Ullman vs. Montréal, Dec. 17, 1967
Floyd Smith vs. Los Angeles, Feb. 1, 1968
Gordie Howe vs. St. Louis, March 16, 1968

1968-69 — Frank Mahovlich vs. Boston, Oct. 31, 1968
Garry Unger vs. Minnesota, Dec. 15, 1968
Frank Mahovlich vs. Minnesota, Dec. 31, 1968
Pete Stemkowski vs. Los Angeles, Feb. 9, 1969
Frank Mahovlich (4) vs. Oakland, Jan. 12, 1969
Gordie Howe vs. Chicago, Feb. 6, 1969
Frank Mahovlich vs. Los Angeles, Feb. 9, 1969
Gordie Howe vs. Los Angeles, Feb. 16, 1969

1969-70 — Gordie Howe vs. Pittsburgh, Nov. 2, 1969
Frank Mahovlich vs. Montréal, Nov. 19, 1969
Garry Unger vs. Oakland, Dec. 28, 1969
Alex Delvecchio vs. Philadelphia, Jan. 3, 1970

1970-71 — NONE

1971-72 — Nick Libett vs. Buffalo, Jan. 27, 1972
Mickey Redmond vs. California, Feb. 6, 1972
Marcel Dionne vs. Montréal, March 19, 1972

1972-73 — Mickey Redmond vs. Vancouver, Jan. 12, 1973
Marcel Dionne vs. Montréal, Feb. 22, 1973

1973-74 — Guy Charron vs. California, Oct. 21, 1973
Guy Charron vs. Toronto, Nov. 11, 1973
Red Berenson vs. Los Angeles, Jan. 12, 1974
Mickey Redmond vs. N.Y. Islanders, Feb. 24, 1974

1974-75 — Mickey Redmond vs. Washington, Oct. 19, 1974
Marcel Dionne vs. N.Y. Rangers, Nov. 20, 1974
Marcel Dionne vs. Boston, Dec. 5, 1974
Phil Roberto vs. Toronto, Feb. 9, 1975
Danny Grant vs. Vancouver, Feb. 14, 1975
Mickey Redmond vs. N.Y. Rangers, March 22, 1975

1975-76 — Michel Bergeron vs. Washington, Dec. 12, 1975
Michel Bergeron (4) vs. St. Louis, March 18, 1976

1976-77 — Dan Maloney vs. Cleveland, Nov. 19, 1976
Dennis Hextall vs. Atlanta, Dec. 18, 1976

1977-78 — Dale McCourt vs. Washington, Jan. 22, 1978
Paul Woods vs. Vancouver, Feb. 12, 1978
Dale McCourt vs. Atlanta, Feb. 16, 1978
Dale McCourt vs. Atlanta, March 22, 1978

1978-79 — Vaclav Nedomansky vs. Chicago, Oct. 28, 1978
Errol Thompson vs. Boston, Dec. 7, 1978
Dale McCourt vs. Vancouver, Dec. 20, 1978
Dale McCourt vs. Pittsburgh, Feb. 18, 1979
Vaclav Nedomansky vs. Colorado, Feb. 25, 1979
Vaclav Nedomansky vs. St. Louis, Feb. 28, 1979

1979-80 — Vaclav Nedomansky vs. Winnipeg, Oct. 17, 1979
Errol Thompson vs. Chicago, Dec. 16, 1979
Mike Foligno vs. Québec, Jan. 27, 1980
Mike Foligno vs. Pittsburgh, Jan. 31, 1980

1980-81 — Dale McCourt vs. Colorado, Dec. 20, 1980
Reed Larson vs. Pittsburgh, Jan. 3, 1981
Dale McCourt vs. N.Y. Rangers, Jan. 19, 1981

1981-82 — Mike Foligno vs. Calgary, Oct. 29, 1981
John Ogrodnick vs. Calgary, Oct. 29, 1981
John Ogrodnick vs. Los Angeles, Nov. 5, 1981
Mark Osborne vs. St. Louis, Dec. 1, 1981

1982-83 — John Ogrodnick vs. Calgary, Dec. 12, 1982
Reed Larson vs. Pittsburgh, Feb. 15, 1983
Ivan Boldirev vs. Hartford, Feb. 20, 1983

1983-84 — Ron Duguay vs. Chicago, Nov. 3, 1983
STEVE YZERMAN vs. Toronto, Dec. 23, 1983
John Ogrodnick vs. Toronto, Dec. 23, 1983
Ivan Boldirev vs. Toronto, Feb. 19, 1984
Ivan Boldirev (4) vs. Los Angeles, March 24, 1984

1984-85 — John Ogrodnick vs. Toronto, Dec. 4, 1984
Lane Lambert vs. Calgary, Dec. 28, 1984
Ron Duguay vs. Chicago, Feb. 17, 1985
Danny Gare vs. Vancouver, Feb. 27, 1985
Reed Larson vs. Vancouver, Feb. 27, 1985
Ron Duguay vs. Minnesota, March 1, 1985
John Ogrodnick vs. Edmonton, March 13, 1985
Ron Duguay vs. Vancouver, March 15, 1985
STEVE YZERMAN vs. Toronto, March 30, 1985

1985-86 — Danny Gare vs. Pittsburgh, Oct. 30, 1985
Warren Young vs. St. Louis, Dec. 7, 1985
Petr Klima vs. Chicago, March 5, 1986
Petr Klima vs. Chicago, March 22, 1986

1986-87 — Shawn Burr vs. Philadelphia, Nov. 13, 1986
Petr Klima vs. Boston, March 2, 1987

1987-88 — Tim Higgins vs. Chicago, Dec. 4, 1987
Gerard Gallant vs. Minnesota, Dec. 18, 1987
Bob Probert vs. St. Louis, Dec. 31, 1987
STEVE YZERMAN vs. Winnipeg, Jan. 3, 1988
STEVE YZERMAN vs. Montréal, Feb. 6, 1988
Gerard Gallant vs. New Jersey, Feb. 12, 1988
Gerard Gallant vs. N.Y. Rangers, March 26, 1988
*Petr Klima vs. Toronto, April 7, 1988
*Petr Klima vs. St. Louis, April 21, 1988

1988-89 — STEVE YZERMAN vs. Philadelphia, Nov. 4, 1988
STEVE YZERMAN vs. Philadelphia, Nov. 12, 1988
Gerard Gallant vs. St. Louis, Jan. 4, 1989
Dave Barr vs. N.Y. Islanders, Feb. 21, 1989
*STEVE YZERMAN vs. Chicago, April 6, 1989

1989-90 — STEVE YZERMAN vs. Chicago, Dec. 15, 1989
Jimmy Carson vs. Toronto, Dec. 27, 1989
Shawn Burr vs. Minnesota, Jan. 9, 1990
STEVE YZERMAN (4) vs. Edmonton, Jan. 31, 1990
STEVE YZERMAN vs. Los Angeles, Feb. 14, 1990

1000 01   STEVE YZERMAN vs Toronto, Nov. 17, 1990
Johan Garpenlov (4) vs. St. Louis, Nov. 23, 1990
STEVE YZERMAN vs vs. Winnipeg, Dec. 22, 1990
STEVE YZERMAN vs. St. Louis, Jan. 26, 1991
Jimmy Carson vs. Québec, March 5, 1991
*STEVE YZERMAN vs. St. Louis, April 4, 1991

1991-92 — Ray Sheppard vs. Calgary, Nov. 12, 1991
STEVE YZERMAN vs. Calgary, Dec. 3, 1991
Paul Ysebaert vs. Toronto, Jan. 3, 1992
STEVE YZERMAN vs. Buffalo, Jan 29, 1992
Kevin Miller vs. Buffalo, Feb. 12, 1992
Jimmy Carson vs. St. Louis, Feb. 15, 1992
STEVE YZERMAN vs. Minnesota, Apr. 14, 1992
*Ray Sheppard vs. Minnesota, Apr. 24, 1992

1992-93 — STEVE YZERMAN vs. St. Louis, Oct. 25, 1992
Jimmy Carson vs. Pittsburgh, Nov. 13, 1992
STEVE YZERMAN vs. Calgary, Jan. 26, 1993
STEVE YZERMAN vs. Chicago, Feb. 14, 1993
*Dino Ciccarelli vs. Toronto, Apr. 29, 1993

1993-94 — Shawn Burr vs. Buffalo, Oct. 18, 1993
Ray Sheppard vs. San Jose, Jan. 6, 1994
VYACHESLAV KOZLOV vs. San Jose, Jan. 6, 1994
Ray Sheppard vs. Winnipeg, Jan. 29, 1994
SERGEI FEDOROV vs. Calgary, Mar. 1, 1994
Dino Ciccarelli (4) vs. Vancouver, Apr. 4, 1994

1995   —   Ray Sheppard vs. Vancouver, Jan. 24, 1995
SERGEI FEDOROV (4) vs. Los Angeles, Feb. 12, 1995
*Dino Ciccarelli vs. Dallas, May 11, 1995

1995-96 — VYACHESLAV KOZLOV (4) vs. Montréal, Dec. 2, 1995
*STEVE YZERMAN vs. St. Louis, May 8, 1996

1996-97 — BRENDAN SHANAHAN vs. Toronto, Nov. 27, 1996
SERGEI FEDOROV (5) vs. Washington, Dec. 26, 1996
BRENDAN SHANAHAN vs. Pittsburgh, Feb. 8, 1997
BRENDAN SHANAHAN vs. San Jose, Feb. 12, 1997

*-Playoffs

ACTIVE PLAYERS IN CAPITALS

REGULAR-SEASON HAT TRICKS: 211
PLAYOFF HAT TRICKS: 17
TOTAL HAT TRICKS: 228
SIX-GOAL GAMES: 1
FIVE-GOAL GAMES: 1
FOUR-GOAL GAMES: 21 (Includes 2 in playoffs)
THREE-GOAL GAMES: 207 (Includes 17 in playoffs)

RED WINGS IN STANLEY CUP PLAYOFFS

Times in Playoffs	46	Games Played	408
Times in Finals	20	Games Won	206
Times Won Cup	8	Games Lost	201
Total Series	83	Games Tied	1#
Series Won-Lost	45-38	Goals For-Against	1137-1091

DETROIT VS. ATLANTA FLAMES

Series Played 1   Won by Detroit 1, by Atlanta 0
Games Played 2   Won by Detroit 2, by Atlanta 0   Goals For-Against 8-5
1978 — Detroit won 2 games to 0

DETROIT VS. ANAHEIM MIGHTY DUCKS

Series Played 1   Won by Detroit 1, by Anaheim 0
Games Played ....4 Won by Detroit 4, by Anaheim 0   Goals For-Against 13-8
1997 — Detroit won 4 games to 0

DETROIT VS. BOSTON BRUINS

Series Played 7   Won by Boston 4, by Detroit 3
Games Played 33   Won by Boston 19, by Detroit 14   Goals For-Against 98-96

1941* — Boston won 4 games to 0	1946 — Boston won 4 games to 1
1942 — Detroit won 2 games to 0	1953 — Boston won 4 games to 2
1943* — Detroit won 4 games to 0	1957 — Boston won 4 games to 1
1945 — Detroit won 4 games to 3	

DETROIT VS. CHICAGO BLACKHAWKS

Series Played...........14   Won by Chicago 8, by Detroit 6
Games Played 69   Won by Chicago 38, by Detroit 31   Goals For-Against..190-210

1934* — Chicago won 3 games to 1	1966 — Detroit won 4 games to 2
1941 — Detroit won 2 games to 0	1970 — Chicago won 4 games to 0
1944 — Chicago won 4 games to 1	1985 — Chicago won 3 games to 0
1961* — Chicago won 4 games to 2	1987 — Detroit won 4 games to 0
1963 — Detroit won 4 games to 2	1989 — Chicago won 4 games to 2
1964 — Detroit won 4 games to 3	1992 — Chicago won 4 games to 0
1965 — Chicago won 4 games to 3	1995 — Detroit won 4 games to 1

DETROIT VS. COLORADO AVALANCHE

Series Played 2   Won by Colorado 1, by Detroit 1
Games Played 12   Won by Colorado 6, by Detroit 6   Goals For-Against 32-32
1996 — Colorado won 4 games to 2   1997 — Detroit won 4 games to 2

DETROIT VS. EDMONTON OILERS

Series Played 2   Won by Edmonton 2, by Detroit 0
Games Played 10   Won by Edmonton 8, by Detroit 2   Goals For-Against 26-39
1987 — Edmonton won 4 games to 1   1988 — Edmonton won 4 games to 1

DETROIT VS. DALLAS STARS/MINNESOTA NORTH STARS

Series Played 2   Won by Detroit 2, by Stars 0
Games Played 12   Won by Detroit 8, by Stars 4   Goals For-Against 40-29
1992 — Detroit won 4 games to 3   1995 — Detroit won 4 games to 1

DETROIT VS. MONTRÉAL CANADIENS

Series Played...........12   Won by Detroit 7, by Montréal 5
Games Played 62   Won by Montréal 33, by Detroit 29   Goals For-Against ..149-161

1937 — Detroit won 3 games to 2	1954* — Detroit won 4 games to 3
1939 — Detroit won 2 games to 1	1955* — Detroit won 4 games to 3
1942 — Detroit won 2 games to 1	1956* — Montréal won 4 games to 1
1949 — Detroit won 4 games to 3	1958 — Montréal won 4 games to 0
1951 — Montréal won 4 games to 2	1966* — Montréal won 4 games to 2
1952* — Detroit won 4 games to 0	1978 — Montréal won 4 games to 1

DETROIT VS. MONTRÉAL MAROONS

Series Played 3   Won by Detroit 2, by Montréal 1
Games Played 7   Won by Detroit 5, by Montréal 1#   Goals For-Against 12-6
1932 — Montréal won 1 game# (total goals)   1936 — Detroit won 3 games to 0
1933 — Detroit won 2 games (total goals)

#-Tie game 1-1 vs. Montréal Maroons March 27, 1932, at Detroit

DETROIT VS. NEW JERSEY DEVILS

Series Played 1   Won by New Jersey 1, by Detroit 0
Games Played 4   Won by New Jersey 4, by Detroit 0   Goals For-Against 7-16
1995* — New Jersey won 4 games to 0

DETROIT VS. NEW YORK AMERICANS

Series Played 1   Won by Detroit 1, by Americans 0
Games Played 3   Won by Detroit 2, by Americans 1   Goals For-Against..........9-7
1940 — Detroit won 2 games to 1

DETROIT VS. NEW YORK RANGERS

Series Played 5   Won by Detroit 4, by Rangers 1
Games Played 23   Won by Detroit 13, by Rangers 10   Goals For-Against......57-49
1933 — Rangers won 2 games (total goals)   1948 — Detroit won 4 games to 2
1937* — Detroit won 3 games to 2   1950* — Detroit won 4 games to 3
1941 — Detroit won 2 games to 1

DETROIT VS. PHILADELPHIA

Series Played 1   Won by Detroit 1, by Philadelphia 0
Games Played 4   Won by Detroit 4, by Philadelphia 0   Goals For-Against 16-6
1997* — Detroit won series 4 games to 0

DETROIT VS. ST. LOUIS BLUES

Series Played 5   Won by Detroit 3, by St. Louis 2
Games Played 29   Won by Detroit 16, by St. Louis 13   Goals For-Against......88-79
1984 — St. Louis won 3 games to 1   1996 — Detroit won 4 games to 3
1988 — Detroit won 4 games to 1   1997 — Detroit won 4 games to 2
1991 — St. Louis won 4 games to 3

DETROIT VS. SAN JOSE SHARKS

Series Played 2   Won by Detroit 1, by San Jose 1
Games Played 11   Won by Detroit 7, by San Jose 4   Goals For-Against......51-27
1994 — San Jose won 4 games to 3   1995 — Detroit won 4 games to 0

DETROIT VS. TORONTO MAPLE LEAFS

Series Played 23   Won by Detroit 11, by Toronto 12
Games Played........117   Won by Detroit 59, by Toronto 58   Goals For-Against ..321-311
1929 — Toronto won 2 games (total goals)   1952 — Detroit won 4 games to 0
1934 — Detroit won 3 games to 2   1954 — Detroit won 4 games to 1
1936* — Detroit won 3 games to 1   1955 — Detroit won 4 games to 0
1939 — Toronto won 2 games to 1   1956 — Detroit won 4 games to 1
1940 — Toronto won 2 games to 0   1960 — Toronto won 4 games to 2
1942* — Toronto won 4 games to 3   1961 — Detroit won 4 games to 1
1943 — Detroit won 4 games to 2   1963* — Toronto won 4 games to 1
1945* — Toronto won 4 games to 3   1964* — Toronto won 4 games to 3
1947 — Toronto won 4 games to 1   1987 — Detroit won 4 games to 3
1948* — Toronto won 4 games to 0   1988 — Detroit won 4 games to 2
1949* — Toronto won 4 games to 0   1993 — Toronto won 4 games to 3
1950 — Detroit won 4 games to 3

DETROIT VS. WINNIPEG JETS

Series Played 1   Won by Detroit 1, by Winnipeg 0
Games Played 6   Won by Detroit 4, by Winnipeg 2   Goals For-Against......20-10
1996 — Detroit won 4 games to 2

*-Final series.

MOST GOALS FOR, ONE GAME: 9
  – vs. Toronto, Apr. 7, 1936, Detroit 9, Toronto 4;
  – vs. Toronto, Mar. 29, 1947, Detroit 9, Toronto 1

MOST GOALS FOR, ONE YEAR: 69
  – 1988 (32 vs. Toronto, 21 vs. St. Louis, 16 vs. Edmonton)

MOST GOALS AGAINST, ONE YEAR: 57
  – 1987 (20 vs. Chicago, 14 vs. Toronto, 23 vs. Edmonton)

MOST GOALS FOR, ONE SERIES: 32
  – vs. Toronto, 1988

MOST GOALS AGAINST, ONE SERIES: 25
  – vs. Toronto, 1942; Chicago, 1989

MOST GOALS FOR, ONE HOME GAME: 9
  – vs. Toronto Apr. 7, 1936, Detroit 9, Toronto 4

MOST GOALS AGAINST, ONE HOME GAME: 8
  – vs. Montréal, Apr. 23, 1978, Montréal 8, Detroit 0;
  – vs. Chicago, April 13, 1985, Chicago 8, Detroit 2

MOST GOALS FOR, ONE ROAD GAME: 9
  – vs. Toronto, Mar. 29, 1947, Detroit 9, Toronto 1

MOST GOALS AGAINST, ONE ROAD GAME: 9
  – vs. Toronto, Apr. 14, 1942, Toronto 9, Detroit 3;
  – vs. Chicago, April 10, 1985, Chicago 9, Detroit 5

FASTEST TWO GOALS: *5 seconds
  – Apr. 11, 1965, second period vs. Chicago
    (both by Norm Ullman, 17:35, 17:40 against Glenn Hall), Detroit 4, Chicago 2

FASTEST THREE GOALS: 1:30
  – Mar. 29, 1947, third period at Toronto
    (Jim Conacher, 17:30, Roy Conacher, 18:30; Ed Bruniteau, 19:00), Detroit 9, Toronto 1

FASTEST FOUR GOALS: 4:46
  – Mar. 23, 1939, third period vs. Montréal Canadiens
    (Syd Howe, 13:44; Syd Howe, 14:39; Sid Abel, 17:02; Ed Wares, 18:30),
    Detroit 7, Montréal 3

MOST POWER-PLAY GOALS, ONE YEAR: 22
  – 1995 vs. Dallas, San Jose, Chicago, New Jersey

MOST POWER-PLAY GOALS, ONE SERIES: 11
  – vs. Toronto, 1988

MOST POWER-PLAY GOALS FOR, ONE GAME: 4
  – vs. Montréal Canadiens Mar. 23, 1939, Detroit 7, Montréal 3;
  – vs. Chicago Apr. 4, 1965, Detroit 6, Chicago 3;
  – vs. Chicago Apr. 10, 1966, Detroit 7, Chicago 0;
  – vs. Toronto, Apr. 29, 1993, Detroit 7, Toronto 3;
  – vs. Winnipeg Apr. 23, 1996, Detroit 6, Winnipeg 1

MOST POWER-PLAY GOALS FOR, ONE PERIOD: 3
  – vs. Atlanta Apr. 11, 1978, Detroit 5, Atlanta 3;
  – vs. Winnipeg Apr. 23, 1996, Detroit 6, Winnipeg 1;
  – vs. St. Louis May 5, 1996, Detroit 8, St. Louis 3

MOST POWER-PLAY GOALS AGAINST, ONE YEAR: 20
  – 1988 vs. Toronto, St. Louis, Edmonton

MOST POWER-PLAY GOALS AGAINST, ONE SERIES:
  – 10 vs. Chicago, 1989

MOST POWER-PLAY GOALS AGAINST, ONE GAME: 4
  – vs. Chicago, Mar. 28, 1963, Chicago 5, Detroit 2

MOST SHORTHANDED GOALS FOR, ONE GAME: 2
  – vs. Toronto, Apr. 5, 1936 (Syd Howe, Bucko McDonald), Detroit 3, Toronto 1;
  – vs. Toronto, Apr. 29, 1993 (STEVE YZERMAN, Paul Ysebaert), Detroit 7, Toronto 3;
  – vs. Winnipeg, Apr. 12, 1996 (Coffey, Brown), Detroit 4, St. Louis 0

MOST SHORTHANDED GOALS, ONE PERIOD: 2
  – vs. Toronto, Apr. 29, 1993 (STEVE YZERMAN, Paul Ysebaert), Detroit 7, Toronto 3

MOST SHORTHANDED GOALS, ONE YEAR: 5
  – 1996 vs. Winnipeg, St. Louis, Colorado

MOST SHORTHANDED GOALS AGAINST, ONE GAME: 2
– vs. Montréal, Apr. 23, 1978, Montréal 8, Detroit 0;
– vs. Chicago, Apr. 11, 1989, Detroit 6, Chicago 4

MOST SHORTHANDED GOALS AGAINST, ONE PERIOD: 2
– vs. Montréal, Apr. 23, 1978, Montréal 8, Detroit 0

MOST SHORTHANDED GOALS AGAINST, ONE YEAR: 4
– vs. Chicago, 1989

MOST PENALTY MINUTES, ONE GAME: *152
– vs. St. Louis, Apr. 12, 1991

MOST PENALTY MINUTES, ONE PERIOD: 114
– vs. St. Louis, Apr. 12, 1991

MOST PENALTIES, ONE GAME: 33#
– vs. St. Louis, Apr. 12, 1991

MOST PENALTIES, ONE PERIOD: 20
– vs. St. Louis, Apr. 12, 1991

MOST CONSECUTIVE VICTORIES, ONE YEAR: 8
– 1952 vs. Toronto, Montréal;
– 1995 vs. Dallas, San Jose, Chicago

MOST CONSECUTIVE VICTORIES: 9
– Eight straight in 1952, first in '53

MOST CONSECUTIVE DEFEATS: 8
– Final four games of 1966 final vs. Montréal;
– First four in '70 vs. Chicago

MOST CONSECUTIVE HOME VICTORIES: 11
– Apr. 16, 1954, vs. Montréal;
– Mar. 22-24, 1955, vs. Toronto;
– Apr. 3-5-10-14, 1955, vs. Montréal;
– Mar. 20-22-29, 1956, vs. Toronto;
– April 5, 1956, vs. Montréal

MOST CONSECUTIVE HOME DEFEATS: 5
– Apr. 22, 1945, vs. Toronto;
– Mar. 24-26, 1946, vs. Boston;
– Apr. 1-3, 1947, vs. Toronto;
– Apr. 28-May 1-5, 1966, vs. Montréal;
– Apr. 11-12, 1970, vs. Chicago;
– Apr. 21-23, 1978, vs. Montréal;
– Apr. 7-8, 1985, vs. St. Louis;
– Apr. 13, 1985, vs. Chicago

MOST CONSECUTIVE ROAD VICTORIES: 4
– Mar. 29-Apr. 1, 1952, vs. Toronto;
– Apr. 10-12, 1952, vs. Montréal;
– Mar. 27-30, 1954, vs. Toronto;
– Apr. 8-10, 1954, vs. Montréal;
– Apr. 10-17, 1966, vs. Chicago;
– Apr. 24-26, 1966, vs. Montréal

MOST CONSECUTIVE ROAD DEFEATS: 8
– Mar. 27, 1956, vs. Toronto;
– Mar. 31, 1956, vs. Montréal;
– Apr. 3-10, 1956, vs. Montréal;
– Mar. 31-Apr. 10, 1957, vs. Boston;
– Mar. 25-27, 1958, vs. Montréal

MOST CONSECUTIVE SEASONS QUALIFYING FOR PLAYOFFS: 20
– 1939 through '58

MOST CONSECUTIVE SEASONS NOT QUALIFYING FOR PLAYOFFS: 7
– 1971 through '77

EARLIEST PLAYOFF DATE: Mar. 19
– 1929 vs. Toronto;
– 1940 vs. New York Americans;
– 1946 vs. Boston

LATEST PLAYOFF DATE: June 24
– 1995 vs. New Jersey

*-NHL record
#-Shares NHL record
ACTIVE PLAYERS IN CAPITALS

—RED WINGS' INDIVIDUAL PLAYOFF RECORDS—

MOST YEARS IN PLAYOFFS: 19 – Gordie Howe

MOST CONSECUTIVE YEARS IN PLAYOFFS: 13 – Ted Lindsay (1945-57)

MOST GAMES, CAREER: 154 – Gordie Howe

MOST POINTS, CAREER: 158 – Gordie Howe

MOST GOALS, CAREER: 67 – Gordie Howe

MOST ASSISTS, CAREER: 91 – Gordie Howe

MOST GAMES, ONE YEAR: 19 – 7 Players on 1996 team

MOST POINTS, ONE YEAR: 24 – SERGEI FEDOROV, 7 goals, 17 assists, 1995, 17 games

MOST GOALS, ONE YEAR: 10 – Petr Klima, 1988, 12 games

MOST ASSISTS, ONE YEAR: 18 – SERGEI FEDOROV, 1996, 19 games

MOST POINTS, ONE GAME: 5
- Norm Ullman (twice), 2 goals, 3 assists Apr. 7, 1963
  and 3 goals, 2 assists Apr. 7, 1964, both vs. Chicago;
- STEVE YZERMAN, 2 goals, 3 assists May 5, 1996 vs. St. Louis

MOST GOALS, ONE GAME: 4
- Carl Liscombe (Apr. 3, 1945, vs. Boston);
- Ted Lindsay (Apr. 5, 1955, vs. Montréal)

MOST ASSISTS, ONE GAME: 4
- Dutch Reibel, Apr. 5, 1955, vs. Montréal;
- SERGEI FEDOROV (twice), Apr. 23, 1996 vs. Winnipeg and May 23, 1996 vs. Colorado

MOST POINTS BY ROOKIE: 9 – Shawn Burr, 1987

MOST GOALS BY ROOKIE: 7 – Shawn Burr, 1987

MOST ASSISTS BY ROOKIE: 5
- Paul Woods, 1978;
- SERGEI FEDOROV, 1991

LONGEST POINT STREAK: 12 games – Gordie Howe, 1964

LONGEST GOAL STREAK: 5 games
- Gordie Howe, 1949, '64;
- Ted Lindsay, 1952

MOST POINTS BY ONE LINE, ONE YEAR: 51
- 1955 vs. Toronto, Montréal, 11 games
  (Gordie Howe, 9-11-20; Dutch Reibel, 5-7-12; Ted Lindsay, 7-12-19)

MOST THREE-GOAL GAMES, CAREER: 3
- Norm Ullman, 2 in 1964, 1 in 1965;
- STEVE YZERMAN, 1 in 1989, 1 in 1991, 1 in 1996

MOST THREE-GOAL GAMES, ONE YEAR: 2
- Norm Ullman, 1964;
- Petr Klima, 1988

MOST THREE-GOAL GAMES, ONE SERIES: 2 – Norm Ullman, 1964 vs. Chicago

MOST POWER-PLAY GOALS, CAREER: 13 – Gordie Howe; Alex Delvecchio

MOST POWER-PLAY GOALS, ONE YEAR: 6
- Andy Bathgate, 1966, 12 games;
- Dino Ciccarelli, 1995, 16 games;
- Dino Ciccarelli, 1996, 17 games

MOST POWER-PLAY GOALS, ONE SERIES: 5[#]
- Andy Bathgate, 1966, vs. Chicago, 6 games

MOST POWER-PLAY GOALS, ONE GAME: 3[#]
- Syd Howe, Mar. 23, 1939, vs. Montréal;
- Dino Ciccarelli (twice), Apr. 29, 1993, at Toronto, May 11, 1995, at Dallas

MOST POWER-PLAY GOALS, ONE PERIOD: 2
- Syd Howe, Mar. 23, 1939, third period vs. Montréal;
- Floyd Smith, Apr. 10, 1966, first period at Chicago;
- Dino Ciccarelli, Apr. 29, 1993, second period at Toronto

MOST POINTS, ONE PERIOD: 3 –
- Ted Lindsay, 3 goals, Apr. 5, 1955, second period vs. Montréal;
- Alex Delvecchio, 3 assists, Apr. 14, 1966, third period vs. Chicago;
- VYACHESLAV KOZLOV, 3 assists, May 21, third period vs. San Jose;
- STEVE YZERMAN, 1 goal, 2 assists, May 5, 1996, first period vs. St. Louis

MOST GOALS, ONE PERIOD: 3 – Ted Lindsay, Apr. 5, 1955, second period vs. Montréal

MOST ASSISTS, ONE PERIOD: 3[#]
- Alex Delvecchio, Apr. 14, 1966, third period vs. Chicago;
- VYACHESLAV KOZLOV, May 21, third period vs. San Jose

MOST POINTS BY DEFENSEMAN, ONE YEAR: 18 – Paul Coffey, 1995, 18 games

MOST POINTS BY DEFENSEMAN, ONE GAME: 5
- Eddie Bush, Apr. 9, 1942, at Toronto (1 goal, 4 assists)

MOST GOALS BY DEFENSEMAN, ONE YEAR: 6 – Paul Coffey, 1995, 18 games

MOST ASSISTS BY DEFENSEMAN, ONE YEAR: 12
- Paul Coffey, 1995;
- NICKLAS LIDSTROM, 1995; 18 games each

MOST ASSISTS BY DEFENSEMAN, ONE GAME: 4 – Eddie Bush, Apr. 9, 1942, at Toronto

MOST GAME-WINNING GOALS, CAREER: 11 – Gordie Howe

MOST GAME-WINNING GOALS, ONE YEAR: 4
- Petr Klima, 1988;
- VYACHESLAV KOZLOV, 1995

MOST SHORTHANDED GOALS, CAREER: 4 – Gordie Howe

MOST SHORTHANDED GOALS, GAME: 1 (several times)
- Recent VLADIMIR KONSTANTINOV, May 23, 1996 at Colorado

MOST OVERTIME GOALS, CAREER: 2
- Leo Reise, Mud Bruneteau, Syd Howe, Ted Lindsay

MOST OVERTIME GOALS, ONE YEAR: 2 – Leo Reise, 1950

FASTEST GOAL FROM START OF GAME: 9 seconds
- Gordie Howe, Apr. 1, 1954, vs. Toronto against Harry Lumley

FASTEST TWO GOALS: *5 seconds
- Norm Ullman, Apr. 11, 1965, second period vs. Chicago, 17:35, 17:40 against Glenn Hall

MOST PENALTY MINUTES, CAREER: 218 – Gordie Howe

MOST PENALTY MINUTES, ONE YEAR: 71 – JOE KOCUR, 1987, 16 games

MOST PENALTY MINUTES, ONE GAME: 29
- Randy McKay, Apr. 12, 1991, vs. St. Louis, 2 minors, 3 majors, game misconduct

MOST GAMES BY GOALTENDER, CAREER: 84 – Terry Sawchuk

MOST GAMES BY GOALTENDER, ONE YEAR: 20 – Mike Vernon, 1997

MOST MINUTES BY GOALTENDER, ONE YEAR: 1229 – Mike Vernon, 1997, 20 games

MOST SHUTOUTS, CAREER: 11 – Terry Sawchuk

MOST SHUTOUTS, ONE YEAR: 4[#] – Terry Sawchuk, 1952 vs. Toronto, Montréal, 8 games

LONGEST SHUTOUT SEQUENCE, ONE YEAR: *248 minutes, 32 seconds
- Norm Smith, 1936, vs. Montréal Maroons

LONGEST SHUTOUT SEQUENCE, ONE GAME: 8176 minutes, 30 seconds
- Norm Smith, Mar. 24-25, 1936, at Montréal; Detroit 1, Montréal Maroons 0;
  winning goal by Mud Bruneteau

SHUTOUT BY DETROIT GOALIE IN PLAYOFF DEBUT:
- Norm Smith, Mar. 24-25, 1936, at Montréal; Detroit 1, Montréal Maroons 0, 6 OTs;
- CHRIS OSGOOD, Apr. 20, 1994, vs. San Jose; Detroit 4, San Jose 0

*-NHL record
#-Shares NHL record
ACTIVE PLAYERS IN CAPITALS

RED WINGS' PLAYOFF SCORING LEADERS

	GP	G	A	PTS
Gordie Howe	154	67	91	158
STEVE YZERMAN	**113**	**46**	**65**	**111**
Alex Delvecchio	121	35	69	104
SERGEI FEDOROV	**88**	**27**	**70**	**97**
Ted Lindsay	123	46	44	90
Norm Ullman	80	27	47	74
Sid Abel	93	28	28	56
VYACHESLAV KOZLOV	**68**	**24**	**26**	**50**
Paul Coffey	49	14	36	50
NICKLAS LIDSTROM	**82**	**16**	**31**	**47**
Syd Howe	68	17	27	44
Bob Probert	63	14	29	43
Carl Liscombe	57	22	18	40
Gerard Gallant	57	18	21	39
Adam Oates	38	12	27	39
Mud Bruneteau	72	23	14	37
Red Kelly	74	16	21	37
Joe Carveth	60	19	15	34
Shawn Burr	79	16	17	33
Dino Ciccarelli	47	24	8	32
Marcel Pronovost	117	7	23	30
Don Grosso	45	15	14	29
Marty Pavelich	91	13	15	28
Petr Klima	31	13	14	27
Steve Chiasson	46	12	14	26
Metro Prystai	43	12	14	26
Brent Ashton	32	11	14	25
DOUG BROWN	**45**	**10**	**14**	**24**
Ray Sheppard	42	14	9	23
Herbie Lewis	38	13	10	23
Floyd Smith	44	12	11	23
Bruce MacGregor	56	9	14	23
DARREN McCARTY	**64**	**11**	**10**	**21**
Marty Berry	23	9	12	21
John Chabot	22	5	16	21
John Wilson	50	11	9	20
Vic Stasiuk	38	10	10	20
John Sorrell	31	8	12	20
Dutch Reibel	32	6	14	20

ACTIVE PLAYERS IN BOLD CAPITALS

DETROIT GOALTENDERS'
ALL-TIME PLAYOFF RECORDS

PLAYER	YRS	GP	W	L	T	GA	SO	AVG
Terry Sawchuk	10	84	47	37		209	11	2.51
Harry Lumley	5	54	24	30		129	6	2.26
Mike Vernon	3	42	30	12		88	2	2.08
John Mowers	4	32	19	13		80	2	2.45
Greg Stefan	5	30	12	17		99	1	3.53
CHRIS OSGOOD	**4**	**25**	**11**	**9**		**49**	**3**	**2.16**
Tim Cheveldae	3	25	9	15		71	0	3.00
Roger Crozier	4	23	9	12		57	1	2.59
Glen Hanlon	3	18	9	6		42	3	2.58
Norm Smith	2	12	9	2		18	3	1.28
Glenn Hall	2	15	6	9		43	0	2.86
Cecil Thompson	2	11	5	6		27	1	2.32
Wilf Cude	1	9	4	5		21	1	2.21
Earl Robertson	1	6	3	2		8	2	1.71
John Ross Roach	1	4	2	2		8	1	2.00
Jim Rutherford	1	3	2	1		12	0	4.00
Ralph Almas	1	5	1	3		13	0	3.00
Hank Bassen	2	5	1	3		11	0	2.44
Bob Champoux	1	1	1	0		4	0	4.00
Connie Dion	1	5	1	4		17	0	3.40
Ron Low	1	4	1	3		17	0	4.25
Vince Riendeau	1	2	1	0		4	0	3.29
Bob Essensa	1	4	0	2		9	0	4.95
Allan Bester	1	1	0	0		1	0	3.00
Alex Connell	1	2	0	1	1	3	0	1.50
Clarence Dolson	1	2	0	2		7	0	3.50
Roy Edwards	1	4	0	3		11	0	3.14
Jim Franks	1	1	0	1		2	0	3.00
Corrado Micalef	1	3	0	0		8	0	9.80
Ed Mio	1	1	0	1		3	0	2.86
Sam St. Laurent	1	1	0	0		1	0	6.00

ACTIVE PLAYERS IN BOLD CAPITALS

SKATERS	GP	YEARS
★ Gordie Howe	22	48, 49, 50, 51, 52, 53, 54, 55, 57, 58, 59, 60, 61, 62, 63, 64, 65, 67, 68, 69, 70, 71
★ Alex Delvecchio	13	53, 54, 55, 56, 57, 58, 59, 61, 62, 63, 64, 65, 67
★ Ted Lindsay	10	57, 48, 49, 50, 51, 52, 53, 54, 55, 56
★ Red Kelly	9	50, 51, 52, 53, 54, 55, 56, 57, 58
★ Marcel Pronovost	9	50, 54, 55, 57, 58, 59, 60, 61, 63
★ Norm Ullman	8	55, 60, 61, 62, 63, 64, 67, 68
STEVE YZERMAN	8	84, 88, 89, 90, 91, 92, 93, 97
John Ogrodnick	5	81, 82, 84, 85, 86
★ Marty Pavelich	4	50, 52, 54, 55
★ Bob Goldham	4	50, 52, 54, 55
Jack Stewart	3	47, 48, 49
★ Sid Abel	3	49, 50, 51
★ Metro Prystai	3	50, 53, 54
Reed Larson	3	78, 80, 81
+ Ebbie Goodfellow	2	37, 39
★ Leo Reise	2	50, 51
★ Tony Leswick	2	52, 54
Bill Quackenbush	2	69, 70
Red Berenson	2	72, 74
SERGEI FEDOROV	3	92, 94, 96
Paul Coffey	3	93, 94, 96
+ Herbie Lewis	1	34
+ Syd Howe	1	39
+ Marty Barry	1	37
+ Larry Aurie	1	34
Bud Poile	1	48
Reg Sinclair	1	52
Bill Gadsby	1	65
Carl Brewer	1	70
Gary Bergman	1	72
Mickey Redmond	1	74
Marcel Dionne	1	75
Dan Maloney	1	76
Nick Libett	1	77
Willie Huber	1	83
Bob Probert	1	88
Steve Chiasson	1	93
NICKLAS LIDSTROM	1	96
VIACHESLAV FETISOV	1	97
BRENDAN SHANAHAN	1	97

> ★-Includes games as member of defending Stanley Cup champions in '50, '54 or '55.
> +-Appeared in Bailey ('34), Morenz ('37), Seibert ('39) benefit All-Star games.
>
> 24 other Red Wings appeared in All-Star games, but only as members of defending Stanley Cup champions in '50, '54 or '55.
>
> ACTIVE PLAYERS IN CAPITALS

GOALTENDERS	GP	YEARS
★ Terry Sawchuk	7	50, 51, 52, 53, 54, 59, 63
★ Glenn Hall	2	55, 56
+ Norm Smith	1	37
Tim Cheveldae	1	92
CHRIS OSGOOD	2	96, 97

COACHES	GC	YEARS
★ Tommy Ivan	4	48, 49, 50, 52
Sid Abel	4	61, 63, 64, 67
★ Jimmy Skinner	2	54, 55
+ Jack Adams	1	37
SCOTTY BOWMAN	1	96

—DETROIT CHAMPIONSHIPS, STANLEY CUP FINALS—

STANLEY CUP: 1936, 37, 43, 50, 52, 54, 55, 97

LEAGUE CHAMPIONS/BEST REGULAR-SEASON RECORD: 1933-34, 35-36, 36-37, 42-43, 48-49, 49-50, 50-51, 51-52, 52-53, 53-54, 54-55, 56-57, 64-65, 95, 95-96

DIVISION CHAMPIONS (REGULAR SEASON): American Division: 1934-35, 35-36, 36-37; Norris Division: 87-88, 88-89, 91-92; Central Division: 93-94, 95, 95-96

DIVISION CHAMPIONS (PLAYOFFS): Norris Division: 1987, 88; Central Division: 95, 95-96

STANLEY CUP FINALISTS:
1934, 36, 37, 41, 42, 43, 45, 48, 49, 50, 52, 54, 55, 56, 61, 63, 64, 66, 95, 97

RED WINGS' ENTRY DRAFT SELECTIONS
(Since inception in 1963)

Round	Overall
1963	
1 Pete Mahovlich	2
2 Bill Cosburn	8
1964	
1 Claude Gauthier	1
2 Brian Watts	7
3 Ralph Buchanan	13
4 Ronald LeClerc	19
1965	
1 George Forge	3
2 Bob Birdsell	8
1966	
1 Steve Atkinson	6
2 Jim Whitaker	12
3 Lee Carpenter	18
4 Grant Cole	24
1967	
1 Ron Barkwell	9
2 Alan Karlander	17
1968	
1 Steve Adrascik	11
2 Herb Boxer	17
1969	
1 Jim Rutherford	10
2 Ron Garwasiuk	21
3 Wayne Hawrysh	33
4 Warren Chernecki	45
5 Wally Olds	57
1970	
1 Serge Lageunesse	12
2 Bob Guindon	26
3 Yvon Lambert	40
4 Tom Johnstone	54
5 Tom Mellor	68
6 Bernard McNeil	82
7 Ed Hays	95
1971	
1 Marcel Dionne	2
2 Henry Boucha	16
3 Ralph Hosiavouri	30
4 George Hulme	44
5 Earl Anderson	58
6 Charlie Shaw	72
7 Jim Nahrgang	86
8 Bob Boyd	100
1972	
2 Pierre Guite	26
3 Bob Kreiger	42
4 Danny Gruen	68
5 Dennis Johnson	74
6 Bill Miller	90
7 Glen Seperich	106
8 Mike Ford	122
9 George Kuzmicz	138
12 Dave Arundel	150

1973	
1 Terry Richardson	11
3 Nelson Pyatt	39
3 Robbie Neale	43
4 Mike Korney	59
5 Blair Stewart	75
6 Glen Cikello	91
7 Brian Middleton	107
8 Dennis Polonich	123
9 Dennis O'Brien	135
9 Tom Newman	138
9 Ray Bibeau	139
10 Kevin Neville	151
10 Ken Gibb	154
10 Mitch Brandt	155
1974	
1 Bill Lochead	9
3 Dan Mandryk	44
3 Bill Evo	45
4 Michel Bergeron	63
5 John Taft	81
6 Don Dufek	99
7 Jack Carlson	117
8 Gregg Steele	134
9 Glen McLeod	151
1975	
1 Rick LaPointe	5
2 Jerry Rollins	23
3 Al Cameron	37
3 Blair Davidson	45
3 Clark Hamilton	50
4 Mike Wirachowski	59
5 Mike Wong	77
6 Mike Harazny	95
7 Jean-Luc Phaneuf	113
8 Steve Carlson	131
9 Gary Vaughn	148
10 Jean Thibodeau	164
11 Dave Hanson	176
11 Robin Larson	178
1976	
1 Fred Williams	4
2 Reed Larson	22
3 Fred Berry	40
4 Kevin Schamehorn	58
5 Dwight Schofield	76
6 Tony Horvath	94
7 Fern LeBlanc	111
8 Claude Legris	120
1977	
1 Dale McCourt	1
3 Rick Vasko	37
4 John Hilworth	55
5 Jim Korn	73
6 Jim Baxter	91
7 Randy Wilson	109
8 Ray Roy	125
9 Kip Churchill	141
10 Lance Gatoni	155
11 Rob Plumb	163
12 Alan Belanger	170
13 Dean Willers	175
14 Roland Cloutier	178
15 Ed Hill	181
16 Val James	184
17 Grant Morin	185

1978	
1 Willie Huber	9
1 Brent Peterson	12
2 Glen Hicks	28
2 Al Jensen	31
3 Doug Derkson	53
4 Bjorn Skaare	62
5 Ted Nolan	78
6 Sylvain Locas	95
7 Wes George	112
8 John Barrett	129
9 Jim Malazdrewicz	146
10 Geoff Shaw	163
11 Carl VanHarrewyn	178
12 Ladislav Svozil	194
13 Tom Bailey	208
14 Larry Lozinski	219
15 Randy Betty	224
16 Brian Crawley	226
17 Doug Feasby	228
1979	
1 Mike Foligno	3
3 Jody Gage	45
3 Boris Fistric	46
4 John Ogrodnick	66
5 Joe Paterson	87
6 Carmine Cirella	108
1980	
1 Mike Blaisdell	11
3 Mark Osborne	46
5 Mike Corrigan	88
6 Wayne Crawford	109
7 Mike Braun	130
8 John Beukeboom	151
9 Dave Miles	172
10 Brian Rorabeck	193
1981	
2 Claude Loiselle	23
3 Corrado Micalof	44
5 Larry Trader	86
6 Gerard Gallant	107
7 Greg Stefan	128
8 Rick Zombo	149
9 Don LeBlanc	170
10 Robert Nordmark	191
1982	
1 Murray Craven	17
2 Yves Courteau	23
3 Carmine Vani	44
4 Craig Coxe	66
5 Brad Shaw	86
6 Claude Vilgrain	107
7 Greg Hudas	128
8 Pat Lahey	149
9 Gary Cullen	170
10 Brent Meckling	191
11 Mike Stern	212
12 Shaun Reagan	233

1983

1 Steve Yzerman 4
2 Lane Lambert 25
3 Bob Probert 46
4 Dave Korol 70
5 Petr Klima 88
5 Joe Kocur 91
6 Chris Pusey 109
7 Bob Pierson 130
8 Craig Butz 151
9 Dave Sikorski 172
10 Stu Grimson 193
11 Jeff Frank 214
12 Chuck Chiatto 235

1984

1 Shawn Burr 7
2 Doug Houda 28
3 Milan Chalupa 49
4 Mats Lundstrom 91
6 Randy Hansch 112
7 Stefan Larsson 133
7 Lars Karlsson 152
8 Urban Nordin 154
9 Bill Shibicky 175
10 Jay Rose 195
11 Tim Kaiser 216
12 Tom Nickolau 236

1985

1 Brent Fedyk 8
2 Jeff Sharples 29
3 Steve Chiasson 50
4 Mark Gowans 71
5 Chris Luongo 92
6 Randy McKay 113
7 Thomas Bjuhr 134
8 Mike Luckraft 155
9 Rob Schenna 176
10 Eerik Hamalainen 197
11 Bo Svanberg 218
12 Mikael Lindman 239

1986

1 Joe Murphy 1
2 Adam Graves 22
3 Derek Mayer 43
4 Tim Cheveldae 64
5 Johan Garpenlov 85
6 Jay Stark 106
7 Per Djoos 127
8 Dean Morton 148
9 Marc Potvin 169
10 Scott King 190
11 Tom Bissett 211
12 Peter Ekroth 232

1987

1 Yves Racine 11
2 Gord Kruppke 32
2 Bob Wilkie 41
3 Dennis Holland 52
4 Mark Reimer 74
5 Radomir Brazda 95
6 Sean Clifford 116
7 Mike Gober 137
8 Kevin Scott 158
9 Mikko Haapakoski 179
10 Darin Bannister 200
11 Craig Quinlan 221
12 Tomas Jansson 242

1988

1 Kory Kocur 17
2 Serge Anglehart 38
3 Guy Dupuis 47
3 Petr Hrbek 59
4 Sheldon Kennedy 80
7 Kelly Hurd 143
8 Brian McCormack 164
9 Jody Praznik 185
10 Glenn Goodall 206
11 Darren Colbourne 227
12 Don Stone 248

1989

1 Mike Sillinger 11
2 Bob Boughner 32
3 Nicklas Lidstrom 53
4 Sergei Fedorov 74
5 Shawn McCosh 95
6 Dallas Drake 116
7 Scott Zygulski 137
8 Andy Suhy 158
9 Bob Jones 179
10 Greg Bignell 200
10 Rick Judson 204
11 Vladimir Konstantinov 221
12 Joseph Frederick 242
12 Jason Glickman 246

1990

1 Keith Primeau 3
3 Vyacheslav Kozlov 45
4 Stewart Malgunas 66
5 Tony Burns 87
6 Claude Barthe 108
7 Jason York 129
8 Wes McCauley 150
9 Anthony Gruba 171
10 Travis Tucker 192
11 Brett Larson 213
12 John Hendry 234

1991

1 Martin Lapointe 10
2 Jamie Pushor 32
3 Chris Osgood 54
4 Michael Knuble 76
5 Dimitri Motkov 98
7 Igor Malykhin 142
9 Jim Bermingham 186
10 Jason Firth 208
11 Bart Turner 230
12 Andrew Miller 252

1992

1 Curtis Bowen 22
2 Darren McCarty 46
3 Sylvain Cloutier 70
5 Mike Sullivan 118
6 Jason MacDonald 142
7 Greg Scott 166
8 Justin Krall 183
8 C.J. Denomme 189
9 Jeff Walker 214
10 Dan McGillis 238
11 Ryan Bach 262

1993

1 Anders Eriksson 22
2 Jon Coleman 48
3 Kevin Hilton 74
4 John Jakopin 97
4 Benoit Larose 100
5 Norm Maracle 126
6 Tim Spitzig 152
7 Yuri Yeresko 178
8 Viteslav Skuta 204
9 Ryan Shanahan 230
10 Jim Kosecki 256
11 Gord Hunt 282

1994

1 Yan Golubovsky 23
2 Mathieu Dandenault 49
3 Sean Gilliam 75
5 Frederic Deschenes 114
5 Doug Battaglia 127
6 Paval Agarkov 153
8 Jason Elliot 205
9 Jeff Mikesch 231
10 Tomas Holmstrom 257
11 Toivo Suursoo 283

1995

1 Maxim Kuznetsov 26
2 Philippe Audet 52
3 Darryl Laplante 58
4 Anatoly Ustugov 104
5 Chad Wilchynski 125
5 David Arsenault 126
6 Tyler Perry 156
7 Per Eklund 182
8 Andrei Samokvalov 208
9 David Engblom 234

1996

1 Jesse Wallin 26
4 Aren Miller 52
4 Johan Forsander 108
5 Michal Podolka 135
6 Magnus Nilsson 144
6 Alexandre Jacques 162
7 Colin Beardsmore 189
8 Craig Stahl 215
9 Eugeniy Afanasiev 241

1997

2 Yuri Butsayev 49
3 Petr Sykora 76
4 Quintin Lang 102
5 John Wikstrom 129
6 B.J. Young 157
7 Mike Laceby 186
8 Steve Wilejto 213
9 Greg Willers 239

SUPPLEMENTAL DRAFT

1987 — Mike LaMoine
1988 — Gary Shuchuk
1989 — Brad Kreick
1990 — Mike Casselman;
Don Oliver
1991 — Kelly Sorensen

──RED WINGS' ALL-TIME PLAYER TRANSACTIONS──

──────────1926-27 SEASON THROUGH 1929──────────

ACQUIRED:

1927 DUKE KEATS and ARCHIE BRIDEN from Boston for Frank Frederickson and Harry Meeking.

1927 RUSS OATMAN sold to Montréal Maroons for $9,500

1927 PETE BELLEFEUILLE from Toronto for Slim Halderson

1927 GEORGE HAY and PERCY TRAUB from Chicago for $15,000

1927 BILL BRYDGE from Toronto for Art Duncan

1927 CARSON COOPER from Boston for Fred Gordon

1927 REG NOBLE from Montréal Maroons for $7,500

1927 STAN BROWN from New York Rangers for Archie Briden

1927 LARRY AURIE from London (Canadian Pro League) for cash

1927 GORD FRASER from Chicago for Duke Keats

1928 JIM HERBERTS from Toronto for Jack Arbour and $12,500

1928 BOB CONNORS and rights to EBBIE GOODFELLOW from New York Americans for John Sheppard

1928 HERB LEWIS from Duluth (U.S. Hockey League) for $5,000

1928 CLARENCE "DOLLY" DOLSON from London (Canadian Pro League) for cash

1929 HAROLD HICKS from Montréal Maroons for cash

1929 BILL BEVERIDGE from Ottawa Senators on loan

──────────────────1930s──────────────────

1930 JOHN SORRELL from London (International League) for cash

1931 LEROY GOLDSWORTHY from London (International League) for Harold Hicks

1931 ALEX CONNELL, HEC KILREA, ALEX SMITH, DANNY COX and ART GAGNE on loan from Ottawa, which folded after 31-32 season

1931 DOUG YOUNG from Cleveland (International League) in inter-league draft

1931 FRANK CARSON and HAP EMMS from New York Americans for Bert McInenly and Tom Filmore

1932 JOHN ROSS ROACH from New York Rangers for $11,000

1932 CARL VOSS from New York Rangers for $5,500

1933 GORD PETTINGER from New York Rangers for cash

1933 FRED ROBERTSON from Toronto for $6,500

1933 COONEY WEILAND from Ottawa for Carl Voss

1934 TED GRAHAM from Montréal Maroons for Stu Evans

1934 WILF CUDE from Montréal Canadiens on loan for season

1934 LLOYD GROSS from Boston for $2,500

1934 TOM ANDERSON and YANK BOYD from Philadelphia (Canadian-American League) for cash

1934 WALLY KILREA from Montréal Maroons for Gus Marker

1934 GEORGE PATTTERSON from Boston for Gene Carrigan

1934 NORMIE SMITH from St. Louis Eagles for Burr Williams

1935 BUCKO McDONALD, DESSE ROCHE and EARL ROCHE from Buffalo (International League) for George Patterson and Lloyd Gross

1935 SYD HOWE and SCOTTY BOWMAN from St. Louis Eagles for Ted Graham and $50,000

1935 MARTY BARRY and ART GIROUX from Boston for Cooney Weiland and Walt Buswell

1935 HEC KILREA from Toronto for $7,500

1935 PETE KELLY from St. Louis Eagles in dispersal draft

1937 KEN DORATY from Cleveland (International League) for cash

1937 RED BEATTIE from Boston for Gord Pettinger

1937 ALEX MOTTER from Boston for Clarence Drouillard

1938 EDDIE WARES from New York Rangers for John Sherf and $12,500

1938 JOE LAMB from New York Americans for Red Beattie

1938 CHARLIE CONACHER from Toronto for $16,000

1938 CHARLIE MASON from New York Rangers for cash

1938 CECIL THOMPSON from Boston for Jim Franks and $15,000
1938 BILL THOMSON and $10,000 from Toronto for Bucko McDonald
1939 PHIL BESLER from Chicago for Charlie Mason
1939 CECIL DILLON from New York Rangers for cash

1940s

1940 HAROLD JACKSON from Providence (American League) for Cecil Dillon and Eddie Bush
1941 DUTCH HILLER from New York Rangers for $5,000
1942 PAT McREAVY from Boston for Dutch Hiller
1942 EDDIE BUSH from Providence (American League) for Bob Whitelaw and Buck Jones
1942 PAT EGAN, MURRAY ARMSTRONG and HARRY WATSON from New York Americans for $35,000 after that club folded
1944 BILL HOLLETT from Boston for Pat Egan
1945 EARL SIEBERT from Chicago for Don Grosso, Byron McDonald and Cully Simon
1945 FERN GAUTHIER and ROLLIE ROSSINGNOL from Montréal Canadiens for Billy Reay
1946 BILLY TAYLOR from Toronto for Harry Watson.
1946 DOUG BALDWIN and RAY POWELL from Toronto for Gerry Brown
1946 ROY CONACHER from Boston for Joe Carvath
1946 PETE HORECK and LEO REISE from Chicago for Adam Brown and Ray Powell
1947 JIM McFADDEN from Buffalo (American League) for Les Douglas and Hal Jackson
1947 BEP GUIDOLIN from Boston for Billy Taylor
1948 GEORGE GEE and BUD POILE from Chicago for Jim Conacher, Bep Guidolin and Doug McCaig
1949 Steve Black from St. Louis (American League) for cash
1949 PETE BABANDO, PETE DURHAM, CLARE MARTIN and JIM PETERS from Boston for Pete Horeck and Bill Quackenbush
1949 JOE CARVETH from Montréal for Calum Mackay and cash

1950s

1950 BOB GOLDHAM, JIM HENRY, METRO PRYSTAI and GAYE STEWART from Chicago for Pete Babando, Al Dewsbury, Harry Lumley, Don Morrison and Jack Stewart
1950 BERT OLMSTEAD and VIC STASIUK from Chicago for Lee Fogolin and Steve Black
1950 LEO GRAVELLE and cash from Montréal for Bert Olmstead
1951 TONY LESWICK from New York for Gaye Stewart
1951 $75,000 from Chicago for George Gee, Clare Martin, Jim McFadden, Max McNab, Jim Peters and Clare Raglan
1952 REG SINCLAIR from New York for Leo Reise
1954 LORNE DAVIS and cash from Chicago for Metro Prystai
1955 DAVE CREIGHTON, BUCKY HOLLINGWORTH and JERRY TOPPAZZINI from Chicago for Tony Leswick, Glen Skov, Johnny Wilson and Benny Woit
1955 BILLY DEA and DOLPH KUKOLOWICZ from New York for Dave Creighton and Bronco Horvath
1955 GILLES BOISVERT, REAL CHEVREFILS, NORM CORCORAN, WARREN GODFREY and ED SANFORD from Boston for Marcel Bonin, Lorne Davis, Terry Sawchuk and Vic Stasiuk
1955 MURRAY COSTELLO and LORNE FERGUSON from Boston for Real Chevrefils and Jerry Toppazzini
1955 METRO PRYSTAI from Chicago for Ed Sanford
1957 TERRY SAWCHUK from Boston for John Bucyk and cash
1957 HANK BASSEN, FORBES KENNEDY, BILL PRESTON and JOHNNY WILSON from Chicago for Glenn Hall and Ted Lindsay
1957 BOB BAILEY, HEC LALANDE, JACK McINTYRE and NICK MICKOSKI from Chicago for Billy Dea, Bill Dineen, Lorne Ferguson and Dutch Reibel
1959 BARRY CULLEN from Toronto for Johnny Wilson
1959 JIM MORRISON from Boston for Nick Mickoski

1960s

1960 MARC REAUME from Toronto for Red Kelly
1960 HOWIE GLOVER from Chicago for Jim Morrison
1960 ALLAN JOHNSON from Montréal for cash
1960 PETE CONACHER from Buffalo (American League) for Barry Cullen
1961 HOWIE YOUNG from Hershey (American League for Marc Reaume
1961 LEO LABINE and VIC STASIUK from Boston for Gary Aldcorn, Tom McCarthy and Murray Oliver
1961 BILL GADSBY from New York for Les Hunt and cash
1961 ED LITZENBERGER from Chicago for Gerry Melnyk and Brian Smith
1961 NOEL PRICE from New York for Pete Goegan and cash
1962 DOUG BARKLEY from Chicago for Len Lunde and John McKenzie
1962 PETE GOEGAN from New York for Noel Price
1962 ANDRE PRONOVOST from Boston for Forbes Kennedy
1963 ROGER CROZIER and RON INGRAM from Chicago for Howie Young
1963 WARREN GODFREY from Boston for Gerry Odrowski
1964 AL LANGLOIS from New York for Ron Ingram
1964 AUTRY ERICKSON and RON MURPHY from Chicago for Ian Cushenan, John Miszuk and Art Stratton
1965 ANDY BATHGATE, BILLY HARRIS and GARRY JARRETT from Toronto for Autry Erickson, Larry Jeffrey, Eddie Joyal, Lowell MacDonald and Marcel Pronovost
1965 BOB McCORD, AB McDONALD and KEN STEPHANSON from Boston for Bob Dillabough, Ron Harris, Al Langlois and Parker MacDonald
1965 PARKER MacDONALD from Boston for Pit Martin
1966 LEO BOIVIN and DEAN PRENTICE from Boston for Gary Doak, Ron Murphy, Bill Lesuk and Rick Smith
1966 HOWIE YOUNG from Chicago for Murray Hall, Al LeBrun and Rick Morris
1967 JOHN BRENNEMAN from St.Louis for Craig Cameron, Don Giesebrecht and Larry Hornung
1967 JEAN GUY TALBOT and DAVE RICHARDSON from Minnesota for Duke Harris and Bob McCord
1968 KENT DOUGLAS from Oakland for John Brenneman, Ted Hampson and Bert Marshall
1968 CARL BREWER, PETE STEMKOWSKI, FRANK MAHOVLICH and GARRY UNGER from Toronto for Floyd Smith, Norm Ullman and Paul Henderson
1968 BOB BAUN and RON HARRIS from Oakland for Gary Jarrett, Doug Roberts, Chris Worthy and Howie Young
1968 TERRY SAWCHUK from Los Angeles for Jimmy Peters Jr.
1968 POUL POPIEL from Los Angeles for Ron Anderson
1969 WAYNE CONNELLY from Minnesota for Danny Lawson
1969 GARRY MONAHAN and DOUG PIPER from Montréal for Bart Crashley and Pete Mahovlich
1969 LARRY JEFFREY from New York for Terry Sawchuk and Sandy Snow
1969 BILLY DEA from Pittsburgh for Mike McMahon

1970s

1970 DALE ROLFE, GARY CROTEAU and LARRY JOHNSON from Los Angeles for Garry Monahan, Matt Ravlich and Brian Gibbons
1970 TOM WEBSTER from Buffalo for Roger Crozier
1970 LARRY BROWN and DON LUCE from New York for Pete Stemkowski and Steve Andrascik
1970 $30,000 waiver price from Buffalo for Bob Baun
1971 BILL COLLINS, GUY CHARRON and MICKEY REDMOND from Montréal for Frank Mahovlich
1971 ARNIE BROWN, MIKE ROBITAILLE and TOM MILLER from New York for Larry Brown and Bruce MacGregor
1971 RED BERENSON and TIM ECCLESTONE from St. Louis for Garry Unger and Wayne Connelly

1971 JOE DALEY from Buffalo for Mike Robitaille and Don Luce
1971 LEON ROCHEFORT from Montréal for Kerry Ketter
1971 AB McDONALD, BOB WALL and MIKE LOWE from St. Louis for Carl Brewer
1971 RON STACKHOUSE from California for Tom Webster
1971 ART STRATTON from Seattle (Western League) for cash
1971 BILL SUTHERLAND from St. Louis for cash
1971 BOB COOK from Vancouver for cash
1971 JIM KRULICKI from NYRangers for Dale Rolfe
1972 RALPH STEWART from Vancouver for Jim Niekamp
1972 RICK NEWELL and GARY DOAK from New York Rangers for first-round pick in 1972 Entry Draft
1972 DENIS DeJORDY and DONN McLAUGHLIN from New York Islanders for Arnie Brown and Gerry Gray
1973 ROY EDWARDS from Pittsburgh for second-round pick in 1973 and '74 entry drafts
1973 BILL HOGABOAM from Atlanta for Leon Rochefort
1973 BRIAN LAVENDER and KEN MURRAY from New York Islanders for Ralph Stewart and Bob Cook
1973 Third-round pick in 1973 Entry Draft and cash from Pittsburgh for Andy Brown
1973 ACE BAILEY and MURRAY WING from Boston for Gary Daok
1973 RICK FOLEY from Philadelphia for Serge Lajeunesse
1973 BRENT HUGHTS from St. Louis for cash
1973 TED HARRIS from Minnesota for Gary Bergman
1973 DOUG ROBERTS from Boston for cash
1973 PIERRE JARRY from Toronto for Tim Ecclestone
1973 MIKE JAKUBO from St. Louis for Dan McPherson
1974 JIM RUTHERFORD and JACK LYNCH from Pittsburgh for Ron Stackhouse
1974 BRYAN WATSON, CHRIS EVANS and JEAN HAMEL from St. Louis for Billy Collins, Ace Bailey and Ted Harris
1974 CLAUDE HOUDE from NY Rangers for Brian Lavender
1974 HENRY NOWAK and third-round pick in 1974 Entry Draft from Pittsburgh for Nelson DeBenedet
1974 DANNY GRANT from Minnesota for Henry Boucha
1974 BRIAN MURPHY from Baltimore (American League) for cash
1974 TED SNELL, BART CRASHLEY and LARRY GIROUX from Kansas City for Guy Charron and Claude Houde
1974 PHIL ROBERTO and third-round pick in 1975 Entry Draft from St. Louis for Red Berenson.
1975 DAVE KRYSKOW from Washington for Jack Lynch.
1975 WALT McKECHNIE from Boston for Earl Anderson, Hank Nowak and third-round pick in 1975 Entry Draft
1975 MIKE BLOOM from Washington for Blair Stewart
1975 Third-round pick in 1975 Entry Draft from Washington for Nelson Pyatt
1975 DAN MALONEY, TERRY HARPER and second round amateur 1976 NHL draft choice from Los Angeles for Marcel Dionne and Bart Crashley
1975 BRIAN HEXTALL from Atlanta for Dave Kryskow
1975 PETER McDUFFE and GLEN BURDON from Kansas City for Gary Bergman and Bill McKenzie
1975 ED GIACOMIN from New York Rangers on waivers
1975 J.P. LeBLANC from Denver (WHA) for cash and second-round pick in 1977 Entry Draft (to Chicago for his rights)
1975 RICK CHINNICK from Minnesota for Bryan Hextall
1975 DON MARTINEAU from Minnesota for Pierre Jarry
1976 BUSTER HARVEY from Kansas City for Phil Roberto
1976 DENNIS HEXTALL from Minnesota for Bill Hogaboam and second-round pick in 1976 Entry Draft
1976 RICK WILSON from St. Louis for Doug Grant
1976 GREG JOLY from Washington for Bryan Watson
1977 TERRY MURRAY, STEVE COATES, BOB RITCHIE and DAVE KELLY from Philadelphia for Mike Korney and Rick Lapointe
1977 RICK BOWNESS from Atlanta for cash

1977 RON LOW from Washington for Walt McKechnie and future considerations
1977 ANDRE ST.LAURENT from New York Islanders for Michel Bergeron
1977 TIM SHEEHY and VACLAV NEDOMANSKY from Birmingham (WHA) for Dave Hanson, Steve Durbano and future considerations
1977 DENNIS HULL from Chicago for future considerations
1978 Third-round pick in 1978 Entry Draft and future considerations from Los Angeles for Danny Grant
1978 ERROL THOMPSON with first-round 1978 and '80 entry drafts, and second-round pick in '78 draft from Toronto for Dan Maloney and second-round draft pick in '80.
1978 ROGIE VACHON from Los Angeles as free agent (Dale McCourt to Los Angeles as equalization)
1979 DALE McCOURT from Los Angeles for Andre St. Laurent and first-round picks in 1980 and '81 entry drafts
1979 GREG CARROLL from Washington on waivers
1979 BILL HOGABOAM from Minnesota on waivers
1979 BARRY LONG from Washington reclaimed prior to 1979 expansion draft
1979 PETE MAHOVLICH from Pittsburgh for Nick Libett
1979 DENNIS SOBCHUK from Philadelphia for third or fourth-round choice in 1981 Entry Draft

1980s

1980 GILLES GILBERT from Boston for Rogie Vachon
1980 Cash from Winnipeg for Barry Long
1980 RICK SMITH from Boston on waivers
1980 MARK KIRTON from Toronto for Jim Rutherford
1981 GARY McADAM from Pittsburgh for Errol Thompson
1981 EARL INGARFIELD from Calgary for Dan Labraaten
1981 BRAD SMITH from Calgary for Rick Vasko
1981 MARK LOFTHOUSE from Washington for Al Jensen
1981 WALT McKECHNIE from Colorado as a free agent
1981 DON MURDOCH, GREG SMITH and first-round pick in 1982 Entry Draft from Minnesota for Detroit's first-round pick in '82
1981 ERIC VAIL from Calgary for Gary McAdam and fourth-round picks in 1982 and '83 entry drafts
1981 DEREK SMITH, DANNY GARE and JIM SCHOENFELD from Buffalo for Dale McCourt, Mike Foligno and Brent Peterson
1981 BOB SAUVE from Buffalo for future considerations
1982 CRAIG COXE, a fourth-round pick in 1982 Entry Draft and fifth-round pick in '83 draft from Toronto for Jim Korn
1982 REGGIE LEACH from Philadelphia as free agent
1982 COLIN CAMPBELL from Vancouver as free agent
1982 TOM ROWE from Vancouver as free agent
1982 STAN WEIR from Edmonton for cash
1982 DWIGHT FOSTER from New Jersey for cash
1982 BOBBY FRANCIS from Calgary for Yves Courteau
1983 IVAN BOLDIREV from Vancouver for Mark Kirton
1983 KEN SOLHEIM from Minnesota for player to be named later
1983 ED JOHNSTONE, ED MIO and RON DUGUAY from New York Rangers for Mark Osborne, Mike Blaisdell and Willie Huber
1983 BARRY MELROSE from Toronto as free agent
1983 BOB MANNO from Toronto as free agent
1983 BRAD PARK from Boston as free agent
1983 ANDRE ST.LAURENT from Pittsburgh for future considerations
1983 BLAKE DUNLOP from St. Louis as free agent
1984 RICK MacLEISH from Philadelphia for future considerations
1984 PIERRE AUBRY from Québec for cash
1984 ROB McCLANAHAN from NY Rangers for future considerations
1984 DAVE "TIGER" WILLIAMS from Vancouver for Rob McClanahan

1984 FRANTISEK CERNIK from Québec as free agent
1984 DARRYL SITTLER from Philadelphia for Murray Craven and Joe Patterson
1984 TODD BIDNER from Edmonton for Rejean Cloutier
1984 DAVE SILK from Boston on waivers
1985 WARREN YOUNG from Pittsburgh as free agent
1985 MIKE McEWEN from Washington as free agent
1985 HAROLD SNEPSTS from Minnesota as free agent
1985 STEVE RICHMOND from New York Rangers for Mike McEwen
1985 BILLY CARROLL from Edmonton for Bruce Eakin
1986 DARREN VEITCH from Washington for Greg Smith and John Barrett
1986 MIKE O'CONNELL from Boston for Reed Larson
1986 DOUG SHEDDEN from Pittsburgh for Ron Duguay
1986 DAVE DONNELLY from Boston for Dwight Foster
1986 TIM HIGGINS from New Jersey for Claude Loiselle
1986 DAVE LEWIS from New Jersey as free agent
1986 GLEN HANLON and third-round picks in 1987 and '88 entry drafts from New York
     Rangers for Kelly Kisio, Lane Lambert, Jim Leavins and fifth-round pick in '88 draft
1986 LEE NORWOOD from St. Louis for Larry Trader
1986 SAM ST. LAURENT from New Jersey for Steve Richmond
1986 DOUG HALWARD from Vancouver for future considerations
1987 DAVE BARR from Hartford for Randy Ladouceur
1987 BRENT ASHTON, GILBERT DELORME and MARK KUMPEL from Québec for John
     Ogrodnick, Basil McRae and Doug Shedden
1987 MEL BRIDGMAN from New Jersey for CHRIS CICHOCKI and third-round pick in 1987
     Entry Draft
1987 Second-round pick in 1987 Entry Draft from Philadelphia for Mark Laforest
1987 JOHN CHABOT from Pittsburgh as free agent
1987 DARREN ELIOT from Los Angeles as free agent
1988 JIM NILL from Winnipeg for Mark Kumpel
1988 JIM PAVESE from New York Rangers for a fourth-round pick in 1989 Enrty Draft
1988 PAUL MacLEAN from Winnipeg for Brent Aston
1988 MIROSLAV FRYCER from Toronto for Darren Veitch
1988 JOHN BLUM from Boston as free agent
1988 BRUCE BELL from Québec claimed on waivers
1989 Tenth-round pick in the 1989 Entry Draft from Edmonton for Miroslav Frycer
1989 Twelfth-round pick in the 1989 Entry Draft from Edmonton for Doug Halward
1989 TORRIE ROBERTSON from Hartford for Jim Pavese
1989 MARK HABSCHEID from Minnesota as free agent
1989 BORJE SALMING from Toronto as free agent
1989 BERNIE FEDERKO and TONY McKEGNEY from St. Louis for Adam Oates and Paul
     MacLean
1989 CHRIS KOTSOPOULOS from Toronto as free agent
1989 JIMMY CARSON, KEVIN McCLELLAND and fifth-round pick in the 1991 Entry Draft from
     Edmonton for Petr Klima, Joe Murphy, Adam Graves and Jeff Sharples
1989 ROBERT PICARD and GREG ADAMS from Québec for Tony McKegney

1990s

1990 RICK GREEN from Montréal for fifth-round pick in the 1991 Entry Draft
1990 BRAD McCRIMMON from Calgary for second-round pick in the 1990 Entry Draft
1990 PAUL YSEBAERT from New Jersey for Lee Norwood
1991 Brad Marsh from Toronto for eighth-round pick in the 1991 Entry Draft
1991 Doug Crossman from Hartford for Doug Houda
1991 Allan Bester form Toronto for sixth-round pick in 1991 Entry Draft
1991 Dennis Vial, Jim Cummins and KEVIN MILLER from NY Rangers for Joe Kocur and Per
     Djoos
1991 ALAN KERR from NY Islanders for Rick Green
1991 BRIAN MacLELLAN from Calgary for Marc Habscheid
1991 Ray Sheppard from NY Rangers as free agent

1991 TROY CROWDER from New Jersey as free agent (Dave Barr and Randy McKay as compensation)
1991 VINCENT RIENDEAU from St. Louis for Rick Zombo
1992 GREG MILLEN from NY Rangers for future consideration.
1992 CHRIS TANCILL from Hartford for Daniel Shank
1992 BOB McGILL from San Jose for Johan Garpenlov
1992 Dino Ciccarelli from Washington for Kevin Miller
1992 Future considerations from Québec for Dennis Vial and Doug Crossman
1992 MARK HOWE from Philadelphia as free agent
1992 DENNIS VIAL from Québec for future consideration
1992 Fourth-round pick in 1993 Entry Draft from Philadelphia for Brent Fedyk
1993 PAUL COFFEY, JIM HILLER and SYLVAIN COUTURIER from Los Angeles for Jimmy Carson, Mark Potvin and Gary Shuchuk
1993 Future considerations from Philadelphia for Bob Wilkie
1993 STEVE KONROYD from Hartford for sixth-round pick in 1993 Entry Draft
1993 Sixth-round selection in 1993 Entry Draft (Detroit's) from Hartford for Brad McCrimmon
1993 STEVE MALTAIS from Tampa Bay for Dennis Vial
1993 AARON WARD and a fourth-round pick in 1993 Entry Draft from Winnipeg for Paul Ysebaert
1993 GREG JOHNSON and future considerations from Philadelphia for Jim Cummins and fourth-round pick (Philadelphia's) in 1993 Entry Draft
1993 KRIS DRAPER from Winnipeg for future considerations
1993 MARK PEDERSON from San Jose as free agent
1993 BOB HALKIDIS from Toronto as free agent
1993 PETER ING from Edmonton for future consideration
1993 TERRY CARKNER from Philadelphia for Yves Racine
1993 Future considerations from Boston for Vincent Riendeau
1994 BOB ESSENSA and SERGEI BAUTIN from Winnipeg for Tim Cheveldae and Dallas Drake
1994 Future consideration from Ottawa for Steve Konroyd
1994 Third-round selection from Winnipeg in 1995 NHL Entry Draft for Sheldon Kennedy
1994 MIKE VERNON from Calgary for Steve Chiasson
1994 MIKE KRUSHELNYSKI from Toronto as free agent
1994 MIKE RAMSEY from Pittsburgh as free agent
1994 BOB ROUSE from Toronto as free agent
1995 BOB ERREY from San Jose for fifth-round pick in 1995 Entry Draft
1995 VIACHESLAV FETISOV from New Jersey for third-round pick in 1995 Entry Draft
1995 STU GRIMSON, MARK FERNER and sixth-round pick in 1996 Entry Draft from Anaheim for Mike Sillinger and Jason York
1995 MARC BERGEVIN, BEN HANKINSON from Tampa Bay for Shawn Burr and third-round pick in 1996 Entry Draft
1995 WES WALZ from Calgary as free agent
1995 IGOR LARIONOV from San Jose for Ray Sheppard
1996 KIRK MALTBY from Edmonton for Dan McGillis
1996 Conditional Draft pick from Tampa Bay for Dino Ciccarelli
1996 BRENDAN SHANAHAN and Brian Glynn from Hartford for Keith Primeau, Paul Coffey and first-round pick in 1997 Entry Draft
1996 Future consideration from Hartford for Stu Grimson
1996 JOE KOCUR signed as free agent
1997 TOMAS SANDSTROM from Pittsburgh for Greg Johnson
1997 Future condiserations from San Jose for Bob Errey
1997 LARRY MURPHY from Toronto for future considerations
1997 BRENT GILCHRIST from Dallas as free agent
1997 Third-round pick in 1998 Entry Draft and second-round pick in 1999 from San Jose for Mike Vernon

A

Gerry Abel, C.....................................1966-67
Sid Abel, C-LW ....1938-39 to 42-43;
                                        45-46 to 51-52
Gene Achtymichuk, C 1957-58
Greg C. Adams, LW.........................1989-90
Micah Aivazoff, LW 1993-94
Gary Aldcorn, LW ....1959-60 to 60-61
Keith Allen, D...................1953-54 to 54-55
Ralph Almas, G 1946-47; 52-53
Dave Amadio, D 1957-58
Dale Anderson, D 1956-57
Earl Anderson, RW 1974-75
Ron Anderson, RW.............1967-68 to 68-69
Tom Anderson, C..............................1934-35
Al Arbour, D ....1953-54; 55-56 to 57-58
Jack Arbour, D-LW 1926-27
Murray Armstrong, C ....1943-44 to 45-46
Brent Ashton, LW ....1986-87 to 87-88
Ossie Asmundson, RW 1934-35
Pierre Aubry, C-LW ....1983-84 to 84-85
Larry Aurie, RW ....1927-28 to 38-39

B

Pete Babando, LW............................1949-50
Ace Bailey, LW ....1972-73 to 73-74
Bob Bailey, RW ....1956-57 to 57-58
Doug Baldwin, D 1946-47
Doug Barkley, D.................1962-63 to 65-66
David Barr, RW...................1986-87 to 90-91
John Barrett, D ....1980-81 to 85-86
Marty Barry, C ....1935-36 to 38-39
Hank Bassen, G ....1960-61 to 63-64;
                                        65-66 to 66-67
Frank Bathe, D ....1974-75 to 75-76
Andy Bathgate, C-RW ....1965-66 to 66-67
Bob Baun, D ....1968-69 to 70-71
Sergei Bautin, D 1993-94
Red Beattie, LW................................1937-38
Clarence Behling, D ....1940-41 to 42-43
Pete Bellefeuille, RW 1926-27;
                                        28-29 to 29-30
Frank Bennett, C 1943-44
Red Berenson, C ....1970-71 to 74-75
Michel Bergeron, RW...........1974-75 to 77-78
Marc Bergevin, D...............................1995-96
Gary Bergman, D ....1964-65 to 74-75
Thommie Bergman, D ....1972-73 to 74-75;
                                        77-78 to 79-80
Fred Berry, C......................................1976-77
Phil Besler, RW.................................1938-39
Pete Bessone, D 1937-38
Allan Bester, G....................1990-91 to 91-92
Bill Beveridge, G...............................1929-30
Tim Bissett, C 1990-91
Steve Black, LW ....1949-50 to 50-51
Tom Bladon, D...................................1980-81
Mike Blaisdell, RW ....1980-81 to 82-83
Mike Bloom, LW ....1974-75 to 76-77
John Blum, D......................................1988-89
Marc Boileau, C 1961-62
Gilles Boisvert, G..............................1959-60
Leo Boivin, D ....1965-66 to 66-67
Ivan Boldirev, C-LW ....1982-83 to 84-85
Dan Bolduc, RW..................1978-79 to 79-80
Marcel Bonin, LW ....1952-53 to 54-55
Henry Boucha, LW..............1971-72 to 73-74
Claude Bourque, G...........................1939-40
Scotty Bowman, D..............1934-35 to 39-40

Rick Bowness, RW 1977-78
Yank Boyd, RW..................................1934-35
John Brenneman, LW 1967-68
Carl Brewer, D...................................1969-70
Archie Briden, LW.............................1926-27
Mel Bridgman, LW-C...........1987-88 to 87-88
Bernie Brophy, C ....1928-29 to 29-30
Adam Brown, LW ....1941-42 to 43-44;
                                        45-46 to 46-47
Andy Brown, G....................1971-72 to 72-73
Arnie Brown, D....................1970-71 to 71-72
Connie Brown, C ....1938-39 to 42-43
Doug Brown, RW/LW ....1995 to 96-97
Gerry Brown, LW 1941-42; 45-46
Larry Brown, D 1970-71
Stan Brown, D 1927-28
Jeff Brubaker, C................................1988-89
Ed Bruneteau, RW............................1941-42;
                                        43-44 to 48-49
Mud Bruneteau, RW...........1935-36 to 45-46
Bill Brydge, D....................................1928-29
John Buyck, LW ....1955-56 to 56-57
Tony Bukovich, LW ....1943-44 to 44-45
Hy Buller, D ....1943-44 to 44-45
Charlie Burns, C................................1958-59
Shawn Burr, C ....1984-85 to 95
Cummy Burton, LW 1955-56;
                                        57-58 to 58-59
Eddie Bush, D......................1938-39; 41-42
Walter Buswell, D ....1932-33 to 34-35

C

Al Cameron, D ....1975-76 to 78-79
Craig Cameron, RW 1966-67
Colin Campbell, D ....1982-83 to 84-85
Terry Carkner, D ....1993-94 to 95
Gene Carrigan, C................1932-33 to 33-34
Billy Carroll. C ....1985-86 to 86-87
Greg Carroll, C..................................1978-79
Dwight Carruthers, D 1965-66
Frank Carson, RW..............1931-32 to 33-34
Jimmy Carson, C.................1989-90 to 92-93
Joe Carveth, RW-C ....1940-41 to 45-46;
                                        49-50 to 50-51
Frank Cernik, LW...............................1984-85
John Chabot, C....................1987-88 to 90-91
Milan Chalupa, D 1984-85
Bob Champoux, G.............................1963-64
Guy Charron, C-LW ....1970-71 to 74-75
Lude Check, LW 1943-44
Real Chevrefils, LW 1955-56
Tim Cheveldae, G ....1988-89 to 93-94
Alain Chevrier, G 1990-91
Steve Chiasson, D ....1987-88 to 93-94
Dino Ciccarelli, RW ....1992-93 to 95-96
Chris Cichocki, RW..............1985-86 to 86-87
Rejean Cloutier, D...............1979-80 to 81-82
Roland Cloutier, C...............1977-78 to 78-79
Steve Coates, RW.............................1976-77
Paul Coffey, D ....1992-93 to 95-96
Bill Collins, RW ....1970-71 to 73-74
Brian Conacher, C.............................1971-72
Charlie Conacher, RW 1938-39
Jim Conacher, LW ....1945-46 to 48-49
Roy Conacher, LW............................1946-47
Alex Connell, G.................................1931-32
Wayne Connelly, RW ....1968-69 to 70-71
Bob Connors, C...................1928-29 to 29-30
Bob Cook, RW 1972-73

Carson Cooper, RW ....1927-28 to 31-32
Norm Corcoran, RW.........................1955-56
Murray Costello, C.............1955-56 to 56-57
Gerry Couture, RW.............1944-45 to 50-51
Abbie Cox, G 1933-34
Danny Cox, LW 1931-32
Bart Cashley, D ....1965-66 to 68-69; 74-75
Murray Craven, LW-C ....1982-83 to 83-84
Bobby Crawford, C 1982-83
Jim Creighton, C ....1930-31 to 31-32
Troy Crowder, RW 1991-92
Gary Croteau, LW 1969-70
Doug Crossman, D ....1990-91 to 91-92
Roger Crozier, G ....1963-64 to 69-70
Wilf Cude, G 1933-34
Barry Cullen, RW.............................1959-60
Ray Cullen, C 1966-67
Jim Cummins, LW ....1991-92 to 92-93
Ian Cushenan, D 1963-64

D

Frank Daley, D-LW 1928-29
Joe Daley, G 1971-72
Mathieu Dandenault, RW...1995-96 to 96-97
Lorne Davis, RW................................1954-55
Bob Davis, D......................................1932-33
Mal Davis, RW ....1978-79 to 80-81
Billy Dea, LW ....1956-57 to 57-58;
                                          69-70 to 70-71
Don Deacon, C ....1936-37; 38-39 to 39-40
Nelson DeBenedet, LW.....................1973-74
Denis Dejordy, G................1972-73 to 73-74
Gilbert Delorme, D ....1987-88 to 88-89
Alex Delvecchio, C-LW ....1950-51 to 73-74
Al Dewsbury, D ....1946-47 to 47-48; 49-50
Per Djoos, D 1990-91
Ed Diachuk, LW 1960-61
Bob Dillabough, LW ....1961-62 to 64-65
Cecil Dilon, RW 1939-40
Bill Dineen, RW ....1953-54 to 57-58
Peter Dineen, D 1989-90
Connie Dion, G...................1943-44 to 44-45
Marcel Dionne, C ....1971-72 to 74-75
Gary Doak, D 1965-66; 1972-73
Dolly Dolson, G ....1928-29 to 30-31
Bobby Dollas, D ....1990-91 to 92-93
Lloyd Doran, C 1946-47
Red Doran, D 1937-38
Ken Doraty, RW.................................1937-38
Kent Douglas, D ....1967-68 to 68-69
Les Douglas, C 1940-41; 42-43; 46-47
Dallas Drake, C-LW ....1992-93 to 93-94
Kris Draper, C....................1993-94 to 96-97
Rene Drolet, RW 1974-75
Clarence Drouillard, C......................1937-38
Gilles Dube, LW................................1953-54
Ron Duguay, RW-C ....1983-84 to 85-86
Lorne Duguid, LW ....1934-35 to 35-36
Art Duncan, D 1926-27
Blake Dunlop, C 1983-84

E

Bruce Eakin, C 1985-86
Murray Eaves, C 1987-88; 1989-90
Tim Ecclestone, RW...........1970-71 to 73-74
Roy Edwards, G ....1967-68 to 70-71;
                                          72-73 to 73-74
Pat Egan, D 1943-44
Gerry Ehman, RW 1958-59
Bo Elik, LW.......................................1962-63
Darren Eliot, G..................................1987-88
Hap Emms, LW ....1931-32 to 33-34
Anders Eriksson, D ....1995-96 to 96-97

Bob Errey, LW ....1995-96 to 96-97
Bob Essensa, G 1993-94
Chris Evans, D 1973-74
Stu Evans, D ....1930-31; 32-33 to 33-34

F

Bob Falkenberg, D ....1966-67 to 68-69;
                                          70-71 to 71-72
Alex Faulkner, C ....1962-63 to 63-64
Bernie Federko, C.............................1989-90
Lorne Ferguson, LW ....1955-56 to 57-58
Sergei Fedorov, C.............1990-91 to 96-97
Brent Fedyk, D ....1987-88 to 91-92
Mark Ferner, D.....................................1995
Viacheslav Fetisov, D..............1995 to 96-97
Guyle Fielder, C.................1952-53; 57-58
Tom Filmore, RW ....1930-31 to 31-32
Dunc Fisher, RW 1958-59
Joe Fisher, RW...................1939-40 to 42-43
Lee Fogolin, D.....................1947-48 to 50-51
Rick Foley, D 1973-74
Mike Foligno, RW...............1979-80 to 81-82
Bill Folk, D...........................1951-52 to 52-53
Len Fontaine, RW...............1972-73 to 73-74
Val Fonteyne, C-LW ....1959-60 to 62-63;
                                          64-65 to 66-67
Dwight Foster, C ....1982-83 to 85-86
Yip Foster, D......................1933-34 to 34-35
Frank Foyston, C................1926-27 to 27-28
Bobby Francis, C 1982-83
Jimmy Franks, G .....1936-37 to 37-38; 43-44
Gord Fraser, D ....1927-28 to 28-29
Frank Frederickson, C 1926-27; 30-31
Tim Friday, D 1985-86
Miroslav Frycer, RW 1988-89
Robbie Ftorek, C ....1972-73 to 73-74

G

Bill Gadsby, D ....1961-62 to 65-66
Jody Gage, RW ....1980-81 to 81-82; 83-84
Art Gagne, RW....................................1931-32
Johnny Gallagher, D..............1932-33; 36-37
Gerard Gallant, LW ....1984-85 to 92-93
Dave Gagner, G 1990-91
George Gardner, G ....1965-66 to 67-68
Danny Gare, RW ....1981-82 to 85-86
Johan Garpenlov, LW...........1990-91 to 91-92
Dave Gatherum, G 1953-54
Fern Gauthier, RW...............1945-46 to 48-49
George Gee, C ....1948-49 to 50-51
Ed Giacomin, G ....1975-76 to 77-78
Gus Giesebrecht, C ....1938-39 to 41-42
Gilles Gilbert, G ....1980-81 to 82-83
Art Giroux, RW 1935-36
Larry Giroux, D ....1974-75 to 77-78
Lorry Gloeckner, D 1978-79
Fred Glover, RW ....1948-49 to 51-52
Howie Glover, RW ....1960-61 to 61-62
Warren Godfrey, D ....1955-56 to 61-62;
                                          63-64 to 67-68
Pete Goegan, D...................1957-58 to 66-67
Bob Goldham, D.................1950-51 to 55-56
Leroy Goldsworthy, RW 1930-31; 32-33
Ebbie Goodfollow, C-D ....1929-30 to 42-43
Fred Gordon, RW 1926-27
Ted Graham, D...................1933-34 to 34-35
Danny Grant, LW ....1974-75 to 77-78
Doug Grant, G ....1973-74 to 75-76
Leo Gravelle, RW...............................1950-51
Adam Graves, C ....1987-88 to 89-90
Gerry Gray, G.....................................1970-71
Harrison Gray, G...............................1963-64
Red Green, LW 1928-29

Rick Green, D..................................1990-91
Stu Grimson, LW....................1995 to 96-97
Lloyd Gross, LW..........1933-34 to 34-35
Don Grosso, C......................1938-39; 44-45
Danny Gruen, LW...............1972-73 to 73-74
Bep Guidolin, LW.............1947-48 to 48-49

H

Marc Habscheid, C/RW......1989-90 to 90-91
Lloyd Haddon, D................................1959-60
Gord Haidy, RW.................................1949-50
Slim Halderson, D...........................1926-27
Len Haley, RW...................1959-60 to 60-61
Bob Halkidis, D ....1993-94 to 95
Glenn Hall, G ....1952-53; 54-55 to 56-57
Murray Hall, C ....1964-65 to 66-67
Doug Halward, D..............1986-87 to 88-89
Jean Hamel, D ....1973-74 to 80-81
Ted Hampson, C ....1963-64 to 64-65;
                                              66-67 to 67-68
Glen Hanlon, G ....1986-87 to 90-91
Dave Hanson, D................................1978-79
Emil Hanson, D 1932-33
Terry Harper, D.................1975-76 to 78-79
Billy Harris, C....................................1965-66
Ron Harris, D....................1962-63 to 63-64;
                                              68-69 to 71-72
Ted Harris, D 1973-74
Gerry Hart, D.....................1968-69 to 71-72
Harold Hart, LW...............................1926-27
Buster Harvey, RW.............1975-76 to 76-77
Doug Harvey, D 1966-67
Ed Hatoum, RW.................................1968-69 to 69-70
George Hay, C-LW ...1927-28 to 30-31; 32-33
Jim Hay, D ....1952-53 to 54-55
Galen Head, RW...............................1967-68
Rich Healey, D 1960-61
Paul Henderson, LW...........1962-63 to 67-68
Jack Hendrickson, D ....1957-58 to 58-59;
                                              61-62
Jim Herberts, C ....1928-29 to 29-30
Art Herchenratter, C..........................1940-41
Bryan Hextall, C................................1975-76
Dennis Hextall, C ....1975-76 to 78-79
Glenn Hicks, LW.................1979-80 to 80-81
Harold Hicks, D.................1929-30 to 30-31
Tim Higgins, RW ....1986-88 to 88-89
Dutch Hiller, LW 1941-42
Jim Hiller, LW....................................1992-93
Larry Hillman, D ....1954-55 to 56-57
John Hilworth, D.................1977-78 to 79-80
Kevin Hodson, G ....1995-96 to 96-97
Bill Hogaboam, C ....1972-73 to 75-76;
                                              78-79 to 79-80
Ken Holland, G 1983-84
Flash Hollett, D..................1943-44 to 45-46
Bucky Hollingworth, D.........1955-56 to 57-58
Chuck Holmes, RW 1958-59; 61-62
Hap Holmes, G..................1926-27 to 27-28
Tomas Holmstrom, LW 1996-97
John Holota, C 1942-43; 45-46
Pete Horeck, RW-LW..........1946-47 to 48-49
Doug Houda, D....1985-86; 1987-88 to 90-91
Gordie Howe, RW ....1946-47 to 70-71
Mark Howe, D ....1992-93 to 95
Syd Howe, C-LW ....1934-35 to 45-46
Steve Hrymnak, D 1952-53
Willie Huber, D...................1978-79 to 82-83
Ron Hudson, RW.................1937-38; 39-40
Brent Hughes, D................................1973-74
Rusty Hughes, D 1929-30
Dennis Hull, LW................................1977-78

I

Miroslav Ihnacak, LW 1988-89
Peter Ing, G 1993-94
Earl Ingarfield, C-LW 1980-81
Ron Ingram, D 1963-64

J

Hal Jackson, D ....1940-41; 42-43 to 46-47
Lou Jankowski, RW 1950-51; 52-53
Gary Jarrett, LW ....1966-67 to 67-68
Pierre Jarry, LW ....1973-74 to 74-75
Larry Jeffrey, LW ....1961-62 to 64-65
Bill Jennings, RW ....1940-41 to 43-44
Al Jensen, G 1980-81
Al Johnson, RW..................1960-61 to 62-63
Brian Johnson, RW 1983-84
Danny Johnson, C.............................1971-72
Earl Johnson, C 1953-54
Greg Johnson, C ....1993-94 to 96-97
Larry Johnston, D...............1971-72 to 73-74
Ed Johnstone, RW..............................1983-84;
                                              85-86 to 85-87
Greg Joly, D ....1976-77 to 82-83
Buck Jones, D ....1938-39 to 39-40; 41-42
Ed Joyal, C ....1962-63 to 64-65

K

Red Kane, D 1943-44
Al Karlander, C-LW ....1969-70 to 72-73
Jack Keating, LW................1938-39 to 39-40
Duke Keats, C ....1926-27 to 27-28
Dave Kelly, RW..................................1976-77
Pete Kelly, RW ....1935-36 to 38-39
Red Kelly, D ....1947-48 to 59-60
Forbes Kennedy, C...1957-58 to 59-60; 61-62
Sheldon Kennedy, RW........1989-90 to 93-94
Alan Kerr, RW 1991-92
Brian Kilrea, LW 1957-58
Hec Kilrea, LW...1931-32; 35-36 to 39-40
Ken Kilrea, C-LW .....1939-40 to 41-42; 43-44
Wally Kilrea, C ....1934-35 to 37-38
Kris King, RW ....1987-88 to 88-89
Scott King, G ....1990-91 to 91-92
Mark Kirton, C ....1980-81 to 82-83
Kelly Kisio, C ....1982-83 to 85-86
Hobie Kitchen, D...............................1926-27
Petr Klima, LW...................1985-86 to 89-90
Mike Knuble, RW...............................1996-97
Joe Kocur, RW.........1984-85 to 90-91;96-97
Steve Konroyd, D...............1992-93 to 93-94
Vladimir Konstantinov, D.....1991-92 to 96-97
Jim Korn, D ....1979-80 to 81-82
Mike Korney, RW ....1973-74 to 75-76
Chris Kotsopoulos, D........................1989-90
Vyacheslav Kozlov, C..........1991-92 to 96-97
Dale Krentz, LW ....1986-87 to 88-89
Jim Krulicki, LW.................................1970-71
Gord Kruppke, D .....1990-91; 92-93 to 93-94
Mike Krushelnyski, LW/C......................1995
Dave Kryskow, LW............................1974-75
Mark Kumpel, RW ....1986-87 to 87-88

L

Leo Labine, RW ....1960-61 to 61-62
Dan Labraaten, LW............1978-79 to 80-81
Randy Ladouceur, D ....1982-83 to 86-87
Mark Laforest, G ....1985-86 to 86-87
Claude Laforge, LW..........................1958-59;
                                     60-61 to 61-62; 63-64 to 64-65
Roger Lafreniere, D 1962-63
Serge Lajeunesse, D...........1970-71 to 72-73
Hec Lalande, C 1957-58
Joe Lamb, LW..................................1937-38

Mark Lamb, C.................................1986-87
Lane Lambert, RW.............1983-84 to 85-86
Al Langlois, D................1963-64 to 64-65
Rick LaPointe, D.................1975-76 to 76-77
Martin Lapointe, RW.........1991-92 to 96-97
Igor Larionov, C..............1995-96 to 96-97
Reed Larson, D.................1976-77 to 85-86
Brian Lavender, LW ....1972-73 to 73-74
Dan Lawson, RW................1967-68 to 68-69
Reggie Leach, RW...........................1982-83
Jim Leavins, D...............................1985-86
Fernand Leblanc, RW ....1976-77 to 78-79
J.P. Leblanc, C.................1975-76 to 78-79
Rene Leclerc, RW...................1968-69; 70-71
Claude Legris, G.................1980-81 to 81-82
Real Lemieux, LW...........................1966-67
Tony Leswick, RW....1951-52 to 54-55; 57-58
Dave Lewis, D...................1986-87 to 87-88
Herb Lewis, LW ....1928-29 to 38-39
Nick Libett, LW ....1967-68 to 78-79
Tony Licari, RW 1946-47
Nicklas Lidstrom, D ....1991-92 to 96-97
Ted Lindsay, LW ......1944-45 to 56-57; 64-65
Carl Liscombe, LW ....1937-38 to 45-46
Ed Litzenberger, RW........................1961-62
Bill Lochead, RW..............1974-75 to 78-79
Mark Lofthouse, RW ....1981-82 to 82-83
Claude Loiselle, C ....1981-82 to 85-86
Barry Long, D 1979-80
Clem Loughlin, D ....1926-27 to 27-28
Ron Low, G 1977-78
Larry Lozinski, G...............................1980-81
Dave Lucas, D 1962-63
Don Luce, C 1970-71
Harry Lumley, G.................1943-44 to 49-50
Len Lunde, C-RW ....1958-59 to 61-62
Tord Lundstrom, LW 1973-74
Pat Lundy, C ....1945-46 to 48-49
Chris Luongo, D 1990-91
George Lyle, LW ....1979-80 to 81-82
Jack Lynch, D ....1973-74 to 74-75
Vic Lynn, D 1943-44

M

Lowell MacDonald, RW....1961-62 to 64-65
Parker MacDonald, LW.......1960-61 to 66-67
Bruce MacGregor, RW ....1960-61 to 70-71
Calum MacKay, LW 1946-47; 48-49
Howard Mackie, RW ....1936-37 to 37-38
Paul MacLean, RW..............................1988-89
Rick MacLeish, LW............................1983-04
Brian MacLellan, LW..........................1991-92
John MacMillan, LW ....1963-64 to 64-65
Frank Mahovlich, LW...........1967-68 to 70-71
Pete Mahovlich, C ....1965-66 to 68-69;
                                                 79-80 to 80-81
Steve Maltais, LW..............................1993-94
Kirk Maltby, LW..................1995-96 to 96-97
Dan Maloney, LW................1975-76 to 77-78
Randy Manery, D ....1970-71 to 71-72
Ken Mann, RW...................................1975-76
Bob Manno, LW-D ....1983-84 to 84-85
Lou Marcon, D........1958-59 to 59-60; 62-63
Gus Marker, RW ....1932-33 to 33-34
Brad Marsh, D ....1990-91 to 91-92
Gary Marsh, LW................................1967-68
Bert Marshall, D ....1965-66 to 67-68
Clare Martin, D ....1949-50 to 50-51
Pit Martin, C.............1961-62; 63-64 to 65-66
Don Martineau, RW ....1975-76 to 76-77
Steve Martinson, D 1987-88
Charlie Mason, RW 1938-39
Roland Matte, D.................................1929-30

Gary McAdam, RW............................1980-81
Jud McAtee, LW ....1943-44 to 44-45
Stan McCabe, LW ....1929-30 to 30-31
Doug McCaig, D ......1941-42; 45-46 to 47-48
Rick McCann, C ......1967-68 to 71-72; 74-75
Tom McCarthy, LW ....1956-57 to 58-59
Darren McCarty, LW ....1993-94 to 96-97
Kevin McClelland, RW........1989-90 to 90-91
Bob McCord, D ....1965-66 to 67-68
Dale McCourt, C.................1977-78 to 81-82
Bill McCreary, LW.............................1957-58
Brad McCrimmon, D...........1990-91 to 92-93
Brian McCutcheon, LW ......1974-75 to 76-77
Ab McDonald, LW ....1965-66 to 66-67; 71-72
Bucko McDonald, D ....1934-35 to 38-39
Byron McDonald, LW 1939-40; 44-45
Al McDonough, RW............................1977-78
Bill McDougall, C..............................1990-91
Pete McDuffe, G.................................1975-76
Mike McEwen, D...............................1985-86
Jim McFadden, C ....1946-47 to 50-51
Bob McGill, D 1991-92
Tom McGratton, G 1947-48
Bert McInenly, LW ....1930-31 to 31-32
Doug McKay, LW 1949-50
Randy McKay, RW ....1988-89 to 90-91
Jack McIntyre, LW ....1957-58 to 59-60
Walt McKechnie, C..............1974-75 to 76-77;
                                                 81-82 to 82-83
Tony McKegney, RW..........................1989-90
Don McKenney, LW 1965-66
Bill McKenzie, G..................1973-74 to 74-75
John McKenzie, RW ....1959-60 to 60-61
Andrew McKim, C..............................1995
Rollie McLenahan, D 1945-46
Al McLeod, D......................................1973-74
Don McLeod, G..................................1970-71
Mike McMahon, D..............................1969-70
Max McNab, C ....1947-48 to 50-51
Billy McNeill, RW...............1956-57 to 59-60;
                                                 62-63 to 63-64
Stu McNeill, C....................1957-58 to 59-60
Basil McRae, LW ....1985-86 to 86-87
Chris McRae, LW 1989-90
Pat McReavy, LW 1941-42
Harry Meeking, LW 1926-27
Tom Mellor, D.....................1973-74 to 74-75
Gerry Melnyk, C ......1955-56; 59-60 to 60-61
Barry Melrose, D 1983-84; 85-86
Howie Menard, C...............................1963-64
Glenn Merkosky, LW..........1985-06; 80 90
Corrado Micalef, G ....1981-82 to 85-86
Nick Mickoski, LW..............1957-58 to 58-59
Hugh Millar, D...................................1946-47
Greg Millen, G...................................1991-92
Kevin Miller, RW ....1990-91 to 91-92
Perry Miller, D....................1977-78 to 80-81
Tom Miller, C 1970-71
Eddie Mio, G ....1983-84 to 85-86
John Miszuk, D..................................1963-64
Bill Mitchell, D...................................1963-64
John Mokosak, D................1988-89 to 89-90
Ron Moffatt, LW..................1932-33 to 34-35
Gary Monahan, LW............................1969-70
Hank Montieth, LW ....1968-69 to 70-71
Alfie Moore, G....................................1939-40
Don Morrison, C ....1947-48 to 48-49
Jim Morrison, D..................................1959-60
Rod Morrison, RW 1947-48
Dean Morton, D..................................1989-90
Gus Mortson, D..................................1958-59
Alex Motter, D ....1937-38 to 42-43

John Mowers, G ......1040-41 to 42-43; 46-47
Wayne Muloin, D 1963-64
Don Murdoch, RW 1981-82
Brian Murphy, C...................................1974-75
Joe Murphy, C-RW ....1986-87 to 89-90
Larry Murphy, D 1996-97
Ron Murphy, LW ....1964-65 to 65-66
Ken Murray, D.....................................1972-73
Terry Murray, D...................................1976-77

N

Jim Nahrgang, D ....1974-75 to 76-77
Vaclav Nedomansky, C-RW .1977-78 to 81-82
Rick Newell, D ....1972-73 to 73-74
John Newman, C 1930-31
Eddie Nicholson, D 1947-48
Jim Niekamp, D ....1970-71 to 71-72
Jim Nill, RW ....1987-88 to 89-90
Reg Noble, D ....1927-28 to 32-33
Ted Nolan, LW 1981-82; 83-84
Lee Norwood, D ....1986-87 to 90-91
Hank Nowak, LW.................................1974-75

O

Adam Oates, C...................1985-86 to 88-89
Russ Oatman, LW 1926-27
Mike O'Connell, D ....1985-86 to 89-90
Gerry Odrowski, D ....1960-61 to 62-63
John Ogrodnick, LW...........1979-80 to 86-87;
                                                            92-93
Murray Oliver, C ....1957-58; 59-60 to 60-61
Dennis Olson, LW 1957-58
Jimmy Orlando, D ....1936-37 to 37-38;
                                                  39-40 to 42-43
Mark Osborne, LW..............1981-82 to 82-83
Chris Osgood, G ....1993-94 to 96-97

P

Pete Palangio, LW 1927-28
Brad Park, D ....1983-84 to 84-85
Joe Paterson, LW ....1980-81 to 83-84
George Patterson, RW 1934-35
Butch Paul, C......................................1964-65
Marty Pavelich, LW ....1947-48 to 56-57
Jim Pavese, D.....................1987-88 to 88-89
Mark Pederson, LW 1993-94
Bert Peer, RW 1939-40
Bob Perreault, G.................................1958-59
Jim Peters, Jr., C................1964-65 to 67-68
Jim Peters, Sr., RW .1949-50 to 50-51; 53-54
Brent Peterson, C...............1978-79 to 81-82
Gord Pettinger, C ....1933-34 to 37-38
Robert Picard, D 1989-90
Alex Pirus, RW 1979-80
Rob Plumb, LW...................1977-78 to 78-79
Nellie Podolsky, LW 1948-49
Bud Poile, RW 1948-49
Don Poile, C-RW 1954-55; 57-58
Dennis Polonich, RW ....1974-75 to 80-81;
                                                            82-83
Poul Popiel, D ....1968-69 to 69-70
Marc Potvin, LW..................1990-91 to 91-92
Dean Prentice, LW ....1965-66 to 68-69
Noel Price, D.......................................1961-62
Keith Primeau, C/LW ....1990-91 to 95-96
Bob Probert, LW-RW ....1985-86 to 93-94
Andre Pronovost, LW ....1962-63 to 64-65
Marcel Pronovost, D ....1949-50 to 64-65
Metro Prystai, RW-C ....1950-51 to 57-58
Cliff Purpur, RW..................................1944-45
Chris Pusey, G....................................1985-86
Jamie Pushor, D ....1995-96 to 96-97
Nelson Pyatt, C....................1973-74 to 74-75

Q

Bill Quackenbush, D...........1942-43 to 48-49

R

Yves Racine, D....................1989-90 to 92-93
Clare Raglan, D 1950-51
Mike Ramsey, D 1995-96;96-97
Matt Ravlich, D....................................1969-70
Marc Reaume, D.................1959-60 to 60-61
Billy Reay, C ....1943-44 to 44-45
Mickey Redmond, RW.........1970-71 to 75-76
Dutch Reibel, C...................1953-54 to 57-58
Gerry Reid, C......................................1948-49
Leo Reise, D ....1946-47 to 51-52
Dave Richardson, LW 1967-68
Terry Richardson, G ....1973-74 to 76-77
Steve Richmond, D 1985-86
Vincent Riendeau, G ....1991-92 to 93-94
Dennis Riggin, G.................1959-60; 62-63
Jim Riley, RW......................................1926-27
Bob Ritchie, LW ....1976-77 to 77-78
Wayne Rivers, RW 1961-62
John Ross Roach, G ....1932-33 to 34-35
Phil Roberto, RW................1974-75 to 75-76
Doug Roberts, RW..............1965-66 to 67-68;
                                                         73-74 to 74-75
Earl Robertson, G...............................1936-37
Fred Robertson, D 1933-34
Torrie Robertson, LW ....1988-89 to 89-90
Mike Robitaille, D 1970-71
Desse Roche, RW 1934-35
Earl Roche, LW...................................1934-35
Dave Rochefort, C 1966-67
Leon Rochefort, RW ....1971-72 to 72-73
Harvey Rockburn, D ....1929-30 to 30-31
Dale Rolfe, D ....1969-70 to 70-71
Rollie Rossignol, LW 1943-44; 45-46
Rolly Roulston, D................................1936-37
Bob Rouse, D ....1995 to 96-97
Tom Rowe, RW....................................1982-83
Bernie Ruelle, LW...............................1943-44
Pat Rupp, G..1963-64
Jimmy Rutherford, G...........................1970-71;
                                              73-74 to 80-81; 82-83

S

Andre St. Laurent, C ....1977-78 to 78-79;
                                                            83-84
Sam St. Laurent, G ....1986-87 to 89-90
Borje Salming, D 1989-90
Barry Salovaara, D ....1974-75 to 75-76
Ed Sanford, C.....................................1955-56
Tomas Sandstrom, RW/LW 1996-97
Bob Sauve, G 1981-82
Terry Sawchuk, G ....1949-50 to 54-55;
                                              57-58 to 63-64; 68-69
Kevin Schamehorn, RW.........1976-77; 79-80
Jim Schoenfeld, D ....1981-82 to 82-83
Dwight Schofield, D.............................1976-77
Enio Sclisizzi, LW ....1946-47 to 49-50; 51-52
Earl Seibert, D....................1944-45 to 45-46
Ric Seiling, RW 1986-87
Brendan Shanahan 1996-97
Daniel Shank, RW...............1989-90 to 90-91
Jeff Sharples, D..................1986-87 to 88-89
Doug Shedden, RW ....1985-86 to 86-87
Bobby Sheehan, C..............................1976-77
Tim Sheehy, RW..................................1977-78
Frank Sheppard, C..............................1927-28
John Sheppard, LW ....1926-27 to 27-28
Ray Sheppard, RW...............1991-92 to 95
Gord Sherritt, D 1943-44
John Sherf, LW ....1935-36 to 38-39; 43-44

Jim Shires, LW 1970-71
Steve Short, D.................................1978-79
Gary Shuchuk, RW...........................1990-91
Dave Silk, RW 1984-85
Mike Sillinger, C ....1990-91 to 95
Cully Simon, D ....1942-43 to 44-45
Thain Simon, D 1946-47
Cliff Simpson, C...........1946-47 to 47-48
Reg Sinclair, RW..............................1952-53
Darryl Sittler, C-LW 1984-85
Bjorne Skaare, C..............................1978-79
Glen Skov, C............1949-50 to 54-55
Al Smith, G 1971-72
Alex Smith, D 1931-32
Brad Smith, RW ....1980-81 to 84-85
Brian Smith, LW...................1957-58; 60-61
Carl Smith, LW 1943-44
Derek Smith, C ....1981-82 to 82-83
Floyd Smith, RW................1962-63 to 67-68
Greg Smith, D ....1981-82 to 85-86
Nakina Dalton Smith, LW 1943-44
Normie Smith, G..............................1934-35;
                       38-39; 43-44 to 44-45
Rick Smith, D....................................1980-81
Ted Snell, RW 1974-75
Harold Snepsts, D...........1985-86 to 87-88
Sandy Snow, RW..............................1968-69
Dennis Sobchuk, C..........................1979-80
Ken Solheim, LW..............................1982-83
Bob Solinger, LW..............................1959-60
John Sorrell, LW ....1930-31 to 37-38
Fred Speck, C..................1968-69 to 69-70
Ted Speers, RW 1985-86
Irv Spencer, D-LW ....1963-64 to 65-66;
                                           67-68
Ron Stackhouse, D ....1971-72 to 73-74
Ed Stankiewicz, LW...............1953-54; 55-56
Wilf Starr, C ....1933-34 to 35-36
Vic Stasiuk, RW-LW..........1950-51 to 54-55;
                          60-61 to 62-63
Ray Staszak, RW 1985-86
Frank Steele, LW 1930-31
Greg Stefan, G ....1981-82 to 89-90
Pete Stemkowski, C ....1967-68 to 70-71
Blair Stewart, LW ....1973-74 to 74-75
Gaye Stewart, LW..............................1950-51
Jack Stewart, D ....1938-39 to 42-43;
                     45-46 to 49-50
Gord Strate, D ....1956-57 to 58-59
Art Stratton, C....................................1963-64
Herb Stuart, G 1926-27
Barry Sullivan, RW.............................1947-48
Bill Sutherland, LW 1971-72

T

John Taft, D..1978-79
Jean-Guy Talbot, D 1967-68
Chris Tancill, C ....1991-92 to 92-93
Billy Taylor, C.....................................1946-47
Ted Taylor, LW 1966-67
Tim Taylor, LW....................1993-94 to 96-97
Harvey Teno, G..................................1938-39
Larry Thibeault, LW 1944-45
Billy Thomson, RW...................1938-39; 43-44
Cecil Thompson, G ....1938-39 to 39-40
Errol Thompson, LW ....1977-78 to 80-81
Jerry Toppazzini, RW 1955-56
Larry Trader, D 1982-83; 84-85
Percy Traub, D ....1927-28 to 28-29
Dave Trottier, LW 1938-39
Joe Turner, G 1941-42

U

Norm Ullman, C ....1955-56 to 67-78
Garry Unger, C ....1967-68 to 70-71

V

Rogie Vachon, G..................1978-79 to 79-80
Eric Vail, LW 1981-82
Rick Vasko, D ....1979-80 to 80-81
Darren Veitch, D ....1985-86 to 87-88
Mike Vernon, G...................1995 to 96-97
Dennis Vial, D ....1990-91 to 92-93
Doug Volmer, RW ....1969-70 to 71-72
Carl Voss, C.......................................1932-33

W

Jack Walker, LW ....1926-27 to 27-28
Bob Wall, D ....1964-64 to 66-67; 71-72
Wes Walz, C 1995-96
Aaron Ward, D...................1993-94 to 96-97
Eddie Wares, RW...............1937-38 to 42-43
Bryan Watson, D ....1965-66 to 66-67;
                                73-74 to 76-77
Harry Watson, LW 1942-43; 45-46
Jim Watson, D ....1963-64 to 65-66;
                               67-68 to 69-70
Brian Watts, LW 1975-76
Tom Webster, RW .....1970-71 to 71-72; 79-80
Cooney Weiland, C.............1933-34 to 34-35
Stan Weir, C......................................1982-83
Carl Wetzel, G 1964-65
Bob Whitelaw, D...............1940-41 to 41-42
Archie Wilder, LW 1940-41
Bob Wilkie, D 1990-91
Burr Williams, D 1933-34; 36-37
Carl Williams, D 1931-32
Dave "Tiger" Williams, LW................1984-85
Fred Williams, C................................1976-77
John Wilson, LW ....1949-50 to 54-55;
                           57-58 to 58-59
Larry Wilson, C....1949-50; 51-52 to 52-53
Lefty Wilson, C..................................1953-54
Rick Wilson, D 1976-77
Murray Wing, D 1973-74
Eddie Wiseman, RW ....1932-33 to 35-36
Steve Wochy, C-RW...............1944-45; 46-47
Benny Woit, D ....1950-51 to 54-55
Mike Wong, C.....................................1975-76
Paul Woods, LW ....1977-78 to 83-84
Larry Wright, RW-C 1977-78

Y

Jason York, D ....1992-93 to 95
Doug Young, D ....1931-32 to 38-39
Howie Young, D.................1960-61 to 62-63;
                               66-67 to 67-68
Warren Young, LW.............................1985-86
Paul Ysebaert, LW..............1990-91 to 92-93
Steve Yzerman, C..............1983-84 to 96-97

Z

Larry Zeidel, D ....1951-52 to 52-53
Ed Zeniuk, D......................................1954-55
Rick Zombo, D....................1984-85 to 91-92
Rudy Zunich, D..................................1943-44

(772 players through 1996-97)

No. 1

Harry Holmes	1926-27 to 27-28
Dolly Dolson	1928-29 to 30-31
Bill Beveridge	1929-30
Alex Connell	1931-32
John Ross Roach	1932-33 to 34-35
Abbie Cox	1933-34
Wilf Cude	1933-34
Norm Smith	1934-35 to 38-39, 43-44 to 44-45
Earl Robertson	1936-37
Jim Franks	1936-37 to 37-38, 43-44
Harvey Teno	1938-39
Cecil Thompson	1938-39 to 39-40
Alf Moore	1939-40
Claude Bourque	1939-40
John Mowers	1940-41 to 42-43
Joe Turner	1941-42
Connie Dior	1943-44 to 44-45
Harry Lumley	1943-44 to 49-50
Ralph Adams	1946-47
Terry Sawchuk	1949-50 to 54-55, 57-58 to 63-64 (Retired Mar. 6, 1994)
Dave Gatherum	1953-54
Lefty Wilson	1953-54
Glenn Hall	1954-55 to 56-57
Bob Perrault	1958-59
Dennis Riggin	1959-60, 62-63
Gilles Boisvert	1959-60
Hank Bassen	1960-61 to 62-63
Roger Crozier	1964-65 to 69-70
Roy Edwards	1967-68, 72-73 to 73-74
Jim Rutherford	1970-71, 74-75 to 80-81
Don McLeod	1970-71
Joe Daley	1971-72
Terry Richardson	1973-74, 75-76
Bill McKenzie	1973-74
Gilles Gilbert	1980-81 to 82-83
Corrado Micalef	1983-84 to 85-86
Glen Hanlon	1986-87 to 90-91

No. 2

Clem Loughlin	1926-27 to 27-28
Percy Traub	1928-29
Harvey Rockburn	1929-30 to 30-31
Alex Smith	1931-32
Doug Young	1932-33 to 38-39
Burr Williams	1936-37
Rolly Roulston	1936-37
John Gallagher	1936-37
Jack Stewart	1939-40 to 42-43, 45-46 to 49-50
Buck Jones	1941-42
Clarence Behling	1942-43
Cully Simon	1943-44 to 44-45
Gerry Couture	1944-45
Bob Goldham	1950-51 to 55-56
Larry Hillman	1956-57
Al Arbour	1956-57 to 57-58

Pete Goegon	1958-59 to 61-62, 65-66
Jim Morrison	1959-60
Noel Price	1961-62
Jack Hendrickson	1961-62
Howie Young	1962-63
Ron Ingram	1963-64
Al Langlois	1963-64 to 64-65
Jim Watson	1963-64
Bob McCord	1965-66
Dwight Carruthers	1965-66
Warren Godfrey	1965-66
Gary Bergman	1966-67 to 74-75
Mike Korney	1973-74
Al McLeod	1973-74
Terry Harper	1975-76 to 78-79
Barry Long	1979-80
Rick Smith	1980-81
John Barrett	1980-81
Jim Schoenfield	1981-82 to 82-83
Larry Trader	1984-85
Barry Melrose	1985-86
Mike O'Connell	1985-86 to 89-90
Brad McCrimmon	1990-91 to 92-93
Terry Carkner	1993-94 to 95
Viacheslav Fetisov	1995-96 to 96-97

No. 3

Slim Halderson	1926-27
Pete Bellefeuille	1926-27
Reg Noble	1927-28 to 32-33
Emil Hanson	1932-33
Carl Voss	1932-33
John Gallagher	1932-33
Stu Evans	1933-34
Ted Graham	1933-34 to 34-35
Bucko McDonald	1934-35 to 38-39
Jack Stewart	1938-39
Scotty Bowman	1938-39 to 39-40
Don Deacon	1939-40
Alex Motter	1939-40 to 42-43
Buck Jones	1941-42
Gordie Sherritt	1943-44
Vic Lynn	1943-44
Murray Armstrong	1943-44 to 45-46
Bill Quackenbush	1946-47 to 48-49
Clare Martin	1949-50 to 50-51
Ben Woit	1951-52
Marcel Pronovost	1952-53 to 64-65
Bill Mitchell	1963-64
Gary Bergman	1965-66
Bert Marshall	1965-66 to 66-67
Bob McCord	1967-68
Jean Guy Talbot	1967-68
Warren Godfrey	1967-68
Bob Falkenberg	1967-68 to 68-69, 71-72
Paul Popeil	1968-69 to 69-70
Jim Watson	1969-70
Gerry Hart	1969-70
Dale Rolfe	1970-71
Jim Niekamp	1971-72

Larry Johnston ....1971-72 to 73-74
Murray Wing..1973-74
Jack Lynch 1974-75
Jim Nahrgang 1974-75,76-77
Larry Giroux ....1975-76 to 76-77
Perry Miller ....1977-78 to 80-81
Rick Vasko 1979-80
John Barrett.......................1981-82 to 85-86
Steve Chiasson ....1986-87 to 93-94
Bob Rouse ....1995-96 to 96-97

No. 4

Harry Meeking 1926-27
Archie Briden.....................................1926-27
George Hay ....1927-28 to 30-31
Herb Lewis.........................1931-32 to 38-39
John Sorrell 1937-38
Gus Giesebrecht 1939-40
Sid Abel 1939-40
Jim Orlando.......................1940-41 to 42-43
Harold Jackson ....1943-44 to 46-47
Jim McFadden....................................1946-47
Doug McCaig ....1947-48 to 48-49
Al Dewsbury 1947-48
Len "Red" Kelly.................1948-49 to 59-60
Marc Reaume....................1959-60 to 60-61
Howie Young.......................................1960-61
Bill Gadsby ....1961-62 to 65-66
Ron Harris 1963-64
Bob Wall 1964-65
Leo Boivin 1966-67
Howie Young.......................................1967-68
Bob Baun............................1968-69 to 70-71
Larry Brown..1970-71
Arnie Brown ....1970-71 to 71-72
Thommie Bergman ....1972-73 to 74-75,
                                                        77-78 to 79-80
Bart Crashley 1974-75
Rick Lapointe ....1975-76 to 76-77
Terry Murray.......................................1976-77
Larry Giroux 1977-78
John Hilworth......................................1977-78
Rick Vasko 1977-78, 80-81
Tom Bladon 1980-81
Hejean Cloutier..................................1981-82
Colin Campbell...................1982-83 to 84-85
Tim Friday 1985-86
Jim Leavins 1985-86
Jeff Sharples 1986-87
Rick Zombo ....1986-87 to 91-92
Bob McGill 1991-92
Mark Howe ....1992-93 to 1995
Jamie Pushor....................1995-96 to 96-97

No. 5

Frank Frederickson 1926-27
Duke Keats ....19-26-27 to 27-28
Gord Fraser ....1927-28 to 28-29
Bill Brydge 1928-29
Bob Connors 1929-30
Ebbie Goodfellow ....1930-31 to 42-43
Pete Bessone 1937-38
John Doran 1937-38
Jim Orlando 1937-38
Buck Jones 1938-39, 41-42

Eddie Bush 1941-42
Doug McCaig......................................1941-42
Clarence Behling...............................1942-43
Hal Jackson.......................................1942-43
Pat Egan 1943-44
Bill "Flash" Hollett...............1943-44 to 45-46
Hugh Millar 1946-47
Al Dewsbury 1946-47
Leo Reise ....1946-47 to 51-52
Ben Woit ....1952-53 to 54-55
Warren Godfrey ....1955-56 to 61-62
Al Arbour 1955-56
Rich Healey 1960-61
Doug Barkley ....1962-63 to 65-66
John Misuk 1963-64
Bob Wall 1966-67
Doug Harvey 1966-67
Bob Falkenberg 1966-67
Bert Marshall 1967-68
Kent Douglas ....1967-68 to 68-69
Carl Brewer 1969-70
Serje Lajeunesse 1970-71
Marcel Dionne....................1971-72 to 73-74
Jean Hamel ....1974-75 to 80-81
Greg Smith ....1981-82 to 85-86
Darren Veitch ....1985-86 to 87-88
John Mokosak 1988-89
Dean Morton 1989-90
Peter Dineen 1989-90
Chris McRae 1989-90
Rick Green 1990-91
Nicklas Lidstrom................1991-92 to 96-97

No. 6

Jack Walker........................1926-27 to 27-28
Larry Aurie ....1928-29 to 38-39
Cumming Burton ....1957-58 to 58-59

No. 7

Russ Oatman 1926-27
Stan Brown 1927-28
Pete Palangio 1927-28
Jim Herberts......................................1928-29
Herb Lewis ....1929-30 to 30-31
Hec Kilrea 1931-32
Art Gagno 1931-32
Leroy Goldsworthy.............................1932-33
George Hay..1932-33
Carl Voss 1933-34
Cooney Weiland.................1933-34 to 34-35
Marty Barry ....1935-36 to 38-39
Alex Motter 1939-40
Don Deacon 1939-40
Sid Abel 1939-40
Ken Kilrea 1940-41
Carl Liscombe ....1940-41 to 45-46
Ted Lindsay........................1946-47 to 56-57
                                       (Retired Nov. 10, 1991)
Billy Dea...1957-58
Hec Lalande 1957-58
Murray Oliver 1957-58
Brian Kilrea 1957-58
Norm Ullman ....1958-59 to 67-68
Garry Unger.......................1968-69 to 70-71
Red Berenson ....1970-71 to 74-75

Dave Kryskow 1974-75
Dan Maloney ....1975-76 to 77-78
Willie Huber ....1978-79 to 82-83
Joe Paterson 1983-84
Milan Chalupa 1984-85
Mike McEwen 1985-86
Steve Richmond 1985-86
Eddie Johnstone 1986-87
Doug Halward ....1986-87 to 88-89
Brent Fedyk 1988-89
Tony McKegney 1989-90
Robert Picard 1989-90
Tom Bissett..1990-91

No. 8

Art Duncan 1926-27
Carson Cooper ....1927-28 to 29-30
Stu Evans 1930-31
Danny Cox 1931-32
Eddie Wiseman..................1932-33 to 34-35
Yip Foster 1934-35
Syd Howe ....1934-35 to 45-46
Don Deacon 1936-37
Billy Rea 1944-45
Cliff Purpur 1944-45
Pat Lundy ....1945-46 to 48-49
George Gee ....1948-49 to 50-51
Tony Leswick ....1951-52 to 54-55
Dutch Reibel ....1955-56 to 57-58
John Wilson ....1957-58 to 58-59
Barry Cullen 1959-60
Murray Oliver 1960-61
Leo Labine ....1960-61 to 61-62
Forbes Kennedy.................................1961-62
Lowell MacDonald ....1961-62 to 63-64
Floyd Smith 1962-63
Art Stratton 1963-64
Claude Laforge..................................1963-64
Pat Martin..........................1963-64 to 64-65
Val Fonteyne......................................1966-67
Gary Jarrett ....1966-67 to 67-68
Bart Crashley.....................................1968-69
Rick McCann ....1968-69 to 69-70
Rene Leclerc 1968-69
Fred Speck 1969-70
Tom Webster 1970-71
Bill Sutherland 1971-72
Dan Johnson 1971-72
Guy Charron......................1972-73 to 74-75
Ted Snell 1974-75
Brian McCutcheon 1974-75
Dennis Polonich ....1975-76 to 80-81, 82-83
Claude Loiselle 1981-82
Joe Paterson 1982-83
Tom Rowe 1982-83
Ted Nolan 1983-84
Dave Silk 1984-85
Ray Staszak 1985-86
Mark Lamb 1986-87
Jim Nill ....1987-88 to 89-90
Bobby Dollas ....1990-91 to 91-92
Gord Kruppke 1992-93
Steve Konroyd 1993-94
Aaron Ward 1995
Igor Larionov......................1995-96 to 96-97

No. 9

John Sheppard ....1926-27 to 27-28
Herb Lewis 1928-29
Harold Hicks 1929-30
Roalnd Matte 1929-30
Bert McInenly......................1930-31 to 31-32
Frank Carson......................1931-32 to 33-34
Tom Anderson 1934-35
Ed Wiseman.......................................1934-35
Wally Kilrea ....1935-36 to 36-37
Pete Kelly 1937-38
Mud Bruneteau...................1937-38 to 45-46
John Sorrell..1937-38
Joe Lamb 1937-38
John Sherf..1938-39
Connie Brown 1938-39
Ken Kilrea 1938-39
Ed Bruneteau 1943-44
Billy Thompson...................................1943-44
Sid Abel 1945-46
Roy Conacher 1946-47
Gordie Howe ....1947-48 to 70-71
(Retired Mar. 12, 1972)

No. 10

Frank Foyston ....1926-27 to 27-28
Frank Sheppard 1927-28
Bob Connors 1928-29
Ebbie Goodfellow 1929-30
Carson Cooper ....1930-31 to 31-32
John Sorrell ....1932-33 to 37-38
Clarence Droulliard 1937-38
Carl Liscombe ....1937-38 to 39-40
Don Grosso ....1939-40 to 44-45
Bill Jennings 1943-44
Billy Reay ....1943-44 to 44-45
Cliff Purpur 1944-45
Steve Wochy......................................1944-45
Fern Gauthier ....1945-46 to 47-48
Gerry Brown 1945-46
Gerry Couture ....1946-47 to 47-48
Max McNab 1948-49
Ed Bruneteau 1948-49
Jim Peters ....1949-50 to 50-51
Metro Prystai ....1951-52 to 54-55
Alex Delvecchio ....1954-55 to 73-74
(Retired Nov. 10, 1991)
Dale McCourt ....1977-78 to 81-82
Mark Lofthouse...................................1981-82
Claude Loiselle...................................1982-83
Ron Duguay ....1983-84 to 85-86
Joe Murphy ....1986-87 to 89-90
Jimmy Carson ....1989-90 to 91-92

No. 11

Hobie Kitchen 1926-27
Jim Riley 1926-27
Bernie Brophy ....1928-29 to 29-30
Jim Herberts.......................................1929-30
Tom Filmore........................1930-31 to 31-32
Frank Steele 1930-31
Art Gagne 1931-32
Carl Williams......................................1931-32

Hap Emms..........................1931-32 to 33-34
Gord Pettinger ....1934-35 to 37-38
Earl Roche...1934-35
Scotty Bowman 1934-35
Wally Kilrea..1934-35
Red Beattie..1937-38
Ken Doraty..1937-38
Eddie Wares ....1937-38 to 42-43
Billy Thompson.....................................1938-39
Sid Abel...1939-40
Adam Brown ....1943-44, 45-46 to 46-47
Jud McAtee 1944-45
Byron McDonald....................................1944-45
Pete Horeck ....1946-47 to 48-49
Barry Sullivan...1947-48
Max McNab..1949-50
Gaye Stewart...1950-51
Marty Pavelich ....1951-52 to 56-57
John Wilson 1957-58
Nick Mickowski ....1957-58 to 58-59
Gary Aldcorn ....1959-60 to 60-61
Vic Stasiuk ....1960-61 to 62-63
Warren Godfrey 1963-64
Irv Spencer........................1963-64 to 64-65
Lowell MacDonald 1964-65
John MacMillan 1964-65
Bob Dillabough....................................1964-65
Jim Watson...1964-65
Val Fonteyne ....1964-65 to 65-66
Pete Mahovlich..................1966-67, 68-69
Jim Peters Jr. ....1966-67 to 67-68
Gerry Abel..1966-67
Gary Monahan....................................1969-70
Gary Croteau..1969-70
Hank Monteith....................1969-70 to 70-71
Don Luce..1970-71
Leon Rochefort ....1971-72 to 72-73
Brian Lavender......................................1972-73
Len Fontaine 1973-74
Chris Evans...1973-74
Hank Nowak..1974-75
Walt McKechnie.................1974-75 to 76-77,
                                                       81-82 to 82-83
Rick Bowness 1977-78
John Taft..1978-79
Lorry Gloeckner 1978-79
Pete Mahovlich..................1979-80 to 80-81
Murray Craven.....................................1983-84
Blake Dunlop 1983-84
Brad Smith..1984-85
Rick Zombo..1984-85
Ted Speers...1985-86
Shawn Burr ....1984-85 to 95
Mathieu Dandenault...........1995-96 to 96-97

No. 12

Fred Gordon 1926-27
Larry Aurie 1927-28
Pete Bellefeuille..................................1928-29
Red Green..1928-29
Jim Herberts...1929-30
Stan McCabe..1929-30
John Sorrell ....1930-31 to 31-32
Walt Buswell......................1932-33 to 34-35

Hec Kilrea ....1935-36 to 39-40
Byron McDonald...............................1939-40
Sid Abel..........................1940-41 to 42-43,
                                                46-47 to 51-52
                                   (Retired Apr. 29, 1995)
Joe Carveth......................1943-44 to 45-46
Glen Skov.........................1952-53 to 54-55
Ed Sanford 1955-56
Metro Prystai ....1955-56 to 57-58
Bill Dineen..1957-58
Tony Leswick 1957-58
Dunc Fisher...1958-59
Gene Achtymichuk...........................1958-59
Stu McNeill 1958-59
Chuck Holmes.....................................1958-59
Val Fonteyne....................1959-60 to 61-62
Alex Faulkner....................1962-63 to 63-64
Pit Martin 1963-64
John MacMillan 1963-64
Bob Dillabough....................................1963-64
Ron Murphy........................1964-65 to 65-66
Bruce MacGregor ....1965-66 to 70-71
Tom Miller 1970-71
Ab McDonald..1971-72
Henry Boucha 1971-72
Randy Manery......................................1971-72
Bob Cook 1972-73
Garnet Bailey ....1972-73 to 73-74
Dan Gruen 1973-74
Marcel Dionne......................................1974-75
Bryan Hextall 1975-76
J.P. Leblanc.........................1975-76 to 77-78
Fern Leblanc..1977-78
Errol Thompson ....1977-78 to 80-81
Brent Peterson...................1980-81 to 81-82
Tom Rowe..1982-83
Ivan Boldirev......................1982-83 to 84-85
Adam Oates 1985-86
Billy Carroll.........................1985-86 to 86-87
Adam Graves.......................1987-88 to 89-90
Sheldon Kennedy...............1989-90 to 90-91
Jimmy Carson ....1991-92 to 92-93
Mile Sillinger...........................1993-94 to 95
Bob Errey..1995

No. 13

Harold Hart 1926-27
Vyacheslav Kozlov.............1991-92 to 96-97

No. 14

Herb Stuart 1926-27
Percy Traub 1927-28
Frank Daley 1928-29
Rusty Hughes.......................................1929-30
Stan McCabe..1930-31
Doug Young 1931-32
Stu Evans 1932-33
Fred Robertson 1933-34
Lloyd Gross 1933-34
Gus Marker...1933-34
Desse Roche..1934-35
Lorne Duguid...1934-35
Wilf Starr 1935-36
Mud Bruneteau....................1935-36 to 37-38
Hal Mackie ....1936-37 to 37-38

Alex Motter	1937-38 to 38-39	Gene Carrigan	1933-34
Sid Abel	1938-39	George Patterson	1934-35
Gus Giesebrecht	1939-40 to 41-42	Lloyd Gross	1934-35
Ken Kilrea	1939-40	Wilf Starr	1934-35
Joe Fisher	1939-40	Pete Kelly	1935-36 to 36-37
Gerry Brown	1941-42	John Sherf	1937-38 to 38-39
Joe Carveth	1942-43	Clarence Droulliard	1937-38
Bernie Ruelle	1943-44	Carl Liscombe	1937-38
Bill Jennings	1943-44	Ron Hudson	1937-38
Ted Lindsay	1944-45 to 46-47	Don Deacon	1938-39
Bep Guidolin	1947-48 to 48-49	Dave Trottier	1938-39
Bud Poile	1948-49	Phil Besler	1938-39
Pete Babando	1949-50	Eddie Bush	1938-39
Metro Prystai	1950-51	Buck Jones	1938-39
Glen Skov	1950-51 to 51-52	Jack Keating	1939-40
Reg Sinclair	1952-53	Connie Brown	1939-40, 41-42
Dutch Reibel	1953-54 to 54-55	Archie Wilder	1940-41
Real Chevrifils	1955-56	Ed Bruneteau	1940-41, 44-45 to 47-48
Lorne Ferguson	1955-56 to 57-58	Ken Kilrea	1941-42, 42-43
Jack McIntyre	1957-58 to 58-59	Bill Quackenbush	1942-43
Claude Laforge	1958-59	Cully Simon	1942-43
Gerry Melnyk	1959-60 to 60-61	Frank Bennett	1943-44
Ed Litzenberger	1961-62	Dalton Smith	1943-44
Len Lunde	1961-62	Billy Reay	1943-44
Bill McNeill	1962-63	Lude Check	1943-44
Larry Jeffrey	1962-63 to 64-65	Larry Thibeault	1944-45
Butch Paul	1964-65	Enio Sclisizzi	1947-48
Billy Harris	1965-66	Fern Gauthier	1948-49
Parker MacDonald	1965-66 to 66-67	Nelson Podolsky	1948-49
Murray Hall	1966-67	Marty Pavelich	1949-50 to 50-51
Doug Roberts	1966-67 to 67-68	Larry Wilson	1951-52
Real Lemieux	1966-67	Alex Delvecchio	1951-52 to 54-55
Craig Cameron	1966-67	Lorne Davis	1954-55
Gary Marsh	1967-68	Larry Hillman	1954-55 to 55-56
Nick Libett	1967-68 to 78-79	Billy Dea	1956-57 to 57-58
Dennis Sobchuk	1979-80	Metro Prystai	1957-58
Alex Pirus	1979-80	Dennis Olson	1957-58
Mike Blaisdell	1980-81	Don Poile	1957-58
Mal Davis	1980-81	Billy McNeill	1958-59 to 59-60
Don Murdoch	1981-82	Jack McIntyre	1959-60
Stan Weir	1982-83	Howie Glover	1960-61 to 61-62
Lane Lambert	1983-84 to 85-86	Charlie Holmes	1961-62
Doug Shedden	1985-86 to 86-87	Wayne Rivers	1961-62
Brent Ashton	1986-87 to 87-88	Pit Martin	1961-62
Miroslav Frycer	1988-89	Allan Johnson	1962-63
Randy McKay	1988-89	Andre Pronovost	1962-63 to 63-64
Torrie Robertson	1988-89 to 89-90	Ted Lindsay	1964-65
Brent Fedyk	1990-91 to 91-92	Irv Spencer	1965-66
Jim Hiller	1992-93	Gary Jarrett	1966-67
Andrew McKim	1995	Ray Cullen	1966-67
Aaron Ward	1996-97	Bart Crashley	1967-68
Brendan Shanahan	1996-97	Galen Head	1967-68
		Ron Anderson	1968-69
No. 15		Fred Speck	1968-69
		Sandy Snow	1968-69
Jack Arbour	1926-27	Hank Monteith	1968-69 to 69-70
Frank Sheppard	1927-28	Al Karlander	1969-70 to 72-73
Pete Bellefeuille	1929-30	Rene Leclerc	1970-71
Roland Matte	1929-30	Robbie Ftorek	1973-74
Jim Creighton	1930-31 to 31-32	Bill Hogaboam	1973-74 to 75-76
John Newman	1930-31	Brian Watts	1975-76
Hec Kilrea	1931-32	Fred Williams	1976-77
Gus Marken	1932-33	Paul Woods	1977-78 to 83-84
Ron Moffatt	1932-33	Claude Loiselle	1984-85
Gord Pettinger	1933-34		

Chris Cichocki.....................1985-86 to 86-87
Mel Bridgman.....................1986-87 to 87-88
Paul MacLean.....................................1988-89
Brent Fedyk.......................................1989-90
Johan Garpenlov................1990-91 to 91-92
Sheldon Kennedy ....1992-93 to 93-94
Mike Ramsey.....................................1995-96
Tomas Holmstrom 1996-97

No. 16

Harold Hicks 1930-31
Leroy Goldsworthy.............................1930-31
Emil Hanson......................................1932-33
Carl Voss...1932-33
Gus Marker..1933-34
Harry Foster 1933-34
Wilf Starr 1933-34
Ron Moffatt..1933-34
Yank Boyd 1934-35
Scotty Bowman ....1935-36 to 38-39
John Gallagher...................................1936-37
Rollie Roulston ....1936-37 to 37-38
Buck Jones..1938-39
Jack Stewart......................................1938-39
Jim Orlando.......................................1939-40
Les Douglas 1940-41
Clarence Behling...............................1940-41
Bill Jennings ....1940-41 to 42-43
Joe Fisher.........................1941-42 to 42-43
Adam Brown ....1941-42 to 42-43
Connie Brown.....................................1942-43
Bill Quackenbush ....1943-44 to 45-46
Rollie Rossignol.................................1943-44
Steve Wochy......................................1946-47
Gerry Couture 1946-47
Lloyd Doran 1946-47
Calum MacKay....................................1946-47
Jim McFadden ....1947-48 to 50-51
John Wilson.......................1951-52 to 54-55
Fred Glover 1951-52
Enio Sclisizzi.....................................1951-52
Norm Ullman ....1955-56 to 57-58
Jack Hendrickson...............................1958-59
Jake McIntyre....................1958-59 to 59-60
Brian Smith ....1959-60 to 60-61
Claude Laforge...................................1960 61
Ed Diachuk 1960-61
Bruce MacGregor...............1960-61 to 65-66
Bob Wall 1965-66
Ted Hampson ....1966-67 to 67-68
Garry Unger.......................................1967-68
Ron Harris.........................1968-69 to 71-72
Henry Boucha ....1972-73 to 73-74
Earl Anderson 1974-75
Michel Bergeron ....1974-75 to 77-78
Andre St. Laurent ....1977-78 to 78-79
Tom Webster 1979-80
Rejean Cloutier..................................1979-80
Jody Gage 1980-81
Mark Kirton ....1981-82 to 82-83
Bobby Francis 1982-83
Kelly Kisio.........................1982-83 to 85-86
Ric Seiling 1986-87
John Chabot ....1987-88 to 90-91
Vladimir Konstantinov.........1991-92 to 96-97

No. 17

Frank Frederickson 1930-31
Leroy Goldsworthy.............................1932-33
Ron Moffatt........................1933-34 to 34-35
Burr Williams.....................................1933-34
Gene Carrigan 1933-34
Ed Wiseman 1935-36
Wally Kilrea 1935-36, 37-38
Art Giroux 1935-36
John Sherf 1935-36
Don Deacon 1936-37
Hal Mackie 1936-37
John Gallagher...................................1936-37
Jim Orlando.......................1936-37 to 37-38
Carl Liscombe....................................1937-38
Ron Hudson.......................................1937-38
Pete Bessone 1937-38
Ken Doraty...1937-38
John Doran 1937-38
John Sorrell.......................................1937-38
Mud Bruneteau 1937-38
Charlie Conacher 1938-39
Cecil Dillion.......................................1939-40
Bert Peer 1939-40
Joe Carveth ....1940-41 to 41-42
Joe Fisher...1940-41
Bob Whitelaw.....................................1941-42
Harry Watson.....................................1942-43
John Sherf 1943-44
Frank Kane..1943-44
Jud McAtee 1943-44
Ken Kilrea 1943-44
Hy Buller 1943-44
Tony Bukovich 1943-44
Billy Thompson...................................1943-44
Steve Wochy......................................1944-45
Earl Siebert ....1944-45 to 45-46
Doug McCaig 1945-46
Gordie Howe......................1946-47 to 47-48
Don Morrison ....1947-48 to 48-49
Pat Lundy 1948-49
Fred Glover.......................1949-50, 51-52
Joe Carveth ....1949-50 to 50-51
Metro Prystai 1950-51
Alex Delvecchio 1950-51
John Wilson 1951-52
Red Almas...1952-53
Larry Wilson 1952-53
Marcel Bonin ....1952-53 to 53-54
Bill Dineen........................1953-54 to 56-57
Forbes Kennedy ....1957-58 to 59-60
Murray Oliver 1959-60
Allan Johnson 1960-61
Claude Laforge 1961-62
Bo Elik 1962-63
Roger Lafreniere 1962-63
Floyd Smith ....1962-63 to 67-68
Ted Hampson 1964-65
Wayne Connelly..................1968-69 to 70-71
Tim Ecclestone...................1970-71 to 73-74
Pierre Jarry ....1973-74 to 74-75
Brian Murphy 1974-75
Ken Mann 1975-76
Bobby Sheehan 1976-77

Steve Coates 1976-77
Al McDonough................................1977-78
Dave Hanson..................................1978-79
Rob Plumb 1978-79
Mike Foligno ....1979-80 to 81-82
Jody Gage 1981-82
Mark Lofthouse 1982-83
Bob Crawford.................................1982-83
Brad Smith.....................................1982-83
Ed Johnstone 1983-84
Gerald Gallant..................1984-85 to 92-93
Doug Brown...........................1995 to 96-97

No. 18

Bob Davis.......................................1932-33
Ron Moffatt....................................1933-34
Rollie Roulston 1935-36
John Sherf......................................1936-37
Charlie Mason 1938-39
Jack Stewart 1938-39
Connie Brown 1938-39, 40-41
Pete Kelly.......................................1938-39
Don Grosso 1939-40
Hec Kilrea......................................1939-40
Dutch Hiller 1941-42
Pat McReavy...................................1941-42
Doug McCaig...................................1941-42
Cully Simon 1942-43
John Holota 1942-43, 45-46
Les Douglas 1942-43
Jud McAtee 1942-43
Bernie Ruelle..................................1943-44
Ed Bruneteau ....1943-44 to 44-45
Hy Buller.......................................1943-44
Gerry Brown 1945-46
Rollie Rossignol..............................1945-46
Jim Conacher.....................1945-46 to 48-49
Doug Baldwin 1946-47
Gerry Couture ....1948-49 to 50-51
Marcel Pronovost 1951-52
Larry Ziedel 1952-53
Bill Folk 1952-53
Jim Hay 1952-53, 54-55
Al Arbour 1953-54
Ed Zeniuk 1954-55
Keith Allen 1954-55
Bucky Hollingworth ....1955-56 to 56-57
Dale Anderson 1956-57
Gord Strate 1957-58
Pete Goegon ....1957-58, 62-63 to 64-65
Gus Mortson....................................1958-59
Jim Morrison 1959-60
Lloyd Haddon 1959-60
Gerry Odrowski...................1960-61 to 61-62
Ron Harris 1962-63
Dave Lucas 1962-63
Ian Cushenan..................................1963-64
John Miszuk 1963-64
Gary Bergman..................................1964-65
Bryan Watson....................1965-66 to 66-67
Ted Taylor......................................1966-67
Warren Godfrey 1966-67
Jim Watson 1967-68
Dan Lawson 1968-69

Ed Haloum 1968-69
Matt Ravlich 1969-70
Dale Rolfe 1969-70
Gerry Hart...........................1970-71 to 71-72
Bill Sutherland 1971-72
Rick McCann 1971-72
Len Fontaine 1972-73
Blair Stewart...................................1973-74
Brian Lavender................................1973-74
Bryan Watson ....1973-74 to 76-77
Kevin Schamehorn............................1976-77
Rob Plumb......................................1977-78
Fern Leblanc 1978-79
J.P. Leblanc....................................1978-79
Mal Davis.......................................1978-79
George Lyle.......................1979-80 to 81-82
Danny Gare ....1981-82 to 85-86
Basil McRae 1986-87
Mark Kumpel ....1986-87 to 87-88
Kris King 1988-89
Kevin McClelland...............1989-90 to 90-91
Alan Kerr 1991-92
John Ogrodnick 1992-93
Chris Tancill 1992-93
Mark Pederson 1993-94
Mike Krushelnyski...............................1995
Kirk Maltby ....1995-96 to 96-97

No. 19

Jack Stewart...................................1938-39
Sid Abel 1938-39
Gus Giesebrecht 1938-39
Ron Hudson 1939-40
Art Herchenratter 1940-41
Hal Jackson 1940-41
Harry Watson 1945-46
Cliff Simpson 1946-47
Les Douglas 1946-47
Tony Licari......................................1946-47
Hugh Millar.....................................1946-47
Max McNab 1947-48
Marty Pavelich ....1947-48 to 48-49
Steve Black ....1949-50 to 50-51
Vic Stasiuk..............1950-51, 52-53 to 54-55
Larry Ziedel ....1951-52 to 52-53
Bill Folk 1951-52
Larry Jankowski...............................1952-53
Steve Hrvmnak 1952-53
Keith Allen 1953-54
Don Poile 1954-55
Jerry Toppazini 1955-56
Murray Costello..................1955-56 to 56-57
Billy McNeill 1956-57, 63-64
Tom McCarthy ....1957-58 to 58-59
Brian Smith 1957-58
Dave Amadio 1957-58
Bucky Hollingworth 1957-58
Gerry Ehman 1958-59
Gord Strate 1958-59
Lou Marcon ....1958-59 to 59-60
Pete Goegon 1959-60
Parker MacDonald............................1960-61
Marc Roileau....................................1961-62
Bob Dillabough 1961-62

Val Fonteyne.....................................1962-63
Wayne Muloin..................................1963-64
John MacMillan 1963-64
Paul Henderson.................1963-64 to 67-68
Pete Stemkowski ....1968-69 to 70-71
Hank Monteith..................................1970-71
Doug Volmar 1970-71
Jim Krulicki......................................1970-71
Bob Wall 1971-72
Gary Doak..1972-73
Rick Foley 1973-74
Ted Harris 1973-74
Jean Hamel 1973-74
Mike Korney.......................1974-75 to 75-76
Barry Salovaara................................1974-75
Mike Wong 1975-76
Rick Wilson 1976-77
John Hilworth...................................1977-78
Dennis Hull......................................1977-78
Roland Cloutier 1978-79
Dan Bolduc.........................1978-79 to 79-80
Mal Davis...1980-81
Gary MacAdam 1980-81
Eric Vail...1981-82
Ivan Boldirev....................................1982-83
Randy Ladouceur.............................1982-83
Steve Yzerman ....1983-84 to 96-97

No. 20

Sid Abel 1938-39
Jack Keating.....................................1938-39
Bob Whitelaw 1940-41
Rudy Zunich 1943-44
Tony Bukovich 1944-45
Gerry Couture 1945-46
John Mowers.....................................1946-47
Red Kelly ....1947-48 to 48-49
Enio Sclisizzi ....1948-49 to 49-50
Larry Wilson 1949-50
Glen Skov 1949-50
Gord Haidy 1949-50
Leo Gravelle 1950-51
Max McNab 1950-51
Jim Hay 1953-54
Jim Peeters......................................1953-54
Marcel Bonin 1954-55
John Bucyk ....1955-56 to 56-57
Don Poile 1957-58
Bob Bailey 1957-58
Len Lunde............................1958-59 to 61-62
Bob Solinger 1959-60
Howie Young......................................1961-62
Parker MacDonald..............1961-62 to 64-65
Don McKenney 1965-66
Murray Hall 1965-66
Dean Prentice ....1965-66 to 68-69
Ed Hatoum..1969-70
Jim Niekamp 1970-71
Mickey Redmond ....1970-71 to 75-76
Dwight Schofield 1976-77
Don Martineau 1976-77
Vaclav Nedomansky............1977-78 to 81-82
Dwight Foster ....1982-83 to 85-86
Tim Higgins........................1986-87 to 88-89

Greg C. Adams.................................1989-90
Marc Potvin 1990-91
Brad Marsh.........................1990-91 to 91-92
Martin Lapointe ....1992-93 to 96-97

No. 21

Pete Kelly...1938-39
Ken Kilrea 1938-39, 40-41
Carl Smith 1943-44
Doug McCaig 1945-46
Rollie McLenahan..............................1945-46
Thain Simon 1946-47
Al Dewsberry.....................................1946-47
Enio Sclisizzi.....................................1947-48
Rod Morrison 1947-48
Lee Fogolin.......................................1948-49
Marcel Pronovost..............................1950-51
Guyle Fielder....................................1952-53
Bill Dineen 1953-54
Earl Johnson 1953-54
Gilles Dube.......................................1953-54
Norm Corcoran..................................1955-56
Ed Stankiewicz 1955-56
Cummy Burton 1955-56
Gerry Melnyk 1955-56
Gord Strate 1956-57
Tom McCarthy 1956-57
Bob Bailey 1956-57
Bucky Hollingworth 1957-58
Jack Hendrickson..............................1957-58
Billy McNeill 1957-58
Charlie Burns 1958-59
John McKenzie...................1959-60 to 60-61
Lou Marcon 1960-61, 62-63
Larry Jeffrey ....1961-62 to 62-63
Eddie Joyal.........................1962-63 to 64-65
Ted Hampson 1963-64
Val Fonteyne.....................................1964-65
Andre Pronovost...............................1964-65
Claude Laforge..................................1964-65
Jim Peters Jr. 1964-65
Andy Bathgate ....1965-66 to 66-67
Warren Godfrey 1967-68
John Brennamen 1967-68
Irv Spencer 1967-68
Pete Mahovlich 1967-68
Jim Watson.......................................1968-69
Gerry Hart 1968-69
Mike McMahon 1969-70
Billy Dea.............................1969-70 to 70-71
Mike Robitaille..................................1970-71
Serge Lajeunesse 1971-72
Ron Stackhouse ....1971-72 to 73-74
Jack Lynch 1973-74
Danny Grant ....1974-75 to 77-78
Roland Cloutier.................................1977-78
J.P. Leblanc......................................1977-78
Dan Labraaten ....1978-79 to 80-81
Earl Ingarfield 1980-81
Mike Blaisdell ....1981-82 to 82-83
Claude Loiselle 1983-84, 85-86
Brad Smith..1983-84
Jody Gage 1983-84
Frank Cernik.....................................1984-85

Adam Oates .... 1986-87 to 88-89
Borje Salming 1989-90
Paul Ysebaert .... 1990-91 to 92-93
Bob Halkidis .... 1993-94 to 1995
Mark Ferner 1995
Bob Errey .... 1995-96 to 96-97

No. 22

Don Deacon 1938-39
Hy Buller 1944-45
Les Douglas 1945-46
Doug McCaig 1946-47
Ed Bruneteau 1947-48
Fred Glover 1948-49
Al Dewsbury 1949-50
Marcel Pronovost 1949-50
Clare Raglan 1950-51
Ben Woit 1950-51
Vic Stasiuk 1951-52
Glenn Hall 1952-53
Len Haley .... 1959-60 to 60-61
Stu McNeill 1959-60
Paul Henderson 1962-63
Gerry Odrowski 1962-63
Bob Dillabough 1962-63
Roger Crozier 1963-64
Harrison Gray 1963-64
Pat Rupp 1963-64
Bob Champoux 1963-64
Carl Wetzel 1964-65
Butch Paul 1964-65
Pete Goegan 1964-65
Ab McDonald .... 1965-66 to 66-67
Howie Young 1966-67
Dan Lawson 1967-68
Nick Libett 1967-68
Ron Anderson 1967-68
Bob Falkenberg 1970-71
Rick McCann 1970-71
Bill Collins .... 1970-71 to 73-74
Blair Stewart 1973-74
Nelson Pyatt 1974-75
Dennis Polonich 1974-75
Larry Giroux 1974-75
Mike Wong 1975-76
Dennis Hextall .... 1975-76 to 78-79
Bill Hogaboam .... 1978-79 to 79-80
Glen Hicks 1980-81
Greg Joly .... 1981-82 to 82-83
Murray Craven 1982-83
Brad Park .... 1983-84 to 84-85
Doug Houda 1985-86
Glenn Merkosky 1985-86
Dave Barr .... 1986-87 to 90-91
Martin Lapointe 1991-92
Dino Ciccarelli .... 1992-93 to 95-96
Mike Knuble 1996-97

No. 23

Enio Schlisizzi 1946-47
Ed Nicholson 1947-48
John Wilson .... 1949-50 to 50-51
Marcel Pronovost 1950-51
Warren Godfrey 1964-65
Bob Wall 1964-65

Gary Bergman 1965-66
Pete Goegan 1966-67
Dave Rochefort 1966-67
Pete Stemkowski 1967-68
Doug Volmar 1969-70
Jim Shires 1970-71
Guy Charron 1970-71
Robbie Ftorek 1972-73
Rick Newell 1972-73
Bill Hogaboam 1972-73
Dan Gruen 1972-73
Tord Lundstrom 1973-74
Nelson Pyatt 1973-74
Nelson DeBenedet 1973-74
Bill Lochead .... 1974-75 to 78-79
Roland Cloutier 1978-79
Glen Hicks 1979-80
Mark Kirton 1980-81
Mark Osborne .... 1981-82 to 82-83
Bob Manno .... 1983-84 to 84-85
Rick MacLeish 1983-84
Basil McRae 1985-86
Rick Zombo 1985-86
Lee Norwood .... 1986-87 to 90-91
Kevin Miller .... 1990-91 to 91-92
Mike Sillinger 1992-93
Greg Johnson .... 1993-94 to 96-97
Mike Ramsey 1996-97

No. 24

Calum MacKay 1948-49
Gerry Reid 1948-49
Al Dewsbury 1949-50
Fred Glover 1950-51
Bob Dillabough 1964-65
Bart Crashley .... 1965-66 to 66-67
Gary Doak 1965-66
Pete Mahovlich 1965-66
Jim Watson 1965-66
Leo Boivin 1965-66
Bob McCord 1966-67
Randy Manery 1970-71
Brian Conacher 1971-72
Ken Murray 1972-73
Brent Hughes 1973-74
Rick McCann 1974-75
Tom Mellor 1974-75
Rene Drolet 1974-75
Frank Bathe .... 1974-75 to 75-76
Jim Nahrgang 1975-76
Greg Joly .... 1976-77 to 80-81
Derek Smith .... 1981-82 to 82-83
Brian Johnson 1983-84
Murray Craven 1983-84
Larry Trader 1984-85
Pierre Aubry 1984-85
Bob Probert .... 1985-86 to 93-94

No. 25

Don Grosso 1938-39
Fern Gauthier 1946-47
Cliff Simpson 1946-47
Tom Gratton 1947-48
Leo Fogolin 1947-48
Ed Stankiewicz 1953-54

Hank Bassen....................................1963-64
Murray Hall........................ 1964-65 to 65-66
Warren Godfrey 1965-66
Jim Peters...1965-66
Doug Roberts 1965-66
Bob McCord 1965-66
George Gardner.................................1965-66
Serje Lajeunesse 1972-73
Tom Mellor 1973-74
Rick Newell 1973-74
Blair Stewart......................................1974-75
Mike Bloom ....1974-75 to 76-77
Dave Kelly 1976-77
Larry Wright 1977-78
Bjorn Skaare 1978-79
Greg Carroll.......................................1979-80
Kevin Schamehorn 1979-80
John Ogrodnick ....1979-80 to 86-87, 92-93
Dave Lewis ....1986-87 to 87-88
Jim Pavese ....1987-88 to 88-89
Randy McKay.....................................1988-89
Mark Habscheid ....1989-90 to 90-91
Troy Crowder 1991-92
Darren McCarty ....1993-94 to 96-97

No. 26

Nelson Pyatt......................................1973-74
Doug Roberts ....1973-74 to 74-75
Al Cameron ....1975-76 to 78-79
Steve Short 1978-79
Jim Korn ....1979-80 to 81-82
Larry Trader.......................................1982-83
Ken Solheim 1982-83
Barry Melrose 1983-84
Ray Sheppard.....................1991-92 to 95
Wes Walz...1995-96
Anders Eriksson................................1996-97
Joe Kocur ....1984-85 to 90-91, 96-97

No. 27

Max McNab 1947-48
Doug McKay.......................................1949-50
Frank Mahovlich.................1967-68 to 70-71
Doug Volmar......................................1971-72
Denis DeJordy 1973-74
Jim Rutherford 1973-74
Brian McCutcheon 1974-75
Phil Roberto ....1974-75 to 75-76
Buster Harvey ....1975-76 to 76-77
Bob Ritchie ....1976-77 to 77-78
Brent Peterson...................1978-79 to 80-81
Brad Smith ....1980-81 to 81-82, 83-84
Reg Leach 1982-83
Pierre Aubry 1983-84
Darryl Sittler.....................................1984-85
Harold Snepsts...................1985-86 to 87-88
Doug Houda........................1988-89 to 90-91
Brian MacLellan.................................1991-92
Jim Cummins 1992-93
Micah Aivazoff 1993-94
Jason York..1995
Mark Ferner 1995
Marc Bergevin 1995-96
Aaron Ward..1996-97

No. 28

Barry Salovaara 1975-76
Reed Larson ....1976-77 to 85-86
Dale Krentz 1986-87; 1988-89
Brent Fedyk 1987-88
Bob Wilkie 1990-91
Sheldon Kennedy 1991-92
Dallas Drake ....1992-93 to 93-94
Tomas Sandstrom 1996-97

No. 29

Terry Sawchuk...................................1968-69
Don Martineau 1975-76
Brian McCutcheon ....1975-76 to 76-77
Fred Berry..1976-77
Tim Sheehy 1977-78
John Hilworth ....1978-79 to 79-80
Joe Paterson ....1980-81 to 81-82
Greg Stefan 1981-82
Ted Nolan 1981-82
Jim Rutherford ....1983-84 to 86-87
Randy Ladouceur ....1983-84 to 86-87
Gilbert Delorme.................1986-87 to 88-89
Chris Kotsopoulos 1989-90
Randy McKay.....................1989-90 to 90-91
Doug Crossman..................................1991-92
Dennis Vial 1992-93
Aaron Ward..1993-94
Sergei Bautin.....................................1993-94
Mike Vernon ....1995 to 96-97

No. 30

Hank Bassen ....1965-66 to 66-67
George Gardner ....1966-67 to 67-68
Roger Crozier 1967-68
Roy Edwards......................1968-69 to 70-71
Jim Rutherford 1970-71
Gerry Gray 1970-71
Don McLeod.......................................1970-71
Al Smith...1971-72
Denis DeJordy 1972-73
Doug Grant...1973-74
Bill McKenzie.....................................1974-75
Terry Richardson 1974-75, 76-77
Pete McDuffe 1975-76
Ron Low 1977-78
Rogie Vachon ....1978-79 to 79-80
Gilles Gilbert......................................1980-81
Corrado Micalef 1981-82
Greg Stefan ....1982-83 to 89-90
Chris Osgood.....................1993-94 to 96-97

No. 31

Andy Brown ....1971-72 to 72-73
Doug Grant.........................1974-75 to 75-76
Ed Giacomin.......................1975-76 to 77-78
Larry Lozinski 1980-81
Claude Legris ....1980-81 to 81-82
Al Jensen...1980-81
Bob Sauve 1981-82
Corrado Micalef 1982-83
Chris Pusey..1985-86
Mark Laforest ....1985-86 to 86-87
Darren Eliot 1987-88
Tim Cheveldae 1988-89

Alain Chevrier....................................1990-91
Scott King 1991-92
Peter Ing...1993-94
Kevin Hodson....................1995-96 to 96-97

No. 32

Bruce Eakin.......................................1985-86
Jeff Sharples.....................................1986-87
Sam St. Laurent................................1987-88
Tim Cheveldae..................1989-90 to 93-94
Stu Grimson ....1995 to 1996-97

No. 33

Bob Manno........................1983-84 to 84-85
Brent Ashton 1986-87
Doug Houda 1987-88
John Blum 1988-89
Yves Racine......................1989-90 to 92-93
Kris Draper........................1993-94 to 96-97

No. 34

Andre St. Laurent 1983-84
Ed Johnstone 1985-86
Sam St. Laurent 1986-87
Jeff Sharples ....1987-88 to 88-89
Daniel Shank.....................1989-90 to 90-91
Greg Millen 1991-92
Steve Maltais 1993-94
Anders Eriksson 1996

No. 35

Ken Holland.......................................1983-84
Warren Young....................................1985-86
Gilbert Delorme................................1986-87
Miroslav Ihnacak 1988-89
Sam St. Laurent ....1988-89 to 89-90
Dave Gagnon 1990-91
Allan Bester......................1990-91to 91-92
Bob Essensa 1993-94

No. 36

Steve Martinson................................1987-88
Per Djoos..1990-91
Dennis Vial ....1990-91 to 91-92

No. 37

Kris King 1987-88
John Mokosak 1989-90
Chris Luongo.....................................1990-91
Vincent Riendeau...............1991-92 to 93-94
Tim Taylor............................1995 to 1996-97

No. 38

Murray Eaves....................................1987-88
Jeff Brubaker 1988-89
Scott King 1990-91
Jason York 1992-93
Bobby Dollas 1992-93
Jason York...1993-94
Tim Taylor...1993-94

No. 39

Dale Krentz.......................................1987-88
Brent Fedyk......................................1988-89
Doug Crossman 1990-91
Aaron Ward.......................................1996-97

No. 40

Rogie Vachon....................................1978-79
Gord Kruppke 1990-91
Jason York 1995
Mark Major 1996-97

No. 41

Ed Mio................................1983-84 to 85-86

No. 42

Bernie Federko..................................1989-90

No. 43

Murray Eaves 1989-90
Bill McDougall....................................1990-91

No. 44

Glenn Merkosky 1989-90
Gord Kruppke 1993-94
Viacheslav Fetisov................................1995

No. 46

Marc Potvin........................1990-91 to 91-92

No. 47

Jim Cummins.....................................1991-92

No. 48

Gary Shuchuk....................................1990-91
Chris Tancill 1991-92

No. 52

Dave Lewis..1986-87

No. 55

Dave "Tiger" Williams........................1984-85
Keith Primeau ....1990-91 to 95-96
Larry Murphy 1996-97

No. 72

Brad Smith..1984-85

No. 77

Paul Coffey........................1992-93 to 95-96

No. 85

Petr Klima...........................1985-86 to 89-90

No. 91

Sergei Fedorov..................1990-91 to 96-97

NORTHERN CONFERENCE

EMPIRE STATE DIVISION

	GP	W	L*	T	GF	GA	PTS
Rochester	80	40	31	9	298	257	90
ADIRONDACK	**80**	**38**	**30**	**12**	**258**	**249**	**90**
Albany	80	38	33	9	269	231	90
Syracuse	80	32	38	10	241	265	74
Binghamton	80	27	40	13	245	300	69

CANADIAN DIVISION

	GP	W	L*	T	GF	GA	PTS
St. John's	80	36	34	10	265	264	88
Saint John	80	28	39	13	237	269	72
Hamilton	80	28	43	9	220	276	69
Fredericton	80	26	46	8	234	283	62

SOUTHERN CONFERENCE

NEW ENGLAND DIVISION

	GP	W	L*	T	GF	GA	PTS
Worcester	80	43	28	9	256	234	100
Springfield	80	41	27	12	268	229	96
Portland	80	37	33	10	279	264	91
Providence	80	35	42	3	262	289	75

MID-ATLANTIC DIVISION

	GP	W	L*	T	GF	GA	PTS
Philadelphia	80	49	21	10	325	230	111
Hershey	80	43	27	10	273	220	101
Kentucky	80	36	35	9	278	284	81
Baltimore	80	30	40	10	251	285	73
Carolina	80	28	48	4	273	303	65

CALDER CUP WINNER: Hershey

*Teams are awarded one point for an overtime loss. 80 game regular season

ADIRONDACK RED WINGS

American Hockey League
Glens Falls Civic Center – 1 Civic Center Plaza – Glens Falls, NY 12801
Capacity: 4,806 Phone: (518) 798-0366 Press Box: (518) 798-3544 FAX: (518) 798-0816

Owner/President .... Mike Ilitch
Owner/Secretary-Treasurer .... Marian Ilitch
Vice-Presidents .... Atanas Ilitch, Chris Ilitch
Senior Vice-President .... Jim Devellano
Governor .... Ken Holland
General Manager .... Don Waddell
Director of Business Operations .... Don Ostrom
Director of Merchandising/Operations Assistant .... David Kolb
Head Coach .... Glenn Merkosky
Assistant Coach .... Murray Eaves
Director of Marketing and Sales .... Dan Long
Director of Public Relations/Broadcaster .... Greg Hallaman
Director of Media Relations .... TBA
Director of Community Relations .... Josh Isenberg
Athletic Trainer .... Piet Van Zant
Equipment Trainer .... Rob Gagne

GLENN MERKOSKY
Head Coach

1996-97 ADIRONDACK RED WINGS' STATISTICS

	Regular Season					Playoffs				
	GP	G	A	PTS	PIM	GP	G	A	PTS	PIM
Paul Brousseau	66	35	31	66	25	4	1	2	3	0
Stacy Roest	78	25	41	66	30	4	1	1	2	0
Mike Knuble	68	28	35	63	54	Det	Det	Det	Det	Det
Allan Egeland	52	18	32	50	184	2	0	1	1	4
Sylvain Cloutier	77	13	36	49	190	4	0	2	2	4
Corey Spring	69	20	25	45	118	4	0	0	0	14
Brent Peterson	52	22	23	45	56	4	3	1	4	2
Jeff Bloemberg	69	5	32	37	24	4	0	3	3	2
Mark Major	78	17	18	35	213	4	0	0	0	13
Brandon Smith	80	8	26	34	30	4	0	0	0	0
Dave Matsos	56	20	12	32	21	4	0	1	1	0
Anders Eriksson	44	3	25	28	36	4	0	1	1	4
Jeff Toms	37	11	16	27	8	4	1	2	3	0
Curt Bowen	78	11	11	22	110	4	0	0	0	2
Colin Cloutier	52	5	15	20	127	2	0	0	0	0
Kevin Grant	53	1	16	17	54	4	1	2	3	6
Yan Golubovsky	62	2	11	13	67	4	0	0	0	0
Sean Gillam	64	1	7	8	50	–	–	–	–	–
Stephan Brochu	18	0	8	8	12	–	–	–	–	–
Steve Sangermano	11	5	0	5	4	–	–	–	–	–
Mike Sullivan	17	1	3	4	2	–	–	–	–	–
Tomas Holmstrom	6	3	1	4	7	Det	Det	Det	Det	Det
Norm Maracle	68	0	3	3	4	–	–	–	–	–
Alexandre Laporte	38	0	3	3	39	–	–	–	–	–
Philippe Audet	3	1	1	2	0	–	–	–	–	–
Daymond Langkow	2	1	1	2	0	–	–	–	–	–
Norm Dezainde	2	1	0	1	4	–	–	–	–	–
Jason Wiemer	4	1	0	1	7	–	–	–	–	–
Maxim Kuznetsov	2	0	1	1	6	2	0	0	0	0
Sean Venedam	13	0	1	1	4	–	–	–	–	–
Jeff Azar	2	0	0	0	0	–	–	–	–	–
Ryan Bach	13	0	0	0	0	1	0	0	0	0
Ryan Brown	6	0	0	0	39	–	–	–	–	–
John Jakopin	3	0	0	0	9	–	–	–	–	–
Marian Kacir	3	0	0	0	2	–	–	–	–	–
Daren Puppa	1	0	0	0	0	–	–	–	–	–
Mathieu Raby	13	0	0	0	28	–	–	–	–	–
TOTALS	80	271	417	688	2025	3	2	3	5	68

GOALTENDERS

Regular Season

	GP	MIN	GAA	W	L	T	EN	SO	GA	SA	SPCT
Norm Maracle	68	3843	2.70	34	22	9	1	5	173	2062	.916
Daren Puppa	1	62	2.90	1	0	0	0	0	3	22	.864
Ryan Bach	13	450	3.86	2	3	1	1	0	29	259	.888
+Tyler Moss	11	507	4.97	1	5	2	0	1	42	301	.860
TOTALS	80	4862	3.05	38	30	12	2	6	247	2644	.907

Playoffs

	GP	MIN	GAA	W	L	EN	SO	GA	SA	SPCT
Norm Maracle	4	191	3.13	1	3	1	1	10	104	.904
Ryan Bach	1	45	3.92	0	0	0	0	3	24	.875
TOTALS	4	236	3.31	1	3	1	0	13	128	.898

+-Traded

PRESS, RADIO, TV INFORMATION

The Red Wings are happy to serve you and appreciate your cooperation. Please phone the Public Relations office at (313) 396-7537 with questions, comments or suggestions. Thank you.

SEASON PASS: Valid for preseason, regular-season games; available only to authorized media covering majority of games.

GAME PASS: Valid for one specific game; available to authorized media covering limited number of games.

HOW TO APPLY: Applications for season or single-game passes must be submitted on company letterhead to Red Wings' Public Relations Office, Joe Louis Arena, Detroit, MI 48226, or by FAX, (313) 567-0296. Single-game passes must be requested 24 hours in advance. Credential requests subject to review by Detroit chapter of Professional Hockey Writers' Association or Detroit Sports Broadcasters' Association. Please enter arena through West Gate press entrance, located on Third Avenue.

PRESS BOX & RADIO-TV BOOTHS: Located at top of arena seats on west side of building and reached by East Gate or West Gate elevator to third floor. Equipped with Charge-a-Call phones, VDT outlets. Coffee, soda, popcorn available. Smoking prohibited in arena. City law prohibits taking beverage cans from press box into arena seating area.

MEDIA LOUNGE: Located in hallway near Red Wings' dressing room on side of arena facing Detroit River. Credentials must be displayed to gain entrance. Opens two hours before game, remains open 45 minutes after game. Hot meals and pizza served before games. Coffee, soda available. Due to limited space, guests are not permitted.

PRACTICE SESSIONS: Dressing room closed to media before and during practice and opens 10 minutes after head coach leaves ice following practice. Access limited to 30 minutes, although exceptions could be made. In event of team meeting immediately after practice, the room opens at conclusion of meeting.

GAME DAY/NIGHT: Room open to media no later than 10 minutes after game and access limited to a 45 minutes, although exceptions could be made.

PREGAME TV-RADIO INTERVIEWS: Television and radio stations seeking live or taped pregame interviews must request coach or player and state specific time of interview to P.R. staff before or during game-day morning skate. Interviews are to be done apart from players' locker area, no later than 5:45 before night game, 11:15 for matinee.

BETWEEN-PERIOD TV INTERVIEWS: Requests are to be made before or during game-day morning skate.

OFF-LIMITS: Not open to media are medical room, weight room, shower and sink area, and players' lounge.

PHOTOGRAPHERS: Those requiring specific vantage points are to phone P.R. office no later than 2 p.m. for night game, 10 a.m. for matinee at (313) 396-7537. Please state how long photographer will stay at game.

PARKING: Reporters/photographers for daily newspapers/wire services or reporters/camerapersons from TV/radio stations who cover majority of games may park at no charge in media section of Joe Louis Arena Garage. City-owned parking garage has limited space and charges P.R. department for each media car parked; therefore, Red Wings regretfully are unable to accomodate everyone for free. Receipts available.

RED WINGS' ATTENDANCE RECORDS

ALL-STAR GAME
*21,002 — Feb. 5, 1980 (Wales Conference 6, Campbell Conference 3)

REGULAR-SEASON GAME
21,019 — Nov. 25, 1983 (DETROIT 7, Pittsburgh 4)

PLAYOFF GAME
20,090 — Apr. 7, 1984 (St. Louis 4, DETROIT 3, 2 OTs)

TOP SEASON TOTALS
819,107 — 1996-97 Season — 19,978 average for 41 games
817,125 — 1995-96 Season — 19,930 average for 41 games
812,640 — 1993-94 Season — 19,820 average for 41 games
808,282 — 1992-93 Season — 19,714 average for 41 games
788,920 — 1991-92 Season — 19,723 average for 40 games
788,102 — 1988-89 Season — 19,703 average for 40 games
786,548 — 1990-91 Season — 19,664 average for 40 games
785,532 — 1987-88 Season — 19,638 average for 40 games

HOME OPENERS
19,983 — Oct. 9, 1996 (DETROIT 2, Edmonton 0)
19,955 — Oct. 10, 1985 (DETROIT 6, Minnesota 6)

OPPOSING TEAMS (Regular Season)
Anaheim — 19,983 — Mar. 25, 1996 (DETROIT 5, Anaheim 1)
Boston — 19,983 — Mar. 19, 1997 (DETROIT 4, Boston 1)
Buffalo — 19,983 — Mar. 27, 1996 (DETROIT 4, Buffalo 2)
Calgary — 19,983 — Mar. 17, 1996 (DETROIT 4, Calgary 2)
Chicago — 19,983 — Apr. 12, 1996 (DETROIT 5, Chicago 3)
+Colorado — 19,983 — Mar. 22, 1996 (DETROIT 7, Colorado 0)
Dallas — 19,983 — Feb. 2, 1997 (DETROIT 4, Minnesota 3)
Edmonton — 20,794 — Feb. 9, 1985 (Edmonton 6, DETROIT 5)
Florida — 19,983 — Feb. 6, 1996 (DETROIT 4, Florida 2)
Hartford — 19,983 — Dec. 31, 1995 (DETROIT 3, Hartford 2)
Los Angeles — 19,983 — Feb. 13, 1996 (DETROIT 9, Los Angeles 4)
Montréal — 19,983 — Oct. 30, 1996 (DETROIT 5, Montréal 3)
New Jersey — 19,983 — Dec. 15, 1995 (DETROIT 3, New Jersey 1)
NY Islanders — 19,983 — Feb. 29, 1996 (DETROIT 5, NY Islanders 1)
NY Rangers — 19,983 — Nov. 25, 1995 (DETROIT 2, NY Rangers 0)
Ottawa — 19,983 — Apr. 11, 1997 (Ottawa 3 , DETROIT 2)
Philadelphia — 20,339 — Feb. 14, 1981 (Philadelphia 3, DETROIT 1)
Pittsburgh — 21,019 — Nov. 25, 1983 (DETROIT 7, Pittsburgh 4)
San Jose — 19,983 — Feb. 12, 1997 (DETROIT 7, San Jose 1)
St. Louis — 19,983 — Mar. 31, 1996 (DETROIT 8, St. Louis 1)
Tampa Bay — 19,983 — Feb. 24, 1996 (DETROIT 2, Tampa Bay 0)
Toronto — 20,328 — Nov. 23, 1984 (DETROIT 6, Toronto 5)
Vancouver — 19,983 — Mar. 2, 1996 (Vancouver 3, DETROIT 2)
Washington — 19,983 — Dec. 26, 1996 (DETROIT 5, Washington 4)
Winnipeg — 19,983 — Mar. 12, 1996 (DETROIT 5, Winnipeg 2)

MATINEE GAMES
19,983‡ — Apr. 13, 1997 (St. Louis 3, DETROIT 1)

FIRST GAME AT JOE LOUIS ARENA
Dec. 27, 1979 — St. Louis 3, DETROIT 2 — 19,742

LAST GAME AT OLYMPIA STADIUM
Dec. 15, 1979 — DETROIT 4, Québec 4 — 15,609

*- NHL Record
+- Formerly Québec
‡- Most recent game

DETROIT RED WINGS'

OZZIE's 100th WIN ↗ (next to Game 1)

GAME	DATE	OPPOSITION	SCORE	RESULT	RECORD	DECIDING GOAL
1	10-1-97	@ Calgary	3-0	W	1-0-0	Shanahan
2	10-3-97	@ Edmonton	8-2	W	2-0-0	Murphy
3	10-8-97	Dallas	3-1	W	3-0-0	Fetisov
4	10-10-97	Tampa Bay	3-0	W	4-0-0	Kocur
OT 5	10-12-97	Calgary	4-4	T	4-0-1	Stillman
6	10-14-97	@ Toronto	3-2	W	5-0-1	Gilchrist
7	10-15-97	Toronto	3-4	L	5-1-1	McCauley
8	10-18-97	Carolina*	4-2	W	6-1-1	Draper
OT 9	10-20-97	St. Louis	3-3	T	6-1-2	Yzerman
10	10-22-97	@ Anaheim	4-1	W	7-1-2	Brown
11	10-23-97	@ Los Angeles	4-1	W	8-1-2	Shanahan
12	10-26-97	@ Vancouver	5-1	W	9-1-2	Lidstrom
13	10-29-97	San Jose	4-3	W	10-1-2	Murphy
14	10-31-97	Los Angeles	1-5	L	10-2-2	Moger
15	11-2-97	Anaheim*	4-3	W	11-2-2	Shanahan
16	11-5-97	@ Carolina	1-3	L	11-3-2	Kapanen
OT 17	11-7-97	Pittsburgh	1-1	T	11-3-3	Shanahan
18	11-9-97	Calgary	6-3	W	12-3-3	Shanahan
19	11-11-97	Colorado	0-2	L	12-4-3	Corbet
20	11-13-97	@ Ottawa	4-2	W	13-4-3	Lapointe
21	11-15-97	@ St. Louis	2-5	L	13-5-3	Hull
OT 22	11-16-97	@ Chicago	3-3	T	13-5-4	Lidstrom
23	11-19-97	NY Islanders	2-3	L	13-6-4	Chorske
24	11-21-97	Dallas	4-2	W	14-6-4	Gilchrist
25	11-22-97	@ Montréal	5-2	W	15-6-4	Holmstrom
26	11-26-97	Ottawa	4-1	W	16-6-4	McCarty
27	11-28-97	Montréal	2-0	W	17-6-4	Shanahan
OT 28	12-1-97	@ Vancouver	3-3	T	17-6-5	Shanahan
29	12-3-97	@ Calgary	4-3	W	18-6-5	Kocur
30	12-5-97	@ Edmonton	1-3	L	18-7-5	Hulbig
31	12-9-97	Vancouver	7-5	W	19-7-5	Maltby
32	12-12-97	Edmonton	2-3	L	19-8-5	McGillis
OT 33	12-14-97	@ Phoenix	3-3	T	19-8-6	Gartner
34	12-16-97	@ San Jose	1-5	L	19-9-6	Nolan
OT 35	12-17-97	@ Colorado	2-2	T	19-9-7	Forsberg
36	12-19-97	New Jersey	5-4	W	20-9-7	Brown
37	12-22-97	@ Boston	4-2	W	21-9-7	Eriksson
38	12-23-97	@ Buffalo	3-1	W	22-9-7	Eriksson
39	12-26-97	Toronto	4-1	W	23-9-7	Maltby
40	12-27-97	@ Toronto	8-1	W	24-9-7	Lapointe
OT 41	12-29-97	Dallas	2-2	T	24-9-8	Zubov

*-Matinee Game

1997-98 SCHEDULE

	GAME	DATE	OPPOSITION	SCORE	RESULT	RECORD	DECIDING GOAL
	42	12-31-97	St. Louis	5-2	W	25-9-8	Brown
	43	1-2-98	San Jose	1-4	L	25-10-8	MacLean
	44	1-4-98	@ Chicago	1-3	L	25-11-8	Amonte
	45	1-6-98	Phoenix	2-0	W	26-11-8	Kozlov
OT	46	1-9-98	@ Dallas	3-3	T	26-11-9	Lethinen
	47	1-11-98	Washington*	2-0	W	27-11-9	Larionov
OT	48	1-12-98	@ NY Islanders	1-1	T	27-11-10	Larionov
	49	1-14-98	Vancouver	4-0	W	28-11-10	Maltby
	50	1-20-98	@ New Jersey	1-3	L	28-12-10	Arnott
	51	1-21-98	Toronto	0-3	L	28-13-10	Korolev
	52	1-24-98	Philadelphia*	1-0	W	29-13-10	Shanahan
OT	53	1-28-98	Phoenix	4-4	T	29-13-11	Lapointe
	54	1-31-98	@ Pittsburgh*	2-4	L	29-14-11	Olausson
	55	2-1-98	@ Washington*	4-2	W	30-14-11	Shanahan
OT	56	2-3-98	@ Florida	1-1	T	30-14-12	Ciccarelli
	57	2-5-98	@ Tampa Bay	5-4	W	31-14-12	Ward
	58	2-7-98	@ St. Louis*	1-4	L	31-15-12	Duchesne
OT	59	2-25-98	Los Angeles	1-1	T	31-15-13	Gilchrist
	60	2-27-98	Florida	3-1	W	32-15-13	Larionov
	61	3-2-98	@ Phoenix	5-1	W	33-15-13	Fedorov
	62	3-4-98	@ Anaheim	2-0	W	34-15-13	Gilchrist
	63	3-5-98	@ San Jose	4-5	L	34-16-13	Marleau
	64	3-7-98	@ Los Angeles*	1-2	L	34-17-13	Blake
	65	3-10-98	Boston	3-6	L	34-18-13	Dimaio
	66	3-12-98	Chicago	3-0	W	35-18-13	Shanahan
	67	3-14-98	@ Philadelphia*	1-6	L	35-19-13	Brind'Amour
	68	3-17-98	Edmonton	4-3	W	36-19-13	McCarty
	69	3-18-98	@ Toronto	5-2	W	37-19-13	Draper
	70	3-21-98	@ NY Rangers*	4-3	W	38-19-13	Brown
OT	71	3-23-98	Chicago	5-5	T	38-19-14	Yzerman
OT	72	3-26-98	Anaheim	3-3	T	38-19-15	Traka
	73	3-28-98	@ St. Louis*	2-3	L	38-20-15	Gill
	74	3-29-98	Buffalo	4-2	W	39-20-15	Draper
	75	4-1-98	Colorado	2-0	W	40-20-15	Fedorov
	76	4-4-98	@ Chicago*	3-2	W	41-20-15	Shanahan
	77	4-7-98	St. Louis	5-3	W	42-20-15	Draper
	78	4-9-98	Phoenix	5-1	W	43-20-15	Brown
	79	4-11-98	NY Rangers*	5-2	W	44-20-15	Lapointe
	80	4-14-98	@ Phoenix	1-2	L	44-21-15	Doan
	81	4-15-98	@ Dallas	1-3	L	44-22-15	Verbeek
	82	4-18-98	@ Colorado*	3-4	L	44-23-15	Forseberg

*-Matinee Game

HOW TO FIGURE . . .

Assist: An assist is awarded to the player or players (maximum of two) who touched the puck prior to the goal, provided no defender plays or possesses the puck in between.

Game Played: A player receives credit for playing in a game if: i) he steps on the ice during time played or; ii) serves any penalty.

Game-Winning Goal: After the final score has been determined, the goal which leaves the winning Club one goal ahead of its opponent is the game-winning goal (example: if Team A beats Team B 8-3, the player scoring the fourth goal for Team A receives credit for the game-winning goal).

Game-Tying Goal: The final goal in a tie game.

Goal: A goal is awarded to the last player on the scoring Club to touch the puck prior to the puck entering the net.

Goals-Against Average: Multiply goals allowed (GA) by 60 and divide by minutes played (MINS).

Goaltender Win/Loss/Tie: A goaltender receives a win, tie or loss if he is on the ice when either the game-winning or game-tying goal is scored.

Penalty-Killing Percentage: Subtract total number of power-play goals allowed from total number of shorthanded situations to get total number of power-plays killed. Divide the total number of power-plays killed by the total number of shorthanded situations.

Plus-Minus: A player receives a "plus" if he is on the ice when his Club scores an even-strength or shorthand goal. He receives a "minus" if he is on the ice for an even-strength or shorthand goal scored by the opposing Club. The difference in these numbers is considered the player's plus-minus statistic.

Power-Play Goal: A goal scored by a Club while it has a manpower advantage due to an opponent's penalty. Following are some examples of what is and is not considered a power-play goal:

- if a Club has an advantage on a minor penalty starting at 2:02 of the period and it scores at 4:02, the goal is not a power-play goal.

- if a Club scores on a delayed penalty, the goal is not a power-play goal.

- if a Club has an advantage due to a five-minute major or match penalty, that Club is always credited with having one more advantage than the number of power-play goals it scores during that advantage, because the penalty does not expire a new advantage begins after such a power-play goal. For example, if Team A scores three goals during a major penalty, it is credited with four advantages.

- if a Club is on a power-play for any length of time it considered to have had an advantage.

- if a minor penalty is incurred by a Club on a power-play due to a major penalty, a new advantage is given to that Club when its minor penalty expires, provided the opponent's major penalty is still in effect.

Power-Play Percentage: Total number of power-play goals divided by total number of power-play opportunities.

Save Percentage: Subtract goals allowed (GA) from shots against (SA) to determine saves. Then divide saves by shots against.

Shooting Percentage: Divide the number of goals scored by the number of shots taken.

Shorthand Goal: A goal scored by a Club while it is at a manpower disadvantage due to an opponent's penalty. The same cases apply in a similar but opposite way for shorthand as for power-play goals.

Shot on Goal: If a player shoots the puck with the intention of scoring and if that shot would have gone in the net had the goaltender not stopped it, the shot is recorded as a "shot on goal".

Shutout: If two goaltenders combine for a shutout, neither receives credit for the shutout. Instead it is recorded as a Club shutout.

Tenths of a Second: If a penalty or goal occurs in the last minute, the time is rounded off to the previous second (ex: if a penalty is called with 12.4 seconds left in a period, the time is indicated as 19:47 and not 19:48.

Tie-Breaking Formula: In the event that two or more Clubs are tied for total points, the order of standings and draft order is determined as follows:

- the Club with the most victories will be placed higher in the standings.

- if Clubs remain tied, the Club earning the most points from the year's head-to-head competition will be placed higher in the standings. In the event an uneven number of home games against one another were played, the first game that created the disparity is discounted. Where more than two Clubs are tied in victories and points, the Club having the greatest percentage of available points earned among each other will be placed higher in the standings.

- if Clubs remain tied, each Club's "Goals Allowed" are subtracted from its "Goals For" during the entire regular season. The Club with the greater differential will be placed higher in the standings.

MEDICAL GLOSSARY

The following information was edited by Dr. Gary W. Dorshimer and used through the courtesy of the Philadelphia Flyers.

Abduction: Movement of a joint away from the center of the body.

AC Joint (Acromioclavicular joint): Joint of the shoulder where acromion process of the shoulder blade and the distal end of the collarbone meet; most shoulder separations occur at this point.

Adduction: Movement of a joint toward the center of the body.

Adhesion: Abnormal adherence of collagen fibers to surrounding structures during immobilization following trauma or as a complication of surgery which restricts normal elasticity of the structures involved; or scar tissue which forms after trauma or surgery which can restrict normal motion.

Aerobic: Exercise in which energy needed is supplied by oxygen inspired and is required for sustained periods of vigorous exercise with a continually high pulse rate.

Anabolic Steroids: Steroids that promote tissue growth by creating protein in an attempt to enhance muscle growth. The main anabolic steroid is testosterone (male sex hormones).

Anaerobic: Exercise without the use of oxygen as an energy source; short bursts of vigorous exercise.

Anterior Cruciate Ligament (ACL): A primary stabilizing ligament within the center of the knee joint that prevents hyperextension and excessive rotation of the joint. A complete tear of the ACL necessitating reconstruction could require up to 12 months of rehabilitation.

AntiInflammatory: Any agent which prevents inflammation, such as aspirin or ibuprofen.

Arteriogram: A film demonstrating arteries after injection of a dye.

Arthrogram: Xray technique for joints using air and/or dye injected into the affected area; useful in diagnosing meniscus tears of the knee and rotator cuff tears of the shoulder.

Arthroscope: An instrument used to visualize the interior of a joint cavity.

Arthroscopy: A surgical examination of the internal structures of a joint by means of viewing through an arthroscope. An arthroscopic procedure can be used to remove or repair damaged tissue or as a diagnostic procedure in order to inspect the extent of any damage or confirm a diagnosis.

Atrophy: To shrivel or shrink from disuse; as in muscular atrophy.

Baker's Cyst: Localized swelling of a bursa sac in the back of the knee as a result of fluid that has escaped from the knee capsule. A Baker's cyst indicates that there is a trauma inside the knee joint that leads to excessive fluid production.

Bone Scan: An imaging procedure in which a radioactivelabeled substance is injected into the body to determine the status of a bone injury. If the radioactive substance is taken up by the bone at the injury site, the injury will show as a "hot spot" on the scan image. The bone scan is particularly useful in the diagnosis of stress fractures.

Bursa: A fluid-filled sac that is located in areas where friction is likely to occur, then minimizes the friction; for example, between a tendon and bone.

Cartilage: Smooth, slippery substance preventing two ends of bones from rubbing together and grating. Most joints use this to cover bones next to each other. A meniscus is made of cartilage.

CAT Scan (Computerized Tomography): Use of a computer to produce a cross sectional view of the anatomical part being investigated from xray data.

Chondromalacia: Roughening of the articular cartilage. Best known for the roughening of the underside of the knee cap, which can occur in any knee cap injury.

Clavicle: Collar bone; the bone connecting the breastbone with the shoulder blade.

Coccyx: The "tail bone," a group of four vertebrae that are fused together to form a small triangular bone, located at the terminal end of the spine.

Concussion: Jarring injury of the brain resulting in dysfunction. It can be graded as mild, moderate or severe, depending on loss of consciousness, amnesia and loss of equilibrium.

Contusion: An injury to a muscle and tissues caused by a blow from a blunt object.

Corticosteroids: Used to suppress joint inflammation and inflammation in a bursa or near tendons.

Cryotherapy: A treatment with the use of cold.

Cyst: Abnormal sac containing liquid or semisolid matter.

Degenerative Joint Disease: Changes in the joint surfaces as a result of repetitive trauma and "wear and tear".

Deltoid Ligament: Ligament that connects the tibia to bones of the medial aspect of the foot and is primarily responsible for stability of the ankle on the medial side. Is sprained less frequently than other ankle ligaments.

Deltoid Muscle: Muscles at the top of the arm, just below the shoulder, responsible for shoulder motions in the front, side and back.

Disc Intervertebral: A flat, rounded plate between each vertebrae of the spine. The disc consists of a thick fiber ring which surrounds a soft gel-like interior. It functions as a cushion and shock absorber for the spinal column.

Dislocation: Complete displacement of joint surfaces.

Electromyogram (EMG): Test to determine nerve function.

Epicondylitis: Inflammation in the elbow due to overuse. Common in tennis players (outer part of elbow) and golfers (inner part of elbow).

Etiology: Study of the cause of injury and disease.

Extension: Action of straightening of a joint as achieved by an extensor muscle.

Fascia: A connective tissue sheath consisting of fibrous tissue and fat which unites the skin to the underlying tissue.

Fat Percentage: The amount of body weight that is adipose, fat tissue. Fat percentage can be calculated by underwater weighing, measuring select skinfold thickness or by analyzing electrical impedance.

Femur: Thigh bone; longest bone in the body.

Fibula: Smaller of the two bones in the lower leg; runs from the knee to the ankle along the outside of the lower leg.

Flexibility: The ability of muscle to relax and yield to stretch forces.

Fracture: Breach in continuity of a bone. Types of fractures include simple, compound, comminuted, greenstick, incomplete, impacted, longitudinal, oblique, stress or transverse.

Glenohumeral: The shoulder girdle; consists of the glenoid capsule, head of the humerus and labrum.

Glenoid: Cavity of the scapula into which the head of the humerus fits to form the shoulder girdle.

Glenoid Labrum: A rim of fibrocartilaginous tissue attached around the margin of the glenoid fossa.

Grade One Injury: A mild injury in which ligament, tendon or other musculoskeletal tissue may have been stretched, but not torn or otherwise disrupted.

Grade Two Injury: A moderate injury in which musculoskeletal tissue has been partially, but not totally torn, causing appreciable limitation in function of the injured tissue.

Grade Three Injury: A severe injury in which tissue loss has been significant, and in many cases, totally torn or otherwise disrupted, causing a virtual loss of function.

Groin: Junction of the thigh and abdomen, location of muscles that rotate, flex and adduct the hip.

Hammer Toe: Condition when the first digit of a toe is at a different angle that the remaining digits of the same toe.

Hamstring: Category of muscle that runs from the buttocks to the knee along the back of the thigh. It functions to flex the knee and is often times injured as a result of improper conditioning or lack of muscle flexibility.

Hemarthrosis: Accumulation of blood within a joint as a result of an acute injury.

Hematoma: Mass produced by an accumulation of coagulated blood in a cavity or in soft tissues.

Hip Pointer: Contusion to the iliac crest.

Hydrotherapy: Treatment using water.

Hyperextension: Extreme extension of a limb or body part.

Iliotibial Band: A thick, wide fascial layer that runs from the iliac crest to the knee joint on the outside of the thigh.

Inflammation: The body's natural response to injury in which the injury site might display various degrees of pain, swelling, heat, redness and/or loss of function.

Isometric Contraction: Muscular contraction in which tension is developed but no mechanical work is done.

Labrum (Labrum Glenoidule): The cartilage of the glenoid cavity in the shoulder. A lipedged or liplike structure.

Lateral Collateral Ligament (LCL): Ligament of the knee along the outer aspect that connects the femur to the fibula. It provides lateral stability to the joint.

Ligament: Band of fibrous tissue that connects bone to bone or bone to cartilage and supports and strengthens joints.

Magnetic Resonance Imaging (MRI): Imaging procedure in which a radio frequency pulse causes certain electrical elements of the injured tissue to react to this pulse and through this process a computer display and permanent film establish a visual image. MRI does not require radiation and is very useful in the diagnosis of soft tissue, disc and meniscus injuries.

Medial Collateral Ligament (MCL): Ligament of knee along the inner aspect that connects the femur to the tibia.

Meniscus: Crescent shaped cartilage, usually pertaining to the knee joint; also known as cartilage. There are two menisci in the knee, medial and lateral. These work to absorb weight within the knee and provide stability.

Metacarpals: Five long bones of the hand, joining the fingers to the wrist.

Metatarsals: Five long bones of the foot, running from the ankle to the toes.

Myositis: Inflammation of a muscle.

Orthotic: Any device applied to or around the body of physical impairment of disability commonly used to control foot mechanics.

Osteochondritis Dessicans: A piece of bone and/or cartilage loosened from its attachment after trauma and a cause of a lesion.

Osteomyelitis: An inflammatory disease of bone caused usually by infection with streptococcus or staphylococcus.

Patella: The kneecap. The patella functions to protect the distal end of the femur as well as increase the mechanical advantage and force generating capacities of the quadriceps muscle group.

Plantar Fasciitis: Inflammation of the plantar (a thick tissue on the bottom of the foot which helps create the arch) fascia; associated with overuse or acute foot injury.

Posterior Cruciate Ligament (PCL): A primary stabilizing ligament of the knee that provides significant stability and prevents displacement of the tibia backward within the knee joint. A complete tear of this ligament necessitating reconstruction could require up to 12 months of rehabilitation.

Quadricep Muscles: A group of four muscles of the front thigh that run from the hip and form a common tendon at the patella; they are responsible for knee extension.

Radius: Bone in the forearm from elbow to the thumb side of the wrist.

Reconstruction: Surgical rebuilding of a joint using natural, artificial or transplanted materials.

Rotator Cuff: Comprised of four muscles in the shoulder area that can be irritated by overuse. The muscles are the supraspinatus (most commonly injured), infraspinatus, teres minor and subscapularis.

Sacroiliac: Junction of the sacrum, the lower back bone, with the pelvis.

Sacrum: Group of five fused vertebrae located just below the lumbar vertebrae of the lower back, which form part of the pelvis.

Scapula: Shoulder blade.

Sciatica: Irritation of the sciatic nerve resulting in pain or tingling running down the inside of the leg.

Sciatic Nerve: Major nerve that carries impulses for muscular action and sensations between the low back and thigh and lower leg; it is the longest nerve in the body.

Shin Splint: A catch-all syndrome describing pain in the shin that is not a fracture or tumor and cannot be defined otherwise.

Spleen: Large, solid organ responsible for the normal production and destruction of blood cells located under the left rib cage.

Spondylosis: Abnormal vertebral fixation or immobility.

Sprain: Injury resulting from the stretch or twist of the joint and causes various degrees of stretch or tear of a ligament or other soft tissue at the joint.

Strain: Injury resulting from a pull or torsion to the muscle or tendon that causes various degrees of stretch or tear to the muscle or tendon tissue.

Stress Fracture: A hairline type of break in a bone caused by overuse.

Subluxation: Partial dislocation of a joint. The term usually implies that the joint can return to a normal position without formal reduction.

Synovial Fluid: Lubricating fluid for joints and tendons, produced in synovium, or the inner lining of a joint.

Synovitis: Inflammation of the synovial lining of a joint.

Talus: The ankle bone that articulates with the tibia and fibula to form the ankle joint.

Tarsals: Group of seven bones of the foot consisting of the calnavicular, talus, cuboid and three cuneiform bones.

Tendinitis: Inflammation of the tendon and/or tendon sheath, caused by chronic overuse or sudden injury.

Tendon: Tissue that connects muscle to bone.

Tenosynovitis: Swelling or inflammation of a tendon sheath caused by calcium deposits, repeated strain or trauma.

Tibia: Shin bone; larger of the two bones of the lower leg and is the weightbearing bone of the shin.

Transcutaneous Electrical Nerve Stimulator (TENS): An electrical modality that sends a mild current through pads at the injury site which stimulates the brain to release the natural analgesic endorphin.

Transverse Process: Small lateral projection off the right and left side of each vertebrae that functions as an attachment site for muscles and ligaments of the spine.

Triceps: Muscle of the back of the upper arm, primarily responsible for extending the elbow.

Ulna: Inner bone of the forearm that runs from the tip of the elbow to the little finger side of the wrist.

Ulna Nerve: Nerve in the elbow commonly irritated from excessive throwing.

Ultrasound: An electrical modality that transmits a sound wave through an applicator into the skin to the soft tissue in order to heat the local area for relaxing the injured tissue and/or disperse edema.

"Wind Knocked Out": Syndrome describing a contraction of the abdominal nerve truck, the solar plexus, as a result of an abdominal contusion.

NHL MANAGEMENT

NATIONAL HOCKEY LEAGUE

Executive Offices — New York
1251 Avenue of the Americas, 47th Floor, New York, NY 10020-1198
(212) 789-2000   Fax: (212) 789-2020   PR Fax: (212) 789-2080

NHL — Montréal
1800 McGill College Avenue, Suite 2600, Montréal, Québec H3A 3J6
(514) 288-9220   Fax: (514) 284-0300

NHL — Toronto
75 International Blvd., Suite 300, Rexdale, Ontario M9W 6L9
(416) 798-0809   Fax: (416) 798-0852

NHL Enterprises, L.P.
1251 Avenue of the Americas, 47th Floor, New York, NY 10020-1198
(212) 789-2000   Fax: (212) 789-2020

NHL Enterprises Canada, L.P.
75 International Blvd., Suite 301, Rexdale, Ontario M9W 6L9
(416) 798-9388   Fax: (416) 798-9395

NHL Europe
Signaustrasse 1, 8008 Zurich — Switzerland
011-411-1-389-8080   Fax: 011-41-1-389-8090

NHL Productions
183 Oak Tree Road, Tappan, NY 10983-2809
(914) 365-6701   Fax: (914) 365-6010

DIRECTORY

Commissioner . . . . Gary B. Bettman
Senior VP and Chief Operating Officer . . . . Stephen J. Solomon
Senior VP Legal Affairs . . . . William L. Daly
Senior VP and Director of Hockey Operations . . . . Brian P. Burke
VP Hockey Operations (Toronto) . . . . Jim Gregory
VP Public Relations . . . . Arthur Pincus
VP Corporate Communications . . . . Bernadette Mansur
VP Broadcasting . . . . Glenn Adamo
VP Television and Business Affairs . . . . Ellis T. "Skip" Prince III
VP and Chief Financial Officer . . . . Craig Harnett
VP Special Events . . . . Frank Supovitz
VP Security . . . . Dennis Cunningham
VP and General Counsel . . . . David Zimmerman
Associate Counsel . . . . Katherine Jones
Executive Assistant to the Commissioner . . . . Debbie Jordan

BROADCASTING/NHL PRODUCTIONS

Vice President, Broadcasting . . . . Glenn Adamo
Coordinating Producer . . . . Ken Rosen
Senior Producer . . . . Darryl Lepik
Director, Broadcasting . . . . Adam Acone
Director, Broadcast Operations/NHLP . . . . Patti Fallick
Director, Scheduling Operations . . . . Steve HatzePetros
Manager, Broadcast Business Affairs . . . . Samuel Esposito, Jr.
Manager, Broadcasting . . . . Todd Goodman

PUBLIC RELATIONS

Vice President Public Relations .... Arthur Pincus
Managing Director, Public Relations (Toronto) .... Gary Meagher
Chief Statistician (Toronto) .... Benny Ercolani
Director, Public Relations .... Andrew McGowan
Manager, Media Services .... Susan Aglietti
Manager, News Services .... Greg Inglis
Public Relations Coordinator (Toronto) .... David Keon
Public Relations Coordinator .... Magdale Labbe
News Services Assistant .... Tamir Lipton
Public Relations Assistant .... Adam Schwartz
Public Relations Assistant (Toronto) .... Chris Tredree

CORPORATE COMMUNICATIONS

Vice President, Corporate Communications .... Bernadette Mansur
Director, Corporate Communications .... Mary Pat Clarke
Director, Creative Services .... David F. Haney
Manager, Corporate Communications .... Tracey Cohen
Publicist, Corporate Communicatons/USA Hockey .... Amy Early
Corporate Communications Associate .... Sandra Carreon
Community Relations Associate .... Adrienne Drennan

TELEVISION AND BUSINESS AFFAIRS

Vice President, Television and Business Affairs .... Ellis T. "Skip" Prince III
Director, New Business Development .... Bryant S. McBride
Manager, Television and Business Affairs,
   International .... Susanna Mandel-Mantello
Manager, Team Television .... John A. Tortora

NHL ENTERPRISES, L.P.

President .... Rick Dudley
Senior VP and General Counsel .... Richard Zahnd
Group VP Marketing .... Ed Horne
VP Youth Marketing .... Dina Gilbertie
VP Consumer Products Marketing .... Brian Jennings
VP Fan Development .... Ken Yaffe
Group Director, Special Projects / Promotional Services .... Glenn Horine
Managing Director, NHL Enterprises, B.V. .... Brad Kwong
General Manager and Executive Producer,
   NHL Interactive CyberEnterprises .... Charlie Schmitt
Director, Club Marketing .... Scott Carmichael
Director, Off-Ice Programs .... Brian Mullen

NHL CLUB DIRECTORY

ANAHEIM MIGHTY DUCKS
Arrowhead of Anaheim
2695 Katella Avenue
Anaheim, CA 92803
(714) 940-2900
General Manager: Jack Ferreira
Coach: Pierre Page
PR Director: Bill Robertson

BOSTON BRUINS
FleetCenter – Suite 250
Boston, MA 02114
(617) 624-1950
General Manager: Harry Sinden
Coach: Pat Burns
PR Director: Heidi Holland

BUFFALO SABRES
Marine Midland Arena
One Seymour H. Knox Plaza
Buffalo, NY 14203
(716) 855-4100
General Manager: Darcy Regier
Coach: Lindy Ruff
PR Director: John Isherwood

CALGARY FLAMES
Olympic Saddledome
P.O. Box 1540, Station M
Calgary, AB T2P 3B9
(403) 777-2177
General Manager: Al Coates
Coach: Brian Sutter
PR Director: TBA

CAROLINA HURRICANES
5000 Aerial Center
Suite 100
Morrisville, NC 27560
(919) 467-7825
General Manager: Jim Rutherford
Coach: Paul Maurice
PR Director: Jim Loria

CHICAGO BLACKHAWKS
United Center
1901 West Madison Street
Chicago, Il 60612
(312) 455-7000
General Manager: Bob Murray
Coach: Craig Hartsburg
PR Director: Jim DeMaria

COLORADO AVALANCHE
McNichols Arena
1635 Clay Street
Denver, CO 80204
(303) 893-6700
General Manager: Pierre Lacroix
Coach: Marc Crawford
PR Director: Jean Martineau

DALLAS STARS
StarCenter
211 Cowboys Parkway
Irving, TX 75063
(972) 868-2890
General Manager: Bob Gainey
Coach: Ken Hitchcock
PR Director: Larry Kelly

EDMONTON OILERS
Edmonton Coliseum
11230 – 110 Street
Edmonton, AB T5G 3G8
(403) 474-8561
General Manager: Glen Sather
Coach: Ron Low
PR Director: Bill Tuele

FLORIDA PANTHERS
100 N.E. Third Avenue
Fort Lauderdale, FL 33301
(305) 768-1900
General Manager: Bryan Murray
Coach: Doug MacLean
PR Director: Mike Hanson

LOS ANGELES KINGS
The Great Western Forum
3900 W. Manchester Blvd.
Inglewood, CA 90306
(213) 419-3160
General Manager: Dave Taylor
Coach: Larry Robinson
PR Director: Mike Altieri

MONTRÉAL CANADIENS
Molson Centre
1260 de la Gauchetière West
Montréal, QUE H3B 5E8
(514) 932-2582
General Manager: Rejean Houle
Coach: Alain Vigneault
PR Director: Donald Beauchamp

NEW JERSEY DEVILS
Continental Airlines Arena
P.O. Box 504
East Rutherford, NJ 07073
(201) 935-6050
General Manager: Lou Lamoriello
Coach: Jacques Lemaire
PR Director: Mike Gilbert

NEW YORK ISLANDERS
Nassau Coliseum
Uniondale, NY 11553
(516) 794-4100
General Manager: Rick Bowness
Coach: Mike Milbury
PR Director: Ginger Killian

NEW YORK RANGERS
Madison Square Garden,
14th Floor
2 Penn Plaza
New York, NY 10121
(212) 465-6486
General Manager: Neil Smith
Coach: Colin Campbell
PR Director: John Rososco

OTTAWA SENATORS
Corel Center
301 Moodie Drive, Suite 200
Nepean, ON K2H 9C4
(613) 599-0306
General Manager: Pierre Gauthier
Coach: Jacques Martin
PR Director: Phil Legault

PHILADELPHIA FLYERS
CoreStates Center
1 CoreStates Complex
Philadelphia, PA 19148
(215) 465-4500
President/GM: Bob Clarke
Coach: Wayne Cashman
PR Director: Zack Hill

PHOENIX COYOTES
America West Arena
One Renaissance Square
2 North Central, Suite 1930
Phoenix, AZ 85004
(602) 379-2800
General Manager: Bobby Smith
Coach: Jim Schoenfeld
PR Director: Richard Nairn

PITTSBURGH PENGUINS
Civic Arena
66 Mario Lemieux Place
Pittsburgh, PA 15219
(412) 642-1300
General Manager: Craig Patrick
Coach: Kevin Constantine
PR Director: Steve Bovino

ST. LOUIS BLUES
Kiel Center
1401 Clark Avenue
St. Louis, MO 63103
(314) 622-2500
General Manager: Larry Pleau
Coach: Joel Quenneville
PR Director: Jeff Trammell

SAN JOSE SHARKS
San Jose Arena
525 W. Santa Clara Street
San Jose, CA 95113
(408) 287-7070
General Manager: Dean Lombardi
Coach: Darryl Sutter
PR Director: Ken Arnold

TAMPA BAY LIGHTNING
Ice Palace
401 Channelside Dr.
Tampa, FL 33602
(813) 229-2658
General Manager: Phil Esposito
Coach: Terry Crisp
PR Director: Gerry Helper

TORONTO MAPLE LEAFS
Maple Leaf Gardens
60 Carlton Street
Toronto, ON M5B 1L1
(416) 977-1641
General Manager: Ken Dryden
Coach: Mike Murphy
PR Director: Bob Stellick

VANCOUVER CANUCKS
General Motors Place
800 Griffiths
Vancouver, BC V6B 6G1
(604) 899-4600
General Manager: Pat Quinn
Coach: Tom Renney
PR Director: Devin Smith

WASHINGTON CAPITALS
USAir Arena
1 Harry S. Truman Dr.
Landover, MD 20785
(301) 386-7000
General Manager: George McPhee
Coach: Ron Wilson
PR Director: Nancy Yasharoff

WESTERN CONFERENCE

CENTRAL DIVISION
Detroit Red Wings
Chicago Blackhawks
Dallas Stars
St. Louis Blues
Toronto Maple Leafs
Phoenix Coyotes

PACIFIC DIVISION
Anaheim Mighty Ducks
Calgary Flames
Colorado Avalanche
Edmonton Oilers
Los Angeles Kings
San Jose Sharks
Vancouver Canucks

EASTERN CONFERENCE

ATLANTIC DIVISION
New Jersey Devils
New York Islanders
New York Rangers
Philadelphia Flyers
Florida Panthers
Tampa Bay Lightning
Washington Capitals

NORTHEAST DIVISION
Boston Bruins
Buffalo Sabres
Carolina Hurricanes
Montréal Canadiens
Ottawa Senators
Pittsburgh Penguins

SCHEDULE

Each team plays 82-game schedule.

Teams in Detroit's Central Division of Western Conference play six games each against three divisional opponents (18 games), five contests each against remaining two divisional opponents (10 games), four games each against seven teams in Pacific Division (28 games) and two contests each against 13 teams in Northeast and Atlantic divisions of Eastern Conference (26 games).

TIE-BREAKER FORMULA

To break tie in final regular-season standings, following methods are used:

1. Most overall victories; 2. Best record in games between tied teams; 3. Best differential between goals for and goals against during 82-game regular season; 4. Meeting or conference call between league general managers.

STANLEY CUP PLAYOFFS

Conference-based system matches No. 1 team vs. No. 8, No. 2 vs. No. 7, No. 3 vs. No.6, No. 4 vs. No. 5. Four division winners receive first two seeds in each conference; No.2 seed could be division winner with fewer points than lower seeds, retaining that seed through conference championship.

All series best-of-seven, with home-ice rotating on 2-2-1-1-1 basis. In series between Central and Pacific division clubs, team with most points could choose to start series at home or on road and opt for 2-3-2 format.

Western, Eastern conference champions meet in Stanley Cup final.

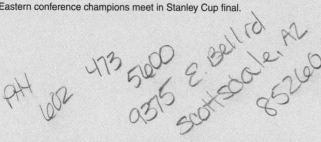

SEPTEMBER

9 Training camps open

9 Hockey Hall of Fame inductees announcement
Toronto

13 First preseason games

27 Unsigned Draft Choices claimed in fourth or subsequent rounds of Entry Draft must be returned to their Junior clubs

30 Unsigned Draft Choices claimed in first three rounds of Entry Draft must be returned to their Junior clubs.

OCTOBER

TBA Waiver Draft

1 81st NHL Regular Season begins

3-4 Game One
Anaheim vs. Vancouver
Tokyo, Japan
NOTE: In Japan, these dates are October **4-5**

NOVEMBER

17 Hockey Hall of Fame Induction Celebration
Toronto

DECEMBER

TBA Board of Governors Meeting

19 Roster Freeze in effect. For all players on an NHL roster as of midnight local time December 19, a roster freeze shall apply through midnight local time December 27, with respect to waivers, trades and any other player assignments; provided, however, that players may be recalled to NHL clubs during this period.

25 World Junior Hockey Championship (through January 3)
Finland

JANUARY

14-18 Pinnacle/NHL FANtasy
Vancouver

17 NHL All-Star Saturday
General Motors Place

18 48th NHL All-Star Game
General Motors Place

FEBRUARY

TBA NHL/CHL Top Prospects Game
Maple Leaf Gardens

8 NHL Winter Break

25 NHL Season Resumes

MARCH

24 Trading Deadline (3 PM ET)

APRIL

TBA Lester Patrick Award Luncheon

19 End of regular season

22 Stanley Cup Playoffs begin

MAY

1 World Championships (through May 17)
Switzerland

TBA Entry Draft Drawing

JUNE

23 Last possible date for completion of Stanley Cup Championship

25 NHL Awards Television Special
Toronto

26 Expansion Draft
Buffalo

26 Top Prospect Preview
Buffalo

27 NHL Entry Draft
Buffalo

JULY

1 Eligible players transferred to free agent list

O C T O B E R

S	M	T	W	T	F	S
			1 CGY 9:00 ★	2	3 EDM	4
5	6	7	8 DAL 7:30	9	10 TB	11
12 CGY 6:00	13	14 TOR 7:30 ★	15 TOR 7:30	16	17	18 CAR 3:30 ★
19	20 STL 7:30	21	22 ANA 10:30	23 LA 10:30	24	25
26 VAN 8:00 ★	27	28	29 SJ ★	30	31 LA 7:30	

N O V E M B E R

S	M	T	W	T	F	S
						1
2 *ANA 3:00	3	4	5 CAR 7:30 ★	6	7 PIT 7:30	8
9 CGY 6:00	10	11 COL 7:30 ★☆	12	13 OTT 7:30 ★	14	15 STL 8:30 ★
16 CHI 8:00 ★	17	18	19 NYI 7:30	20	21 DAL 7:30 ★	22 MTL 7:30 ★◆
23	24	25	26 OTT 7:30	27	28 MTL 7:30 ★	29
30						

D E C E M B E R

S	M	T	W	T	F	S
	1 VAN 10:00	2	3 CGY 9:00	4	5 EDM 9:00 ★	6
7	8	9 VAN 7:30	10	11	12 EDM 7:30	13
14 PHX 9:00 ★	15	16 SJ 10:30	17 COL 9:00	18	19 NJ 7:30	20
21	22 BOS 7:30	23 BUF 7:00 ★	24	25	26 TOR 7:30	27 TOR 7:30 ★◆
28	29 DAL 7:30	30	31 STL 7:30 ★☆			

J A N U A R Y

S	M	T	W	T	F	S
				1	2 SJ 7:30	3
4 CHI 8:00 ★☆	5	6 PHX 7:30	7	8	9 DAL 8:30 ★	10
11 *WSH 3:00	12 NYI 7:30	13	14 VAN 7:30	15	16	17
18	19	20 NJ 7:30	21 TOR 7:30 ★	22	23	24 *PHI 3:00 ■
25	26	27	28 PHX 7:30	29	30	31 *PIT 3:00

F E B R U A R Y

S	M	T	W	T	F	S
1 *WSH 1:30	2	3 FLA 7:30 ★	4	5 TB 7:30 ★	6	7 *STL 3:00 ■
8	9	10	11	12	13	14
15	16	17	18	19	20	21
22	23	24	25 LA 7:30	26	27 FLA 7:30 ★☆	28

M A R C H

S	M	T	W	T	F	S
1	2 PHX 9:00 ★	3	4 ANA 10:30	5 SJ 10:30	6	7 *LA 3:00 ■
8	9	10 BOS 7:30	11	12 CHI 7:30	13	14 *PHI 3:00 ■
15	16	17 EDM 7:30	18 TOR 7:30	19	20	21 *NYR 3:00 ■
22	23 CHI 7:30	24	25	26 ANA 7:30	27	28 *STL 3:00 ■
29 BUF 7:00	30	31				

A P R I L

S	M	T	W	T	F	S
			1 COL 7:30 ★	2	3	4 *CHI 3:00 ■
5	6	7 STL 7:30 ★	8	9 PHX 7:30	10	11 *NYR 1:00 ■
12	13	14 PHX 7:30	15 DAL 8:30 ★	16	17	18 *COL 3:00 ■

■ Home Games ☐ Away Games ★ Denotes Afternoon ☆ Game also on ESPN

WJR All games home and away will be broadcast on Radio 760

★ WAN 50	All Times Eastern	● FOX Sports Detroit (Cable)
◆ CBET Channel 9		■ FOX (National)

RedWings®